Ron,
  Thanks for your commitment to our America...
                    [signature]

THE ENTREPRENEUR'S DILEMMA

Should I Take My Company Public?

Parker H. "Pete" Petit

Atlanta, Georgia
2024

The Entrepreneur's Dilemma
Copyright © 2024 by Parker H. Petit

FIRST EDITION 2024

All rights reserved. No part of this book may be used or reproduced in any manner whatsoever, including electronic or mechanical, including photocopy, recording, or any information storage and retrieval system now known or to be invented, without written permission of the publisher except in the case of brief excerpts embodied in critical articles and reviews.

Published in the United States by
Springdale Publishers, LLC
Atlanta, GA

ISBN 979-8-218-17353-1 - Paperback

ISBN 979-8-320-61324-6 - Hardcover

Cover design by Leaping Cat Graphics, LLC

Manufactured in the United States of America

AUTHOR'S COMMENTS

This is a true story of a portion of my life, particularly my entrepreneurial business activities. I have used my best recollections as well as thousands of emails, other documents, dialogue from conversations and phone calls. I have used company and government documents, where possible, to support other comments. I am sure there may be some slight misinterpretations and misstatements in the text. I apologize for those minor inaccuracies. Of course, the book is written from my perspective and my interpretations of revelent information since I am the person who lived the events.

While some people may not agree with me, the opinions I have expressed here are my honest beliefs. To the extent my opinion was based on a source that was inaccurate, I apologize for my error. I do not intend that anyone rely on such inaccurate information in order to make decisions related to a particular alleged fact or circumstance. Under no circumstances do I intend to cause any unjust harm to any person or entity as a result of the conclusions made or the information provided. Each reader is advised to draw their own conclusions about the information, and before relying on it, to perform their own due diligence.

I sincerely hope this book presents a significant learning experience for all.

Incidentally, my last name is French, and it is pronounced "PE...TEET". You often see it used in describing female sizes of attire but with an "e" on the end to delineate a female adjective meaning small. So much for your French lesson! Thank you.

ADVICE FOR THE ENTREPRENEUR

I wish to begin by providing three documents that have been particularly meaningful during the entrepreneurial portion my life. They are written by Mother Teresa, President Theodore Roosevelt and Rudyard Kipling. These are documents that I gained access to during my entrepreneurial journey, and they became very meaningful at various phases of my life.

I think these documents speak very effectively to the entrepreneur. This is certainly true because most entrepreneurial journeys can be quite lonely, intimidating, thankless and frustrating. As you reflect on these literary creations, I believe it will help you better understand the entrepreneur and the issues that will be associated with their lives and their dilemmas.

Please enjoy!

MOTHER TERESA

The more that I have learned over the years about Mother Teresa, the more convinced I have become that she was one of the most positive and influential individuals who has walked the face of this earth. In her lifetime, she demonstrated numerous attributes and gifts in serving mankind. I believe what was posted in her children's home in Calcutta, India, "Do It Anyway," clearly demonstrates the immense amount of wisdom this Saint possessed.

I will not comment directly in this book on my love of her words. I believe that her statements and their meaning will speak very eloquently, but in perhaps somewhat different ways to each of us.

The prayer, or poem, "Do It Anyway," has been attributed by many to Mother Teresa while others say it was written by a young college student leader. Either way, I believe she strove to live by those words. For me, it is so applicable to what you will read about in this book.

These thoughts have given me real strength and new wisdom during any frustrating periods of my life. Hopefully, they will do the same for you.

Do It Anyway

People are often unreasonable, illogical and self-centered;
forgive them anyway.

If you are kind, people may accuse you
of selfish, ulterior motives;
be kind anyway.

If you are successful, you will win some false friends
and some true enemies;
succeed anyway.

If you are honest and frank, people may cheat you;
be honest and frank anyway.

What you spend years building,
someone could destroy overnight;
build anyway.

If you find serenity and happiness,
there may be jealousy;
be happy anyway.

The good you do today
people will often forget tomorrow;
do good anyway.

Give the world the best you have,
and it may never be enough;
give the world the best you've got anyway.

You see, in the final analysis,
it is between you and God;
it was never between you and them anyway.

THEODORE ROOSEVELT

As another document that has been very meaningful to me in my life, I offer, "While Daring Greatly," by President Theodore Roosevelt. This could have been called, "The Entrepreneur's Inspiration."

WHILE DARING GREATLY

It is not the critic who counts; not the man who points out how the strong man stumbled, or where the doer of deeds could have done them better. The credit belongs to the man who is actually in the arena, whose face is marred by dust and sweat and blood; who strives valiantly; who errs and comes short again and again; who knows the great enthusiasms, the great devotions, and spends himself in a worthy cause; who at the best knows in the end the triumph of high achievement, and who at the worst if he fails, at least fails while daring greatly; so that hisplace shall never be with those cold and timid souls who know neither victory nor defeat.

RUDYARD KIPLING

Rudyard Kipling's poem, If-, was given to me in 1984 in a large frame and signed by over one hundred Healthdyne associates and managers. This was prompted by a number of successful battles that the company had just fought. You can appreciate how much I love the words and the thoughts from our staff.

If-

If you can keep your head when all about you
Are losing theirs and blaming it on you,
If you can trust yourself when all men doubt you,
But make allowance for their doubting too;
If you can wait and not be tired by waiting,
Or being lied about, don't deal in lies,
Or being hated don't give way to hating,
And yet don't look too good, nor talk too wise;
If you can dream - and not make dreams your master;
If you can think - and not make thoughts your aim,
If you can meet with Triumph and Disaster
And then treat those two imposters just the same;
If you can bear to hear the truth you've spoken
Twisted by knaves to make a trap for fools,
Or watch the things you gave your life to, broken,
And stoop and build 'em up with worn-out tools;
If you can make one heap of all your winnings
And risk it on one turn of the pitch-and-toss,
And lose, and start again at your beginnings
And never breathe a word about your loss;
If you can force your heart and nerve and sinew
To serve your turn long after they are gone,
And so hold on when there's nothing in you
Except the will which says to them: "Hold on!"
If you can talk with crowds and keep your virtue,
Or walk with Kings - nor lose the common touch,
If neither foes nor loving friends can hurt you,
If all men count with you, but none too much;
You can fill the unforgiving minute
With sixty seconds' worth of distance run,
Yours is the earth and everything that's in it,
And - which is more - you'll be a man, my son!

TABLE OF CONTENTS

Preface	1
Introduction	2

CHAPTERS

1.	Management Concepts and Personal Development	15
2:	The Tragedy	33
3.	Participative Management	39
4.	The Early Years	51
5.	Growing Up and Going Public	61
6.	Exciting Growth	75
7.	Maturing	91
8.	Matria Healthcare	109
9.	Early History of MiMedx	121
10.	Our Boards of Directors	131
11.	Whistleblowing and Short Selling Begin	143
12.	Channel Stuffing and Revenue Recognition Accusations	169
13.	Short Selling	185

Photos and Figures

14.	The Sally Yates Doctrine and the Whistleblower Laws	207
15.	Protecting Short Selling	219
16.	MiMedx is a Poster Child	227
17.	Opportunists	237
18.	MiMedx Proxy Contest	251
19.	Contributing Factors to the Investigation	265
20.	Accounting Matters	281
21.	MiMedx's Allegations Against Executives	313
22.	Government Charges Against Executives	361
23.	Pre-trial Activities	381
24.	The Trial	397
25.	Incarceration	429
26.	The Summary	437
Acknowledgments		450

PREFACE

I have devoted almost 50 years of my life to serial entrepreneurial activities, the majority of which were healthcare related. During 37 of those years, I functioned as Chief Executive Officer and/or Chairman of the Board of those various companies, all while they were publicly traded. These companies had combined annual revenues of well over $1 billion and employed over 3,500 individuals. All of these companies were successfully sold to larger organizations by mid 2008. Thus, I have an intimate knowledge of most of the issues related to managing a publicly traded company and the pros and cons of that environment.

The principle goal of this book is to better inform entrepreneurs, business executives, their Boards and shareholders of the new and broader risks of managing or investing in a public company in today's legal and regulatory environment. I believe, as do many others, that this is an environment that is now out of control in numerous ways.

I will be highlighting the changes, mostly legal and regulatory in nature, which have driven the risks of entrepreneurship in America far beyond reasonableness. The balance has swung from those who create wealth (and jobs) to those who merely rearrange wealth, namely certain types of lawyers. You will have the opportunity to scrutinize certain aspects of our "new" judicial system, particularly its politicization, as it regulates publically traded businesses.

The story of my last company, MiMedx Group, will be particularly informative and sometimes even shocking! The MiMedx saga will provide substantial insight into the good, the bad and the ugly of managing a public company in America today. There are a great many lessons embodied in those chapters that will be extremely beneficial to those facing The Entrepreneur's Dilemma, which is to decide whether or not to take their company public. If you are already involved with a publicly traded company, these MiMedx chapters should prove to be even more valuable to you!

It is my sincere hope and prayer that the events I have described will provide insights that will help improve corporate performance, prevent unnecessary regulatory and legal actions, and rein in the Wall Street activities that are very detrimental to American businesses and their shareholders.

INTRODUCTION

In the first chapters of this book, I will discuss the history of my personal journey into the entrepreneurial world. Then, I will review some of my management concepts and how we applied those to our fast-growth operations. I will try to differentiate between management, leadership and the administrative qualities that are necessary for success in the entrepreneurial organization. While there are numerous similarities to general management requirements, including leadership and administrative skills, there are some very specific needs for the start-up organization that are not necessarily a requirement in a mature and slower-growth organization. I will share the attributes I have determined, often by trial and my error, that will benefit the small and medium-sized rapidly growing entrepreneurial organizations.

After the initial chapters discussing management, I will review my corporate history and the numerous business transactions and developments that were coordinated over the decades to help build our organizations. These involved financial transactions, acquisitions, divestures and investments in new products and services, as well as two "unfriendly takeovers." I will also discuss "opportunists" and their continuous presence and danger.

In the intermediate chapters of the book, I will discuss some of the successes of my first company, Healthdyne. Healthdyne grew to become four separate publicly traded companies that were all eventually sold to larger organizations. In the mid-1990s, the Board gave, through tax-free dividends, three of the Healthdyne subsidiaries to our shareholders, which broke Healthdyne down into separate companies, all in different facets of healthcare. These companies were Healthdyne Technologies, Healthdyne Maternity Management (later, Matria Healthcare) and Healthdyne Information Enterprises. The other publicly traded subsidiary, Home Nutritional Services, was sold in April of 1994 just prior to the dividending of the other three companies.

As the book unfolds, you will see these and other transactions come out in a number of stories and examples of entrepreneurial initiatives, activities and management. Also, I will discuss a couple of problems we encountered with our acquisitions, all of which related to the honesty and integrity of the management of the companies being acquired.

Generally, all our companies had robust growth rates during most of their maturation. This growth came through very precise sales planning, the development of new medical technologies and services and, in some cases, acquisitions.

Actually, over the decades, our companies acquired 38 other companies. We also divested a number of our companies that were built or acquired and blended. I believe, at last count, there were over eight of those divestitures. We had seven initial and secondary public offerings of Healthdyne and its subsidiaries. We also had two convertible debt offerings.

The last former Healthdyne subsidiary, Matria Healthcare, was acquired in May of 2008 by Inverness Medical. I went into a semi-retirement phase of life after that sale. I set up a family office and was planning to manage the family's portfolio alongside my children. However, after six months, a business opportunity was brought to me by an old friend and fellow entrepreneur, Steve Gorlin.

This business was MiMedx Group, and it was essentially bankrupt. I joined the company in early 2009 as its new Chairman of the Board and Chief Executive Officer and became a major investor as well. After we negotiated an early small acquisition, MiMedx developed into one of the fastest-growing and most successful companies that I have ever known or managed. According to Fortune magazine, MiMedx was the fifth fastest-growing public company in America by 2017, ahead of Facebook and Amazon!

In the fall of 2017, a short seller began to harass MiMedx with numerous allegations and suspicious trading activity. Some of these trading details were given to us by DOJ investigators from the Southern District of New York (SDNY). The short seller's goal was to drive down the price of the company's stock from its high of about $18 per share, which was approximately a $2 billion valuation. Even though they were aware of his activities, there was no regulatory intervention by the Securities and Exchange Commission (SEC) or the Department of Justice (DOJ), and the attacks continued, causing the company, its shareholders and employees substantial damage as the stock traded down to $1 per share. After almost five years from my departing the company, the stock was only trading in the $3 range.

There is currently a very uneven playing field and differing regulatory enforcement for public companies and their officers versus unlawful short sellers and other corrupt Wall Street entities. The lack of federal enforcement surrounding the alleged short selling activities plus a self-serving Board of Directors were the major factors in forcing not only my resignation in June of 2018, but also 19 of MiMedx's other top executives who had spent many years building this very successful and unique company.

The last part of the book covers the MiMedx history and some explanations as to why I and the other top executives were asked to resign. This was effectively a corporate "takeover" by a Board that proved to be incompetent. After about five years, MiMedx had little revenue growth, and their market value was approximately 15 percent of its previous high value!

MiMedx is quite a saga of out of control short sellers, some deceitful sales employees, a paranoid Audit Committee Chairman, a self-serving Board of Directors along with a politically motivated investigation that cost over $200 million in fees for law firms and accounting firms. Also, there were federal regulators ignoring unlawful short selling and federal lawyers working in their own self-interest. Sound interesting? Well, the MiMedx situation will be very, very informative!

Because of what happened to MiMedx, I felt it was very important to document all the issues that transpired to cause the suffering of MiMedx shareholders, management, employees and ultimately our patients. There is extremely important educational information in these later chapters for entrepreneurs, business executives and their Boards, certain types of lawyers, investors, stockbrokers, brokerage house executives, regulators, Congress and even for the Executive Branch of our government.

Today, individuals involved in publicly traded enterprises should be concerned about the current SEC regulations and their enforcement as highlighted by the MiMedx story. MiMedx encountered this "perfect storm" as a result of corruption in today's capital markets, the self-serving activity of government prosecutors in todays "new" justice system and unscrupulous short selling. There will be countless lessons in those discussions, which will be beneficial to you as you face The Entrepreneur's Dilemma of whether to take your company public. As you continue to read, you should realize that MiMedx Group is a superb example of why the majority of small to medium-sized companies should not be publicly traded in today's regulatory and capital market environment.

The Entrepreneurs

Of course, one of the prevalent terms used in this book is "entrepreneur." By definition, an entrepreneur is "an individual who creates a new business, bearing most of the risks and enjoying most of the rewards." But, who exactly is this person? What traits do they possess that lead them to undertake such innovative and risky endeavors? How do successful entrepreneurs take a creative idea and turn it into a functioning and effective operation? How do they cope with the numerous risks associated with entrepreneurship? I hope to convey some answers to these and other important questions.

Individuals who had confidence, courage and a new vision for their future were the principal founders of America. Initially, these individuals were predominantly Europeans who were fed up with the continuous religious conflicts and various governmental abuses, and thus, they developed a vision for "freedom." They sailed away from their heritage and families for potentially a new life in America. Thus, America saw an influx of millions of "risk takers" and "visionaries." Today, America still attracts these types of individuals, and we still call them entrepreneurs. I believe this is the primary reason America has outperformed and outpaced all other countries over the centuries.

As a side note, many people use the word "visionary" to describe entrepreneurs. While that term applies to a degree, it takes a specific type of personality to distinguish "visions" from "hallucinations." Most entrepreneurs begin with a creative vision, but it takes a strong sense of self-confidence, courage and the ability to synthesize to really be successful. The synthesis process combines various concepts into one unified entity. My experience has shown that few people have that ability. The best entrepreneurial managers can view numerous random variables and come up with solutions that can be built into a business plan that their associates can understand, become excited about and align with. A business "vision" is a practical plan that can be brought down to operating reality with revenues and profits. A business "hallucination" is exactly the opposite with the probability of failure or near failure evident to the experienced visionary or business executive!

Over the years, I have spoken to some very intelligent and esteemed professors and advanced degree students at my alma mater, the Georgia Institute of Technology, about their entrepreneurial concepts and endeavors. I always clearly stated to them that the level of intellect in the room was well above mine! However, I was apparently blessed with "common sense" and a keen ability to synthesize. I certainly did not have a photographic memory, like many of the professors did. Therefore, I had to use logic to punch my way through Georgia Tech exams. That is where I began to polish my logical thinking, which I associate with common sense - another vital attribute of a successful entrepreneur.

The management of an entrepreneurial organization necessarily differs from that of a more mature corporate entity. The mature corporation has established processes, procedures and systems that have been previously developed. In addition, in most cases the growth rate is slow to moderate; thus, the hiring and training requirements are significantly different.

On the other hand, with the entrepreneurial organization, the challenge is always satisfying the normal business requirements while simultaneously developing operational and management control systems, dealing with a robust staffing scenario, addressing facilities needs and, finally, raising capital!

As the entrepreneurial enterprise leaves the garage and moves into commercial space, the management tasks and requirements for the new organization escalate rapidly. In those early days of growth, the balancing act between optimizing growth prospects and maintaining adequate controls over the business can be quite daunting. As I will discuss in the early chapters, the entrepreneurial manager has a much more challenging set of responsibilities than the corporate manager who functions within a generally mature organization. And, as I just mentioned, the entrepreneur has the pressing responsibility to raise the necessary funding for the new enterprise to keep its doors open.

In its early development, I strongly believe that an entrepreneurial endeavor should have access to an individual with certain business acumen and experience to help guide key strategic decisions. For instance, is the new concept capable of supporting a business enterprise on its own potential, or should the initial goals focus on a concept that could be sold or licensed as a product line to another business entity? Is the capital required to develop the business capable of being raised without giving up too much ownership and total control? This is where the right "angel investor" can be of help.

When I started my first company, Healthdyne, in 1970, entrepreneurship was well respected and often the subject of much media attention. All of our successes were certainly well documented in the local and sometimes national media. Then, in the late 2000s, the focus began to change, possibly caused by some business scandals, such as Enron or an administrative change in Washington that seemed anti-business…Remember the infamous statement that the president made on NBC News: "If you've got a business, you didn't build that. Somebody else made that happen."

In terms of honoring traditional entrepreneurship, I truly believe that our country has lost its way. Whether entrepreneurs have successes or failures, they should be honored for having the <u>courage</u> to put themselves, as well as their capital, at risk to start a business enterprise that will create jobs for others. Whether it is a bakery shop on the corner or a revolutionary new technology concept, everyone, and particularly the news media, should recognize the importance of America's entrepreneurial heritage and spirit. I pray this book can rekindle the much-needed respect that entrepreneurs received in the past from the press and the public. In addition, I hope it will inform less experienced entrepreneurs and business executives about ways to more effectively manage their organizations and avoid the many potential pitfalls that have developed around America business as well as our citizens. Finally, these disclosures should help focus our

Department of Justice, the other governmental agencies and our politicians on "integrity" rather than "politics."

Recommended Reading

I would like to mention eleven books that I believe would be very informative for you to review in your educational process or curiosity about publicly traded enterprises and how they are affected by our "new" judicial system. The first three books are about corporate DOJ trials, like ours at MiMedx. The last eight are more broadly focused on the general issues associated with wrongdoing in our justice and regulatory systems.

The three books related to corporate trials, *A Matter of Principle* by Conrad Black, *Cardiac Arrest* by Howard Root, and *Uneven Justice* by Raj Rajaratnam, chronicle very similar DOJ cases as that of MiMedx. They all highlight the corrupt actions of federal prosecutors and their support by the respective judges. In all four cases, prosecutors threatened members of corporate management with indictments and intimidated some into supporting the prosecution's version of the truth.

In Black's case, allegations were made against his management of the company by a few self-serving individual shareholders. Black set up a special committee, which hired a former prosecutor and his law firm, who quickly took control and ran up massive legal fees. This committee oversaw their new management destroy almost all of the value in Black's companies.

Black, like me, was naïve about what massive legal fees would be accumulated and the total disregard our Boards would have for their fiduciary responsibilities to shareholders. In my case, I turned over all the allegations and the investigation to the Audit Committee, as required by the Sarbanes-Oxley regulations. Our Audit Committee's actions caused the same results as Black's special committee. When committees bring in a prosecutor as legal counsel, they generally lose total control of the process, as happened with Black's companies and MiMedx. The Audit Committee members or Board may be so inexperienced in corporate governance and so lacking in courage and confidence that they become merely pawns in the legal game that plays out, much to the detriment of the shareholders, employees and the business. These actions primarily benefit the law firms. The federal prosecutors in Black's case, as well as others, went on to high paying positions at large law firms, as they always do!

Howard Root's company, Vascular Solutions, went through five years of legal harassment because of a dishonest sales employee who was terminated for working for a competing company while being simultaneously employed by Vascular Solutions. After he was fired, this employee became a "whistleblower" and presented numerous lies about Vascular Solutions to the DOJ. The DOJ attorneys' personal desire for trial cases motivated them to open a long and ridiculous investigation, which led to a trial against Howard and his company. There are many similarities in this case to our MiMedx situation, except that the Vascular Solutions Board of Directors united behind management. Vascular Solutions and Howard Root beat the government's DOJ prosecutors when they were finally acquitted in their trial in San Antonio, Texas.

In Raj Rajaratnam's book, *Uneven Justice*, you will discover the corrupt practices of federal prosecutors in the Southern District of New York as they tried him, basically, for "insider trading" at Galleon Group. A stream of prosecutor malfeasance resulted in Raj's conviction, but most importantly, it resulted in all three prosecutors in his case quickly moving on to high paying positions at large law firms. Raj's case had the added complexity of the DOJ conducting illegal wiretaps! Either way, you will find many of the same unprincipled actions from the prosecutors in the Southern District of New York in the Galleon case as those we faced in the MiMedx case.

Needham and Company was one of our investment bankers in the 1980s. George Needham was my favorite investment banker because of his experience and character. George hired Raj Rajaratnam in the mid-1980s as a technology analyst, and Raj advanced quickly to become the President of Needham. I enjoyed getting to know Raj because of his engineering background and his integrity. He left Needham in 1997 after 12 years to start his own hedge fund, Galleon Group. He was very successful very quickly and, by 2009, Galleon had over $7 billion under management as a technology focused fund. Raj was respected for Galleon's performance, his ethics and philanthropic generosity. His net worth grew to over $1 billion. Then, on May 11, 2011, Raj was arrested for insider trading. Raj was incensed because he knew he was innocent. He chose to go to trial. He was found guilty and sentenced to 11 years of incarceration. He admits he was naive as to the DOJ's corrupt prosecutorial tactics as were all four of us…Black, Root, Rajaratnam and Petit. I remember listening to the prosecutor's opening remarks at my trial while thinking, "This is not America!"

As I stated earlier, I would recommend reading these three books after you finish my book. Our four books will put in stark perspective the extent to which our judicial system has become out of balance and corrupt relative to corporate law and the enforcement of regulations, particularly for public companies.

For broader enlightenment, please review the book *The Fruits of Graft* by Wayne Jett. This book delves into the real causes of the Great Depression and our recession of 2008-2009. The reason this is important to entrepreneurs and business executives is that it clearly explains the reason our federal government does not attempt to control or prosecute illegal short sellers and other Wall Street crooks. In Chapter 15, Jett gets into a very deep and broad discussion of why we have Wall Street malfeasance that is ignored by our federal government.

The book titled *Naked, Short and Greedy* by Dr. Suzanne Trimbath provides additional insight as it has detailed discussion about illegal "naked short selling" and "fails to deliver." It covers several problems that are caused by the lack of reasonable and workable regulations and the lack of prudent enforcement of the laws that are already in place. This problem is particularly devastating to small and medium-sized publicly traded companies that are attacked by short sellers who use illegal means to perfect their profits. They will generally use "naked short selling," which means that the shares they borrow are not properly delivered to close the transaction. This is illegal. This book clearly highlights the fact that the Securities and Exchange Commission (SEC) has oversight over the Depository Trust and Clearing Corporation (DTCC) and its subsidiaries, which is where this tragic problem needs to be addressed. However, many Wall Street organizations do not have an interest in resolving these corrupt situations because of the massive profits they provide.

My next recommendation is *Conviction Machine* written by Sidney Powell and Harvey A. Silverglate. It is subtitled Standing Up to Federal Prosecutorial Abuse. These two leading authorities describe the problems within the DOJ and in the federal courts, and then offer some practical solutions.

The seventh book is titled *Licensed to Lie*. It was also written by Sidney Powell. In this book, she continues to outline how many of the federal prosecutors in the DOJ have become a cabal of narcissistic individuals who routinely break the rules for their own benefit.

The eighth book, *Three Felonies a Day*, by Harvey A. Silverglate was also a compelling read. Silverglate documents how our federal laws and regulations have exploded in number over the years; therefore, they have become impossibly broad and vague. He points out how the federal criminal justice system has become dangerously disconnected from the common case traditions of "due process" and a fair notice of the law's expectations. The risk is that this further enables federal prosecutors to pin federal crimes on almost any citizen, even for the most seemingly innocuous behavior. I believe the former top executives of MiMedx are an excellent example of the use of this prosecutorial misconduct.

The ninth book is by legal Professor Alan Dershowitz. Professor Dershowitz, who you see on television often, is the author of over 50 books. He has been particularly prolific in the last year or so because of the number of opportunities that have come up for him to give his very logical critique of the changing U.S. judicial system and the development of our accusation culture. I recently finished his latest book entitled *The Price of Principle.* The book has the subtitle *Why Integrity is Worth the Consequences.* His arguments against the current changes in our justice system are very logical and, frankly, provide hope that we will force the Department of Justice and other governmental agencies to become unpoliticized and back on the right track that has served America so well over the centuries.

The last two books, *Political Prisoner* by Paul Manafort and *Abuse and Power* by Carter Page, are examples of the justice system politically focusing on individuals associated with President Donald Trump's 2016 campaign. These books clearly demonstrate the political focus of our new Department of Justice and the corrupt nature of the DOJ prosecutors. There will be facts described which will truly challenge and frustrate your background as an American. This should be the case regardless of your political leanings.

I know that many of you will have the same thoughts that I did as I entered into my indictment and trial process, and as I read several books about what would transpire, particularly related to our "new" Justice Department losing its integrity. Thus, I offer all these other opportunities for enlightenment through numerous other authors.

As another very valuable source of information on this subject, I want to recommend a new HBO Max documentary called "Wall Street Gaming." It is available on the streaming service of HBO. The first part of the movie relates to the background on what I call the trading rebellion related to GameStop and the subsequent activities of the Robinhood brokerage firm. This situation, which developed in late 2019 and into 2020, came about because numerous fans of GameStop products were incensed by the steep price declines that the company's stock had endured. They came together in a social media frenzy, and millions of shares were purchased. This forced the illegal short sellers to begin to have to sell their positions as the stock price began its meteoric rise. Before it was over, hedge funds had been decimated as they had to close out their positions, many of which had been opened with "failures to close" their shorted stock positions which resulted in counterfeit shares being developed. While this was quite a story in its own right because it exposed the huge issues related to illegal short selling and the "fails to deliver" issues associated with it, it was just the tip of the iceberg.

As the program continues, it introduces several very important people who have been especially effective in calling out these issues for many years. First is Wes Christian, a very successful attorney in Houston who has been focused for 20 years on trying to legally thwart these unlawful short selling activities that are supported by Wall Street brokerage houses. Wes is the most successful litigator in the U.S. on these matters. He teamed up in the documentary with David Wenger, who is the founder of a firm by the name of ShareIntel which has been very successful in developing exceptionally sophisticated software that will allow this illegal trading and all of the various supporting schemes to be exposed. In later chapters, you will read where, while at MiMedx, I utilized ShareIntel when our short selling first began in order to develop detailed information on the trading activity in our stock.

The program goes into the activities of both Christian and Wenger. Also, interviews are conducted with Dr. Suzanne Trimbath, the author of *Naked, Short and Greedy*. As I mentioned previously, she is an expert in this area and is very knowledgeable about the lack of action taken by the SEC, FINRA and the Depository Trust and Clearing Corporation (DTCC) and its subsidiaries relative to illegal short selling.

As a future or current entrepreneur or public company executive, you should be sure that your Board members and top management read these books. Then, you should conduct group discussions that will help you assess their acumen and courage to cope. This process should determine which Board members really understand their fiduciary responsibility to shareholders and would take some personal risk to uphold that responsibility. This could also help determine which Board members or management could become opportunists to the detriment of the company.

I sincerely hope that Boards and their executive management will avail themselves of these books to learn defensive techniques.

The Lawyers

As you read this book, you will clearly notice that I have become rather critical of certain types of attorneys, their law firms, as well as the DOJ in general. My criticism stems from the fact that we have many more lawyers in this country per capita than any of the other developed countries in the world. This overabundance of lawyers, which has occurred over the last 40 years, has resulted in some real distortions in our laws, legal processes, justice system and our way of life.

In the early years of my businesses, I was fortunate enough to have met former Georgia Governor Carl Sanders, who was one of the founders of the Troutman Sanders law firm. Carl was an exceptional attorney, but also had the common sense and acumen of a business executive. That was a rare combination, and I was very fortunate to have him on our Boards of Directors for over 20 years. Also, I had access to him as a personal friend. What I witnessed with Carl and the Troutman Sanders attorneys was the epitome of ethics and integrity.

In the 1980s and 1990s, my involvement with attorneys and law firms was very straightforward, and I never ran into a case of unethical behavior or dishonesty. Now, I am not so naïve as to think there was no such dishonesty occurring then, but it was not very widespread. Today, I am afraid this behavior has become more common. There no longer seems to be as much emphasis placed on the importance of integrity in our judicial system as there once was, particularly as it pertains to misrepresentations, manipulations and even lying! I believe the mainstream media has played a part in the increase in this unscrupulous behavior because they do not investigate or publicize it.

Because of my criticisms of our "new" justice department and their judicial processes and pointing out where flaws have developed, I will probably receive some type of retribution. For the sake of this country, I wish to see that these inappropriate activities are properly exposed and their negative effects on Americans and our businesses begin to cease. If that means retribution will come my way, so be it! My fellow Americans deserve to know the truth, if they do not already, that many of the values our country once held dear have significantly deteriorated. I absolutely believe that "integrity is worth the consequences" as Alan Dershowitz states in his new book, The *Price of Principle*. I believe MiMedx will be a "Poster Child" and, as such, will stimulate congressional action and self-reflection by the legal community so that these abhorrent behaviors and activities will eventually come to an end.

Appendices

There are a number of published articles that I consider to be very informative and supportive of some of the issues that I am bringing to light in this book. At the end of certain pertinent chapters, I have included an Appendix that lists the articles by title and author. If you are unable to find these on the internet, I will keep them inventoried on my personal website, petepetit.com.

My personal website was developed over 10 years ago at the request of a number of the large MiMedx shareholders. It presents my entrepreneurial background. Also, I previously began to highlight some of the many issues surrounding improper short selling on the website.

Once you open my website, go to the home page and click on the book title. It will take you to the book's specific site. There you will see "Appendices" in the top navigation bar. Click there and you will find all of the articles I used for the book, grouped by chapter.

Thank You

CHAPTER 1

MANAGEMENT CONCEPTS AND PERSONAL DEVELOPMENT

Upon full retirement, I decided that I had accumulated some valuable personal and business experience that could be very informative to fellow entrepreneurs, public company executives, their Boards and investors. I wanted to share numerous and particularly meaningful experiences that occurred during my long tenure – experiences that should educate, sometimes surprise and, at other times, even irritate and disappoint.

In this process, I want to emphasize some of my personality traits that led to successes and other traits that might have caused some of my failures. These relate to my propensity for management, which to me embodies both leadership skills as well as administrative skills. I find it much easier to break down management into these two skill sets when training and explaining how to obtain optimal results from both those attributes. I believe both contribute to overall management success.

First, I will discuss how I view management with the embodiment of these personal leadership and administrative attributes. I think you will find that this is a rather logical way to discuss the skill sets that managers, leaders and administrators must possess. As an entrepreneur, you will be making numerous decisions about people and your staff, and I believe you will find it easier to understand how to make optimal decisions of this nature by classifying the required skill sets in this manner.

Management

Very simply put, the leadership component of management makes good things happen in the organization, and the administrative component keeps bad things from happening.

I view the leadership component of management as dealing with subjects, such as producing a "vision" or long-term strategy for the organization, inspiring and motivating subordinates, developing creativity and setting examples. In many cases, leadership is involved with the "why" an organization must accomplish certain tasks, goals and objectives, and "why" it is in the employees' best interest to align themselves with these efforts. When leadership is effective, everyone knows and understands where they are going, and they are enthusiastic about participating. Also, good leadership will challenge and produce beneficial "change" in an organization. Generally, leadership <u>makes</u> <u>good</u> <u>things</u> <u>happen</u>.

The administrative component of management is primarily concerned with the setting of goals and the delegation and completion of tasks and projects. This must include the proper levels of authority and controls that allow subordinates to accomplish their delegated responsibilities. The administrative component generally deals with the "what," the "who," the "where," the "when," and the "how" issues related to management tasks. Effective administrators control and solve problems and, in so doing, they create and maintain "order" within an organization, or <u>keep</u> <u>bad</u> <u>things</u> <u>from</u> <u>happening</u>.

If we break up management into these two subcomponents, it is much easier to picture the successes and failures of different management activities. Since management must be carried out by individuals, the ability to recognize their successes and failures and categorize them either as leadership issues or administrative issues is very helpful. Also, since an effective and growing organization must balance "change" and "order," it is imperative that the personality traits that cause these counteracting forces, which result from various individuals' leadership or administrative skills, be clearly understood by the key decision-makers.

Before I delve into the many management situations that will be informative, it will be beneficial to understand a little more about my personality, my DNA and background. So please bear with me as we roll back the decades to the point where I began to have some insight into the traits and talents that I have been given. Then, I will discuss management philosophies in some detail.

My Personal History

I was born on August 4, 1939, at Emory University Hospital in Atlanta. While my parents' families were both from Charleston, South Carolina, they met in Atlanta where my father was the editor of a trade magazine.

Both my grandfathers were entrepreneurs, having started and developed their own businesses. My father's father started a dry goods business in Charleston in his late teens, which was possible because he was fortunate enough to make $1,200 on a horseracing bet that cost him 25 cents. He was a consummate risk taker as he continued to bet on the horses until the Great Depression caused a loss of most of his net worth. In the meantime, he also started one of the first movie theaters in Charleston. And, he was a respected member of the Charleston County Commissioners.

My mother's father somehow became involved in the tobacco business, and he owned a tobacco processing operation. Unfortunately, I do not know much about his business history. He died at the early age of 53, probably as a result of smoking. Sadly, both of my grandfathers passed away before I was born.

My father was a rather risk averse personality, and he did not have his father's propensity for business. However, he had a very strong work ethic and was a gifted salesperson, writer and author. He was also an administrator of "tough love."

As a pre-teen in Jacksonville, Florida, I joined the Boy Scouts. I enjoyed the challenge of proceeding through the six ranks to obtain my Eagle Scout rank. I remained very focused on the Eagle rank, and I achieved it prior to my 15th birthday. I was trying to emulate my father, who was one of the earliest in America to become an Eagle Scout. My son, Bill, and his two sons obtained the Eagle rank, and my youngest daughter, Meredith, has her two sons moving rapidly toward this goal as well.

When I was in the ninth grade, representatives from General Motors made a presentation at my junior high school about the opportunities offered by the Fisher Body Craftsman Guild. The Guild enabled a teenager to design and build a model car for their annual contest and potentially win cash or a college scholarship. I had done well making model airplanes, so I thought this might be something that I would enjoy, and it would potentially have a payoff for college. I made a model car during my sophomore, junior and senior years in high school. My first car won no awards, but my last two won regional awards, which included $250 and a trip to General Motors in Detroit for the convention. That $500 basically paid for my first quarter at Georgia Tech. My last two model cars are shown in Figures 1 and 2.

While in high school in Charleston, South Carolina, I participated in football and track. I was relatively quick, but after about 70 yards, the guys with the long legs would always pass me in the 100-yard dash at the track meets. My football can be summarized by what my high school coach said to me at our 20th year class reunion. He waved me over, and gave me a big hug and said, "Petit, pound for pound, you were the best football player I ever had, but there just were <u>not</u> enough pounds!" I replied, "But, Coach, I always gave 120 percent!" Coach retorted, "Yes, you did, but there were still <u>not</u> enough pounds!"

By my senior year in high school, I had a strong desire to become either an architect or an engineer. I found out about the "cooperative" engineering programs at Georgia Tech, Auburn and Virginia Tech. This allowed an engineering student to work every other quarter in industry and graduate in five years. Since my family had no ability to financially assist with my college education, I knew that I had to pursue the engineering degree as I could not put myself through architectural school. Two of my classmates had decided to go to Auburn on the cooperative program, so I decided to follow them, even though I had also been accepted at Georgia Tech and Virginia Tech. However, I woke up one Saturday morning in July and had an epiphany that my future was in Atlanta and at Georgia Tech. I was born in Atlanta, and Georgia Tech had won eight consecutive football post-season bowl games, thanks to Coach Bobby Dodd. I am sure I had a few other thoughts, but I changed my mind and told my two friends that I was going to Georgia Tech. As it turned out, Auburn won the national football championship in the fall of 1957 and beat Georgia Tech 3-0!

In order for me to obtain a cooperative job in industry and work during the winter quarter, I had to have a 2.0 grade point average. Yes, that is a C average. However, in those days, the student grade point average at Georgia Tech was about 2.2. That equivalent point average today is about 3.1. So let us not frown on my numbers yet! Unlike today, parents received a copy of a student's six weeks grades in the middle of the quarter. I was flunking both math and chemistry at the six weeks point. My father wrote me a very poignant two sentence "tough love" note which read, "Dear Son, We have received your six weeks grades. I will have the army recruiter waiting to meet with you when you come home for Christmas. Affectionately, Dad." Please note that there was no mention of coming home for Thanksgiving!

Well, I was already very motivated to stay in Atlanta during the Thanksgiving break, but I certainly decided **not** to go home after receiving that note. I remained in the dorm and studied for four days. I made a C in both math and chemistry, and I had a 2.4 overall point average for my first quarter. I improved my point average by several decimal points by graduation, and that put me in the top third of the graduating class. I had to put in more study hours than most, but that rigor seemed to agree with me.

My management interest really began to develop at my fraternity at Georgia Tech. It started with the desire to fix a few problems that the fraternity had. Of course, I was beginning to think that I was more motivated to serve than some of the other brothers. I thought my way of doing things would be faster and more effective. So I ran for my first officer position as a third quarter freshman, and I won. I held a second position as a sophomore, and set my sights on being the fraternity President as a junior. In this process, I learned a little bit about politics. When I ran for president, which we called the Archon, I was critical of the seniors because I thought they were not carrying their share of the load given all their experience. That sentiment did not go over very well in the election, and I lost. I ran again my senior year, and I was elected Archon for my last two quarters. I graduated with my Bachelor's degree in Mechanical Engineering in June of 1962.

Please bear with me for a minute while I tell a humorous story that all Georgia Tech graduates will certainly enjoy. It relates to Dean George C. Griffin, who was respectfully called, "Mr. Georgia Tech," and how he taught me a management lesson.

Briefly, Dean Griffin spent almost his whole adult life at Georgia Tech besides his military tours in World War I and II. He came to Tech in 1914 when he was 18 years old. He used to lament that it took him six years to graduate. However, during that period of time he played football, ran track and served in the Navy. After graduation, he stayed on to help Coach Alexander with various athletic coaching activities. He eventually became Dean of Students. In effect, that meant Dean of Men up until the mid-50s when Georgia Tech finally accepted their first co-ed. Dean Griffin went to his office routinely until he neared his final days. He passed away on April 21, 1990.

Dean Griffin was a "tough love" personality, but a very caring individual. He did all types of things to help Georgia Tech students succeed, including bailing them out of jail when necessary.

Dean Griffin was an alumnus of my social fraternity, Pi Kappa Phi. He told me that, when he was a chapter member, Pi Kappa Phi was one of the largest fraternities on campus. However, a disaster occurred in the 1930s when their large house burned down and, unfortunately, the fraternity's treasurer forgot to pay the last insurance payment. Therefore, the chapter lost almost everything. When I joined in 1957, it was a small fraternity, but it had some members that I thoroughly enjoyed and respected. Also, Pi Kappa Phi was founded at the College of Charleston, which was located in the hometown of my mother's and father's families and where I finished high school.

Either way, as I previously mentioned, I was elected the Archon, or President, of our chapter at the end of fall quarter of 1961. At that point, I only had two more quarters until I was to graduate or, as Tech men would say, "Get out!"

This Dean Griffin story will demonstrate my inexperience and over-confidence at the young age of 22. When I came to the fraternity house the first day of the winter quarter, there was a note on the bulletin board, "Petit, come see Dean

Griffin." When any student went to see Dean Griffin, it was always an experience. He was a man of few words, and those words could be very specific and often harsh. But, in this case, I thought he might want to congratulate me on being elected Archon. I was being a little optimistic as that proved not to be the case!

I went "up the hill" to his office and waited in line. When my time came, Dean Griffin gave me the normal greeting with an arm wave, "Petit, come in here." If he did not know you, his greeting was generally, "What do you want, boy?" He was flipping through some school computer printouts as I approached his desk. He looked up and started tapping his pencil on one of the pages. He began with the comment, "Petit, I am blank-blank tired of seeing my fraternity ranked 26 out of 26 of the fraternities on campus in academics." I quickly responded with, "But Dean Griffin, we won the football trophy and the blood drive trophy in the fall quarter." Dean Griffin responded as he more harshly tapped on the page, "I don't give a blank-blank about those things. I want to see you get our fraternity out of last place academically. Now, get your 'A' down this hill and straighten those boys out." I replied, "Yes, sir."

Well, as I walked back down the hill to the fraternity house, I kept thinking to myself that Dean Griffin had just asked me to do an impossible task. We were a group of guys that placed more emphasis on athletics and having a little fun than we did on academics, and I doubted that I would be able to have an impact. However, I let the chapter know in our first weekly meeting what Dean Griffin wanted accomplished. We set up some study halls, and we became more organized about our "files" of old exams. We did all we knew how to do during the winter quarter.

When I came to the fraternity house on the first day of spring quarter, there was a note on the bulletin board, "Petit, come see Dean Griffin." My first thought was to call his secretary and find out what happened with the rankings. When I called and asked, she told me that there was "not much change," but she did not give me the numbers. Then, I asked what did he want to see me about, and she said, "The same thing."

When I arrived at the Dean's office, I stopped by to see his secretary first to ask for the new rankings. She told me that we had gone from 26 out of 26 up to 25 out of 26. We no longer had the lowest average grades of any fraternity on campus! Therefore, I thought I might get some congratulations…my optimistic outlook!

When I walked in, Dean Griffin was looking at the school computer printouts again. I walked up and took the initiative by saying that his secretary had just told me that our fraternity had moved up one spot off the bottom. Dean Griffin looked up at me and said, "Son, that is not what I am talking about." He continued, "I want you guys up here at the top of this list, not hanging out at the bottom."

I responded, "Yes sir, I will take the message back to the chapter and set the top academic spot as one of our primary goals." He then gave me his hand wave, which signaled that we were finished, but I noted that he did have a big smile on his face!

As I walked down the hill back to the fraternity house, I remember thinking I was glad I was graduating at the end of the quarter because reaching this goal was going to be a very hard road. I think that about 25 years later, the chapter finally made it close to the top spot academically; however, I knew this was certainly not going to happen with the group of brothers that were there with me. At that time, we only had one brother that I recall, Bob Snuggs, who was on the Dean's List. Bob went on to get his PhD in Physics, and he had a very esteemed career with the Naval Sea Systems Command.

Well, I learned a lesson in management about responsibility from Dean Griffin. He was holding me responsible for making a significant change to our chapter's goals because of my election as the Archon. Along with titles comes responsibility, whether you want it or not!

My next real experiences in management, leadership and administration came after I graduated and went to ROTC summer camp in order to obtain my second lieutenant's commission. ROTC summer camp was quite a learning experience for all the cadets. You had your normal harassment by the drill sergeants, but you also had opportunities to manage and lead as the command of the company, the platoon and the squads changed daily.

Also, there was a competitive nature to ROTC summer camp as all the universities were competing for the number one position grade-wise. This grading included all aspects of our training. The year prior to this summer camp, Georgia Tech had lost the competition for the first time in many years to the University of Illinois. We had heard about that loss all year long as we prepared ourselves for the 1962 summer camp. I cannot say we did much to pre-prepare for the camp as I later learned the University of Illinois cadets had done. However, we were determined not to lose to Illinois or anybody else again. As it turned out, my platoon commander, Captain Higuard, was an ROTC staff officer at the University of Illinois. So he was very focused on "the competition" for first place and seeing Illinois win again.

Captain Higuard met me one-on-one the first week of summer camp, and he seemed to never forget me, probably because it was a rather humorous meeting. I was sitting alone in our barracks latrine (bathroom) about 10:30 in the morning because I had KP (kitchen) duty that day, and there was no latrine in the kitchen building. So I had to run back to our barracks to take care of my morning "ritual." In those days, there were no partitions in the latrine. There were 12 toilets in a row spaced about 18 inches apart. I was sitting there in the middle of my activity when I heard the door to the barracks burst open and Captain Higuard talking to our platoon lieutenant. I heard his footsteps approaching the latrine, and the next thing I knew he was stepping down into the room with a surprised look on his face. He asked, "What are you doing here?" I explained the situation about my being on KP duty.

The Captain went about his business of finding flaws in the clean-up that we had done the night before, and he used me as a sounding board. He ran his finger up under the bowl in one toilet, and it came out with some colored material on it! Then, he stuck his finger in my face. He made it clear to me that I was responsible to see that, when he did that again the next morning, his finger would come back clean. He also called out a dead fly on the window sill! I continued sitting until he finished his inspection and walked out. I quickly completed my "business" and ran back down to the KP building. That evening, I had a lot to say to the rest of the platoon about how the latrine needed to look the next morning. As I recall, the Captain did not complain the next day so my "latrine leadership" that night apparently solved the toilet cleanliness problem!

So that is how I met Captain Higuard "up close and personal." Toward the end of summer camp, he called me into his office and asked me to close the door. First, he told me that I had come in second place in the platoon behind Cadet Pierre Latour from the Virginia Polytechnic Institute, now Virginia Tech. I considered that flattering because Latour was a very polished cadet, and we had become friends. Actually, his younger brother, Ted, was a fraternity brother of mine at Georgia Tech.

Captain Higuard then told me that the military panel wanted to offer me a regular commission in the Army rather than my maintaining my reserve commission through ROTC. That would require me to put in a commitment for several extra years without any additional special training being given. I was not ready to make that kind of commitment, so I turned down the offer for a regular commission. The same offer was also made to me when I was preparing to come off of active duty some years later. I felt that, since I had a master's degree from Georgia Tech at that point, I needed to find out what that would mean for me career-wise. So I turned down the regular commission offer again. I enjoyed my first military tour and probably would have enjoyed a career in the military. But, as I suspected, there were more important matters in my future.

After asking me that question, Higuard began another conversation, which was intriguing. He told me that he already knew the scores for the summer camp, and that Georgia Tech had come in first and Illinois second. He told me again how hard he had worked his cadets in preparation for summer camp. They were ready with their boots spit shined and other things of that nature that could be done before they arrived at camp. He told me that he thought, for the first two weeks of camp, the Illinois cadets were way ahead of the cadets from Georgia Tech. However, he said it was quite evident after that two-week period there was a difference in the two groups. So he asked me, "What the hell is it about you people from Georgia Tech? Is it your southern heritage?" I said, "Well, sir, I can tell you a few things that being at Georgia Tech does to you in terms of your motivations and management skills. First, you have to learn how to manage your time well. You are always behind and under tremendous academic pressure at Tech. Second, the pressure to perform academically is always present and intense. If a person cannot take that kind of pressure, they just leave. And, finally, there is a great athletic tradition at Georgia Tech, so we are used to functioning and thinking as a team." I said, "I think all those attributes came into play at this summer camp. We could tell we were behind the University of Illinois cadets at the beginning of camp. However, we could also tell that day by day we were learning the ropes faster and beginning to outperform." "Well, I admire you people," the Captain said, "but we will win next year somehow." Fortunately, the Captain did not achieve his goal!

In the fall quarter of 1962, I returned to Georgia Tech to work on my Master's degree in Engineering Mechanics. At that point, I was certain that I wanted to be involved in the aerospace industry working on the space program or something closely related. So I finished my course work for my Master's degree by June of 1963, and I went to work at the Lockheed Georgia Company while I wrote my Master's thesis. After I completed my thesis and obtained my Master's degree, I went on active duty in the Army almost immediately in the summer of 1964.

I was very fortunate to be eventually assigned to army aviation activities at the U.S. Naval Air Station in Corpus Christi, Texas. The Army operation was called ARADMAC. The Army was quite involved in taking over and building up the Navy's aviation maintenance and overhaul facilities at the NAS in order to better prepare for the Vietnam War. At ARADMAC, we were busy repairing and flight-testing all Army fixed wing and rotary wing aircraft. ARADMAC also outfitted a small Navy seaplane tender as a fifth echelon maintenance facility that was to be sent to Cam Ranh Bay, Vietnam. These were very busy and exciting times.

I wanted to return to Lockheed after I completed my tour of duty. However, I received a much better salary offer from General Dynamics in Fort Worth, Texas. So I made a brief stop there before returning to Lockheed in Atlanta in 1968.

While at General Dynamics, I was fortunate enough to be involved with a group that was developing advanced composite materials for the Air Force Materials Laboratory. This was also where I met Dr. James Ashton, who had just graduated with his PhD degree in Civil Engineering from MIT. Jim was the brightest person I had ever met in my life up to that point, and we struck up a personal and family friendship. Also, Jim and I co-authored a book entitled "Primer on Composite Materials: Analysis." We will have more to discuss relative to Jim Ashton in a later chapter.

I returned to Atlanta by accepting a management position with the Lockheed Georgia Company again. I was able to bring to Lockheed my expertise in this new advanced composite material technology. I actually ended up supervising a number of other engineers as we worked on some specific development projects involving these advanced composite materials. So I was beginning to settle into the aerospace career that I had anticipated. I was making a very respectable salary of $14,000 a year, and I managed to buy my first home. That purchase opened up a whole new set of relationships for me.

As it turned out, a young real estate broker by the name of Johnny Isakson sold me my first home. My house was the first that he had sold as a real estate broker, so it was an event for him as well as for me. The house sold for approximately $30,000, and I needed to have a 10 percent down payment, which is all the money I could put my hands on at the time. The closing was being held at a downtown Atlanta law firm, and I had asked Johnny to tell me the exact amount of cash that I had to have for the closing. He did that, and I thought I was all set with my $3,000.

The next scene is a very fancy mahogany legal conference room with me sitting next to Johnny signing papers to close the transaction. When the financial sheet was passed, which had the closing cash I was to provide, I noticed that it exceeded my available cash by $140. I leaned over to Johnny and asked him about the extra $140. He stated that it was for the tax escrow account. I told him that I did not have that much cash. He leaned over and said, "Well, sign it anyway, and I will loan you the money." So, immediately after the closing, we went out into the lobby, and Johnny wrote me a check for $140, which I rushed to deposit in the bank. A few weeks later, when I received my first full paycheck from Lockheed, I paid Johnny back.

Now, fast forward to January 1, 2020, when Johnny Isakson is now our recently retired senior U.S. Senator from the State of Georgia as a result of his Parkinson's disease. He and I had a long relationship over the decades since that day in 1968. How blessed I was to have bought that house with Johnny as my broker. Incidentally, the Senator and I have told this $140 loan story many times in public!

As of today, Johnny Isakson is still one of the most respected men I have ever been associated with in my life. He was the Chairman of the Ethics Committee for the U.S. Senate, and one does not become Chairman of that committee without having great respect from both sides of the aisle. So I have to say again how fortunate I was to have bought that particular house at that point in my life. Unfortunately, Senator Isakson passed away from complications associated with his Parkinson's disease on December 19, 2021.

Flight Instruction

After I returned to Atlanta in 1968, I decided that I wanted to continue flying. So I used part of my G.I. Bill benefits to obtain my civilian flight instructor ratings, both airplane and instruments. On a part-time basis, I began flight instruction for the Atlanta Naval Air Station Flying Club and the Lockheed Flying Club. I bring this up because I learned a few more leadership and management lessons from my early flight instruction.

Learning by making non-fatal mistakes is very important when building flying skills. Flying combines physical as well as mental abilities. The flying principals are relatively simple, but because of the complexities of the feedback that a person needs to understand, it can get complicated. I learned through those few years of part-time flight instruction that allowing a student to continue making a mistake until it scared them was a good teaching scenario. I was willing to take some risk because I knew those situations were the best teaching moments a student could have. Describing and demonstrating to a student a dangerous situation, which I did, never had the impact of them getting themselves into one.

I always tried to keep my hands off the controls until it was absolutely necessary to say, "I got it." The "I got it" command was always a wonderful teaching moment. In my entrepreneur management years as well, I tried to let my subordinates learn by making "controlled" mistakes. I always expressed both in our management booklet and verbally that the company <u>owed</u> its management and employees the ability to make mistakes as long as the process proved to be a learning experience. I said <u>we</u> will chalk up those mistakes as "tuition costs" because we are all still learning. However, in order for us to treat your learning as matriculation, you must literally "attend class" and listen well to constructive criticism so as not to continue to make the same mistakes.

Narcissism

I would like to make a few initial comments about my experience with narcissism. I think this is very important because one narcissistic person can cause irreparable damage to an organization, regardless of whether it is a business, charity, religious group or a family unit.

I have always described a narcissist as a person who has the view that "What's in my brain is correct, and what's in your brain is wrong." Psychologists will use descriptors, such as an immense sense of self-importance, a need for excessive admiration with a general lack of compassion and empathy. They have a need for special treatment and attention.

I have had a number of experiences with narcissistic personalities in my business career. Invariably, they were individuals who could be pleasant conversationalists and even demonstrate charm. However, rather quickly, I would see some of the stressful encounters they had with other people, particularly when we would be in management sessions and trying to develop a consensus. To a strong narcissist, a consensus is merely what they have in their brain. Thus, being a participatory manager, where input from all employees and others is taken into account, is very difficult for narcissist personalities to adequately achieve.

My advice is to always have top managers, executives and Board members screened by an industrial psychologist. Ask specifically for the traits relative to narcissism to be analyzed. And, remember, in their first encounters narcissists can be very charming and convincing. However, they will not contribute very efficiently or effectively to any organization because of their lack of ability to manage and empathize. However, I believe they can be talented individual contributors without being given management responsibilities.

In subsequent chapters, I will discuss a number of narcissists and their impact on a particular situation. I think these examples will help you understand how destructive this personality can be.

Spiritual Philosophy

I added this section after my book was almost complete. Since my attitude about "serving others" comes out in numerous situations that I discuss, it is probably relevant to talk about where that philosophy came from.

As I started the book, I wanted to keep my religion and politics out of the history of my career and the "teaching moments" that I wanted to convey. However, as I began to explain my thinking and actions, it became more difficult to be very specific in certain discussions without some background to draw upon. So here are some personal thoughts on my spiritual philosophy to be followed by a discussion of my political views.

Recall, I wrote this book primarily for entrepreneurs, business executives and their shareholders. I want all my successes and failures to provide good and easily understood "teaching moments" for the reader. I want those to relate to the strengths and weaknesses of the human traits that we discuss. This should help the executive with their hiring (and firing) decisions and with their introspective reflections on their own personality traits. So please be patient…

My mother was Episcopalian and my father Presbyterian. I attended Episcopal churches until high school, and then I became a Presbyterian. I remained a Presbyterian until I was almost 50 when I joined a Methodist church near our new home. Thus, I am certainly a longstanding Protestant.

Mother always stressed "good manners." She literally nagged me about being polite, kind and caring for others. And, Dad was the enforcer! My Boy Scout oath also emphasized being considerate and showing courtesy. As I matured into my twenties, I blended these principles into my Christian beliefs. At some point, I came to the realization that I believed our Creator placed us on this earth "to serve our fellow man" and, in so doing, we "glorify Him." We were all given talents and attributes, which enable us to serve in some way our fellow men as well as our Creator. However, what we have been given is not always used properly. Enough said!

As I became focused in the healthcare field in the summer of 1970, I was driven by a desire to develop products that would save infant lives. As it turned out, I had been given the talent and insight to "engineer" and develop the products and the processes necessary to manufacture and distribute them. As parents' "thank you" letters, phone calls and pictures began to come in after the distribution of our Infant Monitor telling us how SIDS had been prevented with their infants as a result of the Monitor, I began to realize how Healthdyne, my first company, was "serving" these families. I encouraged our staff to understand how blessed we were to be in a position to serve our fellow man in this way. Over the decades, we developed approximately 100 successful products with this servant focus. We acquired 38 other organizations, and we tried to instill the "serving spirit" in everyone. However, we were not always successful at that goal!

I continue to be guided by that principle of "serve your fellow man" on a daily basis. I do my best to counsel, support and assist others. In turn, I seek wisdom from others and also knowledge, which I try to turn into wisdom. I always try to give much more than I get. I call this philosophy "Being a giver, not a grabber."

I began my significant personal philanthropy in the 1970s with donations to SIDS causes. In particular, the SIDS Institute which was founded by Dr. Al Steinschneider. Healthdyne also supported the SIDS Institute and SIDS Alliance programs philanthropically over the decades. As of now, I have donated over 80 percent of my net worth to numerous causes and charities over the decades.

I obtained my aversion to lying from my father. He often said, "First, do not do anything you would need to lie about. Second, never lie because it breaks trust, and trust is the bond for all relationships." During my younger years, he would say, "Do not lie to me because there is nothing you could do that is worse than the lie." As I recall, I never lied to my dad!

When I wrote the Healthdyne Management book, I mentioned lying in this way: If you make a mistake, immediately admit it to your management, and it will become "our" problem to resolve together. If you lie and try to cover it up, it becomes "your" problem, and it defines your character. Thus, it will be dealt with accordingly, and it will probably not be enjoyable.

Political Philosophy

Because of my friendship with Johnny Isakson and his long political career, I was drawn into Georgia politics. I believe it was Johnny who introduced me to Senators Mack Mattingly and Paul Coverdell and Congressmen Newt Gingrich and Dr. Tom Price who became my Congressman after Johnny became our Senator.

As I recall, Paul Coverdell became our second Republican Senator after Mattingly. Paul rose in the ranks of Republican senatorial leadership very quickly. Unfortunately, he passed away at the very young age of 61.

Johnny Isakson served as a State House Representative and Senator prior to becoming our U.S. congressman following Newt Gingrich's retirement. He subsequently became our U.S. senator.

Because he was my Congressman, I developed a relationship with Newt Gingrich as I worked with his Congressional Majority Trust. I actually did some work and studies on our Medicare system for Newt.

I became acquainted with Governor Sonny Perdue during his tenure. Sonny went on to become our U.S. Secretary of Agriculture under President Trump. Actually, Sonny Perdue and our former Senator David Perdue are cousins. I will discuss Senator David Perdue later as he assisted me with some of the MiMedx Group issues.

I believe that during this period of time, Georgia was blessed with some very astute, practical and effective state and federal Republican politicians. I was fortunate to get to know them through Senator Isakson as well as others.

When I first began outlining and then writing this book, I was determined not to bring up national politics. However, that was before Bill Taylor and I were indicted, tried and convicted. As I witnessed so many things taking place that were obviously political in nature, I had to rethink my approach. My goal is for this book to be a teaching and learning document. It will be very hard to cover the various aspects of what transpired without pointing out some of the political issues. However, I will try to minimize my commentary in this area.

I believe I have been blessed with an abundance of common sense, so I have supported candidates and parties that demonstrate a common sense approach to America's issues and problems. I do not like the approach of emotionalizing issues and problems into political agendas. Most often, bad solutions develop when emotion drives decisions and very little logic is utilized. Also, high costs generally result.

Now, I am fiscally conservative, but generally socially moderate. This has left me with a Republican voting record. I simply believe that America is the "biggest business in the world," and it needs a group of experienced business persons to manage and cherish its assets while planning for its growth with productive programs, including social programs.

Unfortunately, I believe the U.S. political system has become very out of control. While our history is full of periods of time when politics became very acrimonious and sometimes possibly unmanageable, I do not think that it has ever reached the level of sophistication that it has today. When any of the critical driving forces that dramatically affect our lives become unbalanced, there will be unpleasant consequences. We are grinding through a period like that right now!

I attribute most of these major changes to the lack of balance and honesty the mainstream media has brought to the process and, of course, the broad and far-reaching nature of social media. When the news media does not accept responsibility for its own integrity, the system quickly becomes corrupted. Thus, their output is "propaganda."

MiMedx, my last company, and I became political targets for the media because of short seller's accusations as well as my political affiliations. I was President Trump's 2016 campaign Finance Chairman for the state of Georgia. Once that became highlighted in the U.S. media, I was branded as a dishonorable business executive in innumerable ways. Subsequently, MiMedx was branded as an unscrupulous healthcare business. Of course, both of those accusations were very incorrect and dishonest.

The individuals or hedge funds, particularly those who are conducting illegal short-selling, use articles written by others to further disrupt and create concerns for the value of a company's stock. As the short sellers working against MiMedx continued to develop their campaign, they enlisted the help of all their journalistic shills. These were people with whom the short sellers had relationships in the past and who had potentially been compensated by the short sellers for their articles. It was in one of these types of articles that I was first called "The Trump of Georgia." That name stuck, and it was used on a number of occasions by other journalists as a negative connotation.

As the book gets into the MiMedx story, I will necessarily make some brief comments about how national politics played a role in the particular issues being discussed. I will try not to overly emphasize, but I will point out the political flaws as those discussions develop.

I hope this is a sufficient review on my politics!

Some Personal Traits

First, I have never had a course in psychology. So the next few paragraphs may be quite odd as I try to highlight my personality traits, particularly those that I think have influenced and affected my business career. So here goes …

Like most men, I believe I am very left brained. I do not think very emotionally, and I am a rather logical thinker, using what I call "common sense." That trait certainly helps me maintain the "courage of my convections."

I believe I received my "tough love" trait from my father. I often used the comment of "get over it" with my children and even the youth football players that I coached. Occasionally, there would be a "just suck it up" comment, depending on the situation! However, I think my children knew I was always there for them with love, but they had to do their part.

I believe that I have an inordinate sense of responsibility. That is a subject on which I received very strong lectures from both my mother and grandmother. So I have never really had a problem stepping up to any form of responsibility.

Along with my sense of responsibility came an awareness of not being selfish. In my business years, being unselfish has manifested itself by always putting my shareholders first. I respected them for their investment and their reliance on management. Also, I never sold any stock over the years except in Healthdyne's initial public offering, which was requested of me by the investment bankers. I waited to allow our various companies to be sold to larger organizations before I ever sold any of my stock. As well, my philanthropy began to play a major role in my decision-making. I felt very blessed by my opportunities and the results. Therefore, I focused myself very often on my philanthropic opportunities.

I always try to listen well because that is when you really learn. You do not learn much when you are talking! I have always tried to associate myself with wise and experienced people because I could ask them those very important and informative questions.

I believe I am more competitive than most. However, I do not take it to a level of being "infected."

I always seem to have a sense of urgency with whatever I am doing. I try to stay on task and on time. I seem to always manage my time really well. MiMedx employees coined the term "SOP." Instead of meaning "Standard Operating Procedure," at MiMedx it meant at the "Speed of Pete!" Also, I trademarked the phrase "Life is a Race, Get in It" and had some tee shirts and ball caps made emblazoned with those words!

I seem to have been given some creative talent. In designing the model cars for the Fisher Body Craftsman's Guild, I had to have some creativity to design the cars and then actually build them. And, I seem to have the ability to visualize well.

Also, thanks to my mother, I believe I was taught and learned to be courteous, kind and compassionate. I actually enjoyed those personality traits as I grew and matured.

I enjoy teaching, which is part of leadership. Early on, I wrote a management manual for my companies. It embodied some of the discussions we will have in Chapter 3.

Over the decades, all of our companies used the "DISC Personality Profile." It only took 15 minutes for an individual to take the profile and have it scored. The profile provided a common language people could use to better understand themselves and those with whom they interacted. This improved our teamwork, our communications and our productivity. When we had management discussions related to personnel, it was always helpful to highlight an individual's personality profile.

People with "D" personalities tended to be managers who were "demanding" and placed a high emphasis on bottom line results.

People with "I" personalities tended to be managers who placed an emphasis on relationships and "influencing" or persuading others, which are conducive to leadership.

People with "S" personalities tended to be individuals who are "stable" and dependable and placed an emphasis on cooperation.

People with "C" personalities tended to place their emphasis on "compliance," quality, accuracy, expertise and competency.

My DISC profile showed that I was a very high "I" and only a moderate "D." That might have surprised some people!

Well, I hope these comments will assist you in better understanding my personality traits. This should be helpful in relating to all the business activities you are about to read.

My Entrepreneurship

We are getting close to the point where my opportunity to be an entrepreneur was thrust upon me in a tragic manner. By June of 1970, my career at Lockheed was beginning to build rapidly. Management accomplishments with my staff and the development projects were going well. I was having conversations with my direct managers that were very flattering in terms of my developing rapidly in the Lockheed management structure. However, my personal situation and life was about to change dramatically.

CHAPTER 2

THE TRAGEDY

On late Sunday afternoon, June 28, 1970, I was sitting on the deck at the back of our house drinking a Coca Cola after I had finished mowing our lawn. I heard my wife scream. I rushed into the house and upstairs to the bedrooms. My wife, JoAnn, was standing in the hall holding our seven-month-old second son, Brett, in her arms, and he was lifeless. I took him from her and put him on our bed where I could administer mouth-to-mouth resuscitation. As I started that process, I told her to call our neighbor, Paul Yokubinas, to drive me to the hospital. However, our four-year old son, Bill, had seen and assessed the situation, and he had already run next door to get Paul.

Paul arrived very quickly. I ran downstairs with Brett, jumped into my car, and Paul started driving us to our local hospital, Kennestone, while I continued mouth-to-mouth resuscitation. Someone had also called an ambulance, which Paul flagged down as it was approaching us. The ambulance did a u-turn, and I jumped in the back with Brett. I continued trying to resuscitate him. When we arrived at the emergency room, the staff took Brett from me.

I waited a couple of hours in the emergency room with no news. The pediatrician finally came out and said that they had managed to get Brett's vital functions started, and he was on a ventilator in the intensive care unit. I went upstairs and saw him. By this time, it was about 10:00 p.m., and the staff recommended that I go home and come back in the morning.

I returned in the morning with my wife, and we spent the day at the hospital. We visited with Brett in the intensive care ward as often as the hospital staff would allow. Brett never gave us any indication that he had any degree of consciousness. We spent that night at the hospital, and early the next morning the hospital pediatrician came down to tell us they had taken Brett off of life support as none of his vital signs showed any sign of being positive.

So, with that event, I was to be thrust into a career of serial healthcare entrepreneurship. That was June 30, 1970. Brett at four months of age is shown in Figure 3.

After Brett's funeral, JoAnn, Bill and I went up to the north Georgia mountains for a few days. While driving along the highway in the mountains, I thought about how useful a simple home physiological monitor could be that would warn a parent if an infant was in physical distress while in their crib. The more I thought about it, the more strongly I felt that a simple system of that nature could be very beneficial. I decided to do some research on crib death and Sudden Infant Death Syndrome (SIDS) and determine if a monitor like this might have a role to play.

After we returned home, I did some reading on these subjects. While there was still a great deal of debate about the causal factors of SIDS, my common sense told me that, regardless of those factors, a monitor for respiration, and possibly heart activity, could be useful. I developed a conceptual picture of the system. See Figure 4. I subsequently called Brett's pediatrician, Dr. Scott James, and asked to meet with him. Dr. James was Chief of Pediatrics at Piedmont Hospital, and he soon became Chief of Pediatrics at the new Northside Hospital. He later became the Chief of Staff at Northside Hospital.

When I met with Scott and showed him the concept, he actually encouraged me, which was probably very unusual at that point in time. However, Scott was a visionary with a great deal of common sense. He told me that he had lost infants in the hospital as a result of apnea, which is the cessation of breathing generally caused by an immaturity of the brain stem. The brain stem eventually matures, and the apnea ceases. He suspected the same thing happens at home, and that assumption turned out to be basically correct, as was determined after many years of SIDS research.

So, with that encouragement from Scott, I continued my product development. I worked nights and weekends on my concept. What I first developed was a soft rubber belt with embedded electronics that would be placed around the infant's chest. It would have stainless steel electrodes on the back that would pick up the cardiac and respiratory signals. The physiological information would be transmitted by telemetry to a monitor by the crib. In addition, there would be a small alarm box that the parent could keep by their side in case they did not hear the alarm from the bedside monitor.

As it turned out, the telemetry link was a step too far in terms of technology. However, by connecting the electrodes to the monitor by a wire, we had a very workable system.

I needed a place to electronically test the Infant Monitor. I enlisted help from one of my college roommates, Ray Pinkerton, who worked at the Georgia Tech Research Center. Ray introduced me to the head electronics technician in the Electrical Engineering department, Paul Branson. Paul agreed to help me with completing the testing of the prototype Monitor in his laboratory. I would go to his laboratory after work, and we worked at night testing the first working prototype, particularly for electrical interference.

Thus, unknowingly, Georgia Tech had its first entrepreneurial healthcare incubator. Of course, those types of incubators are established on most all university campuses today. However, I had to "sneak in" to the electrical engineering lab after my working hours at Lockheed. So I was using a "sneak in" incubator!

I have always been very indebted to Georgia Tech for providing me the ability to obtain my initial education through the engineering cooperative program. Had there not been such a program where I could matriculate and, then on alternate quarters, have a good engineering related job, I probably would never have finished college. Most likely, I would have ended up enlisting in the military as my dad mentioned in his "tough love" letter he sent me during my first quarter. Therefore, as I accumulated some wealth from my entrepreneurial activities, I always found ways to give back to Georgia Tech as well as to Georgia State University, my churches and related charities, and some social entrepreneurial organizations. I consider "giving back" a very important part of one's life!

I initially funded Georgia Tech's second Distinguished Professorial Chair. My Chair was called Engineering in Medicine. This took place in 1985, and it was the second of many of these Chairs that have been given at Georgia Tech over the decades.

Fortunately, Dr. Robert Nerem came to fill that Chair position at Tech. Dr. Nerem was an internationally recognized bioengineering professor, but his best asset was his leadership qualities. He took Georgia Tech's first initiative in bioengineering and turned it into several major programs. Bob's unselfish leadership allowed the development of an important partnership with Emory University Medical School. Later, Bob asked me to fund an endowment for the Institute for Bioengineering and Bioscience. That interdisciplinary concept became an instant success. Subsequently, there had to be a new building to house all of this very focused bioengineering development work. I took a third opportunity to help with the funding of the biotechnology building, which now has my name. See Figures 5, 6 and 7. Thus, I believe that I have now repaid Georgia Tech very substantially for my having used their electrical engineering laboratory as my "sneak in" incubator to complete the development of the Infant Monitor which allowed me to start Healthdyne and my entrepreneurial career.

During the fall of 1970, I spent all my spare time working on the prototype Monitor. I began to develop a plan to leave Lockheed and start a new company to develop, manufacture and market the product that I had named the "Infant Monitor."

I had numerous conversations with myself about leaving a promising aerospace career to start a small company for which I had no experience. There were days that I convinced myself not to take the risk, but there were more days that I convinced myself that "if you can't do this, who can?" I believe I had the "courage of my convictions."

Obviously, I had no experience in start-up businesses whatsoever. I knew that I needed to raise a substantial amount of funding, but I had no idea how much. I had faith in my ability to accomplish adequate product development because I had experience with that in the aerospace industry. However, I realized I knew very little about business.

I never even had an accounting course at Georgia Tech. Therefore, in the late fall of 1970, I decided that I needed to enroll in Georgia State University's MBA program, which could be done by attending classes two nights a week. Some of my Georgia Tech friends were already attending Georgia State on that basis. In fact, Georgia State's business school had a very large student population at night. So, starting in January of 1971, I began attending Georgia State two nights a week and taking two three-hour courses. I decided I was going to focus my MBA in the financial area. My first two courses, which were considered transition courses, were an accounting course and a marketing course.

That certainly turned out to be the right decision as my first finance course was taught by Dr. Al Clark, who was one of the top professors in the business school. Al liked my entrepreneurial story, and he provided me numerous hours of free consulting as I began to plan ahead in terms of the company's fundraising. Al and I kept in contact even after his retirement. He was one of those very special human beings of which you only have a few in your life. Dr. Al Clark retired from Georgia State University in 2010 and passed on March 15, 2018.

I have also felt very compelled to give back to Georgia State University. Had I not been able to enroll in their excellent MBA program and attend classes at night, I would not have obtained my MBA degree in Finance. Therefore, I reacted positively when Georgia State approached me on several occasions to assist with the construction of their new science building and the reconstruction of the former Atlanta Braves baseball stadium into the Georgia State football stadium. In addition, when former Georgia Tech player, coach and friend, Bill Curry, became the first football coach at Georgia State, he interested me in assisting with some of their other football program needs. My name is on their science building and on the football field in their new stadium. See Figures 8, 9 and 10.

Life Systems

I selected the name Life Systems, Inc. as my new start-up company's first name. Relative to raising money for Life Systems (which later became Healthdyne), my only major source of funding was physicians in the Atlanta area who initially knew Dr. Scott James. The only "business person" I knew at that point outside of my executive managers at Lockheed was real estate broker Johnny Isakson.

I needed a working prototype of the Monitor in order to have any credibility for this new entrepreneurial enterprise. As usual, some things did not go according to plan. The prototype device, which at this time was still using telemetry, was not reliable enough yet, primarily because of the telemetry link. In the Georgia Tech electronics isolation labs, we could do things that would interfere with the Monitor transmitting correct signals. Therefore, I reached the conclusion that we needed a system that did not use telemetry.

During the late fall, I found an attorney who had a small law firm that would work with me on setting up the corporation and developing documents that I could use to raise money on a private placement basis.

So, as 1970 ended, I had plans to start night school at Georgia State University in early January, to leave Lockheed in mid-February and to start selling stock as soon as I had the first Infant Monitor prototype device in working order.

I gave notice and left Lockheed on Valentine's Day of 1971. There were a number of people who were interested in listening to me describe the company and the investment possibilities. So I was comfortable that I could begin to close some investments and raise what I hoped to be $100,000.

As you can imagine, my discussions with others, and myself, about my entrepreneurial adventure went on right up to the day I left Lockheed. Obviously, I had developed an optimistic attitude about my chances for success, and I seldom waivered. So, on Friday, February 14, 1971, I began my career as an entrepreneur. The first night after leaving Lockheed, my wife and I played cards with our two neighbors Paul Yokubinas and Bob Potts and their wives. We often had a Friday night card game around our dining room table. About halfway through the evening, someone asked me, and I do not remember who, "Well, Pete, how does it feel to be unemployed?" Well, that "unemployed" word hit me very hard; I never thought about the reality of not having a paycheck in the next two weeks. I remember lying awake that night with some trepidation, but my confidence prevailed with the thought that "you can always go back to Lockheed." However, I had a restless sleep that night realizing that entrepreneurs often do not get paychecks!

Coping with Grief

During the months after Brett's death, I know that my maniacal focus on developing the Monitor was extremely helpful to me in dealing with my grief. I know that my development activities and prototypes also gave my wife some degree of comfort. Thus, we both came through this very traumatic ordeal with our mental health intact. Once I began to develop a real vision for what the Monitor could bring to families, I became very comfortable with why "our tragedy had occurred." I considered myself very fortunate to be able to think through our tragedy with positivity.

My faith allowed me to stay focused on the product development and the related evolution of the business. As things began to come together, my faith grew stronger and stronger relative to why we had lost our second son. I began to realize that my God would be there for me through all the trials and tribulations. And, that is exactly what happened not only for the first few years, but for all the decades until my entrepreneurial activities ceased. Of course, I expect that to be the case for the remainder of my life.

CHAPTER 3

PARTICIPATIVE MANAGEMENT

Now that you have seen how some past experiences may have shaped my personality, I want to provide some basics on the management philosophies that I have developed over the decades. I sincerely believe they allowed our management to maintain order in spite of the very rapid growth rates of my various companies. So these philosophies should be given some consideration for companies growing rapidly through their entrepreneurial phases.

As companies grow, top management naturally becomes further displaced from the majority of their corporate members, and subsequently, more autocratic processes and procedures tend to develop. That phase of an organization's life should be delayed as long as possible because there are substantial efficiencies that come from an organization that utilizes "participative management" principles to function in the entrepreneurial environment.

My interest in participative management became focused in the early 1970s when I read a book called The Human Side of Enterprise by Douglas McGregor. This management classic introduced Theory X and Theory Y, which are two differing approaches to management based on perceived human behavior and nature. Theory X maintains that humans are inherently lazy, and authoritarian management must command and control employees. Theory Y contends that individuals are self-motivated and self-directed. My own ideas about management and employee motivation align primarily with Theory Y because I thought we would hire self-motivated individuals. After reading this book, I developed my own concepts about participative management and eventually wrote a booklet entitled Management-Healthdyne Style.

Most of the material in this chapter will come from that booklet I initially wrote in 1992. It was updated for Matria Healthcare in 2003, and finally updated on February 2, 2010, for MiMedx Group. Of course, the name was changed to Management-MiMedx Style.

Components of Management

As previously mentioned, I developed a philosophy early in my career that management has two components, which are "leadership" and "administration." Over the years, I have seen numerous definitions and books that separate leadership and management as different functions. I have always believed that the leadership function is an integral component of effective management. I do not believe you can manage effectively without leadership. So, in all of the training in our booklet, we take the approach that management will include both the leadership function and the administrative function. It is easy to break these two components down into sub-components and personal traits. Once that is accomplished, it is easier to determine whether the leadership component is more important for a particular job function than the administrative component, and select your candidates for those various positions accordingly.

It is much easier to picture the successes and failures of different managerial activities if you break management down into these two sub-components. Since management must be accomplished through individuals, the ability to recognize their successes and failures and to categorize them into either leadership issues or administrative issues is very helpful. Also, since an efficient and growing organization must balance "change" generally brought about by leadership, and "order," which comes from effective administration, it is imperative that we all understand the personality traits that can cause counteracting forces, which result from leadership and administration.

The excellent manager has a good balance of leadership and administrative skills. There are numerous examples in both business and government of world-class managers. Generally speaking, these individuals get singled out as "strong leaders." However, I submit that they had to be excellent overall managers as well. If they did not also have strong administrative skills, then they were wise enough to surround themselves with people who did. With contemporary business philosophy, however, it is not very "in" to single out a natural "manager" as opposed to a natural "leader."

Over the years, our companies all used the same "Personal Profile System" as a means for managers to better understand themselves, their subordinates, their colleagues and even their bosses. This was a simple personality profile test that could be taken in about 15 minutes. It resulted in a very detailed description of the individual's personality traits, which certainly helped them and management better understand their capabilities for leadership and administration. This generally kept us from making significant initial mistakes in hiring. The system was called the "DISC PROFILE," and I provided some insights in Chapter 1.

Since staffing is one of the most crucial management functions, it is very helpful to understand management in its leadership and administrative framework so that personality types can be blended in an organization to achieve optimal and well-rounded overall management. An individual will usually have a propensity for either strong leadership skills or strong administrative skills. Any organizational unit needs individuals with both of these skills to successfully accomplish its objectives. If both skills are not available in one individual, then the individual responsible for the group must be certain that their skills are supplemented by one or more of their direct reports. Individuals can make much better decisions and choices if they understand both the leadership and administrative components of management and how they will affect their organization's performance.

Leadership

The leadership component of management generally deals with subjects, such as inspiring and motivating subordinates, developing creativity, setting examples and producing a "vision" or long-term strategy for the organization.

There are certain personality traits that leaders should normally exhibit. Some of these are courage, tenacity, persistence, honesty, humility, fairness and the ability to communicate well.

Courage, tenacity and persistence are important because people are seldom interested in following a "short timer." Employees want to follow managers who have either stood the test of time or managers who have those qualities and make them comfortable that they will persevere.

Managers who exhibit humility, fairness, unselfishness and honesty will easily and quickly develop "trust" with those they manage. Narcissism, arrogance and unfairness beget apathy and resentment. The ability to laugh at oneself and not take oneself too seriously is also conducive to the development of trust. Trust is the "cornerstone" of participative management, and we will discuss that in a following section. Unselfishness dictates that leaders should always pass accolades on to their staff. Remember, "Success comes easily when you do not care who gets the credit."

I believe the key process for obtaining consensus and commitment from staff is verbal communication. It is very difficult to lead without the ability to communicate. You cannot communicate effectively without frequently being physically present with your employees. You can supplement your direct presence in communication through voicemail, email, written materials and telephone, but your frequent presence is most important.

The content of your communications is very important if your leadership is to be effective. As a general rule, your communication should be motivational and clearly delineate the "why" message. Your subordinates must know the shared goals within your organization and "why" they are important in order for them to feel they are a part of your team. This is very basic to the inspirational and motivational process.

I also have the view that the leadership skill is very difficult to teach. However, administrative skills are much more easily learned. I have had debates with members of the academic community on this subject, but my experience has shown me that it is much easier to take individuals who have personality traits that are conducive to leadership and school them in administrative skills rather than the reverse. In other words, I believe the major requirements for leadership are embodied in one's DNA.

Administration

I believe that administration, in general, deals with the delegation and completion of tasks, projects and goals and giving proper levels of authority for subordinates to accomplish those activities. As such, the formal organizational structure is utilized to "control" and obtain compliance.

I believe the personality traits that good administrative abilities require include the ability to think logically, to comprehend the interrelationship of tasks, to focus on the critical issues, to organize and develop plans and to possess effective time management skills. Basic intellectual capacity is certainly a requirement, but it is not necessarily a guarantee that an individual can be an effective administrator.

People who can administer effectively have a propensity to organize their own time well. This type of personality will typically keep a daily organizer. Once the individual learns to manage their personal time well, then administrative tasks that occur in the delegation process will be more easily accomplished. One of the key skills a good administrator should master is a "follow-up process" which occurs after the delegation process. They should develop ways to check that the assigned tasks, projects or goals are being worked through properly and on a projected schedule. Good administrators will not accomplish the assigned tasks of their staff, but they will continue a check by several different means to be certain that the project is moving along properly.

I have a favorite phrase, which is, "Delegate. Do not abdicate." Abdication occurs when, after the delegation process, there is no intimate follow-up conducted in several ways. I have often heard the excuse, "Well, I told him what to do." That is a shining example of abdication.

Good administrators have a "sense of urgency" and are always aware that time is working against them. They understand how to set priorities so there is always progress occurring on any given project. They realize how to run parallel courses so that one task is not holding up other tasks of the project. They must strike a balance between being too impetuous and being too indecisive or tentative.

Comparing Leadership and Administration

An effective way to better grasp the differences between leadership and administration is to actually compare them on a functional basis. This can be done by noting the differences in the "setting of goals," the "staffing function," the "delegation process" and the "results" that are obtained through "planning and budgeting."

In the "setting of goals," the administration component of management is concerned with planning and budgeting while the leadership component is concerned with the setting of direction. The planning and budgeting process can be called "tactics" as they generally have a short time frame. Setting direction for an organization involves the development of "strategy," which is very long term in nature. Often this is called "setting the vision."

With planning and budgeting, the administrator and leader go through the process of developing schedules and steps for achieving the desired results with an allocation of resources to achieve the tactical goals. The tactical goals support the strategies for achieving the long-term goals or vision.

On the other hand, leadership is involved with the setting of direction. This is strategy, and it includes the development of the corporate vision and future goals and the techniques for producing the changes needed to achieve that vision.

Relative to the "staffing function," there are also major differences. Administrators are concerned with the development of an organizational structure for accomplishing the tactical goals, the staffing of the structure with qualified individuals, the delegation of responsibility and authority, providing policies and procedures to guide staff and creating methods and systems to monitor the process.

In contrast, leaders align their employees by communicating direction with words and deeds so as to influence the development of coalitions and teams and with education on the vision with a strategy that will achieve the vision.

With the "delegation process," administrators are concerned with controlling and problem solving. They will monitor results versus the plans, identify the deviations and develop a plan to deal with the problems. Administrators attempt to keep "bad things" from happening.

At the same time, leaders must concern themselves with motivating and inspiring their employees. In the process, they try to make "good things" happen by energizing and empowering their employees to overcome bureaucratic, political and other barriers to change.

When we look at the "results" that come from the administration and leadership functions, there are again major differences. The administrative process produces "order" and has the potential of producing consistent results that are expected by the various stakeholders. For instance, for customers we will provide a quality service or product; for shareholders, we will provide financial results that meet their expectations. In contrast to those results, leadership will produce "change." These changes generally will be significant, such as new services, new products and new approaches to changing markets.

Thus, we can see that there are some very different results produced by the administrative and the leadership functions. However, in an efficient and successful organization, there will be a balance of these functions so that "order" is maintained while "change" takes place.

Participative Management

Since the late 1980s, I have attempted to conduct management at all the companies in the style of "participative management." We tried to teach all employees that the company embodied this management philosophy and explain that it is the exact opposite of the philosophy of "autocratic management."

We would make clear that, in an autocratic management system, communications primarily flowed down the chain of command and that, in a participative management culture, communications flow up the chain of command as easily as they flow down. All systems and attitudes are geared to facilitate the task of involving all employees in the management process. All employees should believe that they are valuable contributors, and their ideas are welcome. In this process, we tried to convince all employees that they are respected and treated as the company's most valuable asset. We set up management structures, policies and procedures that allow staff to be heard and actions to quickly result from their input. We tried to convey the fact that participative management embodied living and working in accordance with the golden rule. That is, "Do unto others as you would have them do unto you."

We stressed the fact that becoming a manager at our companies did not mean that an individual received a license to be served by their staff. In fact, we stressed the exact opposite. Managers have the opportunity and basic requirement to serve their staff!

Also, I tried to get across the fact that we should not confuse the principles of participative management with the principles of democracy. In a democracy, all participants have one equal vote. That is not the case in an organization where our type of participative management is effectively utilized. Within each management unit, one person has responsibility for results and authority to develop plans and programs to achieve those results. That person should ask for and receive input from staff, attempt to develop a consensus and then accept responsibility for the decisions. The staff should know their input was considered in the decision. This does not mean, however, that every decision goes to a committee meeting nor does it mean that every person has an equal vote. I stress that a good participative manager keeps a balance and knows when to obtain full staff input, partial staff input and no staff input.

Another major participative management tenant is that it is "all right to make an honest mistake." I would stress that we are all human, and we are all involved in a dynamic and rapidly growing organization. As such, all our skills are challenged, and we must continue to develop and enhance those skills. So mistakes will take place. Of course, when mistakes are made, there are costs to the organization. I characterized those costs as "tuition expenses." These philosophies were directed towards correcting honest mistakes before they caused major problems and discouraging employees to conceal their mistakes. I felt that we would function much more effectively if all employees realized that it was all right to make a mistake and learn from the mistake.

Thus, mistakes would more often be brought to management's attention. Then, the employee would enter a process of instruction and education relative to the mistake so they know they also benefit, which sets the right tone. However, one of the most debilitating problems an organization can face is concealed mistakes. One of the most disappointing issues that transpired at MiMedx was when a corrupt sales manager was selling competitive products on the side and attempting to encourage others to follow his scam. He told the salespeople that executive management knew about the situation and said it was all right for everyone to make a "little extra money." Actually, one of these individuals made over $700,000 of "extra money" in a period of about a year. When the sales employees who knew about this situation were interviewed, I was very disappointed that none of them felt that they should have asked executive management as to whether we really knew about the situation. Had that happened, we would have caught up with this situation sooner than we did. We had very effective systems for reporting, either directly or anonymously, any issues of concern by employees to the Board and the CEO, but it was not used in this case. Our reporting did not even require employees to identify themselves.

We instilled a number of other management approaches that would develop trust within our organization. We worked on easy ways for employees to jump the chain of command when they felt it was necessary. They could come directly to me with what we called a "Dear Pete Letter," or they could go straight to the Board of Directors with a phone call.

I believe that trust is the bonding agent that holds any personal relationship together whether this is in a business environment, a family environment or other organizational environment.

Developing trust involves such managerial qualities as fairness, unselfishness, honesty, integrity, empathy and humbleness. Trust must be earned; it will not truly develop by trying to "buy" employees with rewards. You can ask your staff to give you the "benefit of the doubt" until you have the time to develop their trust, but then set to work to earn it.

I absolutely feel there is a major difference in effectiveness between participative management and autocratic management. An organization that utilizes participative management will be much more efficient and effective than an autocratic organization. I believe that the performance of our organizations over the decades in their fast-growth environments speaks to that belief very well.

I always stressed the fact that I believe, in the entrepreneurial stages of a company's growth, the most valuable asset is the staff. I proved that to myself time after time as we were able to transition through all the major changes in the healthcare system, the regulatory agencies' philosophies and other issues. As I previously discussed, I kept our management team balanced between leaders and administrators over the years. In a few cases, some individuals had both these qualities. However, often a business unit has to have both management skills coming from two different people.

In the entrepreneurial stages of growth, if the staff or management is not very carefully selected, then damage will occur rather quickly. I cannot overemphasize how important the staffing function is in the entrepreneurial phases. I begged our human resource management to find ways to screen new employees for "common sense." I never received any satisfactory recommendations in terms of testing for this. If such a test were available, it would have made a significant difference in our hires.

Also, hiring individuals who have an inherent propensity for honesty and integrity is so important in today's human resources environment. You cannot determine much by looking at an applicant's employment history because most human resources departments will not disclose negative information. You have to be good at reading between the lines in order to assess the virtue of a potential hire. When a miss-hire takes place, the results are more often than not very difficult and time-consuming. From my experience, I would say that common sense with some accompanying business acumen, which includes honesty and integrity, are two of the most important attributes to look for in an applicant. Of course, work ethic comes in a close third.

I am sure you are wondering why I have not highlighted intelligence as an important trait. Well, individuals with Mensa credentials have worked with me over the years, and while I respect their "photographic memory," as I have stated previously, common sense is most important. Often, a photographic memory that we find with many medical professionals and other intelligent people does not necessarily come with common sense. The ability to synthesize without having intimate memory or knowledge of all the variables is part of that common sense provision.

During the Healthdyne years, I relied on both my leadership and administrative skills. However, our executive team consisted of a strong leader, Paul Yokubinas, and our administrators consisting of Brent Burkey, our General Counsel, Terry Dewberry, our Chief Financial Officer, and Don Millard, an individual who later stepped into our Chief Financial Officer role. As individuals, we did not always immediately appreciate each other's contributions, but we certainly respected each other and counted on a balance to come together on critical decisions.

The hiring function was extremely important in those early growth years. We were generally very successful with the vast majority of people we hired, but we had a blunder or two. However, it was a small percentage, considering the thousands of employees we had.

Having used participative management for decades, I believe it is extremely important that it be applied early in the entrepreneurial process. While the very early days may be managed through intimate contact with key subordinates, participative management should start blossoming in those early phases of an entrepreneurial endeavor. As the company grows, a significant distance will develop between the managers and company founders and the rest of the organization, and that is when the advantages of participative management versus autocratic management will be most important.

Managing Narcissism

As I previously mentioned, we relied on the DISC profile for assisting us in categorizing and managing our employees. That profile gave a quick overview of the personality traits of everyone. It was easy to drop individuals into the various categories to be sure we did not have a personality mismatch with the responsibilities of their position.

Thus, when I would encounter a possible personality disorder, such as narcissism, I would manage this issue separately. As I believe I have said, narcissism is one of the most dangerous personality traits that has to be managed. One narcissist in the wrong position with the wrong responsibilities can foul up a very efficient organization quite quickly.

My brief explanation of narcissism is demonstrated by a person who believes that, "What is in my brain is correct, and what is in your brain is not." These individuals never seem to doubt themselves, and they expect special treatment and acknowledgement. Narcissists are also self-centered with little regard for others, and they do not have much compassion for others. The idea of teamwork is foreign to their thought process; therefore, participative management would be an almost impossible task for them to perceive and implement.

Individuals who demonstrate self-confidence can be very beneficial to an organization reaching their goals and objectives. However, one has to be certain that this self-confidence is not driven by any narcissistic DNA. When self-confidence is followed with someone's desire for attention, special appreciation and admiration or other special treatment, you can bet narcissism is at the core of that attribute. However, a person who is self-confident, but not narcissistic, will generally be an effective manager and leader.

This does not mean that narcissists cannot contribute effectively to an organization. However, giving them any management roles will be problematic as they do not have any respect for others, and they lack empathy for others. They will seldom give others credit; they want the admiration and the attention.

"Managing Murphy"

"Managing Murphy" is a term that I coined in the early 1980s to convey to management the necessity for double and triple checking their assumptions and action items on all projects and business initiatives. I have seen too much planning develop around projects with little to no consideration given to Murphy's Law. So I would always begin my review and critique of project plans with my "Managing Murphy" mantra.

Unfortunately, many people feel that, when they have completed a plan, it will be a success. But, often they do not spend as much time developing plans for what the competition or a regulator might do or any of the other negative possibilities. Those possibilities are always just as important to consider, if not more so, as the basic plan itself. Thus, keep your company's strategizing focused on "Managing Murphy" in the planning and implementation processes.

The SIDS Alliance

In the early 1980s, I was interacting with at least five different charitable organizations all of which were focused on trying to resolve Sudden Infant Death Syndrome. Each of these organizations had their own idea as to how they were going to approach this matter. The leadership of these organizations did not necessarily care for each other, and there was a lot of unnecessary bickering and posturing. As I often say, most of these individuals were on "ego trips" rather than on "business trips."

I do not remember why I made the decision, but I decided that I could exert some leadership and bring these organizations together under one name. It took about a year of meeting with all the principals, generally in open sessions, to finally hammer out the bylaws and articles for the incorporation of the "SIDS Alliance." We managed to convince all the organizations to become partners except one. That one was the SIDS Institute, which was founded by Dr. Al Steinschneider. Al just felt that his organization should not be controlled by anyone other than himself, and he wanted to remain independent.

I was elected Chairman of the Board of Directors of this new alliance. I hoped for other leadership to fill that role, but no one volunteered. I functioned in the Chairman role from 1987 until 1997.

To say that there were some diverse personalities involved in these various entities would be an understatement. I often became frustrated when we were trying to align the disparate groups around a common vision and begin making decisions to move the organization forward with charitable and congressional initiatives. All the constituents challenged my patience often, but I managed to meet our goals and objectives, although often later than anticipated.

In terms of management, I always counsel individuals to "understand their limitations." Some of the worst management situations occur when individuals are in over their head, and their job responsibilities are exceeding their capabilities. I can be very honest about the SIDS Alliance because it happened decades ago. I believe there were times that the leadership position exceeded my patience, and my frustration levels became very high. I used to shame myself over my attitude, but some good things came out of having at least four of the organizations aligned and the infighting stopped.

CHAPTER 4

THE EARLY YEARS

Fortunately, the early years of Healthdyne are easy to recount because of the publication of a 25th anniversary book entitled *An Entrepreneurial Adventure*. This book was commissioned by Healthdyne as a gift for our employees. Healthdyne contracted with Mike Shaw, the President and founder of Corporate Issues, a corporate communications firm located in Atlanta. Healthdyne had utilized Mike Shaw's firm over the years, and he was well known to a number of the members of our management staff. Thus, as I try to describe some of the events and management decisions related to those years, I have a book upon which to rely. See Figure 11.

The book was published in 1995, but only about 3,500 copies were printed. While all employees were given a copy of the book, not a large number of copies were retained.

To begin, I will quote verbatim Mike Shaw's opening remarks from the book because they certainly summarize well the birth and early progress of Healthdyne. The first two paragraphs of the book read as follows:

"One man on a single mission touches countless lives. Perhaps we are attracted by the pursuit of the American Dream, or maybe we are drawn by destiny. No matter, we are compelled to take part in the odyssey. Somewhere along the journey, the odyssey gathers enough momentum and support to become a venture, and the venture is molded into a business."

"This business, this entrepreneurial adventure, this Healthdyne, was born out of the passion of one man to resolve the dilemma of sudden infant death syndrome. In pursuit of his dream or destiny, he drew the support of so many – those who would join the business as employees and managers; those who would support it as investors; those with a stake in its success, like patients, parents and physicians. They embraced his mission. They supported his persistence and determination through difficult times. They shared the struggles and celebrated the accomplishments. Together they nurtured and matured this company into a healthcare organization, with more than $250 million in revenues, noted for a rare combination of technological innovation, compassionate care and business savvy."

First Steps

Before I even left Lockheed on February 14th of 1971, I knew that I had to rent some office space so that we could become a functioning business entity with the ability to raise funds. I found a nice space on Highway 41 in Marietta near the Interstate 285 junction that had a small reception area and three offices. At the time, I felt that not only did I need an office, but we also needed an office for our product development activities and an office for potential sales activities.

My major concern was whether or not I could sign a one-year lease for office space in a presentable office park. Since Life Systems had no track record and a very small bank account, I was concerned that I would be unable to rent. But, I felt that I would not be able to raise sufficient funding without an office to show potential shareholders. I do not know how I managed to lease this nice space for one year, but I accomplished just that. The only explanation I have today is "blind luck," or "divine intervention!"

At the time, I sincerely hoped that within that first year we would have our first product, the Infant Monitor, ready to manufacture and place in the market. Therefore, I immediately began to look for production space after we moved into our initial office space.

The first name I chose for the company was Life Systems, Inc. My first lawyer cleared the name, and we were subsequently incorporated. However, about a year after we moved into our first offices, I was at Northside Hospital testing our Infant Monitor when I noticed an infant ventilator that had the name "Life Systems" on the front panel. That name had been trademarked so we had to research another name. I went home that night, took out a note pad, and started looking at alternatives. Within an hour or so, I had created the name Healthdyne. It was my understanding that "dyne" is a Greek word that means "force." I thought that was appropriate. So that is the amount of market research that went into our second corporate name!

Once we moved into our offices on May 1st of 1971, we began to exert a substantial amount of effort in getting the Infant Monitor ready for a more comprehensive product evaluation. Fortunately, Dr. Scott James, who was Brett's pediatrician, was now Chief of Pediatrics at Northside Hospital. He allowed me to come into the Neonatal Intensive Care Unit and test our prototype Infant Monitors. Without that help and assistance, we might never have been successful.

Scott proved to be an extremely bright individual who also had common sense and the ability to synthesize product concepts well. I was looking for some other simple products to perhaps produce as we went through the more lengthy development process for the Infant Monitor. Scott suggested a product, which we eventually named the "Toddler Alarm." This was a safety device that could be placed on the inside of a cabinet door. If a toddler got into the cabinet, the device would set off an alarm after a pre-determined period of time, which was short enough that the child could not potentially harm themselves with the contents of the cabinet. It had an adjustable time delay as well so, with that delay, a parent could open the door of the cabinet, extract what they needed and close the door before the alarm sounded.

In June of 1971, the Infant Monitor's first working prototype reached the development phase where it could be demonstrated. I immediately began to use the prototype in my fundraising activities and became much more effective with my presentation to prospective investors. Beginning on June 1st, I managed to raise approximately $60,000 over the next 12 months. My goal had been $100,000.

This cash shortfall was partially made up by my not taking a salary until mid-1972. My family met our living expenses primarily by building up our credit card debt, which had been almost non-existent previously.

The largest investors I attracted in 1971 were at the $5,000 investment level. We were raising funds at $1 per share, which gave a valuation on the company of approximately $1 million. In other words, approximately one million shares were issued and outstanding and, at $1 per share, that provided a $1 million dollar valuation. We will discuss corporate valuations in more detail in a later chapter.

In 1973, there were only four significant venture capital companies in the United States. Private equity funds had not yet developed. The four venture capital companies were in New York, Boston and on the west coast. There was a Small Business Investment Corporation (SBIC) in Atlanta; however, you had to be an operating business with strong profits in order to be able to qualify for any investment funds from that organization. Therefore, my only source of funding was from what we now call "angel investors." In our first and second private placements, most of our investors were doctors.

After Healthdyne went public in December of 1981, there were three stock splits, and the stock peaked at a price of approximately $40 per share in mid-1983. That put a corporate valuation on the company of $600 million. On our initial shareholders' investment in 1971, we provided approximately a 600 times return on their investment over the next 12 year period!

I managed to sell over $60,000 of the initial $1 per share stock offering by the end of 1971 and $90,000 in a second offering at $2 per share. That cash allowed us to focus heavily on completing our Infant Monitor development so that some clinical evaluations could be conducted. In addition, we began to make plans to manufacture the Toddler Alarm. However, we could not begin that process until we moved into a manufacturing facility, which we managed to do around May 1st of 1972.

During the early part of 1972, I located a satisfactory manufacturing facility in the Windy Hill Industrial Park in Smyrna. It was a 5,000 square foot facility that allowed us to have about 1,200 square feet of office space. At that point, we were ready to begin production of the Toddler Alarm.

Trying to Go Public

As we entered 1973, it was clear that my ability to raise capital in Atlanta through private placements was not going to fulfill the company's need for a several hundred thousand dollar raise which would allow us to bring our products to market, including the Infant Monitor. So I began to focus on raising some capital through a Regulation A public stock offering. Under the Regulation A provisions, up to $500,000 could be raised through a simplified regulatory process.

In the spring of 1973, I had vetted our situation through a number of investment banking sources. I had come to the conclusion that we were not going to be able to attract a well known investment banker to do an offering for such an immature business entity as Healthdyne. Interest was expressed by a small investment banker, H. E. Simpson Securities, in New York to do the regulation A offering only on a "best efforts" basis. They wanted a $5,000 retainer to begin their efforts.

So, in February of 1973, I wrote a $5,000 retainer check to H.E. Simpson Securities in order to initiate activity on a "best efforts" basis "Regulation A" stock offering. We had to begin the process of getting our financial statements in order for the offering. I had been using a local accounting firm, and I asked them to prepare our financial statements for this Regulation A offering.

I had previously retained Powell Goldstein, a large Atlanta law firm, to do some of our legal work. They assisted us in the development of the Regulation A documents and prospectus. We had everything ready to go in September, and we initiated this offering with our submission of documents to the Securities and Exchange Commission (SEC). We received clearance for the offering relatively quickly. In October, November and December, we conducted our marketing efforts.

Early on in this process, I was introduced to Mike Marshall, the founder of First Southeastern Securities in Atlanta. Mike expressed an interest in working with me on the offering, and First Southeastern joined the syndicate. Actually, it was only a two firm syndicate of H.E. Simpson Securities and First Southeastern Securities.

In the fall of 1973, the stock market was in a steep decline. This was primarily because of the oil crisis that was affecting markets worldwide. Obtaining gasoline at the pumps was difficult as most gas stations were not receiving their normal supply of gasoline. Therefore, no company was involved in a public stock offering during the fall of 1973 except Healthdyne, as far as I remember.

The First SEC Inquiry

We managed to raise our minimum of $300,000. However, our first SEC inquiry was opened over a potential new shareholder sending a letter to the Better Business Bureau. That incident provided me the first overview of how the SEC would treat small public corporations.

We had numerous significant shareholders in Dublin, Georgia. The group included a number of doctors, attorneys and a future U.S. Congressman, Dr. Roy Rowland. This group came together as a result of Pete Raymer, who was a homecare dealer that found Healthdyne very early. As we began to interest individuals in purchasing our common stock in this Regulation A offering, we naturally ended up with a number of new shareholders from the Dublin area because of our shareholder base there.

Unfortunately, or perhaps fortunately, one of those individuals who ordered shares in the offering through First Southeastern Securities decided at the last minute that he did not want to buy the shares. Instead of calling First Southeastern and canceling his order, he did not because he thought he would need a valid excuse to cancel.

Instead, he wrote a letter to the Atlanta Better Business Bureau claiming that he never purchased these shares. Of course, the Atlanta Better Business Bureau sent his communication over to the Atlanta SEC office, and our law firm received a call from the Atlanta regional office on December 23rd. My lawyer called me and said they would contact the SEC on December 26th to see what was the reason for this inquiry. Just prior to this, we had been notified by H.E. Simpson Securities that they had raised $300,000, which was the minimum needed in order to close the offering. They were ready to close the offering and start trading the stock.

At this point, Healthdyne was basically out of cash. Some of our Board members and I had guaranteed some corporate notes to the First National Bank of Tucker where Warren Jackson had become President. Warren had been our banker at the Trust Company of Georgia when he accepted the position of the President of the First National Bank of Tucker. We had kept Warren very informed of our progress and financial situation, and he became an advocate for us. Thus, the conversation with the SEC on December 26th was going to be extremely important to the future of the company, particularly if we were unable to take down the $300,000 and start trading the company's stock.

The conversation on the 26th with the SEC outlined to our law firm, Powell Goldstein, the letter received from the individual in Dublin claiming that he did not purchase the stock. Once I had his name, I passed it on to Pete Raymer who knew the gentleman. Pete came back to me saying that this individual merely wanted to cancel his order and did not mean to cause any trouble. I told Pete that he should have called First Southeastern and canceled the order. However, the SEC now had a document to conduct, at a minimum, an inquiry and, at a maximum, an investigation.

Therefore, the SEC told our lawyers that we were not to close the offering, but would have to wait on them to do their inquiry. When I asked our law firm to find out the date the inquiry would be complete, their comment was that the SEC would never give us such a date. That left us in a total state of disarray because the shareholders were expecting the stock to begin trading.

I asked the lawyers at Powell Goldstein to arrange a meeting for me with someone at the SEC in Washington, but they said they could not do that. Their only advice to me was to cancel the offering and refund everyone's money. They also told me that they could not keep pressing the SEC on Healthdyne's behalf as their firm had other much larger clients who needed their help at the SEC. My first thought was that Healthdyne needed a different law firm! I remember thinking that I had never fired a law firm before, but it had to be done! And, it was!

At the time, my father-in-law knew our senior senator, Herman Talmadge. He told me he would call Senator Talmadge and ask him to take a phone call from me, which the Senator agreed to do. I called the Senator, and he said he would arrange a meeting for me with someone at the SEC. After only a day, his office called to say that I should come to the Senator's office on Friday of the following week, and he would have a meeting set up with an official from the SEC.

I went to Washington and to Senator Talmadge's office. The Senator told me that I had an appointment with a top official at the SEC. By this time, the SEC had determined from the individual in Dublin that he merely wanted to cancel his order for the stock and not cause any problems. So I did not understand why this matter could not be settled immediately.

When I met with the SEC official, she told me that it would take an extended period of time for them to complete their inquiry. I remember her saying something like, "Well, we will investigate this area and, if we do not find anything, we will have to investigate this area, and, if we do not find anything, we will have to investigate this area. And, after several of those investigations, then we will finish this inquiry."

I realized at that point that I did not think like a government official, and we were going to have to cancel the offering and refund everyone their money. After nine months of work and expense, we were going to lose $300,000 of very needed cash. I "bit my lip" and thanked this SEC official for her time. Then, I left for the airport.

Once I was at the airport, I had a couple of hours to wait for my flight so I began making phone calls. The first one was to the investment bankers to tell them to do what they needed to do to refund everyone's investment. Then, I called Warren at the bank. I told him that we did not have money for the next week's payroll and that we were going to see the $300,000 evaporate.

Warren told me to come see him the next day, which happened to be a Saturday. He told me to relax. He said that he was committed to helping us and that we would work out these details.

I remember that, after I hung up the phone with Warren, I said a prayer and shed some tears.

A New Start

The meeting with Warren the next day in his offices went well. He said he would loan us some additional money for next week's payroll. I told him I would immediately begin raising funds from the existing shareholders again. I had thought the matter through, and I figured it was probably going to have to be a convertible debt offering that would pay shareholders some interest.

In retrospect, it was probably a blessing that we did not go public at that very early stage of the company's growth. The extra work involved with managing all of a public company's requirements might have been "the straw that broke the camel's back." Either way, as I now reflect on it, I believe it was a blessing. However, I had to go through some more intense periods of raising money.

As we ended 1973, Dick Thomason, a Board member and one of the company's attorneys, developed private placement documents for $150,000 of debt that was convertible to common stock. Dick and I worked through the last weekend in December to complete the documents. So, in early January of 1974, I began raising money for this debt offering. I actually managed to raise those funds rather quickly.

As it turned out, the SEC advised us in June of 1974 that its inquiry was complete and that no action would be taken. That was six months of investigations over one "goofy" incident! The loss of the $300,000 could have put us out of business. However, as I stated previously, I think it was another case of "divine intervention" and actually a blessing.

New Product Development

Through 1972 and 1973, the company's production operations continued to mature. I hired an experienced production manager and some production supervisors. While the Toddler Alarm was beginning to grow in revenues, there was not sufficient gross profit margin in that product to sustain the operations of the company. The Blood Pressure Monitor came into production, but again, it did not have sufficient gross profit margins to support much of the overhead. Not until we were able to get the Infant Monitor and some of our hospital products in the marketplace and develop those gross profits would we be able to support sufficient overhead to add significantly to the staff.

We were pleased when we managed to get the Toddler Alarm into the 1972 J.C. Penney and Sears catalogs. However, the product did not sell very well, and we learned one important marketing lesson. The Toddler Alarm was a proverbial fire extinguisher - everyone thought everyone else should have one. Mothers believed that, by having a Toddler Alarm, they were admitting to not doing a good job of supervising their younger children. See the right center of Figure 11.

The production of the Toddler Alarm positioned the company as an electronics manufacturer. It laid the groundwork for our second product, which we called the

"Blood Pressure Monitor." This was a product concept given to us by Dr. Maxwell Berry, a well known Atlanta internist.

Dr. Berry felt strongly that blood pressure readings were too subjective. His argument was that no two nurses read blood pressure numbers the same because they listen for sounds through a stethoscope. This Blood Pressure Monitor was designed to take those vagaries out of the process.

Initially, buyers for both Sears and J.C. Penney agreed to put the Blood Pressure Monitor in their catalogs. I recall that Sears reneged at the last moment as their corporate attorneys were concerned over liability risks associated with self-diagnostics. They were concerned that Sears would be held responsible if a patient chose not to seek appropriate medical care based on an inaccurate reading of "normal" from the blood pressure monitor and then developed a serious medical problem as a result. This question demonstrated the "risk averse" nature of most lawyers. Of course, home blood pressure monitoring today is routine!

In early 1973, Bill Wood, our new Vice President of Sales, told me that Richard Deborde, the head of the respiratory therapy department at Phoebe Putney hospital in Albany, Georgia, had a new product concept that he thought we could quickly develop. I went to Albany with Bill, and we spent time in the respiratory therapy department with Richard. I was impressed by his vision and creativity. He described a product that was needed to help wean patients off of ventilators. We gave it the name "Intermittent Mandatory Ventilation Controller." That was our first real hospital product, and we introduced it to numerous hospital respiratory therapy departments and distributors who sold into those hospital departments. Richard gave us some other ideas, which we quickly put into development and then production. They were all small monitoring systems that helped his respiratory therapists keep more accurate track of what was going on with each ventilator patient. We always appreciated our relationship with Richard Deborde.

The IMV Controller gave respiratory therapy departments a product to eliminate the weaning problem and provide ventilation intermittently only as a patient needed it. The IMV Controller was simple, easy to understand and operate, and quite effective for what it was designed to do. Thus, Healthdyne's reputation in the respiratory therapy departments of hospitals around the country began to build. In addition, our reputation with distributors who sold these products to hospitals was also becoming very solid.

I remember clearly when we submitted our FDA application for 510(k) clearance to market our microprocessor-controlled ventilators. Apparently, it was the first time the FDA had ever received a request for the approval of a device that was using a microprocessor. Our staff was asked to make some rather bizarre, but educational, steps to assist the FDA staff with understanding how the software in our microprocessor was developed and functioned. We eventually got through the education and submittal process, and we received 510-K clearance for the sale of our line of ventilators.

The use of a microprocessor helped us simplify the controls and monitoring functions of our ventilators considerably. It made the use of our ventilators quite logical and straightforward. Of course, that was the key design philosophy that I tried to convey to our technology staff in terms of "sophistication, but simplicity." I remember being very adamant that our controls and readouts be extremely logical because the operating handbook would probably be lost within about three days of the ventilator being in the respiratory therapy department.

Gross Profit Margins

I would like to make a brief comment on my fixation relative to gross profit margin, which relates to the sales price of a product minus its manufacturing costs. These comments are particularly focused on manufacturing operations and specifically those that are healthcare-related. Because the healthcare system in this country has so many complexities and ancillary costs, gross profit margin is especially important.

In the numerous businesses that I have examined over the decades, I have seen management generally neglect focusing on gross profit margins. To me, this is the most important set of expenses and should be given exceptional focus. If you extract an extra 10 percent or more out of your gross profit line, that leaves a lot of leeway for undertaking new opportunities and resolving mistakes in the other hard expense areas. Spend an inordinate amount of time focusing on improving your gross profit margins because that will pay off richly in countless ways.

CHAPTER 5

GROWING UP AND GOING PUBLIC

In the fall of 1975, because of our rapid growth, Healthdyne was in need of additional capital so we decided to undertake another private placement offering. During this offering, I was introduced to Henry Curtis, the Chairman and CEO of American Business Products, a publicly traded business forms company that his grandfather founded. I thoroughly enjoyed getting to know Henry. He was a very astute business executive and had some interesting family dynamics. He was the first person to advise me that I should establish trusts for my children.

Henry had a large family that had encountered problems over the years because no effective trusts had been set up. He made an interesting and whimsical comment to me that, "You should not want your children to become income poops." When I asked him what was an "income poop," he said it was a child who waited at home every month to receive a check from a trust fund. I told Henry that I absolutely did not want that to happen. He gave me some very good guidance and counsel on how to set up family trusts so that efficient use of those funds in the future by family members would be reasonable and effective.

Briefly, Henry's advice relative to setting up family trusts was to never establish trusts that would send monthly checks to family members. After previously making some mistakes, he created his family's trusts so that each of the principal recipients would get a certain amount of the trust corpus at four different times in their life. He selected the ages of 25, 30, 35 and 40. At each point, depending on the vote of the oversight committee, which was part of the trust, the trust recipient would receive 25 percent of the trust's balance. Henry's attitude was that, if the recipient had taken the money and had not gained the wisdom necessary to manage it by the age of 40, then they should suffer the consequences of their decisions. I was in total alignment with him.

During this particular fund raise, Henry put one constraint on his $50,000 investment. He knew the company needed to raise $150,000. Therefore, he would not allow his $50,000 to go into the offering unless the total $150,000 was collected. I accepted his $50,000 on that basis.

As the expiration date for the offering got closer, which I recall was in mid-December, I was about $30,000 short of the $150,000 total. I realized that I would have to take out a loan on my home for that amount in order for me to buy stock and close the offering. As I cast around Atlanta, I found a "loan shark" who would loan me the money for six months at an exorbitant interest rate. I had to accept his offer.

When I went down to the law firm in Atlanta to sign the documents, I was strongly advised by the closing attorney that the "shark," Mr. B, would take my house on June 15th if this six month loan was not paid in full by then. He advised me not to sign the document unless I was fully prepared to move out of the house. Of course, I signed the document with the expectation that I could get a second mortgage on the house in the meantime. That is exactly what I did! Of course, I never told my wife about the "shark" loan until I closed the second mortgage.

Rapid Growth

Through 1973, 1974 and 1975, Healthdyne continued to develop and place new products in the hospital products market. The company's first hospital product, the IMV Controller, opened up opportunities for the company to present new products to hospital respiratory therapy departments. This included a line of numerous monitoring and controller systems plus three new ventilators for neonatal and pediatric use in the hospital and for transport. In Figure 12, you will see eight of our hospital mini-Monitors and the Infant Monitor in the center of the front row. In addition, you will see our three pediatric and neonatal ventilators. At this point, we had clearly developed an effective hospital product line in addition to our home monitoring system with the Infant Monitor.

In addition, we continued to improve the Infant Monitor and the concept of home monitoring of infants at risk for Sudden Infant Death Syndrome, or SIDS. During that process, I met Dr. Alfred Steinschneider. Al was the foremost researcher on Sudden Infant Death Syndrome, not only in this country, but probably the world. When I first contacted him, he was at Upstate Medical Center in Syracuse, New York. I initially visited with him there; however, he moved to the University of Maryland shortly thereafter. I visited him there on several occasions in 1974, and we would brainstorm concepts for monitoring and managing the data for infants prone to apnea (non-breathing) episodes. Al enlightened me in numerous ways clinically, and I enlightened him in numerous ways from a technology standpoint.

In early 1975, Dr. Steinschneider was awarded a National Institute of Health (NIH) grant, which resulted in his conducting clinical studies on at least 50 infants. For the NIH study, Al had to produce respiratory and cardiac data associated with apnea. Therefore, he challenged us to develop a recording system for the monitor so he could collect the data.

As Al and I talked through these matters, I conceived the idea of a system that would not only serve Al's research study needs by collecting apnea event data, but could also be a reasonably priced product for home use as well. Back at Healthdyne, our technology and production staff developed our pre-production concept.

With a high level of focus on the Infant Monitor that Al desired, we were able to bring him the first prototype in about four months. It embodied monitoring concepts for respiratory and cardiac rates plus the ability to make recordings of events that triggered the alarms. We signed a contract with a cardiology device company to use their small recording system. That recorder fitted nicely into the top of the Infant Monitor, and it could be inserted or removed, depending on the desire of the prescribing physician. See Figure 13. A few years later, microprocessor technology allowed the recording of data to be done internally. Our Smart Monitor was the result of this major step in new technology. See Figure 14.

Over the previous years, we had worked with certain physicians at the American Academy of Pediatrics. Our association with Dr. Scott James helped us create some interest in our Infant Monitor and home SIDS monitoring at the Academy. In 1976, the American Academy of Pediatrics' Apnea Task Force Committee completed a study on the effectiveness of utilizing physician-prescribed home monitoring units for preventing SIDS. They determined that, "The monitoring of infants at home under a doctor's prescription with a device that measures cardiac and respiratory activity was an acceptable alternative to hospitalization."

When the American Academy of Pediatrics issued their opinion, we were the only company that could provide a comprehensive monitoring product acceptable for use in the home. Most importantly, it helped us begin to win reimbursement for home infant monitoring from health plans. At that point, it was relatively easy to interest qualified home healthcare dealers to commit to this new technology for home use.

With these positive actions, the Infant Monitor revenues began to grow very rapidly. Those revenues reached approximately $500,000 in 1977, $750,000 in 1978, $1.25 million in 1979, $2.75 million in 1980 and $7.5 million in 1981. Also, the company's profits grew with this increase in revenues from the Infant Monitors from a loss of $37,000 in 1976 to a profit of more than $750,000 in 1981. Revenues climbed to over $16 million in 1982, and profits more than doubled. Then, our acquisition of Narco Scientific took our revenues to over $100 million. We continued to build revenues to over $400 million over the years. See the early revenues and EPS in Figures 15 and 16.

I believe the Infant Monitor, when sold to a home healthcare distributor, had a gross profit margin of over 60 percent. We probably had the ability to move that up to the 80+ percent range, but I did not have the business insights at that point to do so. I cannot overemphasize the necessity for medical companies, in battling all the regulatory issues, to have gross profit margins of 60 percent, 70 percent and 80 percent to really exploit their products. As you will find out later, MiMedx Group had gross profit margins of approximately 90 percent. However, we worked very diligently to maintain gross profit margins at those levels.

Fortunately, the net profit from the rapid growth in sales of the Infant Monitor provided the cash flow to allow us to focus on the development of other new products. In addition, it gave us the flexibility to look to diversification into other areas of healthcare. In spite of having strong cash flows and a growing staff of product development engineers and technicians, I knew the company was in a very vulnerable stage of growth. We needed to increase our presence with our hospital products, particularly in the pediatrics and neonatal areas. I felt that we needed to stay focused in those areas in order to make rapid progress with the opportunities that we saw. In addition, there were still some interesting product opportunities in home healthcare. Our dealers were becoming comfortable managing high technology home healthcare products. In some cases, this was somewhat of a stretch from selling wheelchairs, crutches and beds. However, the Infant Monitor pushed their learning experience, and they became interested in other high technology products.

In doing our exploratory work, we found out that the KDC Corporation, a small manufacturer of pediatric monitors and transport incubators, was potentially for sale. They had been acquired some years before by the Cavitron Corporation and had subsequently fallen on difficult times. See their infant transport incubator in Figure 17.

I contacted the CEO of Cavitron and went to New York to discuss the acquisition of KDC Corporation. KDC had revenues of only about $2 million at that point, and they had been declining. I told the CEO that we had interest in trying to rebuild this previously well-respected company. We were able to purchase KDC for its hard assets of just inventory. As I recall, we paid less than $500,000 for a company that had revenues in excess of $2 million.

We paid a price of about 25 percent of revenues, which was a good price for this transaction. I am sure we recovered our investment in about one year! We attempted to operate KDC in Anaheim, California for a period of time. However, the state of California had so many odd and restrictive requirements on business that we quickly decided to move that operation to our Atlanta production facilities.

One product that was gaining strong interest in the home healthcare area was oxygen concentrators. These were medical devices that created oxygen from room air. They replaced the cumbersome oxygen tanks that were used by patients who had COPD and other respiratory disorders. These types of products fit our product development capabilities and our distribution through home healthcare dealers.

I learned that the Bendix Corporation, who had one of the first oxygen concentrator product lines on the market, might be interested in selling their product line. They were manufacturing these concentrators in a 25,000 square foot facility in Davenport, Iowa. The product stood about 40 inches high. Today, the latest oxygen concentrators are about 25 percent of the 1982 size. See our production line in Figure 18.

As I recall, a retired military general was running the Bendix division that owned their oxygen concentrator assets. I spent a day in Davenport negotiating with him in the restaurant of our hotel. We paid a little over $3 million for the product line and manufacturing facility. At the time, I believe their revenues were about $6 million so we negotiated another excellent transaction and obtained a building that we quickly sold for about $1.5 million, as I recall.

Today, oxygen concentrators remain a strong portion of the high tech home healthcare business. In fact, Philips Healthcare, who eventually acquired Respironics and Healthdyne Technologies, still produces the oxygen concentrators in a large facility in the north Atlanta area.

Home Healthcare Distributors

We had not necessarily considered acquiring home healthcare distributors, but we knew that there were consolidations taking place in the industry. We had to be careful because our major distributors could be acquired by one or two large entities. However, we were thrust into becoming a home healthcare dealer when our Atlanta dealer, who was managing a large number of Infant Monitors, was about to go bankrupt, which would have left almost 50 families with infants on the monitor without the critical support and service necessary. So we stepped in and began servicing those families after setting up a new home healthcare services subsidiary. We quickly realized the financial leverage that could be achieved with this type of operation, if it was well run. Therefore, we decided to consider other select acquisitions of profitable home healthcare distributors.

Thus, during 1983 we acquired about 15 home healthcare dealers across the country. We only had to pay about one times revenue while our stock was trading at several times that metric. So these acquisitions were not dilutive plus we generally improved their growth rates and profitability.

Corporate Valuations

I want to make some very short and simple comments about my experience relative to Wall Street valuations of companies and company acquisition prices. Over the years, our companies have been analyzed by dozens of analysts. Some were better at figuring out the real pertinent issues than others who were not so efficient.

Normally, there is the "discounted cash flow" model, which has some net present value calculations associated with it. But, basically, the model forecasts the cash flow generated by the enterprise for the next 10 years. That is discounted back to a current valuation based on certain discount rates. The discount rates could change, depending on certain factors associated with the current business and economic environment, such as interest rates.

There are also values added to the business entities, depending on specific asset groups. In addition, the industry segment has certain impact on the valuations, which generally relate to growth rate of cash flows.

The values from the standard discounted cash flow method, primarily relate to the growth rates of revenue and profit. Of course, if the business is balanced properly, operating profits should grow at a faster rate than revenues. However, the business can distort that, particularly if the business's gross profit margins are lower than they should be. Relative to healthcare manufacturing businesses, if you are not producing 60 to 80 percent gross profit margins, issues will develop and opportunities lost, unless there is something else very specific related to that business. Of course, distribution businesses will carry much lower gross profit margins than manufacturing business because of their proprietary asset base.

I have always pushed our operations for higher gross profit margins, which we achieved either by being able to raise sales prices per unit or reducing manufacturing and overhead costs per unit. So always start a business plan by attempting to figure out how to optimize your gross profit margin by increasing revenue per unit as much as possible and reducing the costs associated with producing the product. Often, loss of gross profit is hard to make up with reductions of operating expenses.

After the gross margin optimization has taken place, discounted cash flows will provide values that are higher, depending on the growth rate of revenues and profits. Therefore, increased revenue, profit and cash flow growth or perceived future growth are the simplest keys to obtaining higher valuations.

In the home healthcare sector, most low growth, but profitable, business enterprises will trade or sell at 1.0 to 3.0 times their annual revenues. Of course, profits that are still growing at faster rates than revenues could increase the valuation.

If you begin to increase revenue growth to 15 percent to 25 percent per year, you should see the revenue multiple go up to three to five times the annual revenue. When you start having growth above 30 percent, you could see six and seven times current annual revenue as a valuation. I am always suspicious of valuations above seven times revenues unless there is a new product being introduced that will add dramatically to future revenues.

Therefore, revenue and profit growth should be one area of primary focus relative to business valuations. There is always a balancing act in terms of how that level of growth is achieved. For the entrepreneurial business, you are heavily dependent on the management talent and employee base. For fast-growth business, it is a real challenge to stay ahead of that growth curve with competent and trained personnel and management systems. At my last company, MiMedx, we were very fortunate in that we had dozens of skilled managers and former employees in the Atlanta area who had worked at our previous businesses. Therefore, we were able to pick and choose as we saw the development of our revenues and asset base growing.

Going Public

Healthdyne revenues grew rapidly from 1976 forward. For fiscal year ending April 30, 1977, Healthdyne recorded its first annual profit of $81,000 on $459,000 of revenues. The 1978 revenues were $713,000 with profits of $108,000. The 1979 revenues almost doubled to $1.248 million with a profit of $142,000. The 1980 revenues more than doubled to $2.786 million with profits of $340,000. On April 30, 1981, the company reported annual revenues of nearly $7.5 million with profits of $774,000. We changed our fiscal year end to December 30th in 1982.

The company's net earnings per share (EPS) for 1979, 1980 and 1981 were $.10, $.12 and $.51. On April 30, 1981, the company's weighted average number of common shares and equivalents were 1,517,585. Those rapid increases in revenues and EPS put us in a position to consider going public.

In 1977, Healthdyne moved out of the Windy Hill Industrial Park, where we had our first manufacturing facilities, into a 15,000 square foot manufacturing facility, nearly three times as large, located on North Cobb Parkway in Marietta. Three years later, the company was able to have a building built to our own specifications. It was 70,000 square feet of manufacturing space along with our corporate headquarters.

With this type of progress, the Board decided the company should be in a position to complete a successful public offering of its stock. After discussing the company's progress with a number of investment bankers, the Board selected Bache, Halsey, Stewart and Shields and the Robinson-Humphrey Company as our investment bankers for our initial public offering. After negotiations, the underwriters agreed to take the company public at $17.75 a share. Some of our large early shareholders asked to be able to sell some of their shares in the offering. So 635,000 shares were offered for sale. The company netted $8.275 million from the transaction. On December 8, 1981, Healthdyne became a publicly traded company in the "over-the-counter" market.

One of the country's largest big eight accounting firms, Peat, Marwick, Mitchell and Company, became Healthdyne's auditors a year before the offering. In addition, we hired King & Spalding as our outside law firm. The company's stock traded nicely in the aftermarket. It continued to increase in value as the company announced its quarterly earnings during 1982. The company completed a two for one stock split in July of 1982 at $26 per share.

In August 1982, the company was able to complete a second public stock offering at a price of two times that of the initial offering just nine months earlier. The investment bankers for that offering were the Robinson-Humphrey Company and Robertson Coleman Stephens, a west coast investment banker.

As the company entered 1983, the market continued to show strong interest in the Healthdyne stock. Therefore, in June of 1983, the company successfully completed a third public offering and raised $65 million. At the completion of that offering, the stock reached its high of $41 per share. At that point, stock market valuation of Healthdyne was $600 million. This valuation was over 15 times the value of the company's initial public offering just 18 months earlier. Also, the company had raised approximately $90 million in these three offerings, which were done in late 1981, and mid-1982 and 1983.

Of course, during this year and a half, Wall Street was going through a most enthusiastic period for high technology and healthcare stocks. In fact, we completed our third offering within about two weeks of the market's infamous technology sell off. This resulted in a wholesale flight from technology stocks and many healthcare stocks. I will provide more discussions on this matter in Chapter 6.

The DRG Legislation

As we entered 1983, the U.S. healthcare system was trying to come to grips with providing access to healthcare in spite of the dramatic increases in the cost of delivery. The federal government started with the Diagnosis Related Group (DRG) legislation and then pressed the Health Care Finance Administration (HCFA) to withhold cash payments to home healthcare providers. Thus, numerous changes began to occur as our management tried to understand where these major disruptions were going to lead.

The passage of the DRG legislation was necessary to take away the "blank check" that had been given to hospitals over the years as they charged Medicare for the actual costs of caring for a patient. Instead, the government was stating that they were only going to pay a set amount of dollars for each procedure. If the hospital exceeded this amount, the hospital would have to absorb the costs.

We were rather naive in thinking that the DRG legislation would benefit our home healthcare services operations. Hospitals would have to move patients through their systems more expeditiously and into the home healthcare environment where they would have more cost effective treatments. The result was that the DRGs drove patients out of hospitals "quicker and sicker."

Then, the HCFA struck another blow for cost control. They instructed the insurance carriers who paid their bills to slow down payments to home healthcare providers. There was a particular focus by HCFA on the respiratory care sector of home healthcare because that area had grown very rapidly in prior years. Oxygen delivery products, such as oxygen concentrators, were the mainstay of many home healthcare dealers. Oxygen was also a primary source of revenue for Healthdyne since we acquired the Bendix line of oxygen concentrators in 1982. In addition, we owned home healthcare service dealerships, which rented oxygen concentrators.

Larger Acquisitions

We were always looking for additional products to build our pediatric product line. The largest producer of infant, neonatal and pediatric products in the world was Narco Scientific, which was located in the Philadelphia, Pennsylvania area. They had actually looked at acquiring Healthdyne in 1977, but decided not to do so.

A shareholder of Narco Scientific came to us and offered to sell us their 15 percent ownership in the company in the summer of 1982. That certainly triggered a great deal of exploratory work on our part. This investor, Shamrock Associates from Far Hills, New Jersey, understood that Narco Scientific was undervalued and that someone would take an interest in the company. However, they approached us, which at the time looked like a stretch for Healthdyne. At that point, Narco was a 40-year old corporation traded on the New York Stock Exchange. As I recall, Narco had over $80 million in 1982 revenues. Their revenues were over two times ours, but they had much lower growth rates and profitability. Our market cap was about four times that of Narco because of our rapid growth. Thus, since we were going to offer a stock swap for the acquisition, we would use a high multiple stock for their low multiple stock, which would give us a financial advantage. However, over time, we would have to demonstrate we could improve Narco's revenue growth rate and profitability, or our stock multiple would drop.

Once we locked up the rights to purchase the Narco Scientific shares from Shamrock, we approached Narco's Board of Directors with a $28 per share or $70 million stock offer for the remainder of the company. This was less than one times revenue! Narco stock was trading at about $23 a share at the time. Our offer was quickly rejected.

Once we received the rejection notice, we asked for a meeting with Narco executives to discuss our offer. We had a cordial meeting with Rudy Garfield, the Chairman and founder of the company, and some of their other executives. A couple of days after that meeting, we heard back from them. They basically said, "Thank you for having the foresight to become a shareholder, but we do not plan to provide you any other opportunity." Well, that left us with the unfriendly takeover option through a tender offer to their shareholders as our only alternative. We had our tender offer ready to go, and we went public with it the next morning.

After this meeting with Rudy, Narco stock began to move. The acquisition offer had been publicized and that had motivated arbitrageurs (Arbs) to start trading in the stock. Over the next few days, the Narco stock moved from approximately $23 up to around $31 per share.

In the October 16th issue of the New York Times, it was reported that Narco had communicated with their shareholders and urged them to turn down Healthdyne's tender offer. They called our offer inadequate and not in shareholders' best interest. Narco also stated that they had filed suit in federal district court in New York to block Healthdyne's offer and to force the return of the shares that we had already purchased.

I was very concerned that the upward movement of the stock price could continue to encourage the arbitrageurs and drive the stock price even higher. At some point, the price would be beyond reasonable. I wanted to figure out how to send a message to the Arbs that the price was already above Healthdyne's limit. Note that we were offering a price at about one times their trailing revenues. Normally, a bargain price, but we could only afford a bargain at this point in our history.

I met with our investment bankers and attorneys in Philadelphia. I began by asking advice from Rod Dowling, our investment banker at Robinson-Humphrey. Rod did what would be expected by saying that we would need to make an offer equal to or higher than the current trading price. I told him that I wanted to make a formal offer at a price a couple of dollars <u>below</u> where the stock was currently trading. I felt strongly that it was going to take something like that to stop the speculation. Rod was visibly agitated by my suggestion, and he told me that nothing like that had ever been done before!

Then, Rod called my proposal a "Polish tender offer." In those days, Polish jokes were very popular, and they always indicated some form of foolishness. We had a big laugh about Rod's tender offer name, and we frequently used it when we discussed the successes of our offer.

The Narco stock was trading now at around $30 a share, and we went ahead with our Polish tender offer at $28 per share. Our strategy worked quite effectively, and the price of the stock stopped escalating. Actually, we did raise our bid to $31.50 in our <u>final</u> negotiations with the Narco Board.

We patiently waited over the next week or so to see how our tender offer would be accepted by the Narco shareholders. We would receive daily reports on the number of shares that had been tendered. I remember one night about 6:30 we received a call at the office from Rod. He indicated that we had just received the Teleflex, Inc. shares. The Teleflex CEO, Lennox "Bim" Black, was on the Narco Board of Directors, and apparently he saw the opportunity and tendered his company's 300,000 Narco shares to Healthdyne. That pushed us to over 50 percent ownership, and the battle was basically over.

I expressed my sorrow that this acquisition had to come through an unfriendly takeover. The merger seemed very logical and sensible to me. However, when I met with Rudy, Narco's Chairman and founder, he told me that he had dreamed of being acquired by a large pharmaceutical corporation. Thus, Healthdyne became an "opportunist." Refer to Chapter 17 for more details on opportunists.

I told Rudy that I did not think Narco would have the operational synergy with a pharmaceutical company. On the contrary, I believed the merger of Narco with Healthdyne would dramatically improve Narco's profitability as well as Healthdyne's, and it would benefit both shareholder groups.

After all these years, I certainly do not recommend the unfriendly approach to combining businesses. Even if success does occur, the integration of two organizations with bad attitudes towards each other is always problematic without strong leadership.

The integration of Narco Scientific into Healthdyne went relatively smoothly. We set up a committee of executives from both companies that met weekly and then bi-weekly to work through the integration matters. Our goal was to integrate Healthdyne's hospital products into the sales activities of Narco Scientific and specifically their Air Shields division. See Figure 19 for insight into a typical Narco Scientific product. Their Infant Warmer was used in the neonatal intensive care unit. We also saw some synergies with selling certain Narco products to home healthcare dealers, specifically infusion pumps. Frankly, we also had some Narco divestitures in mind that were not going to fit well with our plan of creating separate operations for hospital products, home healthcare products and services.

As we integrated Narco Scientific into the Healthdyne organization in the fall of 1982, a certain amount of enthusiasm began to develop between the organizations. The Narco management began to understand what we had already built at Healthdyne and our vision for integrating their divisions into our operations. We made the cuts to the top management of Narco in a kind manner, and from that point forward, things began to work smoothly.

One of the first issues we had to plan was our national sales meeting, which was to occur in the month of January. We put a good deal of time into our planning process, and we selected a theme called "The Winning Combination."

In Figure 20, I highlight Margaret Martin receiving a bouquet of flowers for all of the work she and her staff accomplished relative to the 1983 National Sales Meeting. You can see the meeting theme highlighted behind us. Also, it would be appropriate to highlight that Margaret came to work for Healthdyne as an executive assistant. Her talent and leadership abilities quickly showed themselves, and she was promoted into managing our meeting and convention planning department and later our travel department. What is very noteworthy is that Margaret remained employed by Healthdyne, Matria Healthcare and MiMedx Group for 40 years. She finally retired in June of 2022 after dedicating a substantial portion of her life to these companies and all of their associates. Margaret, a very sincere thank you.

Home Infusion Therapy

In early 1983, I had my sights set on the newly developing home infusion therapy area of healthcare. In the home infusion area, we would be stepping into a much larger and rapidly developing market that needed sophisticated systems and management. At the time we were beginning to seriously analyze opportunities in this area. Home Nutritional Services (HNS) also decided that they needed to be acquired in order to grow at a reasonable rate and survive.

HNS was founded by Gene Terry in 1981. Gene was an experienced home healthcare distributor and pharmacist. He heard about and connected with Dr. Robert Winters, who was at Columbia University in New York. Dr. Winters was a professor of pediatrics and was very involved in publishing papers and conducting work on total parenteral nutrition (TPN). This was a very logical opportunity for home healthcare because delivering TPN at home was much less expensive than hospitalizing a patient for administration of these fluids. As it turned out, Gene and Bob decided to start a business, and Home Nutritional Services was born. Their offices were located in Parsippany, New Jersey. HNS began to add operations outside of New York. However, there was a major issue of their obtaining reimbursement from most health plans in a logical and straightforward manner. Even though Medicare had approved payment for total parenteral nutrition (TPN) in the late 70's, health plans were slow to take the initiative.

With cash flow being uncertain and difficult, Gene decided that he should attempt to sell the company. He set up a controlled auction through Smith Barney. There was a lot of interest, and some pharmaceutical companies came to their meetings. However, when we arrived on scene, it was a different ballgame. We had done our homework, and we knew this business opportunity very well.

We made an offer for HNS of $20 million of Healthdyne stock. Gene and Bob accepted the offer in late 1983. When Healthdyne bought HNS, they were completing an $8 million revenue year in 1983. By 1987, HNS had become the third largest provider of home infusion therapy in the United States. After that, we grew HNS revenues rapidly to $132 million in 1993.

As you can imagine, we received both accolades and criticism in 1984 from Wall Street on our acquisition strategy. Our operating issues and revenue growth drop was caused by Congress passing the DRG law in late 1983. This law changed the way Medicare would reimburse for many medical products, and most hospitals almost shut down their purchasing of capital equipment for close to a year. However, our diversification strategy and acquisitions ended up working out well for us. Even when we had to divest companies after only short periods of time, we made respectful profits on our transactions. Of course, if we had only focused on our Infant Monitors, our growth would have slowed, and we might have been forced to sell the company.

During this 1982 and 1983 period, our employee numbers went from about 500 to approximately 2,500. At the end of 1983, we had employees scattered all over the United States, in facilities overseas, and our sales personnel were deployed across the world. We also had a manufacturing facility in Shannon, Ireland for Narco Scientific products.

CHAPTER 6

EXCITING GROWTH

As the company entered 1982, we were headed for an especially rapid growth period. By this point, our revenues were growing very quickly in excess of 100 percent annually, and we were showing good profitability. Recall that we sold our first private placement offering at $1 per share, which gave the company a valuation of approximately $1 million in 1971.

In early 1982, we attracted the attention of a group of well-respected stock analysts, and they created some excitement around the company. By June of 1982, the stock was trading at approximately $26 per share, and we decided to do a two for one stock split.

Our rapid revenue growth continued into 1983, and the stock market was continuing to rise. So, on June 20, 1983, we accomplished a third public offering. That allowed us to raise another $65 million. At the completion of that offering, the stock price was over $40 a share, which approached its all time high of $41. That valued the company at $600 million, which was more than 15 times our initial public offering valuation after approximately a year and a half of being publicly traded.

As I have previously mentioned, within two weeks of completing our June 1983 stock offering, Wall Street's enthusiastic period for high technology and healthcare stocks began to wane. In July, the stock market experienced a significant technology sell off that included healthcare stocks. Our stock price dropped from approximately $40 a share to $25 per share by August 1, 1983. All technology companies and most healthcare companies saw similar price declines, if not more so. During this year and a half period, however, Healthdyne managed to raise $90 million in cash.

The Finality of the Diagnosis Related Group Legislation

Some additional information on the DRG legislation is in order. The majority of healthcare companies enjoyed a period of excellent reimbursement for their products and services from the late 1960s into the early 1980s. This was primarily the result of the federal government paying for Medicare patients based on the cost of their care. In other words, there was an open checkbook for reimbursement of all healthcare costs. Of course, a situation such as this would eventually be brought to closure, and that began in 1983.

This open checkbook policy spread even into private sector health plans. While health plans are notoriously tight and strict with their reimbursement policies, a number of the philosophies of the Medicare system were adopted by certain health plans. Both hospitals and physicians had benefited from this reimbursement era as did medical device, service and diagnostic companies.

During 1983, Congress focused on these out of control healthcare expenditures and enacted what was called the Diagnosis Related Group (DRGs) legislation, which would regulate how the government would reimburse hospitals and physicians for various services for Medicare patients. In effect, these new regulations set limits on reimbursements for the most common medical procedures. Hospitals reacted to these new restrictions by curtailing equipment purchases and services where possible.

I thought that DRGs would be good for the home healthcare services business. The descriptor that was used to characterize the results of this legislation was that patients were forced out of hospitals "quicker and sicker." However, the government realized that these costs could merely be transferred over to the homecare sector of healthcare. Even though costs would be lower in that environment, the Health Care Finance Administration (HCFA) dealt another blow for cost controls by telling certain insurance carriers who paid the bills for Medicare to decelerate payments to providers of home healthcare services. This was an extremely abnormal directive to give. There was no formal announcement; the HCFA just began to hold providers funds. Our accounts receivable aged quickly, and we did not understand why all payers were slowing payments.

Also, it seemed as if there was a focus on respiratory care and oxygen delivery products. At the time, the backbone of many home healthcare businesses was oxygen therapy. Of course, this action reduced the demand for oxygen concentrators. Also, it put growth and profit pressures on all home healthcare dealers.

HCFA put some specific constraints in place relative to oxygen reimbursement. They began requiring doctors and dealers to document the blood oxygen levels, which indicated a patient's need for oxygen. They continued to change those levels to the point that the industry became very frustrated and confused. The most devastating action taken by HCFA was that the changes that were being made were enforced <u>retroactively</u>. This meant that, when therapy was billed, there was no easy determination at what level it would be reimbursed.

This was terribly confusing to the industry. We were unable to get straight answers as to which way these changes were eventually going to go. Finally, Congress passed legislation to prevent HCFA from retroactively changing reimbursement criteria.

Healthdyne had to write off more than $15 million of our oxygen therapy billings from our relatively new home healthcare service operations. Overall, the home healthcare industry had to write off more than $400 million.

Another SEC Inquiry/Investigation

Also, in the fall of 1983, I had begun to realize that, because of the rapid growth of our organization, we were beginning to have a few executive management issues. Our President and Chief Operating Officer and one of my dearest friends, Paul Yokubinas, was beginning to lose his ability to stay on top of all his areas of responsibility. Paul was an excellent operating executive, but he attempted to do more himself rather than delegate and hold people accountable. Because of the rapid growth, we had begun to bring in new management at a fast pace, and Paul was unable to function in the COO capacity as effectively as he had when he was able to manage all the details himself. Therefore, I told the Board that I thought we needed to look for a new President and Chief Operating Officer and give Paul other more specific responsibilities.

About the time I was coming to grips with this issue, I began receiving some communication from Dr. James Ashton, one of my former associates at General Dynamics. Jim and I met after I left the military and went to work for General Dynamics in Fort Worth, Texas. He arrived there at about the same time after having completed his PhD in Civil Engineering at MIT. I have often stated that Jim Ashton was, at that point in time, the smartest individual I had ever met in my life. He obtained his PhD in about 18 months after receiving his Bachelor's Degree in Civil Engineering. Jim told me that the Dean at MIT would not allow him to graduate as soon as he had completed his course work and thesis because no one at MIT had ever accomplished that in such a short period of time.

Jim and I became personal friends, and we actually co-authored a highly technical book together with one other author. It was titled *Primer on Composite Materials: Analysis*.

Initially, Jim did very well at General Dynamics. He was rumored to be headed towards becoming the youngest Chairman and CEO in the corporation's history. General Dynamics sent him to Harvard to get his MBA Degree, and they subsequently began giving him operating assignments in other divisions throughout the company.

However, in 1983, Jim was summarily dismissed as the number two executive at the Electric Boat Division of General Dynamics in Groton, Connecticut. As I recall, I saw the announcement probably in The Wall Street Journal. I called his home phone and talked to his wife, Julie. She explained to me that the dismissal was merely corporate politics. Julie stated that I should know Jim well enough to know that he did not tolerate corporate politics well. That made a little sense to me, but I still found his rapid dismissal confusing. Julie said that he was considering accepting a position at North American Rockwell in Tulsa, Oklahoma. Jim did accept that position but, within about eight months, he was promptly dismissed by North American Rockwell. In my next phone call to Julie, she changed her comments somewhat, but brushed off this recent dismissal as corporate politics as well. She went on to say that she and Jim were getting a divorce as their separate careers had caused them to drift apart. That surprised me.

As I recall, Julie had her PhD in Biomedical Engineering and was quite successfully employed in her field. However, she suggested that Jim should talk to me as he really needed to leave the aerospace industry and start over. So I told her to have him call me, and we would talk about it.

I did get a phone call from Jim, and on that call, he reiterated much of what Julie had said. He made arrangements to come to Atlanta, and we subsequently had a long afternoon meeting at my office. In our meeting, he was still the energetic and self-assured individual that I had known at General Dynamics. He was an attractive and athletic individual who enjoyed playing rugby, and he now had strong, but "intellectual" opinions on business practices because of his MBA degree and some limited experience at General Dynamics.

Jim convinced me that his terminations were merely corporate politics. He stated that, when he witnessed some executives doing something that he deemed inappropriate, he immediately called them out. In both cases, he claimed corporate politics caused him to be dismissed rather than the other executives. When I would attempt to probe deeper, Jim would stop me by saying that he could not risk potential disclosure of inside information on these two large corporate entities by commenting further. Therefore, I could only go so far; I had to rely on my instincts and previous experiences with him. Ultimately, but quickly, I decided to invite him back to meet the Board of Directors, and let them make the decision.

As I expected, Jim made a good impression on our Board, and we all decided that he should be offered the position of President and Chief Operating Officer. As I recall, he started as our President/COO on January 2, 1984. Incidentally, after being terminated from North American Rockwell, he had gone to work for a small private company in Houston, Texas by the name of Space Systems that was planning to put a rocket into space. He was there for only about 60 days when he was dismissed. However, by that time, we had already made the decision to hire him. I do not believe I even asked him what had happened at Space Systems.

For the first several weeks, things seemed to be going smoothly. Jim was quickly absorbing most of the aspects of our business activities. He did not appear to have any issues, and I was able to answer all of his questions. However, when the furnishings for his office arrived, the first odd situation occurred. Jim was Catholic by religion, and on his office walls, he hung two oil paintings of himself that depicted him in a priest's robe. In both paintings, he was the dominant figure with a group of "subjects" in the lower part of the painting. His hands were held up as if he were offering a blessing. I did not say anything about the paintings, but other people took note. Later, I did ask him who the artist was, and he said a friend of his in Fort Worth. That was about all the information he wanted to disclose.

The next incident occurred in his fourth week at Healthdyne. Our head of Human Resources, Joe Clamon, came into my office and closed the door. He said that he had to discuss with me something important about Jim. He showed me a document that Jim had apparently typed himself. The agreement gave Joe a substantial bonus if he could convince me and the other two top executives, Paul Yokubinas, who was the executive Jim had replaced, and Terry Dewberry, the CFO, to resign. He told Joe that I had admitted to him that the company was guilty of some misdeeds and that I would like to quietly resign. Joe could not persuade Jim to tell him any more than that. When Joe pushed back by expressing his familiarity with the integrity of executive management and his knowledge of Healthdyne, Jim offered up a much larger bonus if he could manage to see that these resignations took place.

To say the least, I was surprised and shocked. The allegations were ridiculous, but Jim's proposal to Joe was absolutely bizarre. It certainly showed his lack of business sophistication in terms of corporate governance and a few other dozen issues! This was the type of allegation that should have gone straight to the Board of Directors in normal fashion. So I asked Joe to go back and continue to talk to

Jim and try to collect more information on the supposed corporate issues and to ask for his suggestions on how Joe should approach the Board and me. In the meantime, I would continue to have discussions with Jim to see if he would disclose these matters to me.

I also began to discuss the matter with some of the other Board members, including Rusty French, the attorney on our Board who was with King & Spalding. Everything was quiet for a few weeks.

I had advised Jim that we needed to begin to be conservative about our cash flow because I expected our hospital products revenues to fall fairly substantially during 1984 as a result of the DRG legislation. But, he made some major capital equipment investment decisions without letting me know, and it was going to add a substantial amount of debt to our balance sheet. Our debt went from $15 million to $50 million in the few months Jim was COO as he was making commitments without my knowledge.

When the accounting department came to me about this, I went to Jim and asked him about his spending decisions and his disregard for my direction about managing cash. That is when I first experienced his arrogance and narcissism. He essentially told me that he viewed this as his responsibility and that he would be sure nothing bad happened as a result. I told Jim that he had been on the job for only a few weeks, and he had no idea of the numerous issues with which I already had experience and knowledge. I told him that he did not have the authority to make these kinds of financial decisions as the Board had not yet passed a resolution giving him that authority. But, even that comment did not sway his self-righteousness!

Things settled down for a short period of time until I scheduled a sales and management meeting over a weekend in early March. Because of the passage of the DRG legislation, we had a number of additional plans to complete for our 1984 fiscal year. A dinner meeting was scheduled for Friday night welcoming the members of the corporate management team as well as our sales managers from around the country.

Jim came to me with a request to make a presentation "to everyone on Friday night." I asked him to give me an outline on what he intended to do. As the time for the meeting approached, he still had not given me any information. When I confronted him about it, his argument was that I had to learn to "trust him." He said that he was only going to do something that would motivate and tie the team together. Well, he never did present me with any information other than some generalities. I had some issues to discuss in the opening of the meeting so I figured I would make my points and then see what happened. Well, it was quite a show!

First, recall that Julie, Jim's wife, told me that she was asking for a divorce. Jim never gave me an update on that situation, but he showed up on stage that night attired in a tuxedo when everyone else there was dressed very casually. And, more importantly, he had a young woman with him wearing a cocktail waitress outfit. He introduced her as his "stage assistant" from Fort Worth. I later found out that she was his "girlfriend."

Anyway, as Jim's presentation unfolded, I had never witnessed or even imagined a business presentation more inappropriate.

Jim's behavior that night became more psychotic as his presentation went on. After he introduced his "stage assistant," he began a long diatribe about himself. He described all the large corporate projects with which he had been involved after finishing his MBA at Harvard. He did not mention his dismissals from General Dynamics, North American Rockwell and Space Systems. He made some over the top comments about how successful Healthdyne was going to be now that he was involved. I saw a degree of narcissism from Jim that I had neither previously witnessed nor could have imagined!

Next, Jim stated that he wanted to present some special awards to the executives at Healthdyne. First, he called Yvonne Scoggins, our Corporate Controller, up to the stage. He gave her a hug, and then he stepped back, took a pail of shredded paper from his "stage assistant" and dumped it over Yvonne's head. He exclaimed that he had to do that in order to help her understand that the bureaucracy she created was not welcomed by many. Then, he asked Terry Dewberry, our Chief Financial Officer, to come up on stage and presented him with a five-gallon plastic container of diet pills. Dewberry was an obese individual, but that gift was certainly unwarranted. He also called Paul Yokubinas up to the stage, but I have forgotten what he did to Paul. Jim finished by inviting me to come to the stage. He handed me a foot long piece of a broomstick and asked me to put it in my mouth as a "bite block." He told everyone this was going to be necessary as he made all the changes that he was going to make in order for Healthdyne to be a much better performing company.

I was sitting next to Rusty French, a Board member and our corporate outside counsel, during all this, and he kept leaning over to me with various questions about Jim's behavior. I told him that I had never seen anything like this from Jim. It was very disconcerting, and it was not indicative of the individual whom I had formerly known or of an individual who should be involved with our company. I told Rusty I was now beginning to understand why he had been terminated from three of his previous employers. I also expressed that I was concerned that something in his head had "flipped."

In keeping with the narcissistic personality that I was beginning to understand, Jim had videotaped his show, which came in very handy as I took the tape and gave it to an industrial psychologist. I also asked the psychologist to come to our headquarters and review the two oil paintings that Jim had hung in his office and to discuss Jim's behavior with Joe Clamon and others at the office. I also asked the psychologist to help the Board and me understand what was transpiring with Jim's behavior.

Our industrial psychologist came back with a concern that Jim was exhibiting psychotic behavior. He stated that sometimes extremely intelligent individuals exist on the very edge of psychosis. He said it looked as if, in Jim's case, something had triggered to push him over the line. He also said there was some strong narcissism clearly demonstrated as well as a loss of touch with reality. Hence, his diabolical lying.

About this time, I put in another call to Julie Ashton. I told her that I wanted to advise her of some things, but that I also wanted some straight answers from her. She confirmed that she was in the process of divorcing Jim. After I told her what was happening at the company, she began to cry and told me that she owed me a huge apology. She said that Jim had accused her of being "crazy" sometime prior. She went to see a psychiatrist who gave her a clean bill of health. However, the psychiatrist told Julie that she needed to see Jim, and after visiting with him, she explained to Julie that Jim was in a psychotic state of mind. She also said that it was going to be very difficult to deal with him in family as well as business matters.

Julie said that she had reached the point where she just wanted Jim out of Fort Worth and out of her family's life and that is why she lied to me when she asked me to talk to Jim about a change in career. She had hoped that I might quickly move him to Atlanta. I told Julie that we were probably going to have to dismiss him just as the three previous companies had done. I told her that I would try to smooth out the situation as much as possible, but that we were a public company that had to have sane and effective management. We could not continue to have Jim disrupt the company in this fashion. She apologized again. I told her that I understood, and I forgave her actions. Julie and I connected one more time after Jim's dismissal.

I had a discussion with the Board about the industrial psychologist's report, and Rusty gave input relative to Jim's bizarre behavior at the management meeting. I am not sure if we showed his videotape or not. However, the decision was unanimous that the company needed to give Jim his notice. A decision was made to give him a severance package, in spite of the current problems he had caused and his state of mind.

When Jim was told of his dismissal and the severance package we proposed, he flew into a rage. He requested five years of severance and immediately began to make allegations about improper accounting practices within the company. When I asked why he had not brought those allegations to the Board prior to his termination, he had no answer. That meeting ended acrimoniously, but we proceeded to plan our business activities without Jim being present.

Within about two weeks, we received a call from the Atlanta regional office of the SEC stating that Jim had made a number of serious allegations against the company and that we needed to come visit with them to clarify matters. Rusty and the Audit Committee started the discussions with the SEC. As I recall, I as well as the other corporate executives gave depositions. Personnel from Peat, Marwick and Mitchell, who had been our accountants for a number of years, were also called to testify.

Neither I nor the other executives knew of anything that would cause questions relative to the company's accounting practices. However, after about a year, the SEC asked the company to sign a consent decree. After the full meaning of a consent decree was explained to me, I felt strongly that we should not sign it because the company was not guilty of any misdeeds. King & Spalding explained in every way possible that the consent decree was the easiest way to put the matter behind us. Unfortunately, the Board took the easy way out instead of the right way! That is what most companies did because, with a consent decree, there was no admission of guilt. However, there was a five-year overhang associated with the initial charges the Commission had made. Also, this consent decree was brought up during my trial in 2021 by the DOJ as if it were an admission of guilt! So be wary of consent decrees. It is a method for government lawyers to get some credit when they have no case!

The company signed the consent decree, and the Board decided to give Jim some additional severance compensation. I certainly did not agree with that either.

As far as I know, Jim went on to earn a living by doing individual consulting. I do not know for what or for whom. But, I am certain he never showed up again as a public company officer or the CEO of any meaningful business enterprise. His mental breakdown was a sad ending to such a promising future.

I learned numerous lessons from this particular situation, which included more information than I wanted to know about psychotic and narcissistic behaviors and the clinical and real life implications of these illnesses. I was disappointed in Jim's lack of integrity and his propensity to lie when it was certainly not warranted, but this behavior was apparently driven by his psychosis.

I also began to have some insight into the way the SEC attorneys viewed claims of alleged wrongdoing. They were given the industrial psychologist's report so they knew Jim was not a <u>reliable</u> source of information. That knowledge apparently played <u>no</u> <u>role</u> in their decision to pursue a formal investigation that probably cost millions of taxpayer dollars and wasted huge amounts of time. As I recall, none of our depositions gave the SEC any information that would cause the company or the executives to be charged with any misdemeanors or fraud relative to our accounting. I never felt that they should have any reason to file charges against us. However, the SEC attorneys were adamant that the consent decree be signed, probably in order for them to get "special credit" from their management or to help with their career goal to transition to a private law firm.

This example of a bad hire should tell any entrepreneur, CEO or Board how important it is to have an industrial psychologist review executives as well as Board members prior to engagement offers being made. Of particular concern should be psychoses and other abnormal tendencies. A strong degree of self-confidence, <u>not</u> narcissism, should be present in these individuals.

Also, do not expect the SEC, through its attorneys, to act very prudently with your corporate time and money if they ever have the opportunity to open an inquiry or investigation into your business, no matter how unreliable their source of information may be.

Technology Problems

In 1983 when we started shipping the second version of our Infant Monitor, model 16900, we began to have some technology issues. Reports from the field stated that the monitors were having too many "false alarms."

I had been uncomfortable with my personal testing of this Monitor and had a number of arguments over this matter with our new Vice President of Engineering, Terry Torzalla. We had very proven technology from our first Infant Monitor that had stood the test of time for over eight years. There was some interest in making this second version a microprocessor-based product. However, I was adamant about maintaining the basic monitoring circuitry that we previously utilized. I had many debates with our new VP of Engineering on this subject.

Torzalla was on what I call an "ego trip" rather than a "business trip." Because he was our new VP of Engineering, he was very motivated to see that this decision to make the monitor a microprocessor-based product was his decision. I had basically functioned as our head of engineering up to this point when we brought in our first VP of Engineering from outside of the company.

Remember our discussion about participative management? Well, the company's engineers and its CEO were trying to help Torzalla understand that this new Monitor had problems. He and our staff continued to work on the issues. We totally restructured the project team, and within a few months, all the problems had been tracked down and resolved. I recall during that period of time that we got some "egg on our face" from our distributors and physician customers as we should have. Also, this VP of Engineering did not survive his "ego trip." More narcissism!

An Acquisition Problem

With all the acquisitions that we made over the decades, there is only one that proved to be <u>very</u> problematic. As you will recall, we acquired a number of home healthcare dealers around the country as we built that business. These operations could be nicely profitable and certainly matched with our other major initiatives in developing unique and cost effective products for home healthcare. We acquired at least 15 of these operations and generally paid one times their revenue while our stock was trading at three times our revenue.

We acquired a home healthcare dealership in Paintsville, Kentucky that was jointly owned by a respiratory therapist and a CPA. An audit had been done by a Big Eight auditor so their financials should have been in good order. However, a short time after we acquired the company and made presentations to their staff about our compliance hotline and their ability to send me a "Dear Pete" letter or our Board a private communication without concerns, I received letters from two different employees within a day of each other. Both employees highlighted the fact that we should be aware there were possibly other companies owned by the two principals that were being used to funnel money to doctors. Well, I immediately sent an internal audit team up to Kentucky to quietly see what they could uncover. It took them about a week, but they discovered that there was such a company that, as I recall, supposedly sold office supplies. The owners were funneling money into that business to provide cash to prescribing doctors for oxygen concentrator prescriptions. In fact, the checking account for this false company was held by a bank that was directly across the street from the corporate offices!

We gathered as much of the detailed information as we could, and I asked our internal audit department to put together a package, which we sent to the Department of the Interior, which managed the Black Lung program specifically in these coal mining areas.

We were immediately contacted by agents from the federal government, and we gave them more background information to back up our documented information. After a couple of months, we received a request to come visit with investigators and give depositions. At the time, I was not concerned. However, it shortly became evident that the investigators thought Healthdyne executives had perpetrated this bribery scheme and were trying to cover it up by exposing it in this fashion. It was rather frustrating to see how the information was twisted around to potentially accuse us of being the people who had committed the fraud.

However, within a month or so after that, one of the agents called me and apologized profusely, but he blamed it on the fact that <u>no company</u> had ever come forward and turned in any evidence of fraud being committed in the Black Lung program. He went on to say that, because of what we had done and the ethical manner in which we had handled it, the government had "broken the back" of the corrupt activities against the Black Lung program in Kentucky. He said they found politicians, lawyers and numerous doctors who were involved in this fraud. He thanked me very much and apologized again for initially suspecting us of crimes.

Of course, this disclosure was very detrimental to our business in Paintsville, Kentucky. The two perpetrators of these schemes knew and made it clear that I, in particular, was guilty of blowing the whistle on them. That is when I received two threatening phone calls from anonymous individuals, one of whom said that I should never fly into that airport again because deer rifles on the hills could take care of the airplane. We eventually stabilized the business within about a year.

Other Types of Growth

Our stock price began to rapidly decline in early 1984 caused by the return of numerous Infant Monitors, the DRG legislation reducing our hospital products revenues and the HCFA slowing down payments. The stock actually dropped to $2 per share towards the end of 1984. As I previously said, this was our first real corporate failure after eight years of prosperity. However, we managed to keep everyone motivated and focused during this period. It was not many months before we begin to return to respectable performance.

Healthdyne took Home Nutritional Services (HNS) public in December of 1989. In the transaction, 34 percent of HNS was sold to the public, and Healthdyne retained 66 percent ownership. HNS initially traded at a stock market valuation of $200 million. Healthdyne raised approximately $60 million in cash through the sale of the 34 percent ownership.

Because of the success of HNS going public, it was determined that Healthdyne Technologies was in a position to do the same. However, this time Healthdyne sold only 19 percent ownership to the public. That gave Healthdyne Technologies a market valuation of $100 million initially. The decision to retain 81 percent ownership in Healthdyne Technologies was made in order to be able to consolidate 100 percent of their revenues with Healthdyne's financial statements. Thus, Healthdyne had the advantage of consolidating the full revenue from Healthdyne Technologies. In addition to raising extra cash and owning publically traded assets which added value, namely HNS and Healthdyne Technologies, these spinouts also helped to significantly increase the value of the Healthdyne stock.

Of course, Healthdyne Technologies' management team was quite excited about being publicly traded. See Figure 21. However, I tried to make it clear to them that this was going to take a good deal of extra time on most of their parts. In particular, I told Craig Reynolds, our CEO, that he was going to have to set aside 30 percent to 35 percent of his time just to deal with the rigors of being publicly traded. Craig was rather skeptical of what I said, but he soon learned.

Another area in which Healthdyne Technologies developed an interest was the adult sleep apnea market. A small company in Pittsburgh by the name of Respironics was developing products for this market. We had a discussion with their founder about buying his company. At the time, he wanted $15 million, and the consensus from three members of our executive group was that we should only pay $12 million. Paul Yokubinas and I were willing to pay the $15 million, but Terry Dewberry, Don Millard and Brent Burkey, our General Counsel, aligned behind a maximum of $12 million. So this acquisition was not done.

Respironics grew very rapidly, as did Healthdyne Technologies when we launched our competitive products. However, they were several years ahead of us, and our revenues in adult sleep apnea never caught up with theirs. Figure 22 shows the maturation of the Healthdyne Technology adult sleep apnea system.

Some years later, Respironics acquired Healthdyne Technologies. That full story is told later. It would have been interesting to see how that market would have developed had we been able to combine the two companies together for the $15 million that Paul and I were willing to pay!

Healthdyne reported for its 1990 fiscal year revenues of $138 million, which were up 34 percent, and operating profits of $10.2 million, which were up 51 percent. This significant growth continued when the company reported 1991 revenues of $191 million with operating profit growing 135 percent to $24 million. Healthdyne reported revenues of $247 million for 1992 and revenues of $261 million for 1993.

Healthdyne Technologies demonstrated a nice growth rate in revenues for 1992, 1993 and 1994. The revenues were $54.4 million, $68.6 million and $89.0 million respectively in those three years.

Healthdyne Perinatal Services (Healthdyne Maternity Management) reached a revenue peak in 1992. Their revenues were $69.3 million, $67.6 million, $66.4 million for 1992, 1993 and 1994.

Healthdyne completed the sale of Home Nutritional Services to W.R. Grace for $100 million in April of 1994. HNS revenues peaked at approximately $133 million before the managed care era began to decimate their revenues.

Subsidiaries Being Dividended to Shareholders

As we entered 1995, it was evident to me that Healthdyne had become too complex a company for Wall Street to provide adequate analyst coverage. In other words, we had a subsidiary that manufactured medical devices, Healthdyne

Technologies; we had a subsidiary that was involved in home obstetrical care, which was Healthdyne Maternity Management (previously Healthdyne Perinatal Services); and, we had a subsidiary that was involved with healthcare information technology by the name of Healthdyne Information Enterprises. There was no one healthcare analyst that specialized in all three of these areas of healthcare. Therefore, I decided that we should dividend to shareholders each subsidiary so they would more effectively trade on their own. Then, they would develop their own analyst coverage. That would be much more efficient since Healthdyne did not have adequate analyst coverage because, as I previously stated, no analyst could cover all three companies adequately. This action increased shareholder value initially by doubling and even tripling as each company established their own Wall Street analyst coverage.

So we spun out all of our subsidiary companies to the Healthdyne shareholders. On this basis, we ended up with three separate public companies being traded under their own names. Also, we sold HNS to W.R. Grace before it was spun out. Thus, Healthdyne disappeared as an operating company, and our shareholders received stock in three other public companies as an exchange.

With the three companies trading as independent entities, I felt that I should pass the CEO role to a qualified executive who had helped build each organization. That is what was done as these subsidiaries became separately traded entities. So I became just Chairman of the three Boards, and I reduced my time commitments, just a "little bit!"

CHAPTER 7

MATURING

I want to digress somewhat as I begin this chapter. As I have previously mentioned, Congress passed the DRG legislation in October of 1983. This was primarily directed towards reducing charges to Medicare for numerous hospital procedures. This sent a shockwave through the hospital industry, and hospitals stopped purchasing a number of medical devices. Thus, our hospital product revenues dropped significantly. We could not tell how long these reductions would last; however, I came to the conclusion that the hospital products sector of healthcare would be in the doldrums for a significant period of time. But, many of our other opportunities still looked very bright. For instance, we had just acquired Home Nutritional Services in September, and we were very optimistic about the growth opportunities of the home infusion therapy segment of healthcare.

Thus, we made the decision to divest the businesses that we had acquired through the Narco Scientific acquisition. As usual, we moved quickly. We managed to sell the Pilling Surgical Instruments business on December 31, 1984. As I remember, it was sold to a private equity firm for about $17 million. I believe this was approximately one times revenues since Pilling was not growing very fast at all. We also sold the other two small Narco Scientific subsidiaries in 1984. The crown jewel of Narco was their AirShields subsidiary. We reluctantly sold it to London-based Vickers PLC in September of 1986. And, aside from some product lines that were manufactured by Healthdyne Technologies, that took us out of the hospital products business.

Healthdyne made a reasonable profit on the sale of all the Narco Scientific businesses.

The DRGs and managed care initiatives began to take their toll on our home healthcare services subsidiary. There were still a number of issues that had to be worked out in terms of governmental reimbursement for oxygen concentrators and other high volume home healthcare products. We had acquired a nice national presence with our home healthcare services operation, but we did not want to continue to suffer through this period of uncertainty due to the new managed care era that was being ushered in. Home healthcare services should have been recognized for the significant savings to the healthcare system that it brought by caring for patients in a lower cost home environment rather than in a hospital environment. This finally occurred many years later as the various governmental changes eventually worked their way through the bureaucracy and found actual business solutions to our country's complex healthcare industry.

Thus, in February of 1990, Healthdyne announced the divestiture of our home healthcare services operations. While some of the operations were sold off individually, we sold our major home healthcare service assets to Glassrock Home Healthcare in Atlanta.

Home Obstetrical Care – A New Opportunity

We had been watching the development of a company called Tokos Medical that was in the business of providing home healthcare services to mothers at risk of delivering preterm infants. The company had been drawing some attention from Wall Street and seemed to have a respectable growth profile. About this time, I received a call from David Goldsmith, our healthcare analyst with Robinson, Coleman and Stephens. David was going to be in Atlanta soon, and he wanted to have lunch.

The lunch was devoted primarily to my giving David an update on Healthdyne's progress. However, he disclosed to me that he was on the Board of Directors of Tokos Medical. Although I had done some research on Tokos, I still had a lot of questions, most of which he answered for me.

I can remember driving back to the office after that lunch with the firm belief that Healthdyne needed to enter the home obstetrical care market ASAP. I believe that I had already selected a name, Healthdyne Perinatal Services (HPS), before I even got back to the office!

I began to work on some of our concepts with various individuals in our management group. We developed a business plan and presented it to our Board of Directors in October of 1985. We had the ability to manufacture new technology that could be used in the home to pick up uterine activity contractions from the mother and transmit those to nursing facilities, which we would establish. We continued to work for over a year developing the technology and communication methods between the home uterine activity monitor and what would be our national network of nursing centers.

In looking for business opportunities, I always seemed to gravitate towards new technology developed for use in the home environment in order to improve clinical outcomes and reduce healthcare costs. Having lunch with David Goldsmith increased my enthusiasm for this new opportunity with high-risk pregnancies.

What I felt that Healthdyne could contribute was the development of new technology for use in the home that would be helpful in keeping mothers from delivering their infants preterm. Just like an Infant Monitor alerted the parents to an infant who was having apnea episodes, a uterine contraction monitor could alert a pregnant woman to signs of early labor and transmit that information to our nursing centers for triage.

As I previously mentioned, in late 1985 I assembled a team of individuals to research the viability of home obstetrics care, and we developed business plans related to product development and the supporting service centers. This was called "Project Delta." I asked Marty Olson, who was an expert in clinical matters, Jim Murray, our head of marketing, Mark Finch, one of our experienced product managers, to join the project.

As Project Delta unfolded, it became obvious that there were other obstetrical problems that could be managed from the home. For instance, pregnant women who had developed gestational diabetes or hypertension during their pregnancy could receive nursing attention in the home environment. We determined that our competitor, Tokos Medical, had a very mundane technology that they were employing in the home setting. With our experience in medical electronics and product development, our Project Delta team came up with the development of what we initially called "System 37" for preterm labor only. As we added additional technology to monitor other pregnancy disorders, we renamed the product "OB-1." This gave us a modular home obstetrical monitoring system for all types of high-risk pregnancies. See Figure 23. When we finished the development on that project, we had everything ready for the launch of Healthdyne Perinatal Services (HPS) in early 1987.

Finally, in June of 1987, we formally began operations of HPS. HPS was well received and grew rapidly. We began opening nursing centers across the country, primarily in major cities. However, in January of 1988, we did open a center in a small city, Duluth, Minnesota, because of the available nurse talent. I remember flying up to meet our two nurse managers in a blinding snowstorm. I do not think I ever went to Duluth again!

Our nurses were well trained in teaching pregnant mothers new information about their pregnancies and how to use our home monitoring technology to protect themselves if they experienced preterm labor or had other medical issues, such as gestational diabetes and/or hypertension. The OB-1 System proved to be quite innovative, and it certainly proved to be a system that Tokos Medical could never match.

In its first year of operations, HPS's revenues were about $7 million. In 1989, their revenues doubled to $15 million. However, HPS was still showing a loss as it expanded rapidly into new markets. In 1990, HPS revenues increased to $35 million, but we still posted a small loss. At that point, the company had 28 nursing centers in major cities and one in Duluth, Minnesota. These centers provided the base that increased revenues in 1991 to $65 million, which was an 89 percent increase over the previous year.

While a vast majority of obstetricians were very enthusiastic about HPS and its efficient home healthcare and clinical outcomes, a small group of specialized obstetricians, called Perinatologists, seemed to think that these home obstetrical care operations that focused on preterm labor were a threat to their authority and medical practice.

The leader of these few Perinatologists was Dr. John Hauth, who practiced in Birmingham. To me, he seemed to exhibit strong narcissistic qualities. He was called a nihilist by many of his peers. He became maniacally focused on denigrating home preterm labor management and its contribution to obstetrics.

As I recall, this issue came to a head in 1989 when a malpractice suit was filed against an obstetrician for his patient delivering prematurely. A medical consultant testified that, had the doctor prescribed home uterine activity monitoring from HPS or Tokos Medical, the woman could have delivered a full-term and potentially healthy baby. Unfortunately, to physicians, this was an indication that home obstetrical services were becoming a "standard of care" for high-risk pregnancies.

The Perinatology group, as well as the American College of Obstetricians and Gynecologists (ACOG), did not want to impose the liability on practicing OB/GYNs that comes with the standard of care status. So ACOG immediately adopted a position that home uterine activity monitoring was "investigational" and that considerable more research had to be done to prove its value.

This court trial angered the small group of Perinatologists who were threatened by home obstetrical care, and they held ACOG committee positions. They went to the Food and Drug Administration (FDA) and asked them to deny "approval" for home uterine activity monitors. This was the device in our OB-1 that was used to track uterine activity.

On March 29, 1989, the FDA informed us that they had rejected our pre-market application for approval of our System 37 Uterine Contraction Monitor (UCM) for use on preterm labor patients. They stated that we could not prove that the

UCM prevented preterm births. We pointed out that the doctors' actions resulted in improved birth outcomes, not the Monitor. We never claimed the UCM was anything but a diagnostic tool. We took this disapproval up the chain of command and filed a follow-up appeal with the FDA Chief, Dr. Frank Young.

It did not take long for Dr. Young to understand the misstep that Dr. Lillian Yen, head of OB/GYN at the FDA, had made. Dr. Young granted our appeal.

We went through several more iterations with the FDA on obtaining approval for our System 37 UCM and had one very interesting public meeting during the approval process with the FDA's obstetrical panel. These FDA panels are supposed to be comprised of independent doctors who provide the FDA with their opinions on the results of clinical trials of various healthcare products.

When it came time for the committee head to ask the panel of eight physicians for their opinion of the uterine activity monitor, the first doctor replied something along the lines of, "I cannot remember exactly what Dr. Yen told us last night that she wanted us to say." Well, that was quite a bombshell to drop in this formal FDA public meeting. The panel chairman started scrambling and finally told that doctor to hold his opinion, and she would call on him again later. Then, she went to the other side of the table and began asking the other doctors for their thoughts. It was apparent that they all were saying the same thing, which is what Dr. Yen had told them to say the night before. Dr. Yen violated FDA protocols in giving the panel the words for their impressions of the UCM!

It took us one more meeting after that to obtain our approval, and it ended over five years of a very frustrating approval process for our home uterine activity monitor. It should have been a relatively routine review and approval, but there was this small group of Perinatologists who took self-serving actions to prevent its approval. And, that certainly influenced the way Dr. Yen tried to manipulate our panel. This was one of my most frustrating encounters with the FDA, although we had countless others! However, we were always very persistent and professional in the way we approached the FDA.

Despite not having the blessing of the FDA and ACOG, the HPS revenues increased steadily from the late 1980s to more than $67 million in 1993. The market grew steadily during this period of time, and we approached 50 percent market share by the end of 1994. That put us on an even par with Tokos Medical who had begun many years ahead of us.

Even though some issues developed at the FDA over approving our System 37 UCM for use in the home, that did not deter health plans from realizing the substantial cost savings they would incur if they contracted with HPS. As we mentioned earlier, Dr. Yen allowed certain physicians at ACOG to convince her not to approve the System 37 Monitor because of their concerns that it would become a standard of care. These physicians, all of whom were Perinatologists, had their own interests in mind relative to the treatment of preterm labor patents.

By December of 1990, Healthdyne Perinatal Services had expanded its national obstetrical home healthcare network to 28 monitoring centers and more than 80 other sites of service. Thus, HPS went through a nice growth period from 1987 until it merged with its competitor, Tokos Medical, in October of 1994. At that point, the name of the combined organizations was changed to Matria Healthcare. Over the ensuing years, Matria became more focused on overall disease management and health enhancement rather than just home obstetrical care.

Home Nutritional Services Grows Rapidly

During this period, the home infusion therapy sector continued to rapidly grow. A few months prior to our acquiring HNS in 1983, I made the decision to acquire a small home infusion therapy company, Metabolic Support Associates, located in Atlanta. We made the acquisition, and most importantly, interested the founder of the company, Marty Olson, PharmD, in staying with Healthdyne. Marty proved to be a consummate clinical visionary, and he developed a number of the programs that resulted in successes for HNS and Matria in the following years.

By the end of 1988, HNS had grown from approximately $8 million in annual revenue when we acquired them to $47.1 million. Having a subsidiary perform that well was wonderful, but it could not be properly highlighted because most Wall Street analysts who were covering Healthdyne did not have the breadth of knowledge for all of our subsidiary companies. Therefore, I decided that we should sell a portion of HNS to the public, thus giving us a second publicly traded company. HNS would have their own analyst coverage, and their stock price would increase because of the focus of those specialized analysts. In addition, Healthdyne's stock price would increase as a result of our 66 percent ownership of HNS.

We sold 34 percent of HNS in their initial public offering for $61 million on January 15, 1989, which allowed us to pay off all of our corporate debt and retain a $20 plus million cash position. This put a value of approximately $185 million on HNS, which was about four times their trailing revenue. In doing something of this nature, we should have maintained 81 percent of HNS so we could have fully consolidated all of their revenue with Healthdyne's revenue going forward instead of 66 percent.

HNS continued to be the innovator in the home infusion therapy sector of healthcare. HNS was the first to administer IV drugs to AIDS patients in the comfort and security of their homes. In so doing, they built a network of social workers to support AIDS patients. HNS also bought a stake in a cancer treatment group to bring leading edge, even investigational treatments, to patients in their homes.

After going public in early 1989, HNS continued to grow their revenues at a 25 percent to 30 percent rate until they were sold in 1993. The HNS revenues for 1989 were $64.5 million, for 1990 $81.4 million, for 1991 $103.0 million and for 1992 they were $129.0 million.

The HNS earnings per share for 1988 were 46 cents per share, for 1989 they were 66 cents, for 1990 they were 78 cents and for 1991 they were 97 cents. For 1992, the earnings per share became a loss of 22 cents per share. This was because of the significant write-offs that occurred as health plans began to manipulate their payments to providers of home infusion therapy services.

During this period of time, the escalation of healthcare costs was a major national focus in Washington, which also spread to all private healthcare insurance plans. We had experienced a similar situation when the focus was on the oxygen therapy area some years earlier. It was inevitable that scrutiny would eventually become focused on home infusion therapy because of the growth of that sector.

Of course, the insurance companies were empowered by the healthcare bashing and managed care rhetoric coming from Washington. They began making unilateral decisions related to pricing and ignored contractual requirements to reimburse "usual and customary" fees. When Blue Cross Blue Shield of Massachusetts negotiated a 50 percent discount on home infusion therapies from one small company, it became front-page news. That press release changed the home infusion therapy sector of healthcare immediately. All health plans began to insist on similar discounts. Stock of the largest home infusion therapy company took a 25 percent drop in a single day due to this disclosure and the company's highlighting of how much it would have to write off.

HNS revenues continued to increase in 1992 and 1993, but the "slow pay" and the "no pay" accounts combined to erode profits. By 1993, it was evident that HNS would be entering a period of slow to no growth. When, in the fourth quarter of

1993, HNS revenues actually decreased 21 percent from the same quarter in the previous year, we knew there would be continuing deterioration in revenues.

I felt strongly that these pricing pressures would last for several years, and I recommended to the Healthdyne Board that HNS be sold. In early 1994, National Medical Care, a W. R. Grace subsidiary, bought HNS for approximately $100 million.

Recall, Healthdyne originally paid $20 million for HNS. We raised $60 plus million in the public offering and obtained $100 million in a final sale. We invested less than $20 million in working capital. So we did quite well in terms of return on our investment. However, it was frustrating to see such a promising sector of healthcare become "out of favor" when it was saving substantial healthcare dollars and improving the quality of care.

In 1991, HPS, HNS and Healthdyne Technologies were all enjoying rapid sales and profit increases. Therefore, 1991 was a year that we all took pride in as many years of hard work finally came to fruition. However, there continued to be forces at work within the healthcare sector, in general, and some specifically focused on obstetrical care that were getting ready to cause HPS some problems.

We decided to change the Healthdyne Perinatal Services name to Healthdyne Maternity Management in 1994. That name would better delineate our focus on managed care and disease management.

This name change was also effective relative to a new program that we introduced in 1992. "BabySteps" was a program that we offered to HMOs, health plans and employers that allowed screening of pregnant women for all conditions. When we screened women at the beginning of their pregnancies, we could identify a much higher percentage of those that were "at risk" for complications. In the summer of 1994, BabySteps had been used by numerous HMOs, at least enough to measure its effectiveness. Healthdyne Maternity Management developed significant benefits in terms of cost savings and improved health. The successes were so significant that all those HMOs put out press releases on the outcomes. That publicity was a major benefit to Healthdyne Maternity Management. This also signaled the coming of our other "disease management" programs.

Managed Care and Disease Management

Healthcare costs rose significantly in the country through the 1980s. In most of those years, the country saw double-digit healthcare inflation.

As previously mentioned, in 1983, Congress passed into law the Diagnosis Related Group pricing (DRGs) for hospital procedures that immediately affected purchasing patterns of hospitals and related institutions. In early 1984, the Health Care Finance Administration was encouraging insurance carriers to slow down cash flow to home healthcare providers. Then, by the early 1990s, health plans began to feel empowered to unilaterally and often arbitrarily cut payments to providers and home healthcare organizations. All this activity was grouped into what was called the new "managed care" environment. The primary focus of this was reducing costs while attempting to improve access and quality of care.

These programs reduced costs by paying less for services that were received and by restricting services to only those that were considered "appropriate." There was also a growing interest in encouraging preventative care, which would keep people healthy instead of treating them only when they became sick. These initiatives began to come together in what would soon be called "disease management." That was an area Healthdyne was well prepared to serve as a result of our previous concentration on providing care to patients in low cost environments, such as the home, while collecting patient clinical data and outcomes.

By 1995, the managed care initiatives had not yet shown substantial savings for the U.S. health care system. The major savings were showing up as higher profits for insurance companies and HMOs due to their ability to unilaterally reduce reimbursements to providers. Hospitals, physicians and service providers, like Healthdyne, were left to determine how to attend to their patients' health with substantially fewer dollars for reimbursement of their services.

All of us in the company were very focused on what was transpiring. We knew there would be no change in the general direction; however, we hoped that more "common sense" and "reasonability" would be applied as these major changes worked their way through the healthcare system. Therefore, all the decisions that we made were geared towards reducing our costs and convincing the health plans that our services were very economical. We began doing this by further developing systems for collecting clinical results on our products and services and publishing them so that we could show managed care organizations how cost effective we were.

As mentioned, Healthdyne Maternity Management (HMM) created BabySteps and published the documentation on that program's outcomes. Publishing that data proved that HMOs and health plans would respond to clear, concise and accurate outcomes data in terms of making reimbursement decisions.

Frank Powers, the Healthdyne Maternity Management CEO, and his management staff are shown in Figure 24.

Tokos Medical Merger

To regress somewhat, our major competitor in women's health was Tokos Medical. Tokos was started about five years before Healthdyne Maternity Management. By 1994, the companies were approximately the same size from a revenue standpoint. I thought it would be productive for Tokos to merge with HMM. I called Bob Byrnes, their CEO, to start the conversation. We exchanged some of the typical niceties, but our discussion never went very far. I subsequently contacted David Goldsmith, whom I mentioned earlier in this chapter. David was one of the Tokos Board members whom I had previously known, and we began to have more serious discussions. Some agreements were finally reached which allowed the companies to merge with a future name to be selected and a Board of Directors that had five Board members from each company. Yep! Stay tuned!

We were to retain a business consultant who would help management and the Board make decisions, such as where corporate headquarters should be located, which clinical programs would be emphasized, which ones would be dropped, the management structure, etc. I felt very comfortable with that approach because I thought that we would be the overall benefactors in that process. As the consulting review began, that is exactly what happened. Also, the decision was made in the merger agreement that I would be Chairman of the Board, and Bob Byrnes would be President and CEO. The companies were merged in October of 1994.

The decision was made that the company's headquarters would be located in Atlanta at our offices. One HMM and one Tokos operating executive who would function as executive vice presidents with split responsibilities was also decided. After that, most of the cards fell on our side of the table. Bob managed to get through these disappointments with help from members of his Board of Directors. The name "Matria Healthcare" was selected as a result of an employee-naming contest.

Bob would come to Atlanta from California during the week; however, he would return home for the weekend. I could tell that he was not really interested in moving to Atlanta. Also, his business decisions began to fall short of my and most of the Board's expectations. I ascertained that his Tokos Board members had some frustrations as well. The two companies had a number of disputes, which were often not resolved because the Boards would split 50/50.

After nine months, Bob's CEO position was up for re-election. We presented to the Board a plan that would have Bob step down in favor of Don Millard, the company's current Chief Financial Officer who had been with Healthdyne and HMM for many years. As I recall, when the issue came up for a vote, one of the Tokos Board members was so irritated that he refused to vote. I quickly called the vote for Bob to step down from the CEO role, and it passed five to four! Don was also elected to be the President and CEO, and I remained Chairman. After that, I think the Tokos Board members decided that they should just stay in California! So we entered 1996 with Healthdyne management and Board calling most of the shots!

Matria was really beginning to make headway with our various programs and initiatives. In late 1998, Don thought that the acquisition of a diabetes supply company could be productive because of the diabetes services we offered as part of our disease management. This company had been assembled by an entrepreneur by the name of Mark Gainor. We acquired Gainor Medical in early 1999. We essentially made some small investments in the various components of the company, but ended up divesting all the businesses over the next six years. The largest business was Facet Technologies, and I had installed Bill Taylor as their President in 2000. That became Bill's major promotion relative to executive responsibilities. Facet was sold to a private equity company in 2006 as was DIA REAL, a German services company, and Diabetes Selfcare located in Roanoke, Virginia. We made over a 100 percent return on the sale of the Gainor companies over the years.

Don did not enjoy the workload and responsibilities of the CEO role. The Board was seeing issues, and they asked me to step back in as CEO. Don and I talked through the situation, and he resigned, and I went "back to work" full time! This was in late 1999.

By 2006, Matria Healthcare was performing quite well. The stock price had increased to a high of $45 per share, which was over a $1 billion valuation.

Healthdyne Information Enterprises

With the sale of HNS in April of 1994 leaving Healthdyne with $50 million in cash, I began examining ways to invest those funds. Our thinking kept revolving around managed care and what that was going to present relative to business opportunities. Our executive team began to develop a curiosity about where data gathering systems that turn data into clinical and business information could function in other places within healthcare organizations. Thanks to the vision of Dr. Marty Olson, Healthdyne Maternity Management had been developing clinical information systems since its inception. That service had been beneficial to physicians and all the payers in assessing high-risk pregnancies and providing care plans.

Our former Vice President of Strategic Ventures for HNS, Bob Kelly, conceived a vision for providing information systems to help physicians unite into networks to serve the growing patient populations for the managed care payers. We gave this venture the name "Healthdyne Integrated Alternatives" (HIA). We had briefed the Board a number of times on this emerging vision and received their input. That was fortuitous because Johnny Gresham, one of our long-term Board members, introduced us to Darrell Young, who was an 18-year health industry veteran and the former CEO of HBO & Company. HBO had a strong presence in Atlanta. Also, HBO had developed a strong leadership position in medical information systems in their Atlanta offices. Darrell had recently left HBO to develop his own business plan to address, what he believed would be, the information needs of the new and emerging healthcare system.

Darrell's strategy was to work with provider networks to develop information sharing systems that would address their specific needs. Of course, this was directed towards having more focused care plans and patient data and information, which would facilitate physician decisions. This would also provide a means of showing the payers the results they were getting in their different provider networks. Since there was somewhat of an overlap with Darrell's vision and Bob's HIA venture, we had to make the decision to throw our resources towards one or the other. We decided to sell HIA to another new Atlanta healthcare venture by the name of Preferred Oncology Networks of America. This company happened to be headed by John Anderson, who had been our previous President of HNS.

Healthdyne Information Enterprises (HIE) was incorporated in mid-1994 and was a wholly owned subsidiary of Healthdyne. Darrell was HIE's first President and CEO, and I served as Chairman of the Board. Healthdyne made commitments to invest about $20 million into HIE for their use to develop and also acquire certain specific information technology platforms.

HIE acquired Healthcare Communications (HCI) in 1995. HCI had developed a superior integration engine that allowed numerous and disparate information sources to be smoothly integrated. Their integration engine was called Cloverleaf, and it turned out to be a extremely efficient asset. Today, it is the property of Infor, a large European healthcare information company. It is still in broad use, and it still excels at the exchange of clinical data to help improve healthcare outcomes and other business activities.

As I have previously mentioned, healthcare was beginning go through the managed care crucible in order to reduce overall healthcare costs. One significant cost was the growing necessity to consolidate and integrate all the clinical information and related reimbursement data so that it could be properly managed. I previously mentioned the initiative by the federal government to reduce the soaring costs of Medicare by the passage of the DRG legislation in 1983. In the private sector, the focus was primarily on a need to shift the financial risk of healthcare costs from the payers to the providers who were responsible for directing healthcare expenditures; and, to attempt to begin consolidating healthcare providers into local and regional groups where they became healthcare integrated delivery networks (IDNs). The IDN became a group of healthcare providers who joined together to provide a coordinated and comprehensive continuum of quality healthcare for subscribers through the IDN's healthcare services. During this period of time, a significant number of initiatives were underway, and corporate entities were emerging to attempt to service the obvious future needs of these integrated delivery networks.

During 1994 and 1995, HIE made investments in and acquired certain information technology companies that would support its comprehensive clinical information solutions. As previously mentioned, these included Healthcare Communications who had developed the Cloverleaf integration engine. Cloverleaf proved to be one of the most productive integration engines in the marketplace.

In addition, Dataview Imaging International brought image management tools to HIE. And, Criterion Health Strategies of Nashville, Tennessee brought a physician-oriented clinical management and analysis tool portfolio.

Darrell Young continued to bring talented people over from HBO. These included Robert Murrie who became HIE's Chief Operating Officer and eventually replaced Darrell as the CEO of HIE. Also, Keith Cox was attracted to the company, and he proved to be a multi-talented IT executive who contributed greatly to the future success of the company. In addition, Joe Bleser joined the company as its Chief Financial Officer.

In November of 1995, Healthdyne distributed all the outstanding shares of HIE common stock to Healthdyne shareholders in a spinoff. Thus, HIE traded as an independent company from that point forward. In April of 2000, the name of the company was changed to Healthcare.com Corporation as part of the company's introduction of a new healthcare business-to-business product strategy to complement and extend its existing enterprise wide integration solutions business.

Thus, by early 1997, our business matters were rather stable, and each of the subsidiary companies were on their own with their own Board members who had initially come from the Healthdyne Board.

HIE made steady progress through internal growth and acquisitions. From 1999 to 2000, revenues grew from $25.3 million to $48.3 million, which was a 91 percent increase. Operating earnings reached $3.8 million, which translated into 10 cents per share of diluted net earnings.

In 2001, the Board of Healthcare.com was approached by Quovadx with an offer to acquire the company. The acquisition price was approximately $93 million. Robert Murrie went on to become the Chief Operating Officer at Quovadx.

An Unfriendly Tender Offer

Healthdyne Technologies missed their revenue estimate for the third quarter of 1996. This reduced their stock value significantly. It also attracted an "opportunist," Invacare. Invacare's CEO was Mal Mixon. Mixon was an aggressive executive, but not the astute healthcare executive he needed to be.

On January 2, 1997, Craig Reynolds received a letter from Mixon proposing to have Invacare acquire Healthdyne Technologies at approximately $11 per share. Craig was about to become a real experienced public company CEO because this "Bear Hug Letter" eventually developed into an unfriendly tender offer and a shareholder proxy contest.

The unfriendly tender offer from Invacare to buy Healthdyne Technologies and the resulting shareholder proxy contest became quite an affair in the Atlanta area by the summer of 1997. Healthdyne Technologies was utilizing the Troutman Sanders law firm, which was founded by former Governor Carl Sanders, who was one of our esteemed Board members. Mixon engaged King & Spalding to represent Invacare, and in so doing, he was made aware of a flaw in the Georgia law that allowed a straightforward takeover of a company that did not have a staggered Board provision. Thus, Mixon thought all he had to do was to initiate a proxy contest, and he could assume control of Healthdyne Technologies since we did not have a staggered Board.

Craig and I had an interesting battle ahead of us. Two of the largest law firms in Atlanta were representing the two companies. The media had a field day with all the developments. First, we went to the state legislature to get the misguided corporate law corrected in the Georgia statutes. The Senate immediately recognized the issue and voted to make the correction. However, the House did not vote to make the change because Invacare made a $100,000 donation to a certain coalition so none of the state representatives in that coalition voted for the needed change. And, the resolution did not pass. As I recall, it passed the next year, as it should have.

We were going to end up facing a proxy contest to replace the entire Board with Invacare being the only interested party at that time. In other words, there was not a "White Knight" who could come in and up the Invacare bid. Invacare started their bid in the $11 range, and eventually it was raised to $12.50. Our Board voted that this was an insufficient offer.

So the lines were drawn, and the proxy contest began in the spring. Since we did not have time to locate a White Knight, I focused our efforts on meeting with the arbitrageurs' community. These are stock managers who take a position in a company that is "in play," and they always vote for the acquirer, which is the way they receive their payoff. So for Craig and me to start calling on the Arb community was rather unusual. However, with my optimistic attitude, I thought we could convince the Arbs that the Invacare offer was too low.

By the time Craig and I were ready to "hit the road" and visit the Arbs, that group had already purchased about 51 percent of the company's shares. Thus, we were going to have to convince a significant percentage of the Arbs to vote for the company's slate of directors rather than the Invacare slate. If the Invacare slate won, the new directors would simply accept the Invacare offer to purchase all the company's stock at their final offer price of $12.50. My calculations showed the company should be worth at least $24 per share. Thus, we had to convince this group of sophisticated and independent financial investors that, if they would just give us time, we could find companies that would make offers for Healthdyne Technologies that were almost twice what Invacare was offering. Logically, we had a good argument with the numbers. Mixon was just being too cheap with his offer. He made a <u>serious mistake</u> in undervaluing Healthdyne Technologies and our ability to convince existing shareholders and the new Arb shareholders that his offer was quite undervalued.

We did some work to determine which Arbs were acquiring our stock. We made telephone contact with most of them and set up appointments. Then, Craig and I spent about two weeks in New York and Boston meeting with these arbitrageurs.

I had never before met with Arb funds because I had no need to do so. The Arbs are very much a fraternity with interlocking relationships. I was told numerous times that they voted as a block, and I was wasting our time and theirs by trying to convince them that there would be future valuations much higher than this for Healthdyne Technologies. Nevertheless, we kept to our plan, and in so doing, we got to know a number of shareholders who also learned a great deal about Healthdyne Technologies, which was very enlightening to them.

Over the two-week period, we made a substantial amount of progress. I could not always tell by counting shares whether we were going to be successful, but I had very good feeling about our having convinced a number of the institutions to vote for our slate of directors. This meant they would not quickly get $12.50 for their shares, but if they held their shares for some period of time, they could potentially get substantially more.

We convinced over half of the Arbs to vote for Healthdyne Technologies' existing Board. This surprised many in the Arb group. In fact, on the morning of the shareholders meeting when the proxy vote was to be counted, I was receiving numerous phone calls from Arbs that we had previously visited. One told me that he had <u>never</u> voted for the company in his entire career as an Arb. He had always voted for the "Opportunist." However, he was going to vote for the Healthdyne Technologies slate because we convinced him that the company was significantly undervalued and would produce substantially better results in the future.

At the shareholders meeting, Mixon appeared with about 10 individuals from Invacare and their various law firms. I had received a final vote tally right before the meeting began, and I knew we were going to win. Of course, I think Mixon had been advised by his King & Spalding lawyers that Invacare would win.

Mixon asked for some time to speak to the audience. As Chairman of the Board for Healthdyne Technologies, I was conducting the meeting, and I granted his request. He was his typical arrogant self, giving a few more courteous remarks than he had given to newspaper reporters. However, he was denigrating Healthdyne Technologies and bragging about his and Invacare's achievements, which incidentally, were pretty average and of no real merit. Obviously, he thought that he had won!

I had wanted to do a video of the meeting, but one of our legal advisors, "Finn" Fogg of the Skadden Arps law firm, was absolutely adamant about not having a record of the meeting. He had some concerns about the video being used in the future at an appeal by Invacare. I have always regretted taking his advice and not recording the meeting as it was an interesting and entertaining hour! But, I always had the greatest respect for "Finn" because of his advice during our fight to acquire Narco Scientific in 1982.

Eventually, I announced the results of the voting. Then I asked, "Mr. Mixon, do you have anything else to say?" I do not think he even acknowledged my question; he was busy packing up his notes and getting ready to leave. The next day, the Atlanta newspapers were full of the story. They touted the fact that Troutman Sanders was victorious over King & Spalding!

As it turned out, this battle also made it into the national news and created an interest with Respironics, the company I previously mentioned as one that we had an opportunity to acquire many years prior. We received a call from Jerry McGinnis, their Chairman and founder, asking if it made sense to merge Respironics and Healthdyne Technologies. So, for the next several months, we pursued that opportunity. I saw some real synergism between the two companies, product line-wise and management-wise.

As I negotiated, we began to settle in on a price for the merger for something in excess of $20 per share. After some extended negotiations, the final price agreed upon was $24 per share, which was almost twice what Mixon had offered. This clearly showed a lack of real business acumen from Mixon when he missed value by that amount. The merger with Respironics took place at the end of 1997.

As it turned out, Craig Reynolds and John Miclot, the Healthdyne Technologies COO, ended up running the combined corporations, which they ran for about five years and continued the significant growth rate of both. John eventually became the CEO and Craig became COO, primarily because Craig refused to move to Pittsburgh. Either way, it was a very positive acquisition, and after some years, the combined annual revenues were built to about $1 billion. That is when the Respironics/Healthdyne Technologies combination attracted Philips Healthcare. They acquired the company for approximately $5 billion, which was also approximately five times their annual revenues. Thus, this was a very successful merger with the correct final outcome for everyone…but Mixon!

The Maturing of Our TRAX System

As Healthdyne Maternity Management (HMM) began to mature and further develop its information technology systems, it was evident that there were applications beyond our previous disease management programs. The HMM informatics group was somewhat interdisciplinary. Our operating executives as well as the experienced informatics and IT executives became involved in expanding our systems to integrate other chronic diseases, such as diabetes, chronic obstructive pulmonary disease (COPD) and numerous others. We decided that we would begin to tune our TRAX system to be able to handle these other disease management programs.

I made a comment in the 2003 Annual Report that summarized very well the transition that was taking place in the U.S. healthcare system. I said, "There is a paradigm shift taking place in the way healthcare is delivered in this country. We are in the last phases of the reactive era in which healthcare is primarily available to individuals after an acute episode. The continuing escalation of healthcare costs over the last five years has made it very clear that managing healthcare 'after the fact' is really not managing healthcare at all."

Publications

In the late 1980s and early 1990s, Healthdyne had a great run with their financial performances and successes. In those days, the Atlanta journalistic community focused on real facts, and consequently, Healthdyne received some nice press accolades during this period of time. In particular, Healthdyne was chosen by Delta Air Lines magazine as one of their monthly corporate features. Delta representatives came to my office and presented me with my portrait, including the Healthdyne logo, which was a certainly a surprise to me. We continued to receive a lot of fair and accurate news coverage during the late 1990s and through the late 2000s.

CHAPTER 8
MATRIA HEALTHCARE

Matria's disease management programs were designed to proactively identify and help individuals manage their chronic diseases and other high cost medical conditions so that they could more effectively accept personal responsibility and play a role in improving their health. In these programs, individuals were telephonically connected with a nurse who acted as healthcare coach, mentor and coordinator with their physician. Care plans were developed and goals set, and both of those were routinely monitored. Thus, for the first time, individuals had a medical resource that gave them 24/7 availability for any and all questions regarding their conditions.

We managed to show that approximately 85 percent of the people in these programs reacted positively and began to improve their health status, which reduced their healthcare expenditures. Unnecessary visits to the emergency room and other hospitalizations were rapidly reduced. However, necessary procedures and physician visits were encouraged while the education and motivational process continued. We often commented that disease management is a "common sense" approach to medicine. I certainly felt strongly about that statement.

In 2004, we began to highlight our TRAX system, which we developed as the technology platform for all our disease management processes. This placed Matria Healthcare in a unique position in comparison to the other few companies that were attempting disease management. TRAX simply drew on the technology base and data and information management processes that we had used since we launched Healthdyne Perinatal Services.

At this point, Matria Healthcare consisted of our Health Enhancement and Women's Health segments.

Health Enhancement

Matria coined the term "Health Enhancement" in 2004 to include all processes that improved the health status of a patient. These processes ranged from specific clinical services, such as disease management, case management and utilization management to services that improved wellness, lifestyle and productivity.

After numerous meetings and discussions, management developed the belief that corporate America would make investments of this nature in their employees. Therefore, our management continued to focus strategically on those areas that would allow Matria to serve employees, both private and public, in this manner. Obviously, we initially focused on those programs that would provide to our customers a rapid and very definitive return on their investment. That decision dictated that we focus primarily on disease and case management.

We made statements, such as, "Health enhancement and disease management programs are an effective solution to the rapid escalating cost of healthcare. Corporate America is realizing that programs that improve the health of their employees have an immediate effect on reducing healthcare costs as well as absenteeism and presenteeism. Providing employees the right care at the right time is an investment that has high returns."

I summarized some of our thoughts in this area by saying, "It is simply good business practice for employers to make investments that improve the health of their employees." Generally speaking, the management and employee base is the most important asset of an entrepreneurial business and most businesses.

Thus, Matria Healthcare was created from all the clinical and IT technology systems that were developed for the management of our high-risk obstetrical patients. Our TRAX system started the evolution of these complex management systems.

Acquisitions and Divestitures

We began to look at other small companies that we might acquire to blend into these future health enhancement offerings. We acquired several companies in 2005 and 2006, one of which was Mia Vita located in New York and founded by Mike Milken. We also acquired Winning Habits, which was located in Dallas.

In early 2006, Matria completed the acquisition of Core Solutions, a smaller competitor in the Chicago area. Core Solutions had actually entered the disease management business prior to Matria. However, their growth rate was nowhere near ours because they did not have the technology base that we had. Also, we were able to remove almost $30 million of duplicate expenses predominantly from Core Solutions. This was a natural "roll up" for us.

I thought the due diligence went smoothly, and we negotiated approximately a $500 million acquisition, which was about three times their revenues. By that time, we were performing well enough to borrow almost the total acquisition amount from Bank of America. Borrowing almost $445 million was a new experience for me. While we had some significant loans in the past, we never had anything near that large. However, the process was relatively straightforward.

However, shortly after the acquisition, some of our IT people found a few emails indicating that the executives at Core Solutions and the Chairman of the Board had been exchanging messages with each other about not allowing Matria personnel to see certain communications which were negative in nature. I was appalled that individuals with whom I had developed some trust were that dishonest.

In late 2006, we finished the planned divestitures of Facet Technologies, which was our diabetes product business, and in 2005, DIA REAL, our foreign diabetes services operation in Germany.

During 2006, we also expended a significant amount of effort to integrate our wellness businesses, Mia Vita and Winning Habits, into our TRAX technology platform. In addition, we managed to achieve integration success with Core Solutions. With those integrations complete, the company's common technology, our TRAX system, was able to accept data feeds from all operating units. Also, outcomes reporting, which had been a significant major advantage for us for many years, was now going to be accomplished in a common format which would give us significant competitive advantages against our competition. Our clients' demand for accurate and timely health data from which our nurses could assist participants and their physicians in improving their health status was now available.

Over the years, we had successfully blended our disease management, wellness and health enhancement products and services. By 2007, we had nearly 370 wellness and disease management clients being serviced out of 12 care center locations. Matria Healthcare was serving more than 1 million participants under our disease management programs, more than 4 million participants in our 24/7 nurse triage program and more than 250,000 online participants that had completed our healthy living programs. The systems reached the point where our nurses were managing more than 50 chronic and uncommon conditions and 42 cancer types. We were also using our new technology, OB-1, for home monitoring of our high-risk obstetrical patients, at this time. The Matria field management team is shown in Figure 25.

Illegal Short Selling

In early 2007, the Matria stock price started a steep decline from $45 into the $25 range, and I could not determine the cause of it. I finally received a phone call from an analyst at a hedge fund in Chicago who I had met with numerous times over the previous several years. He told me that Matria was under a short selling attack by about a dozen hedge funds. He also told me that he had seen too much illegal behavior, and he was so distressed by it that he was going to resign. At that moment, I knew exactly what was going on, which was illegal short selling. This will be thoroughly explained in Chapter 13.

My friend said these hedge funds had paid for and were using a publication shill by the name of *Off Wall Street* located in Connecticut. This publication was writing reports on Matria and would initially distribute them to only a select group of hedge funds. The reports were all very negative and full of lies and misrepresentations. One report claimed that the manufacturer of our diabetes products in Japan had just given us notice of cancellation. They claimed that, since this manufacturer had produced the product for us for 15 years, we would be in dire straits. Of course, that was an absolutely false statement.

My analyst friend said that all 12 funds that were receiving this publication knew when these reports were coming out. They would pre-position themselves in the market and develop a short position to help drive down the stock price, which is illegal. He said they would also do naked short selling which, when not closed out, is illegal. Again, he was so disgusted with the behavior that he was going to leave the hedge fund.

I talked to a law firm in Houston, Texas that had achieved good results suing brokerage houses for supporting this type of illegal short selling. We worked on a lawsuit strategy. However, I thought I would try one more approach before I filed a lawsuit. I picked up the phone and called *Off Wall Street* and asked to speak to the CEO.

Their CEO picked up the phone, and I introduced myself. I told him that I had read all the reports he had published on Matria. He responded that the reports only went to subscribers and were kept private. I told him that I had all eight reports so I knew all the lies that he had published and the fraud that was involved. His comments became rather bombastic at that point. Finally, I told him that I had a $200 million lawsuit ready to be filed against his publication by a law firm out of Houston, Texas. After hearing that, he became rather contrite. He probably knew the reputation of that firm. His next comment was, "Who do you think you are?"

And, I replied, "You're going to find out who I am if you write one more article about Matria." Then, he hung up the phone.

In a few days, my friend faxed another article to me written by *Off Wall Street*. The title of the article was, *Off Wall Street is Dropping Coverage on Matria Healthcare*." So that was the way I stopped the substantial manipulations of those 12 hedge funds. The stock began rebuilding itself from the $25 price to which they had pushed it from its high of $45.

The Sale of Matria Healthcare

Matria Healthcare's broadened focus on a number of diseases beyond pre-term labor and pregnancy related hypertension and gestational diabetes began to pay rich rewards during the growth of the managed care era. With all the information technology and healthcare informatics that we had developed over the years, we were able to contract with primarily Fortune 500 employers to help them manage outcomes from the various health plans that they were utilizing. In other words, we could actually benchmark their health plans against each other in terms of how they were managing their diabetic employees, their employees with COPD and other chronic diseases. We would present quarterly comparisons, and it allowed the employer to hold their health plans accountable in the way that they were managing or not managing their employee base. This worked well for many years and allowed us to sign contracts with 243 of the Fortune 500 by 2007.

One of our premier disease management accounts was IBM. Dr. Martine Sepulveda, their Chief Medical Officer, recognized the value that we offered very early, and he became one of the first customers of our disease management and wellness programs. In fact, in 2007, Martine was the individual who called to let me know that he had just been in meetings with representatives from the two large health plans that IBM was utilizing, and he was told by these individuals that they could now offer disease management and wellness programs. My first comment was, "Well, you know that is not true." Martine replied, "Yes I do, but you need to know that this is what they are presenting to the Fortune 500 companies."

I knew this day would probably come, but it came sooner than I expected. Health plans were telling employers that they would give them a discount on their health plan fees if they would give them the disease management and wellness business. This would free the health plans from having to answer every quarter to the reviews that we provided to our Fortune 500 customers.

Of course, we had contracts with some health plans directly. This allowed the health plan to offer our services under their brand. However, none of the big five health plans would want to admit that they did not have their own disease management and wellness programs. So they created very beautiful slide presentations without anything to really back them up.

At a called Board meeting on September 30, 2007, I recommended to the Board that we put Matria Healthcare up for sale on a <u>very quiet</u> basis. If the word leaked out that Matria was up for sale, our few competitors in the wellness and disease management area would have a major advantage over the contracts we were obtaining every month, particularly with the Fortune 500 companies. So secrecy was extremely important as we explored our "strategic alternatives." In order to do that, my recommendation was to hire a small investment banker, who we had previously used very successfully to quietly sell our European diabetes operation, to do this transaction. Some of the Board members wanted to ask investment bankers like Goldman Sachs to handle the sale. However, I finally convinced them that the large investment bankers could not keep a secret for more than about two weeks. As it turned out, we kept our intentions from Wall Street until around January 15th. We finally received a phone call from a hedge fund in New York asking questions about what they claimed they knew. But, by that time, we were well on our way to having our final decisions made and Matria acquired.

We had a very good sales response, having interested Walgreens, Magellan Health, Inverness Medical and a private equity firm. By December, we were going through substantial due diligence meetings with all these organizations. My favorite was Walgreens because of the previous relationship we had with them in the disease management and wellness area. They had a Board meeting on January 6th at which they were supposed to approve the transaction. Their offer was at $31 per share. After they had already completed a substantial and lengthy due diligence, I recall their Board asked management to provide even more information. To me, that was not a positive sign.

Inverness Medical had actually walked away from the deal in mid-December, but by late December, they had re-entered the bidding process. We kept working on them, and they ended up with a bid of $39 per share.

I had an interesting exchange with the private equity firm, who had done many times the due diligence the operating companies normally did, when they returned for visit number five. I sat the principal down and said, "This is your last visit. You have taken many times the amount of time of any other potential suitor. I cannot let you continue to come back and take up any more of management's time." This individual told me that I did not understand. At his firm, management was required to invest in each of their transactions. That meant he was putting his personal money at risk, and he was not going to do that unless things were perfect. I said to him that nothing was ever perfect, and we could not tolerate their lengthy due diligence any longer. I thanked him for the firm's interest and sent them on their way!

When the New York hedge fund began to make public noise after calling us on January 15th, we knew that we needed to go ahead and put out a press release that we were exploring "strategic alternatives." At that point, I wanted things brought to closure before competitors managed to cause new contract problems.

I began pushing hard towards closing either Walgreens or Inverness. We made more progress with Inverness, but I could tell that Walgreens was going to have to wait until they had a subsequent Board meeting before they could make their final bid. I had to tell them that I did not think that was going to work. We would begin losing out on the monthly quotes being requested for disease management and wellness programs since the "word" was out on a pending sale of Matria.

As I recall, the other interested party, Magellan Health, indicated that they would be pricing their offer below $30 per share, which was much too low to be a serious contender. So, towards the end of January, I was not having much interaction with the Magellan executives.

However, negotiations with Inverness were ongoing and very robust. As I recall, they proposed a deal that consisted of 20 percent cash and 80 percent of a new preferred stock. Our shareholders would be given this stock, and it would be traded on a daily basis. We reached agreement on January 29th, and the press release was issued on January 30th. The offer was a purchase price of $39 per share, which put a valuation of $1.2 billion on the deal considering the remaining debt of about $280 million.

Of course, the group of about a dozen hedge funds that I discussed earlier who had taken strong short positions in Matria had a "bad day" when the $39 acquisition was announced. Our stock immediately moved up about 32 percent and was trading at around $33 per share. So here is what I believe these short sellers subsequently orchestrated.

On the night of the announcement, Jim Cramer brought up this offer on his show on the CNBC network. This deal should not have even been on Cramer's radar, but I believe the hedge funds called in some favors with him. Cramer berated the acquisition as something he considered very "stupid" or some similar word. He criticized Inverness for acquiring a service company when they were primarily a products company. He was very critical of Ron Zwanziger, the Inverness CEO, for doing this transaction, and he called on him to back away from it.

I do not know exactly what happened, but the next night Cramer had Ron on a telephone call with him. They debated the pros and cons of the acquisition, and Ron stood his ground on the advantages of the transaction to Inverness.

I thought this behavior was "way out of bounds" in terms of hedge funds, as the result of an acquisition, trying to bring a stock price back down to reverse their final losses. The DOJ should have opened an investigation on the illegal short selling!

The only disappointing part of this acquisition was that it took Inverness about three and a half months to close the deal. The final transaction did not take place until the middle of May. Numerous shareholders complained heavily during the interim period of time that this was an inordinate delay.

The SEC Again

My third encounter with the Securities and Exchange Commission came some time in late 2009. This matter was related to the sale of Matria Healthcare to Inverness Medical, which was closed in May of 2008.

On June 30, 2008, a few months after the announcement of the acquisition, I received the routine notice from FINRA of the list of individuals who had bought shares prior to our announcement. After a major announcement such as this, corporate executives are required to identify any individuals on the FINRA list whom they know, and they must give statements about their contacts with those individuals during the period prior to the announcement. This process is designed to discover possible insider trading cases for the SEC.

When I received the list of shareholder names from FINRA who had bought shares prior to our annoncement, I noted four names that I knew. One of them was one of our Matria managers, one was a consultant to Matria, one was my ex-wife, JoAnn, and one was a friend of mine, Earl Arrowood, a retired Delta Air Lines pilot with whom I had flown on numerous occasions.

I first met Earl when my son and I went to a company that Earl had started by the name of Sky Warriors to do some "dogfighting." Earl had established this successful business at Fulton County Airport which allowed pilots to fly Navy flight training aircraft, namely the T-34, equipped with laser guns and smoke systems so that a close approximation of a dogfight could take place. My son, Bill, and I flew several times at Sky Warriors prior to him leaving for the Air Force flight school.

In this process, we met Earl. Earl had been a Vietnam fighter pilot, and he was also a Georgia Tech graduate. So we became friends as I continued to fly and enjoy the Sky Warrior battles. Sky Warriors held an annual dogfight tournament, which I won in 1992. Earl and I became much better friends after that tournament, and we actually bought a small propeller airplane together.

Earl was not a sophisticated investor. He had faith in my public company experience, and he had invested previously in Matria. The company held its normal quarterly phone call with shareholders at the end of October of 2007. Things were going well for the company in 2007, and it was a positive report. Earl and his wife listened to the report, and they decided to buy some Matria stock at the end of that call. At that time, I had not had any contact with Earl for many weeks.

When I met with Earl in early November to fly my Russian L-39 jet, he made a comment during the preflight of the airplane that made me realize that his name would be on the FINRA list if and when we sold Matria Healthcare. He asked me why the stock price had gone down in the last week or so. I asked him, "Why are you asking?" He replied that he had bought some shares at $25, and they had gone down to $22. So I knew that he would be on my FINRA inquiry. I had to be careful how I even answered that question. I simply blew him off by saying that stocks go up and down, and I cannot tell you why it has come down. He told me that he had bought some shares right after our call with shareholders. I did not know how many shares he bought because I did not ask.

As it turns out, Earl bought some additional shares on December 27th. He never told me that he purchased those shares, but I found out when the SEC opened an inquiry. He later stated that he bought those shares because his Delta Air Lines stock had come down from $21 a share on December 1st to $14 on December 27th. He became disgusted and sold all his Delta shares. He took that cash and bought Matria shares.

Unfortunately, during the last two or three weeks of December, Earl and I were having telephone conversations every day. I was in the process of buying an airplane, and Earl was helping me with all the tasks involved in the purchase. He and I would talk on the phone, and subsequently, I would talk to my attorney who was negotiating the contract with the seller. And, Earl would call the Cessna service center to work through some maintenance issues that had to be corrected. Sometimes, I would talk to the seller after Earl's phone calls. Either way, we did have phone calls in December so there was the possibility that I was passing on inside information to him. Of course, I was not. The pattern of the calls was very clear.

In mid-2009, the FINRA information resulted in the SEC opening an inquiry as to Earl's and my dealings prior to the sale of Matria Healthcare. This was all very bewildering to Earl because he did not know he had done anything wrong, which he had <u>not</u>, unless I had given him information about the potential sale of the company, which I had <u>not</u>!

The SEC began a formal investigation, and we all ended up giving depositions, including my wife, Earl's wife and my children. The SEC had worked up a case over the fact that, because I had a telephone call with Earl on December 27th, I must have given him inside information, which was the reason he sold his Delta stock and bought the Matria stock. Of course, they ignored the fact that the Delta stock was plunging at that time, and Earl was not the sophisticated investor they wanted to make him out to be. Earl had made an emotional decision when he sold all his Delta stock and bought Matria with the proceeds.

As the case went on, I was advised by one of my attorneys that I should take a lie detector test. I said, "Fine, I will do that. However, I want that lie detector test to end the investigation because there is nothing to this."

So I took a lie detector test and "passed it with flying colors." We gave the information to the SEC, and I offered to take another lie detector test, if necessary. They really never responded to us, and they ignored my offer.

That made me realize that the SEC lawyers had <u>no interest</u> in doing anything reasonably related to "justice." They were simply trying to force me to falsely admit to guilt or to sign a consent decree that would basically lock down all the accusations that they had made against me, even though the consent decree would say that I was not admitting to any guilt. I already had experience with a consent decree years before with the Jim Ashton situation at Healthdyne. I told the SEC attorneys that I would never sign a consent decree and that I would see them in federal court. So they filed an action with allegations against Earl and me, and we proceeded towards a court date, which was going to be in mid-June of 2014.

As the trial date came closer, my attorney kept asking me if I felt differently about signing the consent decree or some other settlement. I told him that I did not and that I would sit in front of a jury with this group of SEC attorneys. I felt that I would clearly articulate my case in court. Of course, I told my attorney that I was confident I would win!

About two weeks before the trial date, my attorney received a call from the Atlanta Regional SEC Office. They offered to settle the case. He called me about a settlement, and I told him to tell the SEC that they needed to <u>drop the case</u> as that was the only settlement in which I had any interest. After a few more days, they did <u>drop the case</u>. See the press release mentioned in Appendix 8 at the end of this chapter.

The government wasted four and a half years and a lot of taxpayer money pursuing this case. Earl made $9,890 on the purchase of those Matria shares and their sale after holding them for about eight months. The SEC alleged there were damages of about $98,000. When they made that claim, I thought that they missed the decimal point! This was a totally ridiculous case, but it further demonstrated to me just how far out of reality government prosecutors can go when they are merely trying to enhance their resumes, berate a successful businessperson or play politics.

Fortunately, my legal fees were covered by the company's directors and officers insurance. However, Earl had no insurance coverage, and it cost him about $160,000 in legal fees to remain in the case over those years. Earl did sign a settlement agreement with the SEC about one week before the court date as it was going to cost him another $30,000 to get the legal advice he would need to prepare for the trial. The financial damage this did to Earl was substantial. But, Earl was no different from any other normal citizen. "Most people have no knowledge of the risk of investing in a company where a corporate officer is a friend because, even with casual contact, they could both be accused of insider trading."

After this was over, I sent a letter to Mary Jo White, the SEC Commissioner at the time. I explained to her what had happened in my case, particularly relative to Earl. I suggested that, if she and the Commission wanted to put an end to insider trading of this nature, particularly with uninformed individuals, they should direct all brokerage houses to send a simple statement from the SEC to their clients explaining the risks associated with buying stock in a company where they know a member of the executive group. I told Ms. White that communication such as this could be very effective in helping to stop frivolous cases like what had played out with Earl and me. To me, it was just "common sense!"

After having her Atlanta Regional Office expend four and a half years of effort on this ridiculous and inconsequential matter, I never received <u>any</u> response whatsoever to my proposal from Commissioner White. My simple suggestion would have taken very little effort on the part of the SEC and should have at least been considered. And, after what Earl and I had been put through, a brief letter saying that they were taking my recommendation under consideration would have been appropriate. Of course, having the investing public fully apprised of the Commission's philosophy on alleged insider trading cases like mine would reduce the opportunities the SEC's legal staff would have to file white-collar crime cases to enhance their resumes!

Thus, with the sale of Matria Healthcare, I thought that my final "deal" was done, and I would "retire" (whatever that meant). Obviously, we are only at the end of Chapter 8 so that must mean I flunked retirement!

Chapter 8 Appendix

June 4, 2014 Press Release: The SEC Dismisses Case Against Parker H. "Pete" Petit.

CHAPTER 9

EARLY HISTORY OF MIMEDX

After the sale of Matria Healthcare in May 2008, I semi-retired. I set up a "family office" and began managing my portfolio during the financial crisis. I basically watched everything deteriorate. I did not have any experience in short selling or trading stock options so I took the time to educate myself, and after about 18 months, the portfolio was back to where it started its decline.

In the fall of 2008, the founder of MiMedx Group, Steve Gorlin, brought me the opportunity to finance and manage this company. While MiMedx had the rights to two medical technologies, it was essentially bankrupt with no revenues. I became the company's Chairman and CEO in February 2009. I personally invested substantial amounts of my own capital and raised funds from other angel investors as well. However, I was not able to make sufficient changes in the Board at that time.

Bill Taylor, who had been the President of one of the Matria Healthcare subsidiaries, Facet Technologies, joined MiMedx in the fall of 2009 as our Chief Operating Officer (COO). With the experience and previous success that we both had, we were able to bring in numerous former Matria and Facet managers to help with the growth of MiMedx.

MiMedx Group was already a publicly traded company in the over-the-counter market in the "pink sheets" when I stepped in because the Board had done a "reverse merger" with a publicly traded "shell" corporation, which really had no assets. I do not recommend going public in this manner. As you continue to read, I may have another stronger recommendation! MiMedx suffered early on from a number of constraints and restrictions because the company was taken public in this fashion.

After the change in the administration in Washington. D.C., the company was unable to get our key technology through the FDA process. President Obama appointed Dr. Margaret Hamburg as the new FDA Commissioner, and she told her staff, "The FDA is a regulatory body, and we will regulate." That statement brought on an era of "just say no," which was detrimental to the American public in my opinion. A FDA staff member, whom I had previously known, profusely apologized for the change in their processes. However, we still had to quickly search for additional and allied technology.

We were fortunate enough to find a small company in the Atlanta area by the name of Surgical Biologics that had developed allograft technology manufactured from amniotic membranes. Their revenues were approximately $1.5 million, and they were focused primarily on using their product for eye surgeries. We saw a huge opportunity in wound care and certain surgeries.

I convinced the two founders of Surgical Biologics to allow MiMedx to acquire them in January 2011. This was a stock transaction with a few years of earn-out that embodied three years of additional payments depending on the financial performance of the Surgical Biologics product line. After the earn-out was paid, MiMedx had given up about 10 percent of our stock for assets that developed 100 percent of our revenues! That acquisition combined with our experienced and effective management sparked the growth of MiMedx into the fifth fastest-growing public company in America by 2017 according to *Fortune* magazine. Our revenues were forecast to be $400 million in 2018. We informed shareholders that we planned to have 2020 revenues reach $560 million.

MiMedx was instrumental in changing the future of the advanced wound care sector of healthcare with this new technology. The company became very prolific and efficient in conducting new clinical and scientific studies and publishing these studies. I requested that the company's scientific and clinical staff write a book, which became an industry standard, entitled *"A Primer on Amniotic Membrane Regenerative Healing."* See Figure 26 for a picture of Doctors Jeremy Lin and Tom Koob who primarily co-authored the *Primer*.

MiMedx grew in a stable and orderly fashion through mid-2018. We were able to attract management and other staff ahead of the growth profile requirements. The company met or exceeded its quarterly revenue estimates, which we gave to shareholders, for 29 out of 30 quarters. This was a very exceptional achievement for any public company.

At the end of the second quarter of 2018, Bill and I were both asked to resign because the Board "wanted to take the company in a different direction!" They certainly managed to achieve that goal, but the direction was down…down and down! Those bizarre details and numerous teaching moments are to follow!

Our Rapid Growth

Because of the exceptionally rapid growth rate of MiMedx and the extremely complex factors associated with that growth, I would like to present some paragraphs that came out of our *2017 Business Report* for shareholders. These paragraphs should give you some insight into our many complicated business activities. There are also various comments by a number of our executives in this *Report*. I apologize as some of these paragraphs might not necessarily tie together. However, they will certainly leave you with the understanding that MiMedx was a very sophisticated organization that required experienced executives and managers to produce the performance that took place. Please refer to Figure 27 for the MiMedx revenue growth profile and Figure 28 for a chart on our accounts receivable aging. I will reference these charts several times in the chapters ahead. Figure 29 shows the rapid build-up of our "bad debt" reserves plus our "sales returns and allowances" reserves, which left MiMedx in a conservative financial reporting status. Figure 30 is the MiMedx stock price through December 31, 2018.

So here are the extracts from our *2017 Business Report*:

"As a result of the significant progress that MiMedx has made in the past year, particularly on our strategic issues, we feel it is appropriate to provide our shareholders, employees and other constituents with this special *Business Report*."

"By that we simply mean that going forward, we will not only have products that are in the market regulated under Section 361 of the Public Health Service Act, but we will have products in the market as a result of FDA 'approvals' from our IND/BLA clinical trials."

"MiMedx has a distinct advantage of having a technology platform that includes over 220 proteins that are growth factors, cytokines and chemokines. These proteins act as a milieu of components that enhance healing, modulate inflammation, reduce scar tissue formation and support angiogenesis. With numerous scientific published studies, we have characterized the action of this milieu of proteins as being a 'Stem Cell Magnet.' That is, when placed on an internal wound or site of injury, these proteins act in concert with the local tissue to draw stem cells to the site to create a cascade of actions that are regenerative in nature and can have positive therapeutic effects."

"MiMedx is in a truly unique position in the biopharmaceutical area because of our ability to develop clinical and scientific data with our human tissue, namely amniotic membrane and placenta, and actually use some of those product configurations in medical practice under Section 361. This valuable experience gives MiMedx a great advantage when initiating FDA clinical trials for other products requiring IND/BLA pathways."

"At this point in our history, we have developed five years of clinical and scientific data which has resulted in over 40 publications in peer review journals. Therefore, we have a substantial amount of scientific information helping us characterize the mode of action and other important parameters of our placenta based technology."

"In addition, we have conducted studies on over 2,300 patients at this point, and most of those studies have been published. However, we have two large randomized controlled trials for diabetic foot ulcers and venous leg ulcers we expect to publish this year. That means that MiMedx will have compiled much more published data on our technology than all of our competitors combined. Therefore, our scientists and clinicians know our products very well, although they will continue to conduct studies and gather data for many years in the future."

"MiMedx will enter our first Phase III trial for the indication of plantar fasciitis in the very near future. We expect that trial to be completed and our application for a biologics license to be entered in 2019. However, in parallel, we will be conducting studies on other forms of tendinitis. We also expect to file for the start of an IND study in support of a BLA for applying our injectable products to osteoarthritic knee joint pain by the third quarter this year."

"In the past six years, MiMedx has transformed from a small tissue processor to the world-wide scientific, clinical and market leader in placental tissue."

"Our transformation into the worldwide placental tissue market leader with $245 million in revenues in six years was definitely the result of LEADERSHIP. Each and every member of the team has played an important role in building MiMedx into the preeminent placental tissue company in the world. Thus, positioning MiMedx for its next major transformational move into a biopharmaceutical company."

"MiMedx is a biopharmaceutical leader in placental allografts, and is now developing regenerative and therapeutic biologics. We have supplied over 900,000 amniotic and placental derived tissue allografts as of May 2017 for applications in wound care, surgical, orthopedic/sports medicine, pain management, spinal, ophthalmic and the dental segments of health care. This accomplishment has occurred without any adverse reactions attributed to our products."

"We describe our strategic financial goal as 'three and one in 20' which means we will triple 2015 revenues to $560 million and deliver $1 of adjusted earnings in 2020."

"Pain management, respiratory disease and cardiovascular disease are the large biopharmaceutical opportunities that the Company is focused on to meet the needs of many patients seeking new treatment alternatives in these areas. The Company continues to research new opportunities for placental tissue and fluid, and currently has several additional offerings in various stages of conceptualization and development."

"Overall, MiMedx has achieved reimbursement coverage of over 308 million lives. This includes coverage on all Medicare Administrative Contractors (MACs), the majority of commercial payers and Medicaid coverage in 36 states. When looking at the breadth of coverage, this is primarily for diabetic foot ulcers (DFUs). We have coverage for both DFUs and venous leg ulcers (VLUs) in Medicare, but mainly DFUs in commercial plans. With anticipated publication of a large VLU randomized control trial results in mid-2017, we anticipate achieving an additional 133 million covered lives from VLUs. This additional coverage will extrapolate to a significant revenue opportunity for MiMedx."

"MiMedx continues to devote considerable resources to clinical trials to support coverage and reimbursement of our products, allowing us to confirm an increasing number of private payers that reimburse for EpiFix in the physician office, the hospital outpatient department and ambulatory surgery center settings. Coverage and reimbursement varies according to the patient's health plan and related benefits. To date, more than 800 health plans provide coverage for EpiFix for the treatment of diabetic foot ulcers (DFUs) and venous leg ulcers (VLUs). This translates to coverage availability for more than 207 million lives."

"MiMedx dHACM is the first human amnion/chorion dehydrated membrane to meet the requirements of the United States Pharmacopeia (USP) monograph. This significant achievement is recognized in an official USP-National Formulary (NF) monograph with the online publication of the U.S. Pharmacopeia 40-National Formulary 35.1. This monograph includes our EpiFix and AmnioFix sheet products."

"MiMedx currently has over 30 ongoing clinical trials in various stages of development and execution, with 123 clinical studies under management and 175 doctors currently contracted for research activities. This activity involves over 450 legal agreements and contracts for studies. MiMedx regularly sees protocols from clinicians interested in conducting research across multiple specialties. The chart below further outlines our clinical operations and demonstrates that biopharmaceutical clinical trials require very specific expertise which MiMedx has developed over the years."

"MiMedx manages all clinical trials the Company conducts. We typically do not outsource the management to clinical research organizations (CROs). This is a significant advantage as we can move faster with more responsiveness at a significantly lower cost."

"With the new regulations from the 21st Century Cures legislation and from the new FDA Commissioner's stated belief that products should be on the market after safety is established, the timeline for MiMedx's transition to a biological therapeutic company could become significantly shorter."

"In fact, there is much discussion ongoing that encompasses an alternate approval pathway that will allow a product that has proven safety, like our allografts, to go straight to market while efficacy studies are completed. We developed our plans for future BLAs. We believe that this new FDA legislation will afford MiMedx a tremendous first to market advantage over all of our competition in the HCT/P and biological space."

"MiMedx is compliant with good manufacturing practices per 21CFR 210 and 211. These regulations contain a minimum GMP for methods, facilities and controls to be used for the manufacturing, processing, packaging, or a holding of DRV products to ensure regulatory requirements are met. This milestone is a significant achievement in MiMedx becoming a biological therapeutic company."

"Because of the substantial expertise and investment of time, effort and financial resources required to bring new biopharmaceutical products to the market, the importance of obtaining and maintaining patent protection for significant new techniques, products and processes cannot be underestimated. As of the date of this *Business Report*, we own over 45 issued and allowed patents related to our embryonic tissue technology and products. Over 90 additional patent applications covering aspects of this technology are pending at the United States Patent and Trademark Office, and with various international patenting agencies. The vast majority of our domestic patents covering our core amniotic tissue technology and products will not begin to expire until August 2027."

"Over the last five years, MiMedx has developed the largest placental recovery organization in the United States. Placental tissue is the biological source material for all of our technology. This network consists of overlapping multiyear contracts to ensure uninterrupted supply at approximately 40 hospitals."

"We have several of the top 10 birthing hospitals in the United States under contract and, to our knowledge, our competitors are not contracted with any of the remaining facilities in the top 10."

"MiMedx is honored to be entrusted with a precious gift donated to us by the mothers participating in our GIVE the GIFT of HEALING. In recognition of the placental donations that we are privileged to receive, we formed our Philanthropic Mission and developed the MiMedx HEALING GIFTS Program in 2013."

"Through HEALING GIFTS, MiMedx supports many physician philanthropic endeavors ranging from treating disadvantaged patients across the United States to mission trips to other countries with specific needs in areas in the world that have experienced natural disasters."

The Fifth-Fastest Growing

Describing the attributes of MiMedx and our successes could fill the rest of this book. To become the fifth fastest-growing public company in America in seven years was a tremendous accomplishment as *Fortune* magazine articulated.

From 2011 to mid-2018, MiMedx continued with success after success. The revenue growth chart should speak highly of the company relative to how well we developed and positioned our new product lines. We reached the point where there was an almost insatiable demand for our products when they were presented and distributed properly.

We were able to hire and train our sales force at an especially rapid rate with very few miss-hires, and by July 1st of 2018, we had approximately 435 salespersons scattered all across the U.S. and in Europe. We also had international distributors in numerous foreign countries. And, we developed a training department with a great deal of expertise and enthusiasm to support our sales organization. Figure 31 shows our sales force in January 2016 at the National Team Meeting.

In addition, we were conducting over 30 clinical trials on various uses of our product beyond just advanced wound care. Conducting 30 clinical trials simultaneously itself was a major undertaking. We were very effective in having our clinical studies published in peer-reviewed journals.

If an experienced business executive were to review Figures 17, 18 and 19 and our financial statements up to July 1st of 2018, they would applaud the progress that occurred from a business standpoint. At that point, we had approximately 3,000 different customers ranging from doctors' offices, wound care centers, hospitals and a few distributors both nationally and internationally.

We collected our revenues from these various customers on average in a very efficient manner. Our daily sales outstanding (DSOs) in accounts receivable was at approximately 65 days on June 30, 2018. While our DSOs had been briefly in the high 80 days range in two prior periods, we routinely kept our DSOs below industry averages. Because of the complex healthcare insurance system for reimbursing doctors, wound care centers and hospitals for the use of our products, very often customers wanted to stretch our DSOs up to and past 90 days. We did our best not to allow anyone to get over 90 days, but occasionally those situations would happen. The most important point, however, is that our average DSOs were kept below industry norms. That simply meant that, when we billed a customer, we collected our money in a reasonable period of time relative to healthcare industry standards. Also, we bought $132 million of MiMedx stock in the open market over the years. Thus, we had very strong cash flows.

We were also conservatively reserved in the event a negative issue occurred, such as a customer's bankruptcy. We had conservative reserves in the "sales return and allowances" area and "bad debt" area. This means that we reduced our revenues and profits each quarter by a certain amount to increase our reserves. Thus, we were reducing and understating our actual revenues and profits each quarter. This was very important, and I will discuss it in much more detail in subsequent chapters.

There were many significant achievements by our management team, which should be inspiring and informative to our readers. We fought through situations with competitors who were using dishonest tactics, regulators getting out of bounds, continuing space constraints, huge staffing requirements, rapid build-out of management and information systems, huge training needs plus a few dozen others! We lobbied Congress, and we called out and helped improve a few Veterans Administration procedures.

NASDAQ invited us to ring the opening bell in July 2013. See Figure 32 with Thornton Kuntz (Vice President of Administration), Brent Miller (Vice President of Manufacturing), Bill Taylor (President/COO), Debbie Dean (Executive Vice President), myself (Chairman/CEO) and Mike Senken (Vice President/Chief Financial Officer).

Change of Fortune

As you read further in this book, you will discover that this efficiently run business would be questioned in many ways. This would be a very selfish process by unscrupulous whistleblowers, some dishonest short sellers, some self-serving law and accounting firms and some self-serving federal prosecutors and a couple of members of our Board of Directors who acted in their own self-interests as opportunists.

With the start of a well-orchestrated short selling attack in the fall of 2017, our focus began to change. This destructive process began with a hedge fund that had shorted our stock and an unscrupulous MiMedx salesman who had been terminated for cause in late 2016. He subsequently began communicating with our short sellers. In addition, there was intimidation of our new auditors by one of the short sellers as well as self-dealing by the MiMedx Board. Finally, there was federal prosecutorial overreach. These activities took the stage away from our "excellent operating performance" and this classical "effective entrepreneurship." Many more details later.

The remaining information in this book will provide meaningful analysis on several especially complicated business and legal matters. It will also be an educational forum for pursuing important and necessary changes to benefit American entrepreneurs, businesses, investors and the general public. I hope you will find this very informative and educational in terms of understanding the current complex public company regulatory, accounting, legal and business environment and how it can be most effectively managed from a corporate standpoint.

Many valuable business lessons for public company executives lie ahead as well as some very important lessons for all of us as Americans!

CHAPTER 10

OUR BOARDS OF DIRECTORS

As we will discuss later, the decisions made and actions taken by the MiMedx Group Board of Directors caused severe declines in value and significant reductions in operating efficiencies. To some extent, the CEO of an entrepreneurial stage public company has inordinate responsibilities for the constituents of the Board. However, the Sarbanes-Oxley regulations have taken much of those responsibilities away from the CEO and dispersed them within the Board and its committees. Still, the leadership for key Board matters will come from the CEO from a practical standpoint, unless the Board is populated with experienced and successful CEOs. Having individuals on the Board who have "walked a mile in your shoes" is ideal.

In the case of MiMedx, the Board had already been constituted by the company's founder when I stepped into the role of Chairman and CEO in February 2009. Thus, I had to sort through a number of issues that related to the actual stock holdings of those individuals, their past and potential contributions to the Board and their experience and expertise as public company Board members. To say I faced a "mixed bag" would be an understatement. I asked a few individuals to step down, generally because they had no public company experience or executive experience related to healthcare. So a few changes were made, and I brought in a couple of individuals who I knew had public Board experience or accounting experience pertaining to healthcare businesses. Over time, I was asked by some of the large shareholders to add a couple of other Board members who were not very qualified. I was extremely busy, and the company was performing very well. So I did not put an emphasis on improving the Board, which was a mistake.

Thus, unlike my previous tenure at Healthdyne and Matria Healthcare, I did not have the time to carefully and selectively add to the MiMedx Board. Also, unfortunately, the very experienced, knowledgeable and courageous individuals who had served on the Healthdyne and Matria Healthcare Boards had long passed through retirement age, and they were not interested in serving on a Board of Directors any longer. I did not blame them!

The Sally Yates Doctrine, which is discussed in Chapter 14, puts a great deal of pressure on the Board of Directors of U.S. public companies. In effect, this relatively new directive basically tells a Board that, if there is an "accusation" made against the company, they must hire a law firm to do a full investigation of the allegation. In today's environment, that will necessarily include a forensic audit, which could include examining every email and text message to and from many employees, managers and executives over a significant period of time, meaning many years.

The Yates Doctrine also makes it clear that the top executives of the company should be the "target" of any investigation, even if the allegation points in a different direction. The rationale is that the fines, which can be levied against the company, will be much larger if top executives are somehow involved. As if those directives are not restrictive and dangerous enough, the investigation can limit the company and investigators from allowing the executives "due process." If you look up the definition of due process, you will find that it simply means the accused has the ability to understand and answer the accusations. When an investigation is taking place under the supervision of an ex-prosecutor, who is now employed by a large law firm, there will not be fair and reasonable due process because the ex-prosecutor is often busy creating their own story of what they want to find. One motivating factor for this behavior will be the continuation of the law firm's monthly legal fees for as long as possible. Very simple!

For instance, in the MiMedx investigation which you will read about later in the book, the top two executives of the company and their attorneys were told by an outside counsel that the Board did not need to provide us with due process, and they did not do so. Actually, we never even heard the details of the accusations, except the one related to AvKARE, which was our federal distributor of products to the Veterans Administration hospitals, until the company was having a battle with us and other shareholders in a proxy contest almost a year later. The Board then decided that it was in their best interest to try to discredit me because I was involved in this battle against the company's Board nominees. The Board published a press release with the majority of the allegations. I responded with my own press release, which disputed the top points that they had made. However, we never had a chance to really refute the ridiculous claims that were developed by the King & Spalding prosecutor and partially used by the DOJ prosecutors in their indictments against us.

Of course, this raises the question, why did the MiMedx Board accept the King & Spalding allegations without hearing from the accused? In fact, it also brings up the question of why the Board accepted the claims of a short seller and a dishonest sales employee who was terminated from the company for cause without hearing from the top executives of the company? These questions make it reasonable to discuss in some detail the members of the Healthdyne and Matria Healthcare Boards and the MiMedx Group Board. Also, how the MiMedx Board members with their personalities, business experiences and self-interests potentially influenced the debacle that took place.

The Matria Healthcare Board

The Matria Healthcare Board consisted primarily of individuals who had previously served for a number of years on the Healthdyne Board. When Healthdyne was split into three different public companies in the mid-1990s, its Board members joined the three new Boards of Directors. There were some overlaps from these Board members; however, since Matria was the largest of the subsidiaries that was dividended to shareholders, it retained the largest number of Healthdyne Board members. A brief description of some of the more tenured members should help you put in perspective the experience, personalities and courage of that Board.

I met former Georgia Governor, Carl E. Sanders, in 1984, and we developed a serious and enduring relationship. Carl was not only a successful business leader, but also an extremely respected attorney, and he had developed one of the largest law firms in Georgia, Troutman Sanders. He grew that law firm into having a national presence, and it became one of the larger law firms in this country.

Carl joined the Healthdyne Board of Directors in 1985, and he remained on the Healthdyne and then Matria Healthcare Boards until 2007 when he reluctantly retired. His common sense and practical legal advice over the years was invaluable. "The Governor" passed on November 16, 2014.

In Figure 33, I had just presented the Governor and Dr. Fred Zuspan, who was also a member of the Matria Board, with portraits I had commissioned of the World War II aircraft each had flown. In Figure 34, I had just finished lunch at the Troutman Sanders law firm with Senator Johnny Isakson, Carl Sanders and Johnny Gresham, another Healthdyne Board member.

I met Jacqueline M. Ward in 1984 when both of us became members of the International Business Fellows. We became friends, and she and I and our spouses enjoyed spending time together. Jackie was a consummate entrepreneur who was involved in the founding of an IT technology company by the name of Computer Generation. She was certainly a business visionary. She was aggressive in taking innovative steps and was very successful in doing so.

Jackie was elected the first female Chair of the Atlanta Chamber of Commerce. I happily served as one of her committee chairs during her tenure. She later served on the Board of Directors of the Bank of America, Anthem, Equifax, Flowers Industries and SCI, and subsequently became Chair of the Board of Sysco Corporation.

Guy W. Millner was a very successful entrepreneur, having built a significant executive search firm, Norrell Corporation. He asked me to serve on his company's Board probably a year before his company was acquired by Spherion Corporation. After the acquisition, Guy became a member of the Spherion Board. He also ran unsuccessfully for the governorship of Georgia and for our U.S. Senate position. Guy was a decisive and courageous business leader, and he was always on point by asking, "Why not?" or "Why couldn't we?"

Donald W. Weber was the President and Chief Executive Officer of Contel Corporation, a notable telecommunications company. While Don was not the founder of Contel, he worked his way into the top executive position through years of producing positive outcomes in all his areas of responsibility. Don was a confident decision-maker. With a background in accounting, he served as the Matria Healthcare Audit Committee Chairman.

Frederick E. Cooper was the President and Vice Chairman of Flowers Industries. He was a lawyer by education, but earned his way into the President's role at Flowers from his advisory role as General Counsel. That speaks to his progressive and resolute nature as a proponent of business expansion activities at Flowers Industries. Fred subsequently started his own food products company and investment company.

Morris "Mike" S. Weeden was the retired Vice Chairman of Morton Thiokol Corporation, a huge chemical and rocket propulsion conglomerate. He worked his way up through the chain of command at Morton Thiokol to become its Vice Chairman. Mike was another unwavering and accomplished business executive. Board members described him this way: "He doesn't say much, but when he speaks, everyone listens." Sound familiar? Mike passed away in 2013.

Wayne P. Yetter had a distinguished career in the pharmaceutical industry, having served as Chairman and CEO of several successful pharmaceutical and health related companies. When he served on the Matria Healthcare Board of Directors, he was Chairman and Chief Executive Officer of Savant, Inc., which was a strategic solutions and services partner to the pharmaceutical and healthcare industries. Wayne also served as President and Chief Executive Officer of Novartis Pharmaceuticals Corporation, the U.S. division of Novartis AG. He served on the Board of Directors of several other pharmaceutical and healthcare companies.

Charles Hatcher, MD began his medical management career when he returned to Emory University, his alma mater, in 1962 and accepted a position as an Assistant Professor. Charlie, who was trained in cardiology, performed Georgia's first successful aortic valve replacement, its first double and triple valve replacements and its first coronary bypass. In 1971, he was named Emory's Chief of Cardiothoracic Surgery and, under his leadership, Emory became one of the nation's largest and most effective centers for open-heart surgery.

In 1983, Dr. Hatcher's leadership abilities came to light when Emory President James Laney asked him to serve as Director of the Woodruff Health Sciences Center and Vice President for Health Affairs for Emory University. He retired from Emory in 1996, but he remained the Director Emeritus of the Robert W. Woodruff Health Sciences Center until his death in 2021.

Fred P. Zuspan, MD was a professor and Chairman Emeritus of Obstetrics and Gynecology at Ohio State University. He founded the medical practice of Perinatology, which had a focus on high-risk pregnancies, and he was a respected international scientist. He was accustomed to taking a forceful stance on hard issues and determining responsible actions. Fred passed away on June 7, 2009.

And, finally, Johnny Gresham, the youngest of our astute Board members. Johnny was an all-star halfback on the Georgia Tech football team. He also served as co-captain on the 1964 team with Bill Curry. Johnny obtained his bachelor's degree in Industrial Management and became one of Atlanta's successful real estate developers and an entrepreneur through the formation of his own real estate company.

Johnny served unselfishly on many public boards. He served in the Georgia Legislature and later as Chairman of the Board of the Georgia Department of Transportation. He also was a courageous and motivated risk taker, and he served very capably on the Healthdyne Board. Johnny passed on July 16, 2020.

Three members of the Matria and Healthdyne Boards were World War II veterans. Dr. Zuspan was a Marine Corsair fighter pilot who fought in the Pacific. Governor Sanders was a B-17 Army Air Force bomber pilot, and Mike Weeden was an Army infantry officer. In addition, Wayne Yetter served as an officer in the 4th Infantry Division in Vietnam. Individuals who have been through the rigors of war and military life are rarely timid with their recommendations and actions. As a general rule, they are capable and self-assured, and our veteran Board members always exhibited those qualities in our Boardroom as we analyzed numerous projects and made tough decisions.

The MiMedx Board

The MiMedx Board was constituted in a very different fashion than the Boards at Healthdyne and Matria Healthcare. When the founder of MiMedx asked me to take over the management of the company, he had already placed some of his investors on the Board. That meant these individuals had bought stock, but did not necessarily have any experience relative to the company's technology or its primary focus. There were some individuals who were successful in their own right, but no one had anywhere near the experience and background of the Healthdyne and Matria Healthcare Board members. Of course, it had taken me a number of years to develop those Boards. Also, we were in a different business and regulatory environment after the passage of Sarbanes-Oxley, which meant that I could no longer bring recommended Board members up for consideration without going through the rigors, and sometimes politics, of our corporate governance committee.

An introduction to the MiMedx Board is now in order. This should put into perspective some of the actions they took beginning in February 2018, which caused major problems for the MiMedx shareholders, management and employees.

First, Larry Papasan was an investor in MiMedx. He had previously been the President of the Smith & Nephew medical operations in America. Smith & Nephew is a British company that had a substantial medical technology business in the U.S. Larry had not built that business from an entrepreneurial standpoint; however, he was experienced with managing a mature medical device manufacturing operation that was not publicly traded.

Larry always seemed to bring a good perspective to the Board because of his management experience. However, just prior to the start of the short selling attack against the company, he had a stroke. When he returned to the Board, we were already in the midst of those matters. Larry had become very quiet, and it was obvious that his cognitive abilities had been altered.

Chuck Koob was also an investor in the company. He was a New York attorney and partner with the Simpson Thatcher law firm. He practiced anti-trust law, and although he had many years of practice in New York, he certainly did not have the business understanding and background of Carl Sanders.

I often detected, by his opinions, that he felt he was rather omnipotent. As an example, when the Board finally decided to hire a full-time CEO after my departure, Chuck bragged to some of our large shareholders that he was the person responsible for hiring and developing the compensation package for this new CEO, Tim Wright. Well, the problem with that was Chuck had never done anything of that nature in his life. But, he thought that somehow he knew how to put all the variables together to make this significant hiring decision. Wright did not have sufficient experience to manage a complex and sophisticated fast-growth public company like MiMedx Group. The compensation plan was far too much for his level of experience, and it gave him much too generous a severance package. The company's subsequent very poor operating results demonstrated his lack of experience very clearly over his three years. Wright was not qualified to be a CEO, and he was finally terminated on September 6, 2022.

Bruce Hack was also a MiMedx investor and an entertainment industry executive who had run some entertainment organizations. His latest position was the Chairman of the Board of Technicolor Corporation. Bruce was an aggressive New Yorker who could "raise hell" on numerous business matters, but he rarely exhibited any follow-through so his strong and noisy opinions seldom resulted in reasonable outcomes. A former boss of his said as much to one of our large shareholders. Also, Bruce was not knowledgeable about the healthcare sector of the business.

I placed Terry Dewberry on the MiMedx Board because of his accounting expertise. I had to terminate MiMedx's first CFO when I stepped in to manage the company, and the Board needed an experienced accountant. Dewberry and I were fraternity brothers so I had known him since he was 18 years old. I hired him at Healthdyne as our first Chief Financial Officer about a year before Healthdyne went public in 1981. Dewberry knew accounting very well, having been a manager at KPMG. However, he was also very risk averse and had little courage. Another key issue with Dewberry was that he did not have respect for shareholders and generally refused to talk with them! Dewberry was always a stock options holder, but typically did not invest his personal funds in companies where he was employed or served on the Board. In his later years, he had become very paranoid about a number of matters. In fact, it was almost as though he experienced a personality change. You will see that demonstrated as we discuss the details of the history of MiMedx. He retired from full-time employment back in 1995 when Healthdyne was split into three different public companies.

Joe Bleser was also a stock options holder and usually not an investor. He was an accountant by profession. Joe joined Healthdyne when we started Healthdyne Information Enterprises. He was placed on the Board as HIE's Chief Financial Officer when it went public. I always enjoyed Joe's input because he had good business sense, and he would look at things from a business perspective before simply applying an accounting "opinion." Joe was an ex-Marine, and he was generally very decisive.

Charles Evans joined our Board when one of our largest Atlanta shareholders asked me to give him the experience of being on a public company Board. Charlie spent much of his business career at Hospital Corporation of America (HCA), which is a hospital conglomerate, and he was a typical large company executive. He was politically astute, but not accustomed to the intricate details and complex decisions that had to be made in a rapidly growing organization.

In 2018, the Board decided that they wanted a "lead director" who would help facilitate communications between the Board and management, and Charlie was given the position. He was also appointed Chairman of the Board when I was asked to step down as Chairman and CEO. Thus, being on the MiMedx Board was a learning experience for Charlie. The decisions that he made, which we will discuss later, were generally very poor decisions caused by his lack of experience, and they caused the company substantial difficulties.

Dr. Neil Yeston was not an investor. He was recommended to me by one of our other large shareholders as a potential Board member. They were old friends, and Neil's experience as an MD was noteworthy. While Neil had no business experience, his father was a successful entrepreneur in the New York City area, and Neil inherited his common sense. He developed some rapport with our medical staff, and I frequently called on him to try to put in perspective some of the medical and clinical issues with which we were dealing. Neil was a business professional as much as he knew how to be. During the company debacle in 2018, he seemed to get caught up in the legal issues put forward by the attorneys, and he forgot the business grounding that he should have brought to bear on these matters.

Luis Aguilar was introduced to me indirectly by our Washington lobbyist. He had recently retired after an eight-year stint as a Commissioner for the Securities and Exchange Commission. Luis had spent his early career as General Counsel for Invesco, a large investment company that was founded and grown in Atlanta. Normally, I would not have put a second attorney on the Board, philosophy being that one is more than enough! But, with the unbridled and aparently dishonest short selling attacks that we were undergoing, I thought Luis could contribute because of his intimate knowledge of the rules and regulations the SEC <u>should have</u> been enforcing against these individuals. However, after he was elected to the Board, he made <u>excuses</u> for the SEC's lack of action, such as they did not have sufficient staff, or they did not have sufficient funding, or they could not review two sides of a case at the same time. I became frustrated very quickly with his excuses for the absence of any positive action by such an important government agency. Later, we will discuss the actual reasons for this lack of action by the SEC!

I think from these brief personality profiles you can see the differences in the two Boards. You can begin to understand why one group would probably approach problems, particularly regulatory and legal problems, in a much different manner than the other. The Healthdyne/Matria Board members would have demonstrated courage, confidence and logic in their actions and would not have violated their integrity and fiduciary duty to the shareholders. I think they would have made the same recommendations as I did relative to finishing the company's audit first and then conducting any necessary investigations. This will be discussed in detail in later chapters.

The Atlantic Southeast Airlines Crash

In reviewing the pros and cons of certain personality traits of public company Board members, I reflected on an extremely difficult Board meeting that I was involved in at Atlantic Southeast Airlines (ASA). ASA was one of the fastest-growing regional airlines in the country in the 1980s and 1990s. They were a regional airline that was a feeder for the Delta routes.

The company was run by two experienced airline executives, George Pickett and John Beiser. These two individuals ran a very "tight ship," and the airline was very profitable and building cash rapidly. Their operating profits generally ran between 25 percent and 35 percent of revenues with their cash being approximately equal to their annual revenues of several hundred million dollars.

These executives controlled their expenses very carefully. There were no excesses in the company, as far as I could tell, including their furnishings in the corporate headquarters! I remember asking them at a Board meeting, after I had recently flown the airline, why there were only two blankets on each aircraft. I suggested that most airlines had one blanket for each seat! The Board had some laughs about the frugal nature of these two executives at that meeting!

The Board consisted of these two operating executives plus two executives from Delta Air Lines since they owned about 20 percent of ASA. In addition, there were some other Atlanta business executives on the Board, including myself.

Delta Air Lines eventually acquired ASA when they decided they wanted to roll up their regional feeder airlines. Shortly thereafter, they bought Comair.

I had been on the ASA Board since the company was taken public by Robinson Humphrey. I was the only one on the Board who had actual flying experience as a pilot and flight instructor so I understood the flight principles of aircraft, and I knew aircraft maintenance reasonably well because of my background in Army Aviation and my engineering degrees.

The Board received a phone call from George Pickett one morning in April 1991 that we needed to have an emergency meeting. An ASA flight going into Brunswick, Georgia had just crashed and killed everyone on board. The people on board included Senator John Tower from Texas and his daughter, and the astronaut, Sonny Carter.

George and John described what they knew at the time about the accident. The aircraft was on final approach in clear air to Brunswick Airport and was a little over a mile off the end of the runway at about 500 feet altitude when it rolled inverted and went straight into the ground. To those of us who were experienced, that was a clear indication there was a mechanical failure of some type. A situation like this could have been caused by a propeller reversing on one engine, which immediately causes asymmetric thrust that can roll an airplane on its back and pull the nose toward the ground very quickly. Both George and John felt that something of that nature had occurred, and they highlighted that certain Hamilton Standard propellers had been recently reversing in flight. Therefore, in my mind, I thought we would find out very quickly that this aircraft had a Hamilton Standard prop reversal.

I bring up this incident because of the various behaviors among the Board members at this meeting. As you can imagine, there were numerous concerns from Board members as well as executive management about this incident. Something of this nature could have far-reaching personal consequences for Board members and the company's management, and it could end up causing the demise of the airline.

The dynamics of the meeting were very interesting, and the differences in behavior of the Board members were quite revealing. Certain members of the Board, who generally had no experience with aircraft or flying, were the most panicked and concerned. I could tell they were focused on themselves and what could happen to them as a result of this accident. I could tell from the questions that were being asked that they were in a state of paranoia about the situation. From their standpoint, they had agreed to join the Board of this successful Atlanta company, and now the worst of all things had just happened.

The contrast in demeanor of certain Board members depended on their DNA and personality plus their business experience and practical experience related to aircraft and their operation. It was obvious that, when someone does not have the experience level to analyze facts in a reasonable and productive fashion, they will go into a "protection" mode. Thus, an individual's ability to deal with adversity in a rational way has a great deal to do with their personal fortitude and confidence as well as their experience relative to the situation which they are facing. In regard to this situation with ASA, there were more levelheaded, knowledgeable and courageous Board members than those who were distressed. Fortunately, the situation quickly resolved itself when the accident investigation board determined that there had been a failure in the left propeller control assembly, which caused a prop reversal that rendered the aircraft uncontrollable at such a low altitude.

This ASA incident is just another situation that reinforces the point that the selection of Board members is extremely important, and should be made up of individuals with whom the entrepreneur has gone through some "tough times." You should understand their experience levels but, in particular, their self-confidence and ability to deal with difficult situations without going into a state of panic or paranoia that can cause them to forget their fiduciary responsibility to the shareholders and the company. Without competent leadership, such as an accomplished and tenured Chairman, a previously organized group turns into a destructive rabble! That is exactly what happened with the MiMedx Board!

Final Comment

At a small political event in Atlanta prior to Christmas of 2019, Guy Millner came up to me and said, "Pete, I am sorry for what you and MiMedx are going through. I believe, if you had the Matria Healthcare Board behind you, things would have been quite different. In fact, I know enough about the situation to just imagine what Carl Sanders would have done to push back on all the legal ramifications."

That comment essentially said it all. So let us begin to review some of the specifics of the MiMedx debacle. In the following chapters, I will further discuss the MiMedx "fall from grace" and the causal factors. There will be many lessons to pass on to you. It will be enlightening, and it will certainly cause you to reflect on "The Entrepreneur's Dilemma"… to take my business public or remain private.

CHAPTER 11

WHISTLEBLOWING AND SHORT SELLING BEGIN

The initial catalyst for the negative change in the fortunes of MiMedx was the actions of a hedge fund by the name of Deerfield Management. This fund had followed MiMedx from 2012 on, and they had a "short sell" thesis on the company because they knew reduced pricing for advanced wound care products was being proposed by the Centers for Medicare and Medicaid Services (CMS) in October 2013.

The two healthcare analysts with Deerfield Management, who had covered MiMedx, were charged by the Department of Justice early in 2017 for bribing a CMS official in 2013 into giving them pricing information on the changes that were to occur for dialysis procedures. I have always suspected that Deerfield also obtained pricing change information for MiMedx products. While the new pricing looked negative for MiMedx, it was managed well by the company so the changes did not have a significant impact on our revenue growth or profits after 2013.

MiMedx's shares that had been sold short went from two million to 20 million during the summer of 2013. The majority of that increase was, in all probability, due to Deerfield. In addition to charging their two analysts for using information they obtained by bribery, the SEC fined Deerfield Management $4.5 million in mid-2017 for not properly supervising their two analysts.

In the summer of 2017, MiMedx management was told that Deerfield, because they had amassed short selling losses of over $50 million, was trying to convince other hedge funds to unite with them in a coordinated short sell attack to force the MiMedx stock price down. Apparently, Deerfield achieved that goal, and in addition, another short seller by the name of Marc Cohodes became associated with the short selling of MiMedx stock in September 2017.

A Critical Decision

At the J.P. Morgan Health Care Conference in early January 2017, three of our large institutional shareholders stated that MiMedx was "checking all the boxes" in a very effective manner, but we needed to hire a Big Four auditing firm. These shareholders had been large investors in both Healthdyne and Matria Healthcare so I had known them for decades. Also, I knew that it was dangerous for a public company to change auditors, but I felt strongly that the company was operating so effectively that we should not have an issue with such a transition. Therefore, I discussed it with Mike Senken, our CFO, and I subsequently decided to bring it up with the Audit Committee. When I did, Terry Dewberry, the Committee Chairman, asked me to try to interview the Atlanta offices of the Big Four and to bring back a recommendation to the Audit Committee. I did so in the spring of 2017 in spite of believing that this was Dewberry's job! I came back with a recommendation to engage Ernst & Young (EY). The Audit Committee had subsequent meetings with their representatives, and EY decided they would like to do their due diligence and consider the assignment.

Thus, during the summer, EY finished their due diligence and told the company that they would be very pleased to become our new auditors. The Audit Committee decided that EY would begin to do the company's reviews for the third quarter of 2017 and complete the 2017 audit at the end of the year. I was concerned about the company starting a new auditing firm in the middle of the year, but Dewberry felt that it would not present a problem. During the third quarter, the transition between Cherry Bekaert, our former auditor, and EY seemed to go smoothly.

Now putting everything in perspective, I believe my request to the Audit Committee to consider retaining a Big Four auditor was a crucial mistake with a short selling attack about to begin in September. If I had not pushed this issue, we would probably have been in a situation where Cherry Bekaert, who had done our audits for seven years, would have properly managed Cohodes' allegations against the company. They had audited MiMedx for a lengthy period of time, and they knew management and our capabilities and character very well. I strongly believe that Cherry Bekaert would <u>not</u> have made the same decisions that EY made, and we would have published our 2017 audit on time. We could have subsequently dealt with any investigations of the other allegations that the Board desired after having fulfilled our obligations to our shareholders relative to the annual audit. More details later.

EY completed their first quarterly review of the company's financials. They presented a very positive outlook to the Board at the third quarter meeting in late October 2017. No problematic issues were disclosed, and the financial results were excellent.

In November, I warned the EY partner, Andy Brock, about Marc Cohodes. I told Brock that Cohodes was a "different" type of short seller. I said that I expected him to write EY a threatening letter. This was based on the fact that his attorney had already written threatening letters about our senior senator and congressman because they had assisted the company with an aberrant VA product coverage decision. That VA decision proved to have been manipulated by a competitor, and the VA wrote MiMedx an apology letter.

Brock blew off my concerns by saying, "We are used to this kind of stuff." I suggested that he and Dewberry confer with EY's New York partners to discuss how they would deal with the receipt of such a letter. That meeting never took place as far as I know, and MiMedx suffered the <u>dire consequences</u>.

Whistleblowers

In late 2016 the company uncovered a scheme devised by a sales manager to entice a few MiMedx salespeople into selling competitive products "on the side" through a company he had established! Our review disclosed that this employee told some of our sales associates that executive management knew about this violation of their non-compete agreements, but we said there was nothing wrong with everybody making some "extra money." One sales person made over $700,000 in less than a year on this scheme! The most disappointing part of the scheme, however, was that none of these salespeople reported this breach of company policy through our compliance hotlines. Incidentally, the MiMedx sales organization was one of the highest paid in the industry.

The leader of this group, Jess Kruchoski, who was a regional sales director, made some telephone recordings during 2016 trying to convince other sales management as well as others into agreeing that the company had been "channel stuffing." We obtained some communications that he did this in order to be able to break the "non-compete" clause in his contract and become a legal distributor for other products <u>as</u> <u>well</u> <u>as</u> MiMedx products! This was certainly not a very logical plan!

After Kruchoski made allegations in writing to me of channel stuffing at certain Veterans Administration hospitals in late 2016, I properly notified the Audit Committee as per the Sarbanes-Oxley Act. The Audit Committee engaged our outside counsel, Troutman Sanders, and our auditors, Cherry Bekaert, to investigate. The investigation included extensive document reviews and approximately 15 witness interviews. Troutman Sanders, Cherry Bekaert and the Audit Committee concluded that there had been <u>no</u> channel stuffing or related accounting irregularities. Kruchoski and his attorney did not understand GAAP accounting rules or our policy of never shipping without a purchase order as well as other policies that precluded what was alleged. The company published a press release announcing the Audit Committee's final findings and conclusions on March 1, 2017.

Kruchoski hired an attorney in Minneapolis by the name of Clayton Halunen who had previously represented whistleblowers. This attorney requested a $14 million settlement payment from the company, which was refused. In the mediation hearing, Halunen was told of his client's violations of their non-compete contracts. When the final settlement offer was rejected, which was now down to $8 million, Halunen became upset and told the company's General Counsel, Lexi Haden, and outside counsel, Joe Wargo, that he was going public with all of his client's allegations. When that information did become public in a Minneapolis newspaper, which was in late 2016, it probably emboldened Deerfield to develop their presentation and invite other hedge funds to join with them in a short selling initiative against MiMedx. This publication also forced 3M Corporation to withdraw their offer to acquire MiMedx, which we will discuss later in the chapter. MiMedx executives were told that Halunen contacted the SEC and that Cohodes eventually made contact with Kruchoski and more than likely Halunen. There are much more details in subsequent chapters.

Incidentally, Clayton Halunen was recently "indefinitely suspended" from legal practice in March 2023. The media article stated that it was after "multiple of his employees accused him of sexual harassment."

Short and Distort Campaigns

At this point in my career, I had been managing public companies for 37 years. I had experience with short sellers, and I had always been able to dismantle their allegations. However, I had never encountered a short seller that was as delusional and as maniacal as Cohodes. This behavior, I believe, is a result of a psychosis, some instances of which have been detailed publicly by some of his former friends.

The numerous corrupt issues that can be associated with short selling are clearly summarized in SEC documents and in several excellent publications. I have highlighted these articles by Larry Smith, Walter Cruttenden and Richard Sauer in Appendix 11. Each of these three articles gets into details on this broad subject and all of the various legal and business ramifications. The articles are extremely clear and easy to understand, and they should become part of the education process for any entrepreneur, business executive or public company board member. They should prove to be <u>very</u> valuable and informative.

Most importantly, there are solutions in these articles and in the books that I mentioned that would be easy for Congress to implement to stop the illegal short selling that can affect millions of Americans through their investments and IRAs. I would encourage you to forward these articles to your senators and representatives with a demand for some action through Congress.

At this point a brief review of what the SEC calls "Short and Distort" campaigns is in order.

An illegal "Short and Distort" campaign is composed of two parts. First, there is "Naked" short selling, which results in a "Fails to Deliver" status for the stock. Once a company comes under sufficient short selling, often there are not enough shares in the float to be legally sold short (borrowed). The short sellers will disregard the regulations and do what they need to do to protect their trades, which creates "Naked" or "Counterfeit" shares. In 2018 and 2019, MiMedx had about 40 percent of our shares sold short with "Fails to Deliver." This is an <u>extremely</u> large percentage, and it certainly caused numerous problems in our proxy contest in June 2019, which will be discussed later.

Second, there are other "trading shenanigans," which include developing false and misleading information about a corporate entity; then, advising other members of the cabal, or group, who are participating in the short selling scheme about the publication of the false information and the specific time of publication. This is done in order for them to be able to preposition their short sale prior to the publication. This is called "Front Running," and it is illegal. It is just like disseminating inside information in a normal long trade.

In addition, on the trading day when the information is released, the group of illegal traders will manipulate the stock rapidly down using several techniques, such as "Spoofing," "Layering," etc. "Naked" short selling also generally occurs, which is illegal because of "Fails to Deliver" issues. Refer to Dr. Susanne Trimbath's book, *Naked, Short and Greedy*, for very logical and detailed explanations as well as solutions.

The daily illegal trading schemes can include the following:

- "Painting the Tape" is the illegal practice of traders manipulating the price of a stock by trading it amongst themselves to create the appearance that large amounts of buying or selling are taking place.

- "Layering" and "Spoofing" are the illegal trading techniques used to give a false impression that large amounts of buying or selling of a stock is taking place with the intent to cause the price of the stock to either rise or fall. This is done by entering multiple orders over a set period of time with the intention to cancel them before they are executed. "Layering" is the practice of entering multiple buy or sell orders at prices away from the current market, whereas "Spoofing" is the practice of entering multiple buy or sell orders at the current market.

- "Offering Out Loud" large blocks is the practice of entering large sell orders away from the current market with no intention to execute on these orders. This is designed to frighten away buyers.

Of course, when the public sees a significant stock price decline, uninformed shareholders panic and sell their stock, and other uninformed investors do not buy the stock. The resulting increase in selling and the decline in buying make it easier for rogue traders to continue to manipulate the stock price lower.

Regulatory Indifference

In late 2017, I asked Marlon Paz, one of our outside counsels in Washington, to assist me in drafting a letter to the SEC with all the information we gathered demonstrating what we believed to be illegal short selling, to include daily trading information on the cabal that was apparently working with Cohodes. This included trading data that we had developed from ShareIntel that should have been very easy to analyze by both the SEC and FINRA.

I sent the letter to SEC Commissioner Jay Clayton on January 3, 2018. See Appendix 11. I also wrote a letter to the President of FINRA and copied NASDAQ officials. I even visited with NASDAQ in Washington. I never received any response from either SEC Commissioner Clayton or the FINRA President relative to the data and information that was outlined in those letters. At the recommendation of Paz, some large shareholders also filed formal complaints with the SEC relative to

Cohodes' short selling techniques, and to my knowledge, they also <u>never</u> received any response. The NASDAQ officials never responded in a substantive manner.

Because there was no action taken by the SEC or DOJ, MiMedx developed a policy of posting on its company website the Cohodes allegations that had meaningful legal and regulatory implications along with the company's corrections and clarifications of those allegations.

Those responses by the company turned the tide in terms of Cohodes' accusations going uncorrected. The stock returned to the $18 range in late January 2018, which was approximately a $2 billion valuation, from its low of $12 in December 2017. The information refuting the Cohodes allegations was forwarded on a routine basis by Lexi Haden, our General Counsel, to the SEC Regional Office in Denver.

In February 2018, Cohodes did exactly what I told Brock he would do. I believe that Cohodes sponsored and/or wrote an 18-page letter through *Aurelius*, which is one of his literary shills, threatening EY. That letter was preceded by dozens of emails to EY with the same misinformation. Had there been any reasonable response from federal agencies, it might have deterred Cohodes and his partners from presumably making all those allegations about MiMedx to our new auditors. Had EY let MiMedx management know about receiving these emails, we could have provided very clear explanations. I cannot imagine why they did not!

Of course, had EY not panicked when they received the *Aurelius* letter, it would have allowed the company to finish its 2017 audit and to conduct any investigations that the Audit Committee or Board deemed reasonable without turning control of the company over to an auditing firm that was acting in their own self-interest and then to law firms who were doing the same. EY resigned in November 2018. They had billings of approximately $5 million and <u>never</u> finished an audit that was to cost less than $1 million. Perhaps, this was their motivation!

As mentioned earlier in the chapter, when Halunen obtained publication of his client's allegations of channel stuffing by the company in the Minneapolis newspapers, it caused the termination of an offer of nearly $1.4 billion that 3M Corporation had recently made for their acquisition of MiMedx Group. 3M had spent three months with approximately 90 people conducting a due diligence on the company. The pricing was in final negotiations. 3M is headquartered in Minneapolis, and they withdrew their offer in early 2017 when the Kruchoski allegations were published in the local newspaper.

In this process, I received a real surprise, which is that the American judicial system allows attorneys to go public with allegations merely disclosed to them by their clients. There is, unfortunately, no responsibility for due diligence or verification of the allegations. I was told that this is unlike any other judicial system in any developed country in the world! Has the U.S. legal system become unbalanced? Many judges think so! Frankly, I do too!

The Board's Disastrous Decisions

As I just mentioned, I believe Cohodes sent EY an 18-page threatening letter in February 2018 through *Aurelius*. On a February 6th conference call, EY informed the Audit Committee and some of the Board members that, because of Cohodes' old accusations, they would not finish the 2017 audit that was due in approximately two weeks. They also faulted the Audit Committee for not conducting a thorough investigation of the allegations of channel stuffing made by Kruchoski principally because no expensive forensic auditor was hired. But, there was no need for such a large expense because the allegations were very easy to disprove, were very inaccurate and came from noncredible sources.

After EY delivered their "stop the audit" ultimatum to the Board and departed the call, I told the Board that I did not expect EY to ever finish the audit. Dewberry, the Audit Committee Chairman, adamantly disagreed. I stated to the Board that, as soon as one set of Cohodes' claims was investigated, he would make more, and EY was so fearful of SEC and PCAOB oversight they would insist that each new allegation be investigated before they would complete the audit. I predicted that EY would resign from the account rather than finish the audit under those circumstances. Again, Dewberry adamantly disagreed. However, that is exactly what happened in November 2018 with many millions of dollars in EY charges that later evolved.

As a side note, in late January and early February, John Cranston, our Controller, duly noted that questions coming in from the EY accounting staff was indicating to him that EY was way behind in the auditing process. John told Mike Senken, our CFO, the questions they were asking should have been brought forward a month prior. He did not see how they were going to complete the audit by the end of February with these open issues. This raises numerous integrity questions related to EY and their audit process.

On the February 6th call, I also suggested that the Board terminate EY and bring back Cherry Bekaert to complete the 2017 audit, which I felt could take place within 60 days, and then consider switching to a new Big Four auditing firm for 2018. I mentioned that we could conduct any necessary investigations while the audit was being completed. I proposed another Board meeting the next week to make the final decisions when I returned from my vacation. However, Dewberry immediately hired King & Spalding within two days of that call while I was still on vacation. I had some support for my proposal, but with Dewberry's paranoia and CYA attitude, the majority of the Board decided to stick with EY and meet all their demands -- and the lengthy, costly and destructive saga that has been MiMedx's recent five year history began.

Dewberry launched into a solution to "protect" himself. He spoke up at two subsequent Board meetings saying, "I am not going to let the SEC put me in jail." Incidentally, the SEC charges individuals civilly and does not put them in jail! Dewberry was admonished by me as well as legal counsel each time he made that comment. But, that did not keep him from over controlling the investigation, including hiring King & Spalding and negotiating their contract, which I believe was not seen and properly reviewed by our General Counsel and the outside Board members. This was not proper and effective corporate governance.

Since Dewberry's management of the previous investigation had been questioned by EY, why would the outside Board allow him to conduct a much more complex investigation where he might be a subject or where an investigation with intimate Board oversight would be in order? A "good question" that should have been asked! Of course, I was not in a position to pursue the issue because I was a potential subject. This lack of judgment was an early sign of an inexperienced and disinterested Board or of an opportunistic group preparing to act. As an entrepreneur and business executive, keep the potential for this type of problem always in mind. I will propose some solutions later.

The "opinion" by certain members of the EY staff that the investigation conducted a year earlier by the Audit Committee was insufficient also resulted in the company basically terminating our 30-plus year relationship with the Troutman Sanders law firm in Atlanta. I was informed by David Ghegan, our lead attorney at Troutman Sanders, that Brock had visited with him. Ghegan stated that the meeting was very acrimonious with Brock being especially accusatory in terms of the way Troutman Sanders and the Audit Committee had conducted the whistleblower investigation. Brock's <u>narcissism</u> was blossoming! He made the same point that Ghegan should have forced Dewberry to hire an independent auditor to do a <u>forensic</u> <u>audit</u>. Of course, that was way out of line considering that the channel stuffing allegation was easily refuted by merely reviewing our accounts receivable and cash collections. Also, the allegation had been made by individuals who were terminated, according to MiMedx, for well-documented "cause" and were trying to extort their way out of their non-compete contracts.

I believe it was Brock's communications with Dewberry plus encouragement from King & Spalding that indicated the Board needed to terminate Troutman Sanders as its outside law firm. I am sure Dewberry thought that Troutman Sanders might "call him out" on his manipulations of the investigation. And, that played into the hands of Lexi Haden desiring to hire her former "college friend," Isaac Greaney, and his Sidley Austin law partners from New York. Thus, Troutman Sanders was dismissed as our outside counsel after over 30 years. Another serious mistake.

From that point forward, the Audit Committee was in total charge and had full responsibility for the investigation and ensuing audits. Dewberry <u>never</u> prepared a written scope and budget for this expensive project. As mentioned, he selected King & Spalding (the Sally Yates law firm; see Chapter 14), and their partner, Paul Murphy, a former prosecutor, to conduct the investigation and KPMG (his former employer) to conduct a forensic audit.

The Audit Committee and Board effectively turned over most of the company's key audit decisions and many of its <u>business</u> decisions to EY, King & Spalding, KPMG and Sidley Austin. In addition, the Board was being "encouraged" to select a new corporate law firm to replace Troutman Sanders. The decision was eventually made to retain Sidley Austin after my departure on June 30th.

After the termination of Troutman Sanders, I told Lexi that she could bring the Sidley attorneys in temporarily until I went to New York to select a new law firm. During the first month of Sidley's involvement, Greaney told me about a conversation he supposedly had with Brock. When I tried to verify the conversation, I was told by Brock that no such conversation ever took place. When I confronted Greaney with Brock's comment, he had nothing to say for himself. Obviously, he was trying to manipulate the situation under review, which was the issuance of a press release. The Sidley partners had just presented the Board with a lengthy "no communications whatsoever to shareholders" document, which had been under great debate. We did, however, publish this particular press release!

In March 2018, I finally had the time to visit New York and interview law firms to potentially become our new corporate counsel. I selected Simpson Thatcher, which was the firm where Chuck Koob, a Board member, had spent his career. I told Lexi of the decision, and I directed her to stop giving assignments to the Sidley Austin staff. I stated that Simpson Thatcher would be the new corporate attorney. Lexi asked if she could continue to give Sidley the SEC and DOJ assignments related to the investigation. All of that, I told her, needed to be transitioned to Simpson Thatcher. She did not do that; she kept favoring Greaney and the other three Sidley attorneys.

At the Board meeting review of the 2017 year-end results in late February 2018, the Board held its normal Compensation Committee meeting to review management's recommendations for raises. Thornton Kuntz, the company's Vice President of Administration, always had very detailed information and metrics on the proposed raises. Over the decades, our Comp Committees never had any changes of any significance to management's recommendations. However, at this meeting, Dewberry, who was also on the Compensation Committee, drove a major change in the compensation that management had recommended for Lexi Haden.

After the Compensation Committee had its meeting with Lexi taking the minutes, Bill and I were called back into the Board room, and Lexi was asked to leave. Dewberry, apparently speaking for Compensation Committee Chairman Joe Bleser, stated that they had decided to give Lexi a significant increase to her proposed raise. He said they had decided to double the raise that management had proposed. I pointed out that she had been recommended for a 12 percent raise, which was an extremely high raise considering the situation. I asked why the Comp Committee had decided to double it. Dewberry corrected what he said to state that it was only a 22 percent raise.

I questioned the Compensation Committee as to why they did not ask executive management to come back into the room before they made this decision with only Lexi present. I reminded the Committee that there had never been anything of this nature to take place with any of the companies of which I was Chairman or CEO over the decades. I added that I considered what they had done to be way out of line, and I asked them never to take this type of action again without first discussing the matter with executive management. I stated that they had <u>no idea</u> of Lexi's capabilities and her ability to conduct the day-to-day management of the legal department. There were a number of problematic issues that I had been attempting to coach her on without the results that I had expected. Lexi later admitted to her management shortcomings in a session with our DOJ prosecutors. We received those details in the Brady information prior to our trial. I admitted at the Compensation Committee meeting the fact that she worked very hard, as did the rest of management, and that was the reason for giving her a substantial 12 percent raise. However, I was adamant that the way the Comp Committee had made this decision was destructive, particularly with Lexi in the room and not first discussing it with executive management.

I later understood that this was Dewberry's way of building rapport with Lexi so that she would support him and his way of conducting the investigation, which was in a CYA mode for himself and the Audit Committee. I had never witnessed Board behavior of this nature at any of my previous companies or at any of the public Boards of which I was a member. I had never seen Dewberry violate corporate governance or good business practice like this either! But, I believe his paranoia caused by his lack of courage and self-confidence was driving his self-serving and destructive behavior.

At this point, Greaney had already misled me about his conversation with Brock. And, I had other frustrations, as did other Board members, relative to the way this group of Sidley Austin attorneys were conducting themselves. All four were very narcissistic personalities with little common sense or business acumen. Bruce Hack, one of the Board members, once told one of the Sidley attorneys on a telephonic Board meeting to shut his "blanking" mouth and quit wasting the Board's time. Shortly, a second significant lie would be told to the Board and me by another Sidley partner, David Rody.

Visit with DOJ Investigators

In early 2018, DOJ investigators familiar with Cohodes' activities against other public companies asked us to come to a meeting at the Southern District of New York (SDNY) DOJ offices in New York. Bill, Lexi and I met with these three DOJ investigators. The meeting was led by Kurt Hafer, Criminal Investigator, Securities and Exchange Fraud Unit, Department of Justice. The agents began by stating that they were not being given enough credit for how much work had been done and how much they knew about Cohodes' unlawful activities. I took those remarks to indicate that the DOJ prosecutors were ignoring their findings and the allegations they had developed. This statement is a key to related comments we will have in subsequent chapters.

The meeting lasted over an hour as both groups shared information on Cohodes' short selling activities. According to the investigators, Cohodes' activities also included international money laundering. They mentioned that they were in communications with European and Canadian authorities reguarding Cohodes activities. They asked us to simply document for them any fraudulent activities that we were sure Cohodes had conducted against our company.

Upon our return to the MiMedx offices, I asked Lexi to extract from the company's website the information that Cohodes had published along with the company's counters to his allegations and to prepare that information to be sent to Hafer. Lexi suggested that she involve the Sidley attorneys in this activity, which I approved. It took an inordinate amount of time for Sidley to take the information from the website and condense it into a document for submission to the DOJ.

About the time the documents were prepared, I received a call from David Rody, one of the four Sidley lawyers that had been recently involved with the company on these matters. I asked Lexi to join the call. Rody made some very confusing statements to me. He said that he had called AUSA Brendan Quigley, with whom he had previously worked at the Justice Department at the SDNY. He said that Quigley told him he <u>did</u> <u>not</u> want our documents on Cohodes' activities against the company sent to the investigators. When I asked why not, Rody told me that Quigley was responsible for the Cohodes investigation, and he was not ready to receive such information. I stated that we had been asked by another DOJ official to forward the information, and I wanted to do so. Rody then admitted that Quigley did not seem to know anything about the investigation. That brought up further questions! I told Rody I was going to send the information anyway because I had been given direction by Hafer to do so. Lexi then got involved and suggested vetting the matter with the Board of Directors.

That happened some weeks later, and I was <u>very</u> surprised to have the Board recommend that the information <u>not</u> be sent to Hafer because a Sidley lawyer, Rody, said it should <u>not</u> be sent! This lack of response from the company to a request by a federal regulator was very confusing. I knew the Board had been manipulated, but I did not have the time to follow up until later.

After my departure from the company, I asked my personal attorney to verify with Quigley and Rody what had happened because I suspected some type of ulterior motive from the Sidley lawyers. As I expected, AUSA Quigley responded quickly to an email sent by my lawyer with a <u>written</u> response saying that he did <u>not</u> have a discussion of that nature with Rody. When Rody was confronted with what Quigley had said, he stated that he would provide an answer shortly. That was over three years ago; we are still waiting!

It is very important to note that something transpired in this situation that should not have. The company never forwarded to Hafer any of the misinformation and inaccurate statements that Cohodes published. The major question, "Why?," has never been answered. I clearly believe this is another indication that the DOJ <u>prosecutors</u> wanted to <u>protect</u> Cohodes for their own benefit. At the time, no one wanted me to know that Cohodes and all short sellers were <u>to</u> <u>be</u> <u>protected</u> as per DOJ "unofficial directives." Much more discussion on this subject later.

The AvKARE Decision

In March 2018, Dewberry essentially directed the activities of King & Spalding and KPMG without much involvement from the rest of the Audit Committee or the Board of Directors. I called him out on that in April, and he then began to involve the Audit Committee, and finally, the Board. During this period, I am certain that Dewberry was educated by the King & Spalding and Sidley attorneys on the "playbook" for the Yates Doctrine. That Doctrine gave him the coverage he felt that he needed because of his paranoia. Thus, Dewberry pushed the investigation towards finding issues for which the Board could terminate executive management and tell federal regulators that they had fulfilled their responsibilities under the Yates Doctrine. As previously discussed, this Doctrine directs companies to retain a large law firm to conduct investigations focused on the top executives. There was apparently no focus on Cohodes' specific allegations as had been requested by EY. I do not know if the EY staff was aware that short sellers were being protected or if they ever questioned why Cohodes' allegations were not being investigated by King & Spalding. Although, this could have been the real reason EY resigned in November 2018.

In a large meeting at the King & Spalding office tower in Atlanta on May 23, 2018, with over 30 people present, KPMG made a presentation arguing that, in their "opinion," management had somehow violated the contract with the company's federal distributor, AvKARE, and we needed to have revenues restated for six years from an accrual basis to a cash basis. Neither executive management nor financial management was involved in that review or decision until after the fact. Management was given a short time to respond to numerous emails and slides that had been prepared by KPMG. However, many of those documents were physically withheld from management.

Accounting management responded at a Board meeting on June 7th. During their financial presentation, I could tell that the Board did not seem to be paying attention to Mike, our CFO, or John, our Controller. I found out later that the Board had previously made their decision to terminate Mike and John that day. At the recommendation of EY, the Board had been in contact with Alvarez & Marsal, a business-consulting firm, since the middle of May. They had also planned to terminate the company's top two executives, Bill and me. However, the demand for our resignations did not occur until June 30th. Again, at that point, neither one of us had given any testimony whatsoever to King & Spalding or KPMG, and we knew of no issues or concerns other than the AvKARE six-year restatement with which we adamantly disagreed. Thus, Dewberry was moving quickly on his personal CYA agenda, and the "takeover" of MiMedx by the outside Board was building momentum.

Of course, this six-year restatement should have reflected directly on the Audit Committee. However, by alleging that a key document, namely the weekly FDA "implant report" that came from AvKARE, was the primary cause of the restatement and because that document had not been disclosed to accounting or to the Board, management was alleged to be hiding accounting information. We were not involved in a cover-up because we never believed that the weekly report documenting tissue implant code numbers for the FDA had any accounting implications whatsoever. In addition, accounting received copies of these reports. In fact, I still feel very strongly that this FDA document should not have been considered a part of our GAAP accounting. This was clearly a King & Spalding and KPMG manipulation! Much more later!

The fact that AvKARE decided to write checks most weeks, generally of the approximate dollar amount of tissue they determined had been implanted, was merely their way of easily deciding check amounts and managing their cash flow. Also, AvKARE had directed to us in writing that their payments were always to be allocated to the oldest invoices because their accounting system was not mature enough to match our invoice numbers with their cash disbursements. We held AvKARE accountable for the amount and aging of their accounts receivable because they were always merely managing their cash flow like every customer. How they did that was their own business as long as we were obtaining satisfactory payments in a timely fashion and their accounts receivable aging stayed in a reasonable range. Chapter 21 will review these issues very thoroughly.

In fact, when I had lunch after my resignation with David Coles, the temporary CEO who was hired from Alvarez & Marsal, he told me the shareholders would be frustrated when they finally saw the minor changes that were going to occur in the financial statements as a result of the restatements related to AvKARE. This was because the company had basically collected all the cash that it had booked as revenues in a reasonable time period. I will get into these details in Chapter 12.

So why did the Audit Committee recommend to the MiMedx outside Board that it adopt this new opinion of how revenues from AvKARE should have been booked for over six years? That occurred because it matched Dewberry's CYA goals of shifting any blame for the EY opinions to executive management, which would result in dismissals. Like EY, the Audit Committee and Board were intimidated by the short seller's allegations, and they must have decided that it was safer for them to "scapegoat" top management for those imaginary wrongdoings than to defend against them. I also believe King & Spalding was pushing the Sally Yates Doctrine since she had recently returned to King & Spalding from the DOJ after President Trump fired her for not enforcing his border policies. I believe Yates had developed a hatred for President Trump and anyone associated with him… like his 2016 Georgia Campaign Finance Chairman…"Pete" Petit.

As another motivation to terminate executive management, there were certain individuals interested in filling those CEO and COO roles. First was Charlie Evans, who had never been on a public Board until one of MiMedx's largest shareholders asked me to consider him for a position. After my departure, Evans was elected Chairman of the Board. At that time, Evans did not have a job, according to the executive assistant to the CEO of his former employer. The Chairmanship allowed him to hold a position that he had never previously held and be financially compensated for it. Also, the temporary CFO, Ed Borkowski, began to immediately campaign for the permanent CEO role, for which he had no qualifications.

The first step in this process was accepting the "opinion" from KPMG that a non-accounting document that came in to the company weekly for FDA regulatory purposes actually did have GAAP accounting implications. I am certain that, had other auditors' "opinions" been obtained, the decision could have been different. However, Dewberry convinced the Board, without the operating executives being present, into buying into the six-year restatement. That gave him what he needed to ask the Board to dismiss the top two financial executives and three weeks later dismiss the CEO and COO. Thus, a "takeover" took place by a Board comprised of individuals who had no experience managing companies like MiMedx. Dewberry commented at the June 7th Board meeting that, "When a company has to restate six years of revenue, people must go." That comment basically exposed Dewberry's CYA actions and "takeover" plan.

Dismissals

At the Board meeting on Saturday, June 30, 2018, the Board informed Bill and me that they were requesting that we resign because, "They wanted to take the company in a different direction." When they made their intentions clear, I told them there was a way this process was normally conducted, and I wanted to understand their plans for carrying it out. They did not tell us the truth about their plans because they said the Board was going to do a CEO search. However, they had already made the decision to bring in a temporary CEO from Alvarez & Marsal. In fact, David Coles was to start that next Monday, July 2nd.

I continued to inquire how they intended to manage the company until a permanent CEO could be found and transition all the complexities of running this business from the top two operating executives they were asking to resign. Both Bill and I routinely worked 60-plus hours a week, and it would be impossible to manage all those daily activities with one individual. I explained that the normal process would be to notify the executives that you wish to have resign of their termination, and then ask them to remain with the company until the new executive arrives. This would provide a transition period where the new executive is fully briefed by the former executives on the complexities of the daily operations, management strengths and weaknesses, tactical and strategic plans and many other issues. The terminated executives would then depart.

Several of the Board members spoke up and said, "That makes a lot of sense." I replied that this is the way a major transition is normally done! I then suggested that Bill and I and our attorneys leave the room so the Board could discuss if that would be the appropriate method for them to consider. I also informed them that I had just been diagnosed with bladder cancer, and I would be more than happy to step down and pass the CEO responsibilities on to a qualified candidate. I said that, with the right search firm, this could probably be completed by the first of September or certainly by the first of October. I emphasized that I would be happy to exit at that point, but I felt that Bill might prove to be very valuable to the new CEO, and he might consider staying on in his previous role or as a consultant. Obviously, it was disappointing to realize how little this Board understood about this process and what they were doing!

We took an hour break for lunch and came back to the meeting. When the meeting was reconvened, Dewberry spoke up first. He said that they had considered our recommendations and decided that they would continue the process they had previously agreed upon. At that point, we did not know there would be a temporary CEO arriving on Monday morning. Thus, the Board was not truthful with us.

I later talked to Chuck Koob and asked him why the Board decided not to conduct this process in the normal fashion. He said Dewberry told the Board that he had been informed by King & Spalding that they had discovered new issues relative to us and that the Board should not allow us to stay on during this interim period of time. I asked Chuck, "What were these new issues?" Chuck said that Dewberry did not tell them! Well, I do not think I need to say much about that statement with regard to the total lack of corporate governance associated with it. This shows the disjointed nature of this investigation and the inordinate control that King & Spalding, the other lawyers and Dewberry had over these business matters. None of these Board members were experienced enough to make these types of business decisions individually. The Board, at this point, was <u>totally</u> abdicating its responsibilities related to corporate governance and <u>their</u> fiduciary duties to shareholders. However, a "takeover" of the company was underway.

At that meeting, the Board advised us that, if we resigned, they would be in contact with us immediately relative to the implementation of our severance packages. I naively accepted that as being truthful. However, in spite of our attorneys being very proactive in the following weeks with attempting to obtain specifics on the severance package, which would include our stock option and stocks grants, they were continually given excuses for the delays. Around the middle of September, we finally received some feedback. The company had decided <u>not</u> to provide any severance packages. Also, they stated they were going to take away all our stock options and stock grants because they had now decided our terminations would be "for cause."

During the first few years of my involvement with MiMedx, I worked at salary levels that were approximately one half of what they had been at Matria Healthcare. Consequently, MiMedx supplemented those low salaries with stock options rather than cash. The company's cash was very limited in our early years. For the Board to take away those specific stock options is particularly galling since I sacrificed so many years for the company at low salaries. Also, my 60-plus hour work weeks and the company's excellent performance should have been a determinant in the Board's decisions!

After my resignation as Chairman and CEO, I continued to send numerous emails to the Board advising them on key issues, but they ignored my advice and warnings. Their disastrous decisions caused major problems for the company. The stock dropped during 2018 from approximately $18 per share at its high down to below $1 per share as the Board made these significant blunders. I remained on the Board until mid-September 2018. I resigned because I was planning on participating in a proxy contest with the other major shareholders to replace certain directors.

As I previously stated, I inherited the MiMedx Board when I stepped into the role of Chairman and CEO. Since I recommended that the Board have staggered term limits to protect the company from corporate raiders, I could only request Board changes periodically. I made some immediate changes, but never had the time to create a very experienced Board like the ones I had assembled at Healthdyne and Matria Healthcare.

I discussed in Chapter 10 the Boards that I developed at Healthdyne and Matria Healthcare. These Boards included numerous successful entrepreneurial business executives, such as Jackie Ward, Guy Millner, Fred Cooper, Don Weber, Wayne Yetter, Johnny Gresham, and finally, former Governor Carl Sanders who built a major law firm, Troutman Sanders. These individuals had the business and in some cases legal acumen to have managed the Cohodes allegations and EY debacle quickly and effectively rather than making self-serving decisions, which were the wrong decisions for shareholders, employees and customers.

Six weeks prior to the departure of Bill and me on June 30, 2018, the Board had begun making plans to bring in David Coles, a temporary executive, who had no healthcare experience, to run the company. No transition time was allowed for Bill and me to bring Coles up to speed on the numerous intricate issues that the company's executives dealt with on a weekly basis. Therefore, he came in and began to struggle with the complexity of the company and the Board. He did have separate lunches with Bill and me. Coles said there was no need for a turnaround at MiMedx because it was a well-run and efficient company. As mentioned earlier, he also said that, when the shareholders saw the revenue restatement and what the revenue changes were going to be, they would be very frustrated with all the commotion over just moving revenue around somewhat.

Subsequently, the Board began to make serious judgmental mistakes beyond bringing in a turnaround manager with no healthcare experience and providing him no transition time. The next thing that occurred was that Evans allowed Borkowski to go to NASDAQ in mid-September with several lawyers from the Sidley Austin contingent to try to convince NASDAQ that the company could finish its 2017 audit by February 2019. I was still on the Board at that time, and I requested that, before Borkowski and the Sidley lawyers were allowed to proceed, the presentation that would be made to NASDAQ be presented to the Board. Evans overruled my request because he said it was a "management prerogative" matter. As previously mentioned, Evans had no experience in public company governance. I was concerned that the presentation that would be made could be very flawed. Within about 45 days, the Board had to admit to NASDAQ that the information Borkowski and the Sidley lawyers had presented was incorrect, and there would be no 2017 audit completed by February 2019. As matters turned out, the 2017 and 2018 audits were not finished until March 2020.

NASDAQ immediately delisted the company, and the stock plunged. Recall that there was never a budget, schedule and scope prepared by Dewberry, Evans or Bleser, the individuals who made up the Audit Committee, to control and manage the audits or the investigation. In their March 2020 Form 10-K, the company estimated that the investigation and resulting audits would cost approximately $125 million. This was based on very unprofessional and self-serving business decisions that would result in a "takeover" of the company. That estimate was later raised to $150 million and then to $200 million-plus!

The next issue that caused an even larger drop in the company's stock price was the resignation of EY as the company's auditors on November 5, 2018. This occurred just as I told the Board on the February 6th board call that it would. There were never any "real" reasons given for their resignation. By this time, EY had probably invoiced the company five times their original quote for the audit. My guess is that the decision could have related somewhat to their frustration with the lack of audit management processes as developed by Dewberry and King & Spalding's lack of focus on Cohodes' allegations.

Next, the Board allowed Coles and the two inexperienced operating executives they had selected, Mark Landy and Ed Borkowski, to convince them that the company needed to terminate 24 percent of the workforce, including the sales force. I sent the Board a memo asking them to wait until they obtained the 2019 financial forecast and budgets at their December 13th Board meeting before making such a decision. As usual, my advice was ignored, and the termination announcement was made on December 5th. Frankly, that is a ridiculous date to announce a major layoff for any company. They should have waited until January 2nd. The company had a disastrous December in terms of sales because of the morale issues associated with the layoffs. The recent financials disclosed that the company had about $45 million in cash as of December 31, 2018. So what was the rush?

These obvious Board blunders during the summer and fall of 2018 made it very difficult for the Board to do an adequate recruiting job for the full-time CEO position. From my discussions with Board members, it was evident they were having trouble finding someone interested in filling this role. Those inadequacies continued into early 2019. Apparently, Chuck Koob was given the task to conduct the initial interviews, and that is when Tim Wright's name came up. I was told that Wright was about number nine on their list of choices. However, the Board themselves were totally responsible for all of the poor decisions they made and the resulting publicity which made most qualified candidates understand clearly that this was not an organization where a competent Board was in place. Therefore, the Board's mistakes and the ensuing publicity severely constrained their ability to effectively hire an experienced and effective CEO. Recall King & Spalding's advice to the Board to not let Bill and I remain until the new CEO was hired. This is typical of the poor business advice the Board accepted from lawyers, which generally became business disasters.

Proxy Contest

Because of the continual Board blunders, the long-term shareholders of the company kept asking me what could be done to rectify the Board's incompetence. I worked with some of the shareholders to develop a proxy contest to force the company to hold the <u>overdue</u> 2018 shareholders meeting, which would provide an opportunity to elect a few new Board members. About the time we were getting ready to take some legal action to demand the meeting, a Florida investment fund and shareholder, Hialeah Management, filed a lawsuit in Florida to force the company to hold the meeting. I and the other large shareholders joined the effort, and I personally employed law firms in Florida and New York to assist.

In spite of the Board's efforts to fight the holding of a shareholders meeting, the Florida judge ordered the company to hold the 2018 meeting on June 17, 2019. At that meeting, three of the original eight outside Board members who asked for the resignations of Bill, Mike, John and I were replaced. Subsequently, another Board member resigned. Thus, there were only four of those original Board members left, and at least one was to be replaced at the 2019 meeting, which the company committed to hold in December 2019. Of course, the Board broke their commitment and did not hold the meeting at that time.

In Chapter 18, I cover the details of our proxy contest.

Short Selling Schemes

As Cohodes started his campaigning, he began calling some of our former sales employees who had been terminated. He clearly highlighted on a phone call with Jeff Schultz, a MiMedx salesperson, his relationship with Ty Cottrell from the Denver SEC office. He was giving Cottrell's phone number to MiMedx salespeople who had been terminated for cause by the company. We were told that Cohodes was encouraging them to talk to Cottrell about filing a whistleblower action. He was promoting this as if he and Cottrell had become very well acquainted. Some of these terminated employees subsequently filed whistleblower actions.

It should be noted that, in Canada, Cohodes improperly interacted with one of their regional SEC personnel, and that individual was fired. It is not known what action the Canadian government took against Cohodes.

If Cohodes had been contacted by any of the regulators, such as the SEC, he probably would <u>not</u> have sent that threatening and inaccurate letter to EY through *Aurelius*. Had EY not panicked when it received the Aurelius letter containing inaccurate financial and corporate information about Mimedx, they probably would have finished the 2017 audit in a timely manner, which would prove that 2017 was another <u>very</u> positive year. The company could have investigated any other allegations over time. The shareholders of this company would <u>not</u> have been devastated as they have been. And, the short sellers would not have made <u>fortunes</u> with the collapse of the MiMedx stock. Where is the justification for what has happened to an extremely efficient and effective public company that was being run by very experienced and honest healthcare executives? We will get into more details on why short sellers are protected by the SEC and DOJ in Chapter 15.

It is a travesty to allow a short seller to control so much of the environment within which a public company has to operate. The way short sellers conduct their <u>unlawful</u> activities is quite easily verifiable. If any short seller is publishing information in today's environment, it is probably laced with false information and innuendo. The most important regulatory issue is that there <u>will</u> <u>be</u> <u>coordinated unlawful</u> <u>trading</u> on the day of any published announcement. The cabal can be determined relatively easily by FINRA and the SEC reviewing trading data and the "Fails to Deliver." That is, if they are so motovated!

Whistleblowing is Becoming a "Racket"

The whistleblower laws have become a huge "windfall" for legal fees. Also, they provide some basis for government attorneys to file lawsuits. Then, there are huge fees paid by the company to their outside attorneys for representation in such cases. This is just another shining example of how over the last 20 years the pendulum has swung against American business.

It is quite easy to find some of the statistics, but here is a quick summary. In 2021, the SEC received over 12,200 whistleblower tips. That is up 76 percent over 2020. From the SEC's fiscal year 2012 until 2021, the number of whistleblower tips received by the Commission has grown by approximately 300 percent.

As I am trying to emphasize, this is one of the most dangerous impediments to U.S. business. This system is so out of balance that it will soon become a "racket" as I have described the "strike suits" against American businesses for stock price declines. This situation will continue to grow rapidly into a racket unless numerous whistleblowers are held accountable for lying to the federal government and are prosecuted.

As in our case, employees and former employees can be manipulated by a short seller to file whistleblower claims. Cohodes went on a rampage of talking to former sales employees trying to continue to build some allegation against the company. I have documents that Cohodes created by doing <u>supposed</u> interviews with former MiMedx salespersons that were terminated for cause. Cohodes and one of his employees would conduct the interviews and make suggestions and claims that led to false allegations aganist MiMedx. However, Cohodes would still send these documents to the SEC, the DOJ, EY and King & Spalding. While these interviews were so superficial and easily refuted, that did not happen prior to them being circulated to these federal agencies. I bring this up to point out how easily the system can be manipulated today by unscrupulous individuals. And, the latest whistleblower laws have done nothing but increase the power that emanates to the whistleblower. Of course, the short sellers connect with them, as happened in our case, and the manipulations and misinformation developed at a rapid rate.

There is information available describing what a corporate entity should do to protect themselves from this new "threat." However, much of it goes back to setting up a proper compliance reporting system. In our case, we had such a perfected system. It had been used for decades, and there was never any retribution of any kind to the employees. However, Jeff Schultz, one of our salespersons, who became a federal DOJ witness through their intimidation, was asked in cross-examination by our attorney, if the company was conducting corrupt activities, why did he not report them. Schultz's response was that he was afraid of being fired. How so if his name <u>did not</u> have to be disclosed on the report? Also, there was never any record of our system being used in that way because it had been used to perfection. Unfortunately, you have to be in a position to refute employees' whistlebloweer allegations and other misinformation they try to purvey.

You would think that the federal government and the Department of Justice would have enough business acumen to understand what they have built with the whistleblowing legislation. However, it is certainly very well constructed to benefit the law firms, the federal prosecutors and the SEC and the DOJ. Thus, there is nothing more to say!

Other Informative Sources

The Center for Prosecutor Integrity has developed a list of the most serious types of prosecutorial misconduct. One of those is "allowing witnesses who they know or should know are not truthful to testify." This is a lesson that also should be learned by the news media, particularly media members who associate themselves with illegal short sellers. These journalists are notorious for finding individuals who are themselves corrupt and quoting them in publications when they are trying to defame some corporate entity that the illegal short sellers are in the process of attacking.

In the case of MiMedx, there were two of these journalists from New York who were employed by large news media firms. Both of these individuals knew Cohodes well, and they were prone to write articles about public companies whose stock he was shorting.

In her book, *Licensed to Lie*, Sidney Powell asks the question, "Why do prosecutors engage in misconduct?" She commented that The Center for Prosecutor Integrity provides an answer:

> "Prosecutors are subjected to a variety of powerful incentives that serve to reward zealous advocacy: the gratitude of victims, favorable media coverage, career promotions, appointments to judgeships, and the allure of high political office."

In their book, *Conviction Machine*, Sidney Powell and Harvey A. Silverglate comment:

> "Because it is so easy under the broad and vague federal criminal code to turn even facially ordinary daily activity into a prosecutable offense, and because slipshod ethical codes allow prosecutors to get witnesses to 'sing and compose,' as professor Alan Dershowitz has felicitously put it, there is never a slow season for federal prosecutions. And the revolving door leading from high profile prosecutions to lucrative partnerships in 'white shoe' law firms or high positions in government give prosecutors all the initiative they need to go after 'high value' targets."

In subsequent chapters, we will discuss the personal motivations that many attorneys at the DOJ and SEC have to bring white-collar crime cases to trial. I have now provided comments from Sidney Powell, Harvey Silverglate and others on this issue. I think the only way to resolve matters of this nature is through management of the situation, to include holding prosecutors accountable for not properly assessing the evidence in a case and for focusing only on the subject who they wish to convict. Frankly, it might be too difficult because of the restrictions of the civil service and government employment system to ever adequately hold these attorneys accountable. However, President Trump certainly dealt with similar issues at the Veterans Administration so there are ways to assure proper behavior from government officials.

I would like to mention that AUSA Brendan Quigley left the SDNY DOJ after seven years to join a New York law firm when he finished a case in 2019 for Osiris Therapeutics. Osiris settled an SEC claim of channel stuffing and accounting fraud, was ordered to pay a $1.5 million penalty and their former CFO pleaded guilty to lying to Osiris' auditors. This is a recent and very relevant example of a DOJ assistant U.S. attorney departing the agency after obtaining their white-collar crime case. I will discuss what transpired with our three prosecutors in a later chapter.

Chapter 11 Appendix

Larry Smith. *Illegal Naked Short Selling Appears to Lie at the Heart of an Expensive Stock Manipulation Scheme.*

Walter Cruttenden. *Shorting America.*

Richard Sauer *Counterfeiting Stock.*

Petit, *Letter to the SEC* Dated January 3, 2018.

CHAPTER 12

CHANNEL STUFFING AND REVENUE RECOGNITION ACCUSATIONS

Over the last couple of decades, the definitions and interpretations of the term "channel stuffing" have evolved. One of the first cases was at Sunbeam Corporation. In that instance, product was actually loaded onto trucks, and the trucks were parked away from the manufacturing facilities until the end of a quarter. Sunbeam would bill for these products and book the revenues. Then, the trucks would return after the quarter end and offload the product.

Over the years, more sophisticated methods of inappropriately increasing revenues on a quarterly basis were discovered. For example, in 2001, Bristol Myers Squibb was accused of placing as much as two years' worth of product into their distributors' warehouses and booking those revenues. Other schemes developed over the years. However, in all these cases, there was always a "day of reckoning" when the product was not paid for or was returned by a distributor because the distributor did not wish to pay for and hold that much product in inventory. Thus, the inflated revenues would generally be reflective of a substantial increase in the accounts receivable day sales outstanding (DSOs) and revenue drops in future quarters as return product was received and credit issued. Also, cash collections would begin to slow down.

More recently, channel stuffing began to be defined as ANY PROCESS OR PROMOTION THAT BOOKED REVENUE AHEAD OF NORMAL REVENUE GROWTH AND PRODUCT DEMAND. Fortunately, the market had an almost insatiable demand for MiMedx's new and effective technology. Thus, revenues quickly developed when appropriate sales focus was employed. So what was "normal demand?" See References at the end of the chapter for more discussion.

MiMedx executives have categorically denied knowingly taking any actions that could be defined as channel stuffing. The two formal investigations of the company both came to the same conclusions.

MiMedx Sales Processes and Procedures

MiMedx managed to grow revenues at very rapid rates from 2011 through the second quarter of 2018 under the management of me, Bill Taylor and the other top 18 managers who were dismissed or left. This growth rate occurred because of the significant attributes of the company's product line and the efficient and effective management of the company by experienced business executives. If channel stuffing had taken place, it would have been exposed during this period of time by the accounts receivable growing and remaining high and quarterly revenue growth fluctuating, which did not happen. Naturally, as the company's revenues grew, the revenue <u>growth</u> <u>rate</u> came down in an orderly manner. However, the number of units being shipped by the company kept increasing at a rapid rate.

When a company with these business attributes is well-managed, maintaining a track record of meeting or exceeding 29 out of 30 quarterly revenue forecasts is achievable with competent management. If channel stuffing had occurred during this period of time, there would have been quarterly revenue fluctuations at some point when product was returned for credit, and there would have been a significant growth in the accounts receivable. For instance, a smaller competitor of ours, Osiris Therapeutics, saw their accounts receivable grow from 80 to over 150 days sales outstanding (DSOs) because of their illegal channel stuffing schemes. MiMedx had maintained DSOs in a range of approximately 60 to 90 days over the years with the later years' average being closer to 70 days. For the second quarter of 2018, which was my last quarter as CEO, I believe the DSOs were approximately 65 days.

Figure 28 from Chapter 9 is a chart of the MiMedx day sales outstanding in accounts receivable over the years. You will see an uptick in the DSOs in 2015, which was predominantly caused by the company notifying AvKARE, its Federal Supply Schedule (FSS) distributor, that MiMedx had obtained its own FSS contract and would, therefore, be terminating their distributor relationship over time. At that point, AvKARE became upset with the company, and they began to slow down their payments. At about that time, MiMedx made commitments to additional accounts receivable staff and new management, which also quickly changed the inflection point and brought the aging of our accounts receivable down in a very substantial manner.

Another telltale sign of channel stuffing is a decrease in overall cash flow because the DSOs in accounts receivable are increasing. During these years, MiMedx actually purchased over $130 million of its stock in the open market. The company continued to see strong cash flows, which is certainly an indicator that there was no channel stuffing since the company was being routinely paid for products it had shipped.

The basic underlying growth and growth potential of the MiMedx product line was substantial. Because of the business experience of executive management, we were able to manage this growth potential of revenues, EBITDA and cash flow quite effectively. We also managed the company's commitment to rapidly increase health plan coverage, conduct numerous clinical studies, increase production efficiency, grow sales and marketing activities and routinely improve the quality assurance and regulatory systems.

With my prior public companies, I was used to having very detailed information on the selling activities. Therefore, MiMedx began early to develop our own quite sophisticated sales management system using the Salesforce.com product as a base. The company's sales executives were always inquisitive during and at the end of each quarter because of this system.

Because my previous company, Matria Healthcare, was one of the country's largest providers of healthcare "Informatics," I brought some of those management and staff persons to MiMedx to help create the sales management system that served our sales functions so efficiently. As the company grew, the sophistication and expanse of that system allowed the company to focus very carefully on new sales territories and the demographics associated with them. Thus, this made our sales personnel additions and their placements relatively easy and our sales function quite efficient.

Also, because of the development of the sales management system, the quarterly and annual revenue forecasting became much more accurate and efficient over the years. This enabled the company's quarterly revenue forecasts to become more and more precise as the years passed.

Our sales management process would involve every sales territory, region and area bringing their revenue estimates for the quarter to the corporate sales executives within the first couple of days of a new quarter. Significant analyses took place, and both under and over optimistic forecasts were scrutinized. Subsequently, the corporate executives would analyze the results and trim the revenue estimates by certain amounts for conservatism. That conservative forecast would be presented to shareholders by around the tenth business day of the new quarter. Because of the accuracy of the sales management system and this "bottom up" sales management discipline, the company sustained a very accurate track record of predicting quarterly revenues. In fact, MiMedx only missed quarterly revenue estimates <u>one time</u> out of 30 quarters while we were in our executive roles.

However, the King & Spalding investigators alleged that we missed our forecasts in three quarters of 2015 due to misinterpretation of some revenue recognition rules, which was an indicator of fraud! Those allegations were not true. We will discuss these accusations thoroughly in the following chapters.

To the best of my knowledge, the company's processes and procedures for revenue recognition were disciplined. MiMedx never booked revenues without a purchase order from the final customer or the distributor and without documentation of shipment. At the end of each quarter, the operating executives, the CFO and Controller all discussed the addition of "sales returns and allowances" reserves and "bad debt" reserves. Our public company experience allowed us to accurately add to these reserves, which reduced revenues for the quarter by the increase in the "sales returns and allowances" reserves. THUS, MIMEDX NEVER HAD ANY SIGNIFICANT DIFFERENCES IN ITS PUBLISHED REVENUE AND THE CASH IT COLLECTED IN A REASONABLE TIME FRAME FROM THOSE REVENUES. Also, Bill and I were very involved every month with the assessment of the collectability of our accounts receivable and would use that assessment to work with accounting to increase the "bad debt" reserves, which reduced quarterly operating profit.

If you were to step back and analyze the company's reported revenue and cash collections, you would see that those numbers are very close to each other. Also, if you analyze the quarterly build-up of the company's "sales returns and allowances" reserves and the "bad debt" reserves, you would see that the company's revenues and profits were generally conservatively reserved over this lengthy eight-year period. In fact, the company's 10-K filing of March 10, 2020 stated on page F-27: "DESPITE THESE (CREDIT LIMIT) OVERRIDES, THE COMPANY RECOVERED THE MAJORITY OF ITS BILLINGS MADE BETWEEN 2012 AND 2017 WITH INSIGNIFICANT WRITE OFFS RECORDED."

Thus, with the King & Spalding AvKARE accusations, the Audit Committee and Board made the decision to re-audit these years on a "cash basis" in spite of any significant disparity between booked revenue and cash collected! More discussions on that bizarre and destructive decision to follow!

Accusations

I want to review where the accusations of MiMedx's channel stuffing initially emanated. These charges were first made public by Clayton Halunen, the Minneapolis attorney who represented MiMedx regional sales manager, Jess Kruchoski, Mike Fox, his boss, and Luke Tournquist, his subordinate. In December

2016, these were the first individuals that MiMedx terminated for selling competitive products while being full-time company employees. At the mediation meeting, Halunen demanded that MiMedx pay Kruchoski and Tournquist a total of $14 million for them to drop the accusations of channel stuffing. The company refused to pay for the elimination of those accusations. Subsequently, Halunen went public with these <u>undocumented</u>, <u>unproven</u> and <u>false</u> allegations.

Halunen went to the Minneapolis papers shortly after the mediation meeting with these baseless allegations. MiMedx immediately filed lawsuits against Kruchoski, Fox and Tournquist as well as a number of other salespeople who were also involved in this corrupt sales scheme.

Generally speaking, in the ensuing legal discovery process, the depositions of these terminated employees were very revealing in terms of their lack of understanding of the company's revenue recognition and billing processes. It was also disclosed that one individual admitted that he had been lying, which "he did for his own benefit." In another case, one of the individuals said that he did not believe there was any channel stuffing at MiMedx. None of these individuals or their attorneys had enough accounting background to understand the meaning or implications of the term channel stuffing.

I was told that this particular sales manager, Kruchoski, was upset about the increased oversight on the part of corporate executives into the selling processes and into holding the sales force <u>accountable</u> <u>for</u> <u>their</u> <u>forecasts</u>. As MiMedx matured, our sales management system improved at a rapid pace. This allowed corporate executives to monitor relatively accurately the actual sales activities and expectations for each territory, region and area. That amount of management oversight was disconcerting to the individuals who were involved in the activity of selling competitive products on the side. Recall that one of these individuals made approximately $700,000 of extra pay from these impermissible sales. He settled the company's lawsuit by agreeing to pay the company $350,000! He testified that there was no channel stuffing taking place, and he even stated that he would like to come back to work for the company!

Relative to the accusations of "overstocking" Veterans Administration (VA) hospitals, called channel stuffing by these individuals, I offer the following. The individuals who were involved in this behavior had worked together at Pfizer and Advanced Bio Healing. They had long-term personal relationships with each other. And, they had a long history of working with the podiatry departments at the VA hospitals. They had very little experience working with the surgical or dermatology departments. Thus, when sales management requested and later demanded that all VA salespeople make routine calls on these two other departments, it caused pushback from some of these individuals. They basically wanted to devote all their time to the podiatry departments where they had relationships and could manage their selling of competitive products. They <u>did</u> <u>not</u> want to make calls on these other departments to introduce broader use of our product line.

In the majority of the company's VA sales force, there was compliance with our "No Department Left Behind" sales program, and revenue was rapidly growing in these other VA departments. There was always oversight on this program by management, which led to subsequent complaining by the few VA salespeople who were involved in selling competitive products. These particular employees were always trying to deflect management's attention from their violation of their employment agreements and from their not taking direction to support education initiatives in other VA hospital departments.

Thus, the accusations of channel stuffing from these <u>few</u> individuals relate to our insistence on them calling on two other departments in the hospital and being certain that there was product available for in-service and use in those departments. <u>No</u> product was ever shipped to a VA hospital by MiMedx without a <u>purchase</u> <u>order</u> from AvKARE <u>or</u> from the hospital unless it was a "sample."

Our sales personnel would request additional consignment inventory as they saw demand developing in podiatry and other departments, and AvKARE would either sign off and issue a purchase order, or they would not. Numerous times AvKARE <u>would</u> <u>not</u> issue new purchase orders because their inside sales personnel thought there was sufficient inventory at that facility to cover current as well as future use. Thus, under no definition of channel stuffing would MiMedx be guilty of improper business activity. Please note that MiMedx began to take purchase orders <u>directly</u> from certain VA hospitals after the company obtained its own FSS contract in 2014. In the case of our placing consignment inventory at a hospital, those sales were <u>not</u> <u>billed</u> and counted as revenue until the product was used and a purchase order was received at MiMedx from the VA hospital.

There is one instance of a sales initiative for the VA "Limb Salvage Program," and it fell short of expectations. In March 2016, MiMedx aligned a sales promotional program with the VA's Limb Salvage initiative. Our larger allografts, primarily the 7x7s, were the ones that were best utilized for venous leg ulcers (VLUs) because of the large size of the wounds. VA physicians felt that utilizing our EpiFix tissue on VLUs was very productive in stopping wounds from growing, which could prevent amputations. Thus, MiMedx established a sales program in the spring of 2016 to match with the VA's Limb Salvage initiative. During the latter part of the first quarter, a substantial number of 7x7s were shipped; however, they were only shipped to approximately 20 of the 160 VA hospitals where we had coverage.

A couple of months later, the national VA headquarters in Washington <u>dramatically changed</u> the payment process for <u>any</u> "implants" that cost more than $3,500, which caused issues with these large EpiFix sizes. This affected pacemakers, stints and numerous other medical implants, including our allografts. The payment change process caused a huge problem across the country with a number of medical device manufacturers. Medtronic, who is the largest medical device manufacturer in the world, even had issues, and they filed complaints.

MiMedx's large allografts became much more difficult for doctors to utilize because of the extra paperwork associated with this new VA payment directive. So in these 20 hospitals that had received the 7x7s, the larger size tissues were not being used. Doctors would use several smaller size tissues instead, which was generally more expensive for the hospital. We decided in the third quarter of 2016 to take those large 7x7s tissues back in exchange for other inventory or for credit.

Management had <u>no way</u> to know that this major change in utilization and reimbursement procedures was going to take place, and when it did, we reacted appropriately. First, the reserves were sufficient to cover the returns. Second, "sales reserves" <u>were further increased</u> (which reduced quarterly revenues) as well as "bad debt reserves" (which reduced profit). At no point during this period should MiMedx have had any concerns about misrepresenting revenue trends, profits or cash collectability to our shareholders.

We always made demands on our distributors to keep up a reasonable revenue growth rate. When the company was growing revenues at about 50 percent annually as in 2015, we expected our distributors to maintain some close but lesser revenue growth rate in their exclusive territories. We expected them to continue to invest sales time in our product line. When they did not, we requested that they add salespeople, sales focus, time and enough inventory to increase their growth rate. Some distributor's contracts required certain revenue growth rates over time anyway.

MiMedx Revenue Restatement

In regard to the "opinion" that KPMG developed during the <u>early</u> investigation relative to restatement of 2012 to 2017 revenues for AvKARE, there are numerous extenuating factors. In making this decision, KPMG alleged that, in 2012, executives in the company knew that AvKARE intended to pay the company for its invoices only after the tissue was implanted at the VA hospitals. That was absolutely not the case. If it had been, that would have required the company to only book revenues when the cash was received. In other words, MiMedx would be booking revenues on a cash basis rather than on an "accrual basis." However, the company's other numerous emails and testimony clearly indicated that this key KPMG allegation was incorrect. I am afraid… purposely incorrect.

The KPMG decision primarily hinged on their review of a 2012 email from an administrator at AvKARE indicating that they would like to pay their invoices once they had notification from the VA that the tissue was implanted. Also, a report came in weekly from AvKARE to the MiMedx Compliance Department on "Tissue Implants." This was a report that was required by FDA regulations. The report was not an accounting document nor did it have the accuracy of data that would be definitive for accounting information. VA hospitals seldom notified AvKARE or us on a timely or particularly routine basis of their implants. Also, AvKARE could manipulate the data and/or make mistakes, as they often did.

However, this non-accounting document that came in weekly to the Compliance Department was utilized as proof by KPMG that MiMedx should have booked AvKARE revenue on a cash basis. But, there were never any written or verbal agreements from the management of MiMedx agreeing to that. In fact, there were specific emails to the accounting department indicating that AvKARE wanted their weekly payments to be allocated to the oldest invoices, not the tissue that had been recently implanted. Also, there were documents showing that AvKARE responded to requests from executive management to bring their accounts receivables aging down when, on two different occasions, approximately $2 million was paid on their account irrelevant to any tissue implantation schedule. There were many other instances where calls from the MiMedx accounting staff to AvKARE resulted in reductions to their accounts payable to us. In addition, there was a period when AvKARE slowed down payments significantly when MiMedx first notified them that the company had obtained its own FSS number and would be winding down our business relationship. Thus, AvKARE became upset with MiMedx and began slowing down payments in 2015.

Like any growing small business, AvKARE probably had its cash flow issues. They had a number of manufacturers for whom they were selling products in the VA hospitals, and they would balance their payments accordingly. This is normal business practice. MiMedx had other dealers that would also attempt to slow down payments. But, MiMedx had a disciplined process of tracking accounts receivable and making phone calls or written demands when appropriate. Bill and I attended monthly meetings on reviews of all accounts receivable, and occasionally we would make collection calls to the larger accounts ourselves.

Also, there were two addendums added to the AvKARE contract in 2014 and 2016. If a procedure change of this importance had really been accepted, then I know that AvKARE would have demanded the new procedure be put in these amendment documents. That would have made the contractual change that KPMG alleged. The supposed change was not put in the amendment documents because AvKARE made no request to do so! Therefore, the alleged "pay when paid" concept, which would not have allowed AvKARE revenue to be booked on shipment, did not exist.

It was the opinion of executive management that the "opinion" by King & Spalding and KPMG relative to 2012 to 2017 revenues being collected on a cash only basis for AvKARE had no rational accounting foundation. I believe that other auditing firms would also have come to a different conclusion. It was certainly executive management's conclusion that there was no reasonable or documented proof that management had agreed to accept weekly payments only on tissue implants at the VA. In fact, the contract with AvKARE specifically stated that, upon shipment, invoices were due and payable. The email question from the AvKARE administrative person did not cause a "course of dealing" issue and that was not sufficient to modify the written agreement.

I believe the development and acceptance of this KPMG and King & Spalding "opinion" was pushed by the Audit Committee Chairman for his own personal reasons in May 2018. He wished to deflect any concerns over revenue recognition to executive management rather than to himself or to the Audit Committee. Once that "opinion" was accepted by the Board, then they could point to "for cause" terminations of certain financial managers, and later, executive management. THUS, A "TAKEOVER" BEGAN OF THE COMPANY BY A FEW INEXPERIENCED BOARD MEMBERS USING THE AVKARE RUSE AND INVESTIGATION AS A MANIPULATIVE TOOL. THIS TAKEOVER WAS LED BY THE AUDIT COMMITTEE CHAIRMAN, TERRY DEWBERRY. The Board's subsequent business decisions were disastrous and very damaging to the company, its shareholders and its employees on a long-term basis. This approach that was dictated by a paranoid Audit Committee Chairman and the Sally Yates Doctrine (Chapter 14) was so unnecessary!

Public Company Auditing is a Science??

When I was on the Board of Guy Millner's company, Norrell, I experienced a situation in which they had changed auditors, and the Board was enmeshed in the infighting between the two auditing firms. I have never seen anything so childish as accountants arguing over their "opinions" of how Norrell should deal with specific issues. To me, it was a group of individuals on "ego trips" rather than "business trips." So I witnessed firsthand what changing auditors could do to a company with the resulting confusion and the lack of ability to mediate the situation.

I should have taken this situation into account when I recommended to the MiMedx Audit Committee that it was time to bring in a Big Four auditor because our largest institutional investors were making that request. Of course, I felt the company was operating very efficiently, and I anticipated no accounting issues. Now being able to put everything in perspective, I believe my request to the Audit Committee to consider retaining a Big Four auditor was a crucial mistake. I was badly mistaken about possible accounting issues caused by the future creation of false allegations by alleged illegal short sellers, by resentful sales employees who had violated company and VA policies and had been terminated, and the political and fee motivations of the King & Spalding investigation team.

One of the key problems that public companies have today is the fact that the Big Four auditors are doing their best to turn accounting into a "science," not a profession of "opinions." That will never take place because it is a profession of "opinions." Each client has different business factors that make accountants' "opinions" necessarily focused on that client's particular situation. This makes things problematic for auditors because their oversight groups, the PCAOB and the SEC, continually question their accounting "opinions." I understand where they are coming from by trying to get many accounting principals that are "opinions" accepted as if scientific equations are governing. This would reduce the criticism from the PCAOB and SEC.

As we get deeper into a number of the issues that caused MiMedx to have many of these problems, you will find that they basically stem from the fact that one auditor's opinion went one way, and another auditor's opinion went the other way. Unfortunately, when you change auditors, the new auditor generally will call the shots. There is no way to mediate that. Scott Taub, our revenue recognition expert, reiterated that public companies should do their absolute utmost to NEVER CHANGE AUDITORS. He said that, generally speaking, not much good comes out of that change. MiMedx is another shining example!

Of course, when you have a self-serving Board and political motivations, real complex problems will develop.

No Channel Stuffing?

I want to bring out one of the very key issues associated with the fallacy of Bill Taylor, Mike Senken, John Cranston and me being guilty of accounting fraud related to the recording of revenues. As we continue, I will get into more detail about these allegations. However, the very crucial argument that refutes all those related allegations is a statement that the company was probably forced to make in their March 2020 10-K that was published for their 2017 and 2018 financial statements.

Recall that King & Spalding recommended to the Audit Committee and the Board that the company needed to restate six years of revenues because of the AvKARE contract. We will discuss that later in some detail to point out what a farce that was. However, in preparing this 10-K, I imagine the company's new auditor, BDO, went through numerous headaches restating almost 3,000 customers' revenues to a cash basis for this six-year period. As David Coles told me at lunch, shareholders will be quite frustrated with the small amount of change in revenues associated with this restatement.

I can imagine the auditors who replaced Ernst & Young having the same frustration. After accomplishing all that work, which cost the company approximately $80 million, the accountants are the ones who probably decided that this very key statement needed to be put in the 10-K filing to the SEC. I will refer to this statement many times in the following chapters because it essentially shows that the company, because of a number of issues, was conducting a revenue restatement unnecessarily. In other words, the AvKARE allegations that resulted in the termination of the first four top officers of the company were false. That shows what this expensive investigation, which was caused by the unnecessary desire of the Audit Committee's Chairman to protect himself, did to MiMedix. This KEY and defining statement from the 10-K is "DESPITE THESE (CREDIT LIMIT) OVERRIDES, THE COMPANY RECOVERED THE MAJORITY OF ITS BILLINGS MADE BETWEEN 2012 AND 2017 WITH INSIGNIFICANT WRITE-OFFS RECORDED."

If management was guilty of accounting fraud related to channel stuffing, this statement should not have been put into this important filing with the SEC. This series of events, while they fed off of each other, were all misguided, and all the people involved in the investigation should have known that they were wrong. The accusers were either acting in their own self-interest or that of their corporate entity.

My key question is why did the company have to spend $80 million on a revenue restatement in order to determine that it was not necessary. Under ordinary circumstances, this allegation should never have been made. However, once Dewberry employed King & Spalding to do an investigation, the die was cast. Under the Sally Yates Doctrine, some type of allegation against the top executives of the company was going to be found. More than likely, that Doctrine fed the numerous allegations and misinformation that the short sellers were promoting.

The next question is why would EY refuse to complete the 2017 audit because of the allegations of an unreliable and obviously self-motivated source? Well, I am afraid that goes back to the oversight power of the PCAOB and the SEC as it relates particularly to the Big Four auditors who are usually the scapegoats for any new issues that these agencies wish to emphasize. However, what EY did to MiMedx and the damage it caused is unconscionable. This tragedy would not have happened had it not been for the "protect ourselves at all costs" and "forget the customer" philosophy we witnessed from EY.

As previously discussed, this investigation was driven by Dewberry trying to protect himself as witnessed by him saying at two Board meetings, "I'm not going to let the SEC put me in jail." He had total disregard for his fiduciary duties to the shareholders of the company and anyone else except himself. Of course, I stated to him and the Board that his concerns were unfounded, which the 2017 and 2018 10-K certainly supports. Our attorney told him the same thing.

Cohodes' allegations of channel stuffing might not have been made if he had just understood how to read public company financial statements and if he had not believed a non-credible source, namely Kruchoski. When a company is engaged in channel stuffing, their days sales outstanding (DSOs) in accounts receivable will go up dramatically after they start such a process because the clients who are allowing them to "park" product are not generally going to pay for them in a timely manner. That is why I kept referring people to our financial statements when they brought up the accusation of channel stuffing. Incidentally, Cohodes tweeted many times that our actual revenues were only 50 percent of our published numbers! That was his "revenue lie" as we called it!

Cohodes is probably inexperienced enough to think that any public company auditor can be duped into not seeing those accounting parameters (DSOs) rapidly change, which would bring up more auditing scrutiny. Actually, he knows the value in making as many unfounded allegations as possible in order to catch everyone's attention.

KPMG and King & Spalding finally came to the conclusion that no channel stuffing had occurred. In fact, I read that in the written statements they made to the Board of Directors. I was later told by a board member that Dewberry immediately instructed King & Spalding to restart the investigation.

The lack of finding of channel stuffing by King & Spalding certainly vindicated the Audit Committee and Troutman Sanders' investigation of the whistleblowers in 2017, which EY alleged was flawed. EY claimed that an expensive forensic audit would have been required for that investigation!

I expect this very important statement in the company's 10-K would have also been a game changer at Bill's and my trial. Of course, we did not testify or offer any witnesses because the judge had manipulated the trial to the point where there was only about a week left for the defense to present its case before the judge wanted his courtroom to shut down due to COVID. That would <u>not</u> have been sufficient time for our testimony and the defense's closing statements to be presented. The prosecutors presented their case for four weeks! Much more detail later!

Had we been allowed to provide testimony to King & Spalding and the Board, and receive due process of the law, we would have brought this investigation, under normal circumstances, to a <u>halt</u>. However, there were so many "interested parties" with personal and political agendas that the bizarre process may have continued anyway.

I have to say that during the initial investigatory phase, from mid- February until June 7th, I was somewhat complacent and rather naive in terms of where this process was going to go. Knowing what I knew about our accounting and business practices, I saw no real issues. I assumed that the investigation would debunk the numerous Cohodes allegations and clear up those matters. However, I was not aware of the Sally Yates Doctrine at that point. Also, I did not realize that she had returned to King & Spalding during our investigation. While I pushed Dewberry to develop a set of goals and objectives, a schedule and a budget for the process, I stayed out of the activities because that was the proper thing to do from a corporate governance standpoint. Also, I still had a great respect for attorneys based on my long experience with Carl Sanders and his law firm. I could never have imagined the injustice I was about to witness perpetrated by former and current prosecutors.

My recommendation to others would be to involve yourself in investigations until you exceed the comfort level of the Audit Committee or Board. The reason for that simply relates to the fact that issues will evolve where there is a lack of leadership in any process. With a lack of leadership, normal and truthful outcomes generally do not happen. Our Audit Committee and Board lacked the experience, courage and leadership to manage these complexities.

Tissue Tagging

Some explanation is probably in order because of the accusations that came from some of the terminated sales employees on "tissue tagging." Cohodes built this allegation into a massive case of the company manipulating revenues to show more sales for wound care than for surgical procedures. He tried to make the point that the company had some motivation to show more wound care sales versus sales for surgical procedures. That was not the case. In fact, if there was any motivation, it would probably have been the other way around to demonstrate that the company had opportunities in a totally new sector of healthcare related to numerous surgical procedures. However, this was all nonsense because it related to our two sales organizations, wound care versus surgical, fighting over whether a tissue was implanted as a wound care product or a surgical product. While EpiFix was generally used for wound care and AmnioFix for surgical procedures, we discovered that the sales force was actually manipulating some of those procedures in order to garner sales commissions. So fights would start between members of the surgical sales force and wound care sales force. While both sales groups could be in one hospital, the MiMedx products would generally be in one department or the other. If a doctor needed a product, they would learn to get it from the other department if it was not available in theirs. Therefore, the sales force had to keep track of the tissue implants, which was called tissue tagging.

It took us awhile to get a system set up to stop the bickering and finger pointing. However, this was an administrative issue, and it had nothing to do with GAAP accounting. It had to do with sales commissions being paid to the wrong salesperson from time to time. The commission expenses were <u>still</u> <u>there</u> and <u>booked</u>, but they were paid to the wrong person.

By Cohodes listening to the biased accounts and inaccurate claims of former salespeople and having a propensity for alleging accounting fraud, he developed a story that supposedly distorted our revenue by some amount that would have been consequential. The truth is that these sales commission mis-tags would have had an unnoticeable effect on our category of revenue or profits.

Chapter 12 Appendix

Edwards, Jim. (2010, July 12). *Did the federal courts just legalize channel stuffing? One big pharma lawyer thinks so.*

Loughran, Maire. *What to look for when you audit revenue.* Dummies.com.

Rosen, Al & Mark. (2016, October 21). *When revenue recognition is questionable.*

Senogles, Geoffrey & Glowka, Maja. (2013, August). *Aggressive accounting vs. fraudulent accounting.*

Stuffing the Channel. Theinnerauditor.com. cwl890. (2016, June 25).

CHAPTER 13

SHORT SELLING

Because of the disclosure I was given by three DOJ investigators when I met with them in New York at the DOJ offices, I will occasionally use the word "unlawful" and sometimes "illegal" to describe the alleged short selling conducted by Marc Cohodes. This DOJ meeting was discussed in Chapter 11.

To say that Cohodes was effective in achieving his goals would be an understatement. I believe that his psychotic behavior is quite intimidating to most people, and they do not want to offend him because, more than likely, he will immediately strike out at them.

Among the approximately 30 companies that Cohodes attacked in Canada and those he subsequently attacked on the U.S. stock market, he created chaos and huge losses for probably millions of shareholders. The idea that he is doing the public a service by finding and calling out corporate misconduct is a farce. He generally shows up late in the accusatory process and increases the pressure on a stock by his self-serving short selling. In addition, he generally leads the tweeting and podcast activity against the company. To him, public service is about increasing his net worth and self-perceived reputation! He ignores the tragic financial losses to shareholders and to the government for capital gains taxes and corporate taxes.

What I have seen is a person who is detached from the truth. I have read documents that he has written about issues that have been told to him by unreliable sources without any verification. He writes false tweets that he dreams up, and he will encourage other people to write false information as well. None of that seems to bother him. He calls out, verbally and in writing, honorable people and accuses them of doing illegal things without any proof. For instance, he had his attorney write a letter with unfounded allegations about our senior senator, Johnny Isakson. Senator Isakson was Chairman of the Senate Ethics Committee and was on another senatorial committee at the time. You do not become Chairman of the Senate Ethics Committee without having strong support from both sides of the political aisle as well as being a man of integrity. Another letter was written by Cohodes' attorney where he made accusations about the improper behavior of two FBI agents who visited Cohodes' home to advise him to stop threatening my life on Twitter! Generally, Cohodes' written and verbal creations were placed on a website he created named "PetiteParkerTheBarker.Com"!

In this chapter, I will make some additional educational points on the differences between "unlawful" short selling and short selling. In addition, I will give some examples of my allegations of Cohodes' unlawful short selling. I believe we gave to the SEC sufficient information that related to his developing false information and giving it to his cohorts prior to publication. Cohodes' deceit is most visible in the falsehoods he spreads through his tweets and blogging. I believe those activities satisfy certain psychotic personal needs.

I will present some of Cohodes' misinformation as well as the truth that debunks his allegations. You will see that the quality of his information is very tainted. In addition, you will get a feel for the quantity of information he produces daily. I think you will be astounded by both the lack of credibility of his information and the volume of his communications. Also, you will see that he has a couple of shills who will also write about his targets.

Short and Distort Campaigns

As a result of my personal experiences and conversations with numerous attorneys and others, I would allege that Cohodes and his Cabal orchestrate and participate in short selling attacks commonly referred to by the SEC as "Short and Distort" campaigns. These attacks could involve Cohodes and several of his shills, such as Viceroy Research and Aurelius Value. See Appendix 13. These shills publish pseudo-research to include articles and other internet and social media communications that drive down the stock price of a targeted publicly traded company. I believe that Cohodes along with his trading partners, who probably include hedge funds and other individuals, act in a coordinated effort to drive down the stock price of a targeted publicly traded company after they have prepositioned their short sale trades of the company's stock.

The actual orchestration of this type of campaign can vary depending on whether or not there is already public information questioning if a company has violated regulations and/or laws. Some of Cohodes' shorting schemes have worked effectively because he has simply jumped into the fray when corporate wrongdoing has already been alleged and exposed by others. His Cabal then attacks with a combination of coordinated media or pseudo-research reports in addition to targeted social media activity, all of which are aligned to benefit his trading activities on the attack day.

In the MiMedx case, allegations of channel stuffing were initially brought by sales employees who were terminated for violations of their non-compete contracts and who we sued. They subsequently filed whistleblower lawsuits. I believe Cohodes and his Cabal used those allegations to begin their attack. A few other sales employees had also been previously terminated for performance issues, violations of federal regulations or company policies. Cohodes eventually contacted most of these former employees, and I beleive he assisted them in filing whistleblower lawsuits. MiMedx answered the many allegations from Cohodes and his associates with correct and documented factual information, which was initially posted on the company's website under "Short Selling Commentary."

As previously mentioned, in 2017, MiMedx was named the fifth fastest-growing public company in America by Fortune magazine. This is a tribute to our excellent product and technology platform, management's operational experience and employee dedication. All of these contributed to a significant increase in MiMedx's revenues and stock price from 2012 until 2018. This resulted in substantial losses for short sellers, like Deerfield Management, who bet against the company beginning in 2012. Reference Chapter 11. I believe that Cohodes could have possibly been compensated by certain hedge funds that had amassed substantial losses over the years by short selling MiMedx, although I have no proof of this.

In the case of MiMedx, all of Cohodes' aligned publicists with their "Short and Distort" themes have now been identified, with the exception of Aurelius. I believe that Aurelius is merely a sponsored website that is used by people who are aligned with Cohodes' interests for their publications. Importantly, the individuals behind Viceroy were unmasked. See Appendix 13.

One of Cohodes' associates in his trading activities is an individual by the name of Fraser Perring. As I just mentioned, Perring was finally disclosed as being the individual behind Viceroy Research. In addition, there were two other analysts that worked with him through Viceroy Research. Perring was mentioned numerous times in an article entitled Zatarra. This article is also referenced in Appendix 13.

There have been multiple attempts to damage MiMedx, and I believe the motivations to damage MiMedx come from short sellers engaged in Short and Distort campaigns. For example, there was a memo ostensibly from a current MiMedx employee alleging all types of misconduct. This was published and sent to major media sources, regulators, and competitors. For a number of reasons, the memo was determined to be fraudulent by the MiMedx Board and management from the simple corporate mistakes.

Another early attempt to damage MiMedx was to set up a false email account in my name, and subsequently begin communicating with one of the company's most respected Wall Street analysts. The analyst became suspicious after he received several emails from the fraudulent email account so he reached out to me. You can imagine the severe ramifications that could have occurred if false information was communicated to this analyst supposedly from me.

Up to this point, this discussion should clearly assist in understanding how I allege these publications with false information were created, which is with the full knowledge of the short sellers. I believe they knew when false information was going to be released. In other words, they had in-depth knowledge as to when the attacks would occur, and they could preposition their stake in the company's securities for their benefit. In effect, this is a form of trading with "inside information." This is often referred to as "Front Running."

In a "Short and Distort" campaign, when the publication with possible false information is ready for public dissemination, the hedge funds and individuals involved in the particular attack go into the trading market and preposition their trades. This can be done by short selling the stock or by buying or selling puts and calls in the options market. On the day of the attack, these trading partners will execute trades to force a rapid decline in the company's stock. It is these trading schemes that cause the majority of the rapid decline, and they keep up the pressure that enhances the decline. The publication on that date is merely the "starting gun" and the referenced catalyst for the decline. However, it is the coordinated attack with false social media and publications and the short sellers' activity that cause the majority of the stock price decline.

This coordinated and planned activity to push a company's stock price lower is not only illegal, but also abusive short selling. The SEC has published several memos and white papers that clearly delineate what makes that particular activity illegal. While the SEC has published several documents referring to this activity as a "Short and Distort" campaign, the SEC has taken enforcement action against only a few very small perpetrators, probably just to cover themselves.

By using my involvement as President Trump's 2016 Georgia Finance Chairman, Cohodes could stimulate reporters' interest in his allegations. As is now well known, President Trump went through several years of media and other harassment over supposedly "Russian collusion" and other false allegations. Thus, calling me "The Trump of Georgia" developed media attention quite easily. As an example, I will give you some quotes from one Atlanta Journal/Constitution article:

> "But his detractors received more validation on Monday. Following further discoveries in the biopharma company's own ongoing investigation, Petit abruptly stepped down, ending his nine-year run, leading what Fortune magazine once ranked the fifth fastest-growing public company, ahead of Facebook and Amazon. On Monday, the MiMedx stock dropped 38% to $3.93 a share."

"Petit, 78, has been among metro Atlanta's business elite for decades, having started his first company, called Healthdyne Inc., in the early 1970s, and establishing a track record of turning health industry startups into billion-dollar companies."

"Feisty and politically connected, he served as Donald Trump's campaign finance chairman in Georgia and has connections to U.S. Senator Johnny Isakson, and former U.S. Secretary of Health and Human Services, Tom Price."

Another one of Cohodes' destructive tactics was to encourage as many of our terminated sales employees as he could to call the SEC to file whistleblower actions. Since, at that point, we had approximately 430 salespersons, we had necessarily terminated a few of them. Some of those terminations were for performance issues as well as for breaking their legal agreements with the company, such as the non-compete restrictions of their employment contracts, or for violating government regulations. Of course, that included the individuals who had been convinced by Kruchoski to join him in his scheme. We heard about Cohodes' contacts with these individuals through our other sales employees.

As a matter of fact, Cohodes made numerous phone calls to Jeff Schultz, one of our sales staff in Chicago, whom I mentioned earlier. He literally kept nagging Schultz to file a complaint with Ty Cottrell, a SEC official in Denver. He gave Schultz the phone number and other contact information for Cottrell.

Cohodes tried to influence Schultz by telling him that he knew from information he had been given that the company was going to blame all of its "illegal" problems on Schultz and "throw him under of the bus." Schultz kept us informed of the conversations. In one case, Schultz had one of the other sales managers listen to a phone call from Cohodes.

Some of Cohodes Allegations

The best way I can convey to you what MiMedx faced as we became the short selling target of Marc Cohodes is to give you a recent example of his behavior related to a situation that occurred beginning in 2005. In this situation, Cohodes was one of the defendants in a lawsuit that Overstock.com had filed against his group. This was a case that Overstock.com filed against Gradient Analytics, Rocker Partners, Rocker Management, Rocker Offshore Management Company, David Rocker, Marc Cohodes, and others. Generally speaking, the case related to short selling activities including the supporting misinformation that had been promulgated against Overstock.com. Overstock.com was victorious in the case, and I have read where Cohodes was fined approximately $5 million. Of course, it cost other people involved in these organizations also.

On January 13, 2022, during a Twitter Space Call, Cohodes made statements regarding the Overstock.com case and one of their attorneys, James W. "Wes" Christian. Cohodes became very vocal with allegations regarding Wes Christian and other members of the plaintiff's attorneys. He made numerous accusations and engaged in unsavory name-calling. However, in the process, he violated state defamation laws for Texas as well as California. Wes wrote Cohodes a letter, which is in the public domain, dated February 1, 2022, demanding that he cease and desist all false statements regarding him. Wes also demanded that within seven days from the receipt of this letter, Cohodes make a public retraction regarding each of the 12 statements that were identified in his letter including the alleged threats that Wes supposedly had made against Cohodes' children.

In the last paragraph of his letter, Wes Christian stated: "I take these matters that attempt to stain my professional character and reputation very seriously and even more so when those allegations are based on lies. Moreover, dragging the names of deceased persons, a plaintiff who sued you, and a former friend of mine, and misusing and misrepresenting the facts of their own tragedies to support your own lies on my reputation and attempt to thwart an ongoing attorney-client relationship extremely seriously. If you continue to make these false claims, I will not provide any further notice to you, and we'll take immediate legal action."

Cohodes did correct the numerous statements that he made regarding Wes Christian. I took Cohodes retractions from his podcast, and they are shown below:

"So during my Respensis Space Call on Twitter on January 13th of this year, I made a few statements about Wes Christian that were incorrect, and I'm now retracting them. Specifically,

1. I said, 'Wes Christian is lucky he wasn't disbarred for the shit he pulled.' I retract that statement.

2. I said, 'Wes Christian is a despicable and unethical lawyer.' I retract that statement.

3. I said, 'This whole [inaudible].' To the extent that statement referred to Mr. Christian, I retract it.

4. I said, 'This is a despicable group.' To the extent that statement referred to Mr. Christian, I retract it.

5. I said, 'If Wes Christian represents this group or has anything to do with this group, I am officially gone, that is how bad he is.' I retract the statement that Mr. Christian is bad.

6. I said, 'The whole crew is as bad as can possibly be.' To the extent that statement referred to Mr. Christian, I retract it.

7. I said, 'Wes Christian is as big and bad of a scumbag as you can find.' I retract that statement.

8. I said, 'John O'Quinn miraculously had an auto accident, and he perished so Overstock got rid of Wes Christian and the late O'Quinn.' I retract that statement.

9. I said, 'All you need if you talk to Wes Christian, please give me the story how he threatened to kill Cohodes' kid.' To the extent that statement referred to Mr. Christian threatening my kids, I retract it.

10. I said, 'It happens to be true, you can Google Mary Helborn, Encans, Wes Christian, John O'Quinn.' To the extent this statement implied that my statement about Mr. Christian were facts, I retract it.

11. I said, 'He is lucky he still has his law license.' I retract this statement.

And finally,

12. I said, 'I am just bringing it up, certain things you don't forget.' To the extent that I referred to Mr. Christian, I retract it.

That is all I have to say on that famous January 13th Space Call."

This particular situation related to Wes Christian will help you put in perspective the numerous similar instances that occurred surrounding MiMedx Group as Marc Cohodes began his improper short selling activities. After Bill and I resigned, our Board was too inexperienced, intimidated and weak to do what Wes did.

After watching Cohodes' behavior since September of 2017, I believe he is psychotic. I have read his tweets and articles. I talked to one of his former friends, and they said the same thing. In particular, his <u>disconnection from the truth</u> is very problematic. He comments without even considering what he is saying or writing. I can give examples of that because of the many accusations he made against MiMedx and our management that were obviously untruthful and were exposed on our website. As always, reflect on his retractions of his comments about Wes Christian.

Wes has advised me on legal issues over the years. MiMedx should have retained him. I will certainly do so <u>personally</u> if the need arises!

One very obvious example of Cohodes' psychosis is when he confronted me at the question and answer session at our J.P. Morgan Healthcare Conference presentation in early January 2018. As soon as I started the session, he stood up in the back of the room and began ranting about numerous issues. When I told him to stop, he asked if he could come up to the front table and shake my hand. I said, "Certainly." He came up, and I shook his hand while others were taking pictures. But, about two hours later, he tweeted that, "Petit refused to shake my hand." Then, when a number of people sent pictures of the two of us shaking hands, his retort was "Well, Petit's hand was shaking." Of course, this was his second lie to cover his first lie!

Second, because Cohodes is becoming very bald, he apparently felt that he had to make it appear that I was also becoming bald. He tweeted in early 2020 that he knew I wore a toupee. He also made some comment that most business executives wear one. Well, in my case, that is absolutely false. But, I believe that is the kind of commentary he has to create in order to make himself feel better for his perceived issues and shortcomings…in this case, his balding. I believe that is certainly psychotic behavior.

In late 2017, Cohodes threatened my life with two of his tweets. His first tweet basically said, "I am going to bury the little fella in a shoe box." He followed that up with, "My gun is cocked and loaded."

Since I was developing concerns about the psychological stability of Cohodes, I asked our senior senator, Johnny Isakson, if there was something here that the

FBI should check out. He said that he thought so, and he would see if they would check into the matter. A few weeks later, two FBI agents came to Cohodes' home. In essence, they told him he could not be tweeting life-threatening comments on the internet. He began accusing the FBI agents of being MiMedx "goons." He claimed the FBI had mistreated him and his family, and he tweeted about the incident. Afterward, his lawyer, David Shapiro, wrote very accusatory letters to the FBI and Senator Isakson. He also wrote me and said that Cohodes' statements were <u>not</u> threats against my life! Cohodes later corrected that misstatement!

As publicized in the San Fransico media, Cohodes was having dinner with a friend in 2019. The friend apparently disagreed with his thoughts on some issue, and Cohodes struck him in the face and broke his eye glasses. Psychotic issues are definitely involved here, and I hope, for his own sake and that of his family, he puts himself under the care of a psychiatrist to resolve his issues. However, he also needs to be held accountable for his alleged breach of numerous SEC and DOJ regulations and laws against numerous public companies.

By October of 2017, we had become very frustrated with all of the misrepresentation that we believed that were being tweeted and published by Cohodes, Aurelius and Viceroy. It was particularly frustrating because Aurelius and Viceroy were totally anonymous entities, and we could not find out who was responsible for these claims. Therefore, MiMedx posted an article on our website. I have some excerpts from that article, which should be informative.

Here are the excerpts from that MiMedx article:

> "Also, shareholders should consider the source of any information they are reviewing. When you review MiMedx's press releases, SEC filings and corporate documents, please clearly understand that the officers of a public company must abide by numerous rules, regulations and laws. If they do not, they can be fined, incarcerated and sanctioned so they cannot play a role in a public company again. Mr. Petit, the company's Chairman and CEO, has been the Chairman and/or CEO of public companies for 36 years. He clearly understands his fiduciary obligations to his shareholders as well as his legal obligations to the regulatory organizations."

> "On the other hand, purveyors of misinformation such as Viceroy Research and Aurelius Value do not have the same regulatory and legal obligations. These type of groups can allege they are engaging in 'freedom of speech,' and in many cases they are not held accountable

for publishing misinformation. They do not have to report all their activities to the SEC on a routine basis. They stay hidden in the shadows and throw out their misinformation and innuendo. Many of them try to remain anonymous. They can act in concert with others to manipulate the market price for a company's stock using their misinformation and innuendo. It is very difficult to find out who they are, and thus, prove what they are doing with their illegal trading."

"Legitimate research organizations do not hide the author's names, do not hide their domiciles, nor do they admit in their disclaimer that their articles do not contain 'statement of facts.'"

"In fact, registered research analysts employed by FINRA member firms have to verify by law that the facts in their report are true and their opinions offered are reflective of their belief and views at the time of the writing. They further certify that their opinions are not influenced by potential for financial gain either to them or the firm that employs them. They are required to do so to ensure those who rely on their due diligence, opinion and reports to make investment decisions are basing their investment decision on truthful facts and analysis. These 'authors' have not done this. They are not employees of a legitimate FINRA member firm. They are not registered with FINRA as research analysts. They have no qualifications that allow them to offer investment advice or opinion. Most troubling, they state that they stand to benefit financially from the publishing of their reports."

It would be very difficult for me to adequately convey to you the disgust and frustration of seeing numerous tweets and other verbal provocations of Cohodes and his Cabal during the fall of 2017 and throughout 2018. Their comments also found their way onto the website that Cohodes created just to promote his campaign against MiMedx. In addition, he prepared other documents, which he continued to feed to Ernst & Young, King & Spalding and governmental agencies during 2018. His publications included his tweets, documents he developed from interviews he had with former MiMedx salespersons as well as other documents he would create. There is not much logic to the documents because most of the statements are not factual; they are not true. However, I think he certainly believed that the more misinformation he could publish the further down the MiMedx stock price would be pushed and the more money he would make from his efforts.

I will present just a very few of the comments that Cohodes and his Cabal created to give you an idea of the disjointed, dysfunctional and corrupt commentary that he developed. Many were very bizarre comments like he made against Wes Christian. Now, I do want to say that he put in tremendous amounts of time and effort in orchestrating his campaign. He is certainly maniacal in his endeavors, and his "activities" earned a huge return – I believe over $50 million!

Let me start by giving you some quotes that he placed on his website. One of the most notable was that he declared that MiMedx revenues were almost all fraudulent, and he expected that our reported revenues were only about 50 percent real. He later changed that to 70 percent real. These comments are literally hallucinations! Cohodes ignored eight years of our audited financial statements!

Of course, both the Audit Committee's investigation in 2017 and the King & Spalding investigation disclosed that there was no channel stuffing at the company. In fact, the company had to admit in their March 10, 2020 10-K filing that, "Despite these (credit limit) overrides, the company recovered the majority of its billings made between 2012 and 2017 with insignificant write-offs recorded."

What follows are some of Cohodes' comments from emails he supposedly received from our terminated sales employees which he sent to EY and King & Spalding:

Former Employee Comment:

"I heard last week that the field was given direction that sales reps can no longer make up their own purchase orders and that it has to be issued and signed off by the customer."

Cohodes Response:

"Interesting...They were putting in fake purchase orders...That's really dumb. And, companies can catch that easily."

Of course, this is a lie, but it is also so ridiculous it should not have been brought up. However, it shows you the lack of real business acumen that Cohodes applies to his allegations. To my knowledge, MiMedx never shipped or billed products to anyone without a purchase order from a valid customer. Our many years of audits certainly documented that fact.

Here is a comment from Cohodes, which he sent to EY, after having a conversation with his "Confidential Witness Number Six:"

Cohodes Comment:

"This is just one more conversation with CW-6...This person is a former and would like to help in the various investigations but is afraid of retaliation..."

CW-6 Comment:

"I will and can go very deep with the wrongdoing but it needs to be in a discussion format. The retaliation that Parker Petite (Cohodes' own spelling) uses against formers has people scared to come forward to you and when 'Dear Pete' letters are written, within two days to three weeks those employers are terminated."

In the history of all my companies, <u>no one</u> had been terminated for sending a 'Dear Pete' letter. In late 2016, some salespersons were terminated for breaches of their non-compete contracts by selling competitors' products on the side and some for violating VA regulations. These former employees created numerous false allegations, and apparently Cohodes does not bother to verify anything if it sounds like an allegation he would want to make.

Here are some comments directly from Cohodes from one of his interviews with CW-6. He is responding to a question about his upcoming "Periscope Broadcast."

Cohodes Comment:

"It's going to be really a storytelling thing, it's going to include some BA (maybe a typo; perhaps BS), it's going to include ABH, and it's going to include what a piece of s____ this thing was before you hired the ABH people, and basically brought in a bunch of criminals to jack the s____ out of sales, through all sorts of illegal means. Doing this or that or the other."

"I'm going to cite examples of what is done and that this whole thing should be shut down because it's frankly a big criminal operation. There's no science here, there's no medical here. All the clinicals and all the posters are done by guys who MiMedx pays off, but no one knows because they don't report on the sunshine."

There is not a word of truth to this dishonest palaver!

The following is from an email that Cohodes sent to Andy Brock at Ernst & Young and to King & Spalding:

"I hope you guys are taking this information seriously.

Even the head of the FBI, Christopher Wray, came out of the big law stalwart King & Spalding. That firm counts as a client medical company MiMedx; the FBI recently raided a short seller's house for sending a threatening tweet about MiMedx's CEO."

Well, at least Cohodes is finally admitting that he sent what most people would view as a "life-threatening" tweet directed at me. Of course, that is the reason the FBI came to simply gave him a warning (no raid) to stop sending life-threatening tweets.

On July 30, 2018, Cohodes wrote a letter to NASDAQ officials and Ty Cottrell, at the SEC in Denver, Colorado. This letter included the following commentary:

"I urge NASDAQ to delist MiMedx as soon as possible to prevent more damage to investors."

This is a disingenuous and ridiculous statement and an obvious untruth relative to what would happen to our shareholders (investors) when the company was delisted. The MiMedx stock price actually dropped approximately 30 percent when the delisting occurred so Cohodes' short position was even more valuable!

Cohodes made three written accusations to EY and King & Spalding about the company's operating activities. These included:

1. "Channel stuffing to inflate revenues. The company has apparently conceded that it engaged in illegal channel stuffing, despite its former CEO's attacks on me and other critics."

That is absolutely not the case. The initial investigation done by the Audit Committee pointed out that there was no channel stuffing, and that was put in a press release on March 1, 2017 before Cohodes started his attacks. Also, King & Spalding finally admitted to the Board in writing that there was no channel stuffing. Plus, the company's March, 2020 10-K document made it clear that all reported revenues were collected in cash except for inconsequential amounts.

2. "Bribery. On May 8, 2018, three employees of the Veterans Administration were indicted by a federal grand jury in South Carolina for accepting bribes from MiMedx employees. The indictment is enclosed. MiMedx has never disclosed any information about the company's practice of bribing government officials or explained the specifics underlying this incident."

The incident was well publicized. Our salesperson, who was involved in this incident of violating VA regulations by paying for meals and other expenses for VA employees, was terminated for violating those VA rules. Also, he certainly became one of the disgruntled sales employees making allegations against the company in coordination with short sellers.

> 3. "Selling unapproved drugs. On March 28, 2018, Petite announced at a healthcare conference that Forms 483 issued to MiMedx by the FDA in 2016 were 'rather routine' and the company 'cleared all those up.' But the Forms 483 that were issued to MiMedx identified 13 separate deficiencies ranging from sterility and purity issues tied to the company's own manufacturing processes to a lack of validated procedures and patient safety issues. MiMedx never told the public about the FDA inspection or the results. Instead it responded to a short seller exposé of the problems on this trash-talking, anti-short seller website and referred to a 2012 interaction with the FDA."
>
> "None of this has been adequately disclosed by MiMedx. Instead, short seller analysts obtained the information through FOIA requests and other legal investigative techniques. And, that means MiMedx has been selling unapproved drugs for years, and neither the patients nor the investing public truly understand that fact."

All of those statements are basically lies, and they were explained and exposed on the MiMedx website. Cohodes routinely made false and unsubstantiated allegations, which we discussed on the MiMedx website.

As another example of a Cohodes' associate, Viceroy, making other untruthful allegations, I present the following…

> Viceroy Allegation:
>
> "Repeating a statement by a terminated former employee claiming that the MiMedx relationship with former distributor CPM somehow was a 'channel stuffing' arrangement because it involved exclusive territory rights and volume-based pricing."
>
> MiMedx's Response:
>
> "This is yet another example of the author trying to turn a legitimate, legal and common business practice into something 'nefarious.' It is perfectly legal to have a relationship with a distributor whereby the

company grants an exclusive territory to said distributor in return for committed purchases. It is also quite common to have volume-based pricing with distributors, where the higher the volume of purchases, the lower the prices. This occurs regardless of when in the quarter the distributor makes purchases."

Here is another example of a Viceroy claim that MiMedx challenged...

Viceroy Allegation:

"The stark denial of our evidence about MiMedx's management indicate they are uninterested in investigating these allegations. As such, we believe channel stuffing and kickback schemes are being conducted in FULL KNOWLEDGE of management."

MiMedx's Response:

"As discussed previously, the allegations by former employees of 'channel stuffing' have been thoroughly reviewed and investigated. The result of the investigation was that there was no wrongdoing found. As to the Viceroy allegations, they are nothing but a short seller's fantasy. They are inaccurate, misleading and false. There are NO MiMedx's kickback or channel stuffing schemes."

"As previously discussed, the DOJ office in Washington investigated claims brought by an executive at a competitor several years ago that included kickback claims in his qui tam suit, and the DOJ found NO merit to those claims and declined to intervene in the case. We likewise do not believe there is any merit to these recent channel stuffing claims."

On November 8, 2017, MiMedx posted on its website the following commentary:

"We note that Mr. Cohodes and others have tweeted portions of an amended legal complaint filed by Mike Fox, who was terminated for cause, and they are asking for a 'response.' The proposed counterclaim contains 'allegations,' not facts, and they are merely repetitions of the same allegations made in other terminated employee litigation. After posting these allegations, Mr. Cohodes again calls for an internal investigation. As Mr. Cohodes is aware and has repeatedly ignored, MiMedx undertook an internal investigation when these allegations were first raised almost a full year ago."

"Mike Fox never used the compliance systems that MiMedx's employees have access to in order to report their concerns about any issues."

"The Audit Committee completed its investigation and confirmed there is no credible evidence of any wrongdoing on behalf of members of the MiMedx's management, and the audit result was published. The lawsuits for these former employees are ongoing and management continues to believe that the employees' counterclaims and accompanying allegations are without merit."

"In September, Mr. Fox filed counterclaims containing numerous accusations which reasonable due diligence would have proven to be without merit. Therefore, the company put Mr. Fox's attorneys on notice that MiMedx would be bringing a Rule 11 motion requesting that such allegations be withdrawn because they lack support and were brought to harass the company. In response to that notice, Mr. Fox withdrew those meritless pleadings."

Mr. Halunen, who was also Mike Fox's attorney, was "indefinitely suspended" from legal practice in March 2023 according to news media reports.

More Allegations of Channel Stuffing…

Aurelius Claim:

"The court documents filed by the whistleblower alleged that CPM Medical received 'significant product discounts as well as exclusive territory rights within Texas, in exchange for CPM Medical placing large orders for MiMedx's products at the end of quarters. Specific order amounts are included with totals implying that CPM was over a 5% customer for MiMedx during 2015. For example, the whistleblower states that CPM made roughly $2.5 million of purchases immediately before the end of Q1 2015, an order that would have been directly responsible for MiMedx's ability to meet its guidance of $40.8 million during that quarter."

MiMedx:

"Pricing based on volume is perfectly acceptable and legal. Our contract with CPM ended in 2015. As is common in any industry, pricing discounts are given with higher volume. There is nothing wrong or illegal with such orders."

"Distributors with good business practices do not buy inventory they cannot sell in a reasonable period of time. Distributors were less than 5% of our 2017 revenue. Also recall that MiMedx filed lawsuits against certain former employees for violation of their non-compete contracts and other grounds. Only after these lawsuits were filed did those former employees countersue MiMedx with complaints about alleged business practices, including 'channel stuffing.'"

More Cohodes Misinformation…

Cohodes Tweet:
"See the adverse effect in the FDA Adverse Event Reporting System (FAERS). MiMedx best start reporting or shredding. This is part of the poll."

MiMedx Response:

"Cohodes once again is purposely trying to mislead shareholders. The FAERS system is designed for pharmaceutical adverse event reporting by companies, health care providers and consumers. MiMedx's current products are HCT/Ps (human tissue products). Any adverse conditions related to the use of an HCT/P are required to be reported as adverse reaction reporting for HCT/Ps. MiMedx complies with these FDA reporting requirements. Also note that health care professionals (physicians, nurses and others) can and do report safety concerns directly to the FDA. If MiMedx somehow avoided reporting such adverse reactions, there would still be a record of the health care professionals submitting their complaints to the FDA. The facts are that after over one million allografts distributed, MiMedx's products have a stellar safety record, and the allegations that MiMedx destroys records of adverse reactions is patently absurd and false. If MiMedx's products were not safe, there would be thousands of complaints by health care professionals directly to the FDA, and MiMedx would have no way to prevent those complaints from going to the FDA."

Another Viceroy Idiotic Claim…

Viceroy Claim:

"As can be seen, the net reimbursement is positive, meaning the physician actually made money from the Medicare reimbursement. This is conclusive evidence that MiMedx's

EOB's are intended to exploit federal billing systems."

MiMedx:

"FALSE. Viceroy is demonstrating a total lack of knowledge of the U.S. healthcare system. The U.S. healthcare system <u>does</u> reimburse doctors for their services and the products they use."

"As per the CMS website, 'Where applicable, the payment amounts in the quarterly ASP files are 106% of the average sales price (ASP) calculated from data submitted by drug manufacturers.' The 6% addition shows that Medicare expects that physicians will make money on products they use."

"Wounds are not square and round. They're extremely variable in shape, surface area and depth. Therefore, it is a physician's choice to select the tissue size that they can best work with in terms of covering the wound surface area as well as the depth." "MiMedx offers more sizes and shapes of grafts than any other manufacturer in this category. That has been one of the principle features of our product lines since it was introduced in 2011. The large number of size offerings has the effect of reducing costs to the health care system because it makes our products very cost-effective."

"Viceroy does not understand the CMS claims and adjudication systems that are managed by the Medicare intermediaries (Medicare administrative contractors or MACs). Those systems will make changes to payments if mistakes have been made."

Another Untruthful Allegation from the Cabal...

Social Media Claim:

"There have been recent posts on social media accusing MiMedx of not properly reporting consulting payments as per the Sunshine Act."

MiMedx:

"This allegation is FALSE, as usual. At a minimum, the writers do not understand the requirements under the Sunshine Act. Part of the Act requires companies to report physician payments if they are an 'applicable manufacturer,' as defined in the Act."

"As per cms.gov, The Sunshine Act 'requires applicable manufacturers' and applicable group purchasing organizations (GPOs) to report certain payments and other transfers of value given to physicians and teaching hospitals, and any ownership or investment interests physicians, or their intermediate family members, have in their company. This information must be reported every year."

"Manufacturers of products under the HCT/P classification per Section 361 of the Public Health Service Act are not 'applicable manufacturers' under the Act. MiMedx received confirmation of this directly from CMS in 2013."

On a different subject related to the King & Spalding investigation…

In mid-September of 2018, Bill Taylor, our attorneys and I had a conference call with the Sidley Austin attorneys who represented the company. After that telephone call, Bill Weinreb, our attorney with Quinn Emanuel, put out a press release. His initial quote was:

"Today's announcement that former MiMedx Chairman and CEO, Parker H. 'Pete' Petit, and former MiMedx President and COO, Bill Taylor, were dismissed 'for cause' is deeply disappointing. Regrettably, public companies facing government investigations into alleged wrongdoing have developed a standard playbook: identify purported 'wrongdoers' among top management, dismiss them without severance, and then argue that the 'problem' has been fixed and there is nothing more for the government to do. Our clients Mr. Petit and Mr. Taylor are the latest victims of this unfortunate practice. The company effectively accused, tried, and convicted them of unspecified inappropriate conduct without first giving them notice of the 'charges' or a fair and meaningful opportunity to respond."

This press release calls out the unbalanced and self-serving nature of the Sally Yates Doctrine, which focuses on corporate executives. Thus, executives are "targeted," and there is no "due process" of the law required. Also, there is no consideration for the tens of thousands of shareholders and their losses on the subsequent drops in the stock price when executives are accused.

Cohodes developed his own MiMedx related website called "PetiteParkerTheBarker.com." He posted on his website all of his articles and tweets about MiMedx as well as those of his journalistic shills. Over time, he has erased some of the most bizarre comments, and he took the website down in early 2022. My attorney copied the site before it was totally taken down.

In 2021, I was given copies of over 200 emails and documents that Marc Cohodes had sent to the staff at Ernst & Young and King & Spalding about MiMedx and its employees. These particular emails began in the fall of 2017 and went through 2018. In spite of the fact that he struck a huge blow to the price of the company's stock when EY stopped the audit two weeks prior to its scheduled completion, Cohodes was not satisfied. He continued to send emails and documents through the remainder of 2018 until the stock price had dropped to approximately $1 per share. It would have been professional for EY to have shared those documents with executive management for our review.

After having read through all of Cohodes' emails to EY, King & Spalding, the SEC and DOJ, I will simply say that I was astounded at the dishonesty of his comments. However, I must say that a tremendous amount of work was put into his creating more and more allegations about MiMedx as 2018 played out. Cohodes literally interviewed almost every salesperson that we had ever terminated. He would conduct interviews with these individuals and create documents supporting the interviews. He was effective at manipulating people who were irritated at the company because we terminated them for cause related to their violation of government regulations and laws or corporate rules.

In addition, I have previously mentioned Cohodes' numerous emails to EY. One of his emails, dated December 18, 2018, stated the following:

> "You did the right thing and saved your firm. I'm in Atlanta on December 18-20 if you would want to meet up."

That congratulatory comment about "saving your firm" should say it all about Cohodes' threats he made to manipulate EY into stopping our 2017 audit and devastating MiMedx. Of course, this also devastated 15,000 other people, namely our shareholders. Plus, it deprived the federal government and state governments of over $500 million of capital gains and other taxes.

The Fruits of Graft

I would like to remind you of a book that would be very informative reading for educating yourself on the many issues related to the possible corruption in our financial markets. The book is entitled *The Fruits of Graft*, and it is written by

Wayne Jett. You will find that Chapter 15 in the book entitled Third Millennium Mercantilism will outline several instances where, as a corporate officer or Board member, you should be aware of the history of some of our Wall Street corruption.

This chapter of Jett's book begins by highlighting how the SEC has "green-lighted" "Naked" short selling. This is information in which I have gained some insight over the last several years, but I do not have the in-depth background and knowledge of Jett. I recall that it is very clear the SEC has allowed the "prime brokers" of Wall Street to have their own way relative to "Naked" illegal short selling and all the ramifications associated with that activity. Those ramifications are very problematic.

I believe that all short sellers are very knowledgeable about the "tricks of the trade" outlined in Wayne Jett's Chapter 15. Even with the passage of Reg SHO by the SEC, none of that has really had any effect on stopping the continuous growth of illicit short selling activities. There are some interesting disclosures in Jett's Chapter 15 related to the SEC and most of their senior officials resigning in 2007 over some of these untoward activities.

There are also some interesting disclosures about how the legal "strike suits," which I discuss in Chapter 17, are really managed. It turns out, these strike suit firms are very intimately connected to the firms that are doing the "Naked" and illegal short selling. It gives them an advantage to have their plaintiffs take small positions in those stocks so that when the stock is pushed down, they have a lawsuit ready to file with their plaintiffs. In doing this, they are accomplishing "Front Running," <u>which</u> <u>is</u> <u>illegal</u>. See the Chapter 13 Appendix for a full story on a broad illegal short selling cartel called "Zatarra." This information will definitely allow you to make more informed business and financial decisions, both professionally and personally.

Shorting America

I recommended that you read the article entitled "Shorting America" by Walter Cruttenden. In this article, the development of short selling is historically revealed. See Appendix 11. In the past, one of the key components that held short sellers in proper balance was the "uptick rule." However, this rule was eliminated when Congress passed some new regulations, Reg SHO, that supposedly eliminated the need for this rule. But, once the uptick rule was eliminated, more companies filed for bankruptcy in the subsequent three years than had ever transpired previously.

Cruttenden presents a very clear and common sense solution, if Congress was so motivated, to stop the very negative issues associated with short selling. Since most investors do not realize the shares that they have paid for and own are being loaned to short selling entities for the conduct of this business, it would make sense to have each shareholder approve that their shares can be loaned for such purposes. However, most investors realize these loans are not in their self-interest. That would bring this corrupt Wall Street process to an end.

If you happen to be an officer in a public company now, and you suspect illegal short selling is occurring, there are ways to gather that trading information and have it very well analyzed. There is a company by the name of ShareIntel that can do much of the analysis on your company's day-to-day trading activities. There is another company by the name of URVIN.AI, which is very effective in analyzing the "Spoofing" and "Layering" that occurs in the daily trading malfeasance. Connect with those organizations to see whether they can provide the definitive information necessary to take your case to the SEC and FINRA as we did. However, when you take your cases to those two regulatory agencies, you need to be certain you connect with your senators and congressmen. Hopefully, they will be on a committee that can force the right kind of regulatory and prosecutorial review of the information that you provide.

In the last chapters of the book, I discuss details of the MiMedx investigation into the short seller accusations as well as the Department of Justice initiatives. The DOJ eventually indicted me and Bill Taylor. Our subsequent trial in the Southern District of New York quickly revealed the misconduct in our "new" weaponized justice system.

It was revealing to see the manipulations that took place by the court as well as the prosecutors so that we never had a chance to testify. We were found guilty on one of the accusations and were sentenced to one year in a federal prison camp, which is a low security facility, rather than a prison. In my case, I went to a medical facility because of my bladder cancer. I made some wonderful friends during my actual six months of incarceration. My remaining six months of penalty time was spent under home confinement.

Chapter 13 Appendix

Zatarra. See my website, petepetit.com

Photos & Figures

Fig. 1: Model Car 1956 Hardtop

Fig. 2: Model Car 1957 Convertible

Fig. 3: Brett Petit

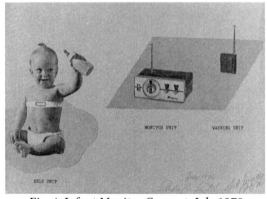

Fig. 4: Infant Monitor Concept, July 1970

Fig. 5: BioTech Building on the Georgia Tech Campus, Opened in 1999

Fig. 6: BioTech Building/ Front View

Campaign Quarterly

The *Campaign Quarterly* Interview
Pete Petit reflects on decades of philanthropy

Parker H. "Pete" Petit, ME 1962, MS EM 1964, is the chairman and CEO of MiMedx. The company develops biomaterial-based products that serve to regenerate damaged or diseased tissues in multiple therapeutic areas, including spine and orthopedic implants, ophthalmology, and urology. Petit has been a leader in the health care industry since 1970, when he founded Healthdyne and invented a home monitor used for infants at risk of developing Sudden Infant Death Syndrome. In 2011, he established the first endowed director's chair for a research institute at Georgia Tech. But he is perhaps best known for his visionary philanthropy that began back in 1986 when he endowed a distinguished chair for engineering in medicine, and later, with the creation of the Parker H. Petit Institute for Bioengineering and Bioscience (IBB), an interdisciplinary research facility that continues to anchor Tech's research enterprise in all bio-related fields. Petit's service to Georgia Tech stretches back for decades as well, including the Georgia Tech Foundation Board, the Georgia Tech Advisory Board, the Alexander-Tharpe Board, and the Biomedical Engineering Advisory Board. Petit also served as chair of both his 40th and 50th Reunion Committees. He and his wife, Janet, live in Atlanta.

CQ: For three decades, you have been a steadfast supporter of and advocate for biomedical engineering research and education at Georgia Tech. Why has this field been so important to you as a philanthropist?

PP: In the early 1970s, medical technology was in its infancy. By the mid '80s, I was very interested in supporting a faculty chair in engineering and medicine. That early chair came with a caveat from me, which was that Georgia Tech and Emory Medical School would come together in some manner to help enhance the future of the biomedical programs at both universities. The rest is history. Robert Nerem came to Tech not only very well credentialed in biomedicine, but also with very effective leadership qualities. From that point forward, Bob Nerem, Robert Guldberg, and the leadership at Georgia Tech and Emory launched one of the most effective biotechnology programs in the country.

I was approached on two other occasions to fund other programs as these programs grew and prospered, and I said yes. It was, and continues to be, gratifying to see the results of the second and third investments as well.

CQ: What is your vision for the future, not only for biomedical engineering and the biosciences at Tech, but also for Georgia Tech as a whole?

PP: I have no doubt that Georgia Tech will continue to set the standard for innovative, multidisciplinary, biotechnology academics and research. We have had strong leadership since the first initiative in 1986, and that certainly continues. With strong and unselfish leadership, rapid and sustained progress ensues.

Georgia Tech's progress escalated dramatically under the leadership of Wayne Clough, and has continued under the leadership of Bud Peterson. I expect that Georgia Tech will remain one of the most respected institutes for higher learning in this country, and in fact, worldwide. For the 20th century, Georgia Tech was known for graduating academically well-trained individuals who were seasoned and matured from the pressures of the Tech system. As such, they were prepared to play very key roles in the industrial setting. Moving forward, I hope that will not change, in terms of what the "Tech graduate" means to industry.

CQ: You have played a significant role in Campaign Georgia Tech, as well as in the campaign that preceded it ending in 2000. With the conclusion of the current Campaign just months away, what strikes you the most about what has been achieved?

PP: First, John and Mary Brock — and Al West before them — have taken Campaign Georgia Tech to new levels in commitment, execution, and performance. I think it is an indication of what can be accomplished in terms of increasing our permanent endowment when strong leadership enhances Tech graduates' philanthropy even further. I believe that Tech graduates are a special breed of individuals, and with the right leadership, they will continue to take Tech to new levels relative to the growth of our endowment.

CQ: Intercollegiate athletics has also been a major philanthropic priority of yours for many years. Why do you think it is important for Tech to build and maintain a great athletics program, in terms of both on-the-field success and academic excellence?

PP: Athletic achievements have been one of the cornerstones of Tech's illustrious history. There are very few universities with the academic reputation of Georgia Tech that also have the superb athletic programs and athletic history. While the students today may not know our athletic history, I certainly did when I chose Georgia Tech over Auburn in 1957. I believe many of our involved alumni place a great deal of emphasis on this particular cornerstone of Georgia Tech.

CQ: You have been engaged with the life of the Institute for decades, and in a variety of capacities. What has it meant to you, personally, to be so deeply connected to your alma mater?

PP: Georgia Tech has been a key part of my life since the fall of 1957. If not for Tech's co-op program, I probably would not have been able to attend college. I owe Georgia Tech for giving me a means to obtain a college education and then polishing my perseverance and tenacity. Also, my time at Georgia Tech allowed me to begin to exert my management and leadership skills at my fraternity and other campus organizations. Living in Atlanta and being able to remain connected with my Georgia Tech family has been a blessing in so many ways. Next to my own children, grandchildren, and my business associates, Georgia Tech has and will continue to play a key role in all my thoughts and activities.

CQ: Is there anything you would like to add?

PP: Georgia Tech graduates all seem to be "kindred spirits" because they survived and "got out." The vast majority of us have retained a loyalty and giving spirit because of our experiences there. That loyalty and spirit have allowed Tech to continue to raise its endowment and post achievements beyond most of our expectations. I would encourage all of you to find ways to make those investments in Tech and other worthy causes because the rewards are very gratifying.

> "Being able to remain connected with my Georgia Tech family has been a blessing in so many ways."
> ~ Parker H. "Pete" Petit

Fig. 7: Philanthropy Article in Georgia Tech Magazine

Fig. 8: Georgia State University Science Center, Opened March 2010

Fig. 9: Georgia State University Science Center Entrance

Fig. 10: Georgia State University Magazine Cover Fall 2005

Fig. 11: The Healthdyne 25th Anniversary Book

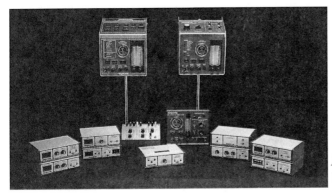

Fig. 12: Monitors and Ventilators

Fig. 13: Infant Monitor and Recorder, 1975   *Fig. 14: Smart Monitor, 1985*

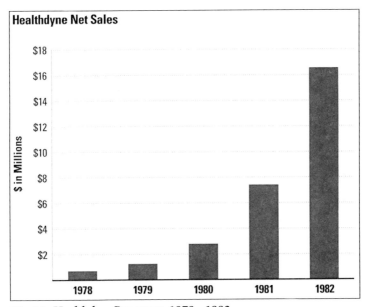

Fig. 15: HealthdyneRevenues, 1978 - 1982

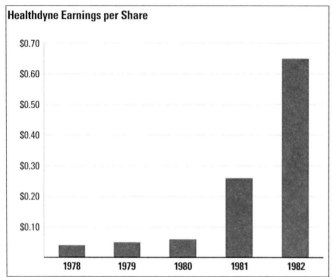

Fig. 16: Healthdyne Earnings Per Share, 1978 - 1982

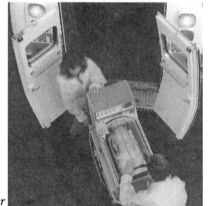

Fig. 17: KDC Transport Incubator

Fig. 18: The Oxygen Concentrator Production Line

Fig. 19: Infant Warmer

Fig. 20: Margaret Martin Recognition

Fig. 21: Healthdyne Technology Management, 1990

Fig. 22: Adult Sleep Apnea Systems

Fig. 23: The OB-1 Modular Home Obstetrical Management System

Fig. 24: Matria Healthcare Management, 1992

Fig. 25: Matria Field Management, 1992

Fig. 26: Drs. Jeremy Lin and Thomas J. Koob speak and sign copies of the "Primer on Amniotic Membrane Regenerative Healing", at Fall SAWC 2015

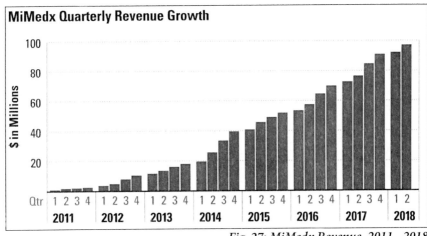

Fig. 27: MiMedx Revenue, 2011 - 2018

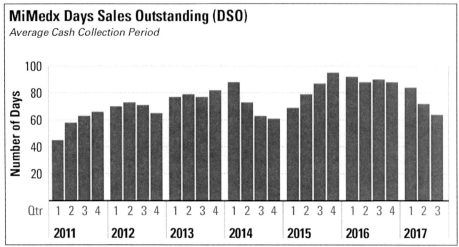

Fig. 28: Mimedx Accounts Receivable Aging (Days Sales Outstanding), 2011 - 2017

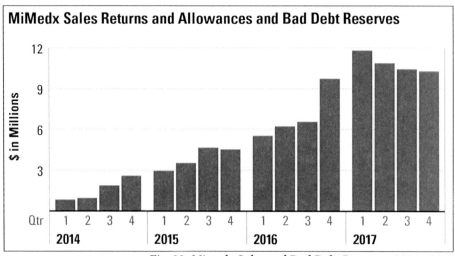

Fig. 29: Mimedx Sales and Bad Debt Reserves, 2014 - 2017

Fig. 30: MiMedx Stock Price 2010 - 2018

Fig. 31: MiMedix Sales Force, 2016

Fig. 32: NASDAQ opening July 11, 2013

Fig. 33: Carl Sanders and Dr. Fred Zuspan

Fig. 34: Senator Isakson, Carl Sanders, Pete Petit and Johnny Gresham, October 2012

CHAPTER 14

THE SALLY YATES DOCTRINE AND THE WHISTLEBLOWER LAWS

The Sally Yates Doctrine

Sally Yates returned to Atlanta in early 2018 to join her former law firm, King & Spalding, after President Trump terminated her for refusing to enforce his border policy. From a business perspective, her major contribution to our judicial system as Deputy Attorney General was her Yates Doctrine.

Unfortunately, the majority of public company executives are not aware of the implications of the Sally Yates Doctrine. See Appendix 14. Because of this Doctrine, being the CEO, COO or CFO of a public company in America has become extremely risky. In fact, if most public company officers or aspiring officers knew the full implications of this Doctrine, they would likely refuse to accept those responsibilities.

The Yates Doctrine basically dictates to all Department of Justice attorneys, public company officers and Board members that, if there is an allegation made against a company, the Board of Directors should retain an experienced law firm to do a formal investigation, which should probably include a forensic audit. The Doctrine explains that, if this process is followed, then the DOJ will "go easy" on the company in terms of levying fines and other punitive measures. Of course, most Boards will not ask the tough questions and push back on this unbridled authority. The inexperienced Board will be intimidated into following this directive and go through a very expensive investigation, which is supposed to be particularly targeted on the top executives of the company according to this Doctrine.

This Doctrine requires the focus of these investigations be on the top executives because the fines should prove to be much higher once those executives are convicted of a crime. The Doctrine recommends "targeting" the top executives from the start of an investigation. It also allows the Board to basically conduct an investigation without "due process" for these executives.

In addition, according to the Yates Doctrine, the results of the investigation against a corporate entity are to be given to the DOJ or SEC. Thus, the federal attorneys have very little work to do on their own because they are given a case that has already been investigated by a large law firm and for which huge legal fees have been paid by the company. Since the company is encouraged by this Doctrine to find fault with top executives, anything that may have happened that violated rules or regulations is going to be attributed to them legally, regardless of whether or not they are guilty or even knew about the violation. Besides, when a law firm is paid $25 million to $50 million to do an investigation, they are under pressure to provide results and often do present findings of corporate malfeasance, particularly when accused management is given no due process to understand and refute the allegations!

There have been a number of philosophical and direct changes to the Sally Yates Doctrine since it was first published in 2015. Before Deputy Attorney General Rod Rosenstein left the DOJ to also join King & Spalding, he went public with comments that the DOJ would relax the rigid approach required by the Yates memo and sensibly return some flexibility and discretion to government investigators.

Primarily, these changes were focused on the "all or nothing" approach to permitting corporations to receive credit for their cooperation only if they identify individuals who are significantly involved in or cause a criminal act. In addition, they were going to permit greater flexibility and discretion in awarding cooperation credit in civil cases. However, Rosenstein emphasized they would continue to focus on individuals in their white collar investigations which amounts to "targeting" the top executives of business organizations.

Also, on September 15, 2022, Deputy Attorney General Lisa Monaco delivered some remarks on new philosophies related to corporate criminal enforcement. In my opinion, she is merely reiterating that their top priority remains pursuing individuals who are in the best position to commit and profit from corporate crime. That means their policy of "targeting" corporate executives still remains intact. Monaco did bring up some philosophy changes relative to the history of misconduct, voluntary self-disclosures and compliance monitors.

Monaco pointed out how the DOJ now wanted to shift the burden of corporate financial penalties away from shareholders, who frequently play no role in the misconduct, to those more directly responsible. What infuriates me about that comment is that it ignores the illegal short selling and untruthful whistleblowing activities that directly penalize American shareholders and the government's taxes!

I know the Department of Justice is quite informed on illegal versus legal short selling and its associated whistleblowers, and yet, like the SEC, they are ignoring this whole area of malfeasance. It is my belief that Marc Cohodes could have made approximately $50 million for his 16 months of work short selling MiMedx.

Monaco also said they would be asking Congress for another $250 million to enhance their actions in this area. This request needs a strong and thorough congressional review!

Most importantly, all of the issues that I have discussed in this chapter need to be reviewed by Congress before they give additional funding to the DOJ. While the discussions and commentary from Deputy Attorney Generals Rod Rosenstein and Lisa Monaco clearly delineate some of the key legal problems with the Sally Yates Doctrine, they do not discuss the other key problems which relate to this Doctrine causing corporate America to be fleeced by dishonest whistleblowers, illegal short sellers, corrupt opportunists and now the government as they "target" top corporate executives.

Another factor that weighs heavily <u>against</u> the actual truth being determined by the Yates Doctrine is that it is not in the corporate investigators' interests at the law firm to quickly determine fact from fiction. Having experienced this type of investigation at MiMedx, I can tell you that we never had a chance to correct the record for the 2015 allegations because there was <u>no due process</u> of the law. In fact, we were advised that this type of investigation did not have to abide by due process requirements in preparing the legal case. Thus, the two most informed individuals relative to the MiMedx case were never allowed to explain the facts or correct the assumptions and allegations that were being made. Had we been able to do so, it would have put into perspective the ridiculous assumptions that were made. In fact, we never knew the actual accusations, aside from the AvKARE situation, until almost 15 months after the investigation was started.

Regardless of the motives of King & Spalding's former prosecutor and his staff in terms of prolonging the investigation and increasing the invoicing for their legal fees, the Board of Directors should have stepped in and required reasonable due diligence on all the exploratory work that was being done. Of course, there is no natural or normal motivation for a large law firm with expensive hourly legal rates to not do, in their mind, a "very thorough" investigation. However, when an Audit Committee and Board of Directors do not prepare a <u>formal business plan</u> with costs for these types of expenditures, the law firm will realize that they have an open checkbook. That is exactly what happened at MiMedx.

I have made the point several times that our federal agencies generally do not hold their management accountable for misdeeds or mismanagement. There may be a very few instances where accountability has taken place, but it was always something extremely egregious that was well publicized by the press. One of the most egregious issues that I can recall, came about when the Department of Justice obtained approval of several FISA warrants allowing the government to spy on one of our citizens, Carter Page. Carter Page was a minor player in former President Trump's 2016 campaign. As you will recall, his story was woven into the Russian collusion scam that persisted for about three years against President Trump.

At a Senate hearing in August of 2020, Sally Yates testified, "As the Deputy Attorney General and the number two person at the Justice Department, I was responsible for the actions of every single employee at DOJ, all 113,000 of them. That includes everybody at the FBI and the DEA and the ATF and all the US Attorney's offices and all the lawyers at the Department of Justice. I was responsible, in that sense, for the actions of all of them." Senator Josh Hawley then discussed the role of Christopher Steele, a former British spy who compiled the unverified dossier, a document to be used as opposition research for the Hillary Clinton campaign. The FBI used the dossier for their evidence for obtaining the FISA warrant against Carter Page. Hawley then brought up that Deputy Attorney General Yates told the DOJ Inspector General that she was not aware of who Steele worked for, but she thought he could have been working for the Republicans. Well, if this process had been managed well, that is certainly a key question that should have been answered before going forward. Senator Hawley pointed out to Yates that Steele had told the FBI in July of 2016 that he had been hired by Democrats. Most importantly, Yates direct report, Bruce Orr, knew about this situation because he was arranging contacts between Steele and the FBI and State Department. Yates responded that she was "Completely unaware of Bruce Orr's actions." That clearly demonstrates a detachment from the broad responsibilities that she shouldered as Deputy Attorney General. In any management role, you certainly need to be capable of at least understanding clearly what projects your direct reports are working on, their goals and objectives and the progress being achieved.

I think most of us realize the far-ranging implications of our Department of Justice not managing situations of this nature effectively, or being on a political "witch hunt" whereby they are ignoring and covering up the DOJ malfeasance that is taking place.

If this had been a situation where the CEO of a public company told DOJ prosecutors that "I did not know what was transpiring as my direct report broke the law," they would still have been indicted. Our laws are now constructed so that the top business executive would be held accountable legally for any transgressions. Therefore, why should not government managers and officials be also held accountable on this same basis?

THE SALLY YATES DOCTRINE FINANCIALLY BENEFITS LAW FIRMS, ACCOUNTING FIRMS AND FEDERAL PROSECUTORS TO THE DETRIMENT OF PUBLIC COMPANIES, THEIR EXECUTIVES AND STOCKHOLDERS AND THE FEDERAL GOVERNMENT'S TAX REVENUES. In addition, there are significant legal issues that can be called into question as clearly outlined by Professor Katrice Copeland from the Penn State Law School in her article entitled *The Yates Memo: Looking for "Individual Accountability" in All the Wrong Places*. In addition, Latham & Watkins Client Alert Commentary entitled *USA Deputy Attorney General Monaco Announces Revised Policies on Corporate Crime* is very enlightening on the shortcomings of the Sally Yates Doctrine, but the malfeasance that is blatant relative to corporate injustice is not discussed. The business issues are clearly discussed in Howard Root's article entitled *Sally Yates' Legacy of Injustice at the Department of Justice*. See Appendix 14.

In the 10-K SEC report that MiMedx filed on March 10, 2020, it is possible to determine that the company estimated expenditures of $125 million would be spent on the investigation and related audits for law firms and auditors! My first thought was "irresponsible." However, with no budget, schedule or scope, this was to be expected as I pointed out to the Board numerous times in early 2018. It also clearly demonstrates the focus of Dewberry and Borkowski, acting Chief Financial Officer, on themselves with total disregard for their fiduciary responsibility to shareholders and employees. This Board should be ashamed of the travesty caused by their mismanagement. Later comments by the company have indicated that these expenditures will exceed $200 million. Remember, the alleged accounting fraud involved about $9 million of revenue that was collected, but was supposedly booked in the wrong quarter. This was also not true!

Also, remember that some members of the MiMedx Board and their new management were acting in their own self-interest, and that caused the misalignment with former management, which enabled this corporate takeover. Because the Board and management remained aligned at Vascular Solutions, Howard Root's company, their ordeal only cost $25 million in legal fees, and they won their DOJ trial.

MiMedx Board's behavior should not be the concern of a regulator; however, some common sense should be applied to passing legislation like the whistleblower laws and developing doctrines of the Sally Yates nature. There are very few Boards of Directors of public companies that will have enough business experience, legal experience and courage to see this process for what it is, and call a "timeout." Of course, there is always the distinct possibility that some Boards and Board members will become opportunists and take advantage of the investigation for themselves to the detriment of their tens of thousands of shareholders.

If a large law firm is paid $25 million to $50 million to investigate the top officers of a public company, they will find something of which to make an issue. As a general rule, these investigations are conducted by former prosecutors who can investigate under a prosecutor's bias. Thus, companies, their shareholders and employees can be severely damaged by overly ambitious and unscrupulous former federal attorneys who may be working with inaccurate and misleading allegations from dishonest whistleblowers, unlawful short sellers and opportunists.

These unreasonable and unfair prosecutorial procedures need to be corrected for the benefit of all American public businesses, their shareholders and our capital markets. It is the large law firms that are the primary benefactors of the Sally Yates Doctrine. I will provide later in this chapter an analysis of where the actual money went in the MiMedx case. The federal government with their loss of tax revenues!

Perhaps this is where a number of the readers of this book would be able to make a difference in terms of the DOJ's lack of focus on these corrupt individuals who destroy shareholders' net worth by unlawful short selling. It should only take a conversation with properly motivated top federal officials to begin a process to stop this horrible and destructive trend that is changing America.

The Whistleblower Laws

Any employee, former employee, competitor or other individual can file a whistleblower action against a company. The whistleblower laws have become broader and more profitable for individuals and their law firms while being much more detrimental to the corporate entity. Whistleblowers can obtain up to 30 percent of any damages the government recovers from the information that the whistleblower has exposed. The critical problem is that the whistleblower can even bring lies and false information to the federal government, but they are not held accountable. That is a clear motivational factor that can encourage unethical people to bring unwarranted and untruthful claims against corporate entities in the United States. Thus, federal attorneys can open an investigation from unreliable sources who have presented deceitful and dishonest information to the government. Reflect on that fact!

Incidentally, my comments all relate to my experiences relative to whistleblowing in the private sector. There have been a number of changes in the rules, regulations and laws related to how whistleblowers are treated, particularly related to confidentiality. There is now a rapidly developing legal system that is totally focused on whistleblowing. There has been a book written to assist the whistleblowers. However, one must differentiate between whistleblowing in the governmental sector and in the private sector relative to the regulations and laws.

In 2006, a federal judge made very strong negative comments to me about the whistleblower laws. The judge stated that he felt the whistleblower legislation was some of the worst legislation Congress had ever passed because of its possible misuse by corrupt individuals. In our case, the lady who had caused some Medicare mis-billing for the business Matria Healthcare had recently acquired was going to be terminated because of her mismanagement. When she found out what was about to happen, she retained a lawyer who advised her to file a whistleblower lawsuit, or qui tam action, against the company. Therefore, even though she had caused the incorrect billings that the company was going to have to repay and for which they would be fined, she was going to get 25 percent of the settlement amount and her attorney about one half of her settlement! That infuriated this judge as it did our general counsel and me. However, that is perfectly "legal and just" relative to the way the whistleblower laws are written.

There is another major problem associated with the administration of whistleblower actions. That relates to the fact that many attorneys at the DOJ and SEC are aggressively seeking white-collar crime cases to litigate. These types of cases give them a "ticket" to leave the federal agencies and go to work for large law firms. These young attorneys relentlessly look for any information that would allow them to start an investigation, and perhaps, file indictments against a corporate entity and their officers. They wish to leave the government and significantly increase their annual salaries. Therefore, there is a great deal of <u>overzealousness</u> associated with this group of assistant U.S. attorneys (AUSAs) attempting to find cases to investigate and to subsequently file litigation. Again, I will call your attention to the books written by Howard Root, Lord Conrad Black, Raj Rajaratnam, Sidney Powell and Harvey Silverglate that I mentioned in the Preface.

The whistleblower laws have become a huge windfall for lawyers and their legal fees. Also, they provide some basis for government attorneys to file lawsuits. Then, there are the huge fees actually paid by the company to their outside attorneys for representing them in such cases. This is just another shining example of how over the last 20 years the pendulum has swung against American business and its executives.

As stated in Chapter 11, it is quite easy to find some of the growth statistics, but here is a quick summary. In 2021, the SEC received 12,220 whistleblower tips.

That is up 76 percent over the prior year. From the SEC's fiscal year 2012 until 2021, the number of whistleblower tips received by the commission has grown by approximately 300 percent!

I am trying to emphasize that this law will become one of the most dangerous impediments to U.S. business. This system is so out of balance that whistleblowing will soon become a "racket" like the "strike suits" against American business for stock price declines. This situation will continue to grow rapidly into a racket unless numerous whistleblowers are prosecuted for lying to the federal government and Congress balances the law.

As happened in our case, former employees were interviewed by a short seller and encouraged to file whistleblower claims. Then, Cohodes would send these documents to the SEC, the DOJ, Ernst & Young and King & Spalding. While these interviews were so superficial and easily refuted, none of that happened prior to them being circulated to these federal agencies. I highlight this to point out how easily the system can be manipulated today by unscrupulous individuals. And, the latest whistleblower laws have done nothing but increase the power that goes to the whistleblower. Of course, if the short sellers connect with them, as happened in our case, then the manipulations and misinformation develop at a rapid rate.

As mentioned, there is information available describing what a corporate entity should do to protect themselves from this whistleblower "threat." However, much of that goes back to setting up a proper compliance reporting system. In our case, we had such a perfected system that had functioned efficiently for over 20 years. It had been used on occasions, and there was never any retribution of any kind to the whistleblower. However, Jeff Schultz, one of our salespersons who became a federal DOJ witness through their intimidation, was asked in cross-examination by our attorney if company executives were conducting corrupt activities why did he not report them? Schultz's response was that he was afraid of being fired. However, there was never any record of our compliance system being used in that way, and besides that, employees do not have to put their names on the forms! You have to keep yourself in a position to refute whistleblower allegations and other misinformation at all times.

You would think that the federal government and the Department of Justice would have enough sense to understand what has been developed with these whistleblower laws. However, they are certainly very well constructed to assist law firms, the SEC and the DOJ and their attorneys. There is no balance at all for corporate America, their shareholders and even the government with their loss of tax revenues!

Where the Money is Going

We have discussed and will discuss further the major changes that have taken place in the U.S. justice system over the last several decades. They have been broad and far-reaching, resulting in processes that affect individuals as well as corporate entities. The significant changes have been very advantageous for the government, its prosecutors and even the law firms that represent the government's targets, namely the defense attorneys and public defenders.

Relative to American citizens, we need to note that the U.S. has approximately 25 percent of all the incarcerated prisoners in the world! However, we only have 5 percent of the world's population. Think of the annual legal fees expended in this monstrous incarceration process and the massive infrastructure build-out required to house this rapid addition of inmates. Today the Supreme Court is reviewing old congressional legislation that has placed many inmates in prison with sentences that are many times longer than should be allowed. This review is being forced by the First Step Act, which was President Trump's initiative. Prosecutorial bragging rights for obtaining excessively long sentences will be reduced considerably across the board with full enactment of the First Step Act.

With regard to American business, the Sally Yates Doctrine has basically brought the coupe de grace to any balance for corporate entities fighting corrupt whistle blowers, illegal short sellers and takeover attempts by opportunists. Once any "allegation" is made against a corporate entity, this Doctrine becomes applicable.

This Doctrine will be very intimidating to most public company directors – hopefully, a lot less after reading this book and the Black, Root and Rajaratnam books. Now, the Board may get advice from their outside law firm to support the Yates Doctrine because it will mean a significant revenue windfall for that law firm. It will mean an even larger revenue windfall for the firm doing the investigation. Incidentally, do not use a former prosecutor for the investigation. They will have too many corrupt investigatory habits and a strongly narcissistic personality!

You should understand how heavily the deck is stacked against the corporation and management once the Yates Doctrine is triggered. I believe that Sally Yates and the DOJ lawyers view corporate America as a money pit to be plundered primarily for the law firms. And, they have become very good at this unscrupulous process.

As mentioned earlier in the chapter, one of the key dictates of this Doctrine is that it tells the investigators not to focus on who has been accused of malfeasance, but rather focus on the top executives. That is called "targeting," and it is corrupt, as pointed out by Attorney General Robert Jackson in 1940. The Yates' Doctrine states, "That aim will result in recovering as much money as possible for the public fisc." Yes, primarily money for law firms and short sellers and much less for the government. The majority of the cash losses come from the shareholders, the employees, and surprisingly, the government.

If the executives have broken the law, they should be fined and incarcerated. However, what about the tens of thousands of shareholders who simply took some "risk" to make a "return" by buying some stock in an interesting company? What about the employees who joined the company because of the innovation and growth prospects? These are the real losers because of the dramatic stock depreciation and loss of jobs associated with allegations and the subsequent investigations and the illegal short selling.

Let us analyze the Yates Doctrine quote, "That aim will result in recovering as much money as possible for the public fisc." Her innuendo would be that the government would recover more in fines and penalties from indicting the top officers than from lesser managers. Let us review the numbers in the MiMedx case for a good perspective on where this money <u>really goes</u>. These numbers are certainly approximate!

MiMedx paid $1.5 million in fines to the SEC. I paid $1 million in fines to the government, and Bill paid $250,000. We also paid approximately $3.25 million to the SEC. That is a total of $6 million paid to the government. The company paid over $200 million in fees to over a dozen law firms and a few accounting firms. So is Yates looking out for the federal government or for large law firms, like King & Spalding, and large accounting firms?

Now, let us review in our case where the federal government really lost dramatically...that was with capital gains taxes and other related taxes. Over an eight-year period, the MiMedx stock went from approximately $0.50 per share to $18 per share. A tremendous amount of capital gains and ordinary gains taxes accrued over that period for over 15,000 shareholders. I would estimate that tax accrual could have been approximately $375 plus million. As the stock plummeted down to less than $1 per share, that tax accrual disappeared. Many shareholders would have sold after having losses, which further decreased future government tax revenues. Those losses would be carried forward and could have been another $100 plus million loss, which brings the total to possibly $475 million. Then, the fees paid to law and accounting firms turned MiMedx from a very profitable tax-paying business into one with huge losses! MiMedx would have paid over $25 million in income taxes for 2018 and beyond if the Audit Committee Chairman had not hired King & Spalding and accepted the Sally Yates Doctrine. That is a total loss of approximately $500 million for the federal government and an average of 3% of the gains for the states. Also, MiMedx was not profitable for five years after we left!

Now those government taxes lost from MiMedx and its shareholders were partially offset by taxes from the salaries and bonuses from the law and accounting firms resulting from the $200 million plus paid to them by MiMedx. Also, there were the taxes on the huge gains from the short sellers, which I assume were paid.

It just takes a little arithmetic and common sense to see what Yates did in her few years as deputy attorney general to assist our federal government with her Doctrine. In the MiMedx example, the government gained $6 million in penalties and <u>lost</u> perhaps $475 million in capital gains and ordinary income taxes from MiMedx shareholders and $25 million from MiMedx 2018 profits. Since the MiMedx stock went from approximately $18 per share to less than $1 per share from February to December 2018 because of terrible Board decisions, the government not only lost future cash from the accrued capital gains and ordinary gains, but built up a future loss of taxes because many shareholders sold their stock at a loss. The law and accounting firms gained over $200 million from their fees, which could have provided approximately $60 million in taxes for the government. All the short sellers could have made at least $200 million on their gains. This would result in approximately $40 million of federal taxes as a result of the short selling. Thus, the final result is a gain of approximately $106 million and a loss of $500 million for the government. So much for the Sally Yates Doctrine being a boost to federal income or the "public fisc" in the MiMedx case! I expect this phenomenon will occur in the majority of "corporate accusation" cases where the Yates Doctrine is utilized.

So how could Sally Yates ever think her Doctrine would be good for the federal government? While she may not have any business experience, certainly she or some member of the Justice Department staff could add and subtract the tax implications. Frankly, I believe it comes down to the old adage, "Lawyers do not create wealth…they rearrange it." The Sally Yates Doctrine is a huge gift to law firms at the expense of our public companies, who are the job creators and backbone of our economy, and our federal government's tax revenues. So her statement, "That will result in recovering as much money as possible…," must be referring to fees for law firms and accounting firms!

Possible Solutions

Finally, in today's public company environment, I think that only a few percent of the Boards are properly prepared to deal with the Sally Yates Doctrine. However, an attack utilizing the Doctrine will be more damaging to the small and medium sized businesses just due to the more limited assets that can be focused on all of the issues and due to the concentration of short sellers on these size businesses.

As an entrepreneur or business executive, a thorough review of your Board members' relative to their experience, self-confidence, risk aversion and attitudes toward governmental overreach is certainly in order. Then, a well-planned education program on how accusations develop and how they can be managed would be the second step. You will be surprised how out of balance the whistleblower laws and the deference to short sellers, illegal and legal, from the governmental agencies have become. After the Board's education, members should either be ready to support the company and its shareholders or consider retirement.

There are ways to properly educate employees to support their company with a compliance reporting system that will help preclude issues developing that could lead to "investigations" and devastating legal and possible accounting fees. These could result in the cutting of expenses elsewhere that result in layoffs of dedicated employees or in failure of the company. If you have the ability, please talk to your U.S. congressmen and senators about the very unbalanced nature of the whistleblower laws. I think real momentum is building relative to the U.S. having an epidemic of qui tam/whistleblower actions. The damage to shareholders and companies can be very disproportionate to the supposed violations and the fees collected by the government.

Chapter 14 Appendix

The Sally Yates Doctrine. Justice.gov.

Latham & Watkins (Sept. 27, 2022). USA Deputy Attorney General Monaco Announces Revised Policies on Corporate Crime. *White Collar Defense & Investigations Practice*, Client Alert Commentary Number 3013.

Professor Katrice Copeland. *The Yates Memo: Looking for Individual Accountability in All the Wrong Places.*

Howard Root. *Sally Yates's Legacy of Injustice at the Department of Justice.*

CHAPTER 15

PROTECTING SHORT SELLING

My termination from MiMedx and the terminations and departures of the other top 19 executives at the company were a direct result of alleged unlawful short selling that went unchecked by the U.S. regulatory agencies, namely the Securities and Exchange Commission and the Department of Justice. MiMedx provided substantial information about the unlawful short selling of our stock to the SEC, but to my knowledge there was never any action taken. In addition, two of our other corporate executives and I had a meeting at the DOJ offices in New York where we were told by three of their <u>investigators</u> that they had substantial information on Marc Cohodes that indicated securities law violations and money laundering. Again, as far as I know today, there has never been any action taken as a result of those investigations.

Without any regulatory action, it became possible for Cohodes to intimidate Ernst & Young to the point that they stopped our 2017 audit in February just two weeks before it was due. Subsequently, Cohodes sent a congratulatory email to Andy Brock at EY in December 2018, which thanked him for saving EY supposedly from his wrath if they had finished our audit and not allowed our stock to drop below $1.00 per share. Also, recall that EY pressured the MiMedx Audit Committee with claims that they had not done a thorough job a year prior when investigating a whistleblower allegation of channel stuffing. That allegation, which was <u>ridiculous</u>, nonetheless threw the Audit Committee Chairman, Terry Dewberry, into a state of paranoia. From that point forward, the Audit Committee's actions and those of the Board were out of control resulting in disastrous results for the company, its shareholders, employees and executives. However, this action probably resulted in Cohodes making over $50 million in short sale profits!

Concealed Government Policy

Let me remind you of the excellent discussions and specific details in our recommended books of how certain Wall Street organizations and federal government departments work together and keep unlawful short selling as a major tool for Wall Street wealth creation.

Now, I wll present four cases that happened at MiMedx to document the partnership between the government agencies and the short sellers who engage in unlawful means to short publicly traded corporate entities. I will give several examples of activities that clearly show this unspoken and concealed policy of protecting unlawful short sellers to the detriment of public companies, their shareholders and the government.

Case 1

One of the first directives that Paul Murphy of King & Spalding gave to the MiMedx Board was to have management remove the section on the company's website that countered the important Cohodes allegations. Management had established this, with a section of the website entitled "Short Selling Commentary" in order to provide proof countering Cohodes's allegations. We only placed information on the site that alleged a violation of Federal regulations or laws. Cohodes' <u>numerous</u> other published personal insults and misinformation were generally not posted and were ignored.

Once the company developed this section for our website, our stock price began to retrace the drop that had occurred when Cohodes began to make his allegations. This commentary was the only information our shareholders had that refuted and corrected all of these allegations. By the end of January of 2018, our stock was back up in the $18 range from the low of approximately $12.

In April 2018 when Charlie Evans, acting as lead director, told me that King & Spalding wanted the Cohodes section removed, I asked him for the reason. He said they did not give one; they just wanted it taken off the website. I told him to get a rational answer because taking it down would be very detrimental to the company's ability to respond to the false allegations. I said that, if there were statements on the website that were incorrect, then any legal ramifications of that were already in the market. So, if there was a mistake, there was nothing we could do about it, even if we took the rebuttals of Cohodes allegations off our website.

I also stated that I did not want Cohodes declaring a victory and pushing our stock price down further just because King & Spalding thought there might be "some legal risk." After about another week, Evans came back with the demand that the website <u>must</u> be taken down. Again, I asked for the reason. Evans said that King & Spalding did not give a reason, but they wanted it taken down, and if we refused, they told the Board that executive management should be fired!

My first thought was, "They are allowing Murphy to run this company?" I said to Evans, "Well, there is something going on here that I believe is wrong and could be very detrimental to the company." I hoped that the Board would have enough business sense to demand an explanation. Perhaps an explanation was given, but if so, King & Spalding advised the Board not to tell me knowing I would have created havock by exposing this behavior, as it protects unlawful short sellers.

Now, after all this time has passed, I believe I know the reason why King & Spalding wanted to remove the points we were making relative to Cohodes allegations. I BELIEVE THAT THERE IS AN UNSPOKEN POLICY AT THE SEC AND DOJ THAT PROTECTS SHORT SELLERS, EVEN THOUGH THESE AGENCIES KNOW THAT MANY OF THESE GROUPS ARE VIOLATING FEDERAL LAWS AND REGULATIONS. This behavior is allowed because the SEC and DOJ believe that unlawful short sellers bring them information with which they can open investigations. Without unlawful short sellers making unverified and inaccurate allegations, many investigations would never be initiated. The same goes for whistleblowers making allegations, whether the allegations are true or false.

Thus, these two groups, unlawful short sellers and whistleblowers, are viewed by the DOJ and SEC regulators as catalysts for the goals that they wish to achieve, both personally and otherwise.

Unfortunately, many of those goals are driven by ambitious attorneys at these agencies who are looking for that one white-collar crime lawsuit that will create interest in their resume from some large law firm. That case, whether won or lost, will be their ticket out of the federal government's employment to a large law firm with all the future possibilities of becoming a partner with large salaries and partner payouts. This "concealed policy" by these federal agencies is extremely destructive to our capital markets, American public companies and their shareholders.

The goal of protecting the flow of information from dishonest whistleblowers and short sellers can be easily achieved in a manner that does not allow the government to "look the other way" when illegal acts are taking place, federal laws are being broken, and public company shareholders are being devastated.

These government agencies could simply pay unlawful short sellers a "whistleblower fee," which could be paid once a case is tried and convictions take place. The fee may even be in the multi-million dollar range. However, most short sellers, when they attack a company like MiMedx, will have returns in the hundreds of millions of dollars. Therefore, unlawful short sellers want the system to remain exactly as it is.

Without any reasoning for the company to remove the Cohodes section from our website, I believe that the King and Spalding directive is another example of the government attempting to protect short sellers. I believe this directive could have come from Sally Yates advising Murphy or from his communications with the SDNY prosecutors.

Case 2

On January 3, 2018, I wrote a letter to Jay Clayton, who was the Commissioner at the SEC. See the Chapter 11 Appendix. A notebook with a substantial amount of trading information and details on the unlawful short selling that had transpired in the MiMedx stock during the fall of 2017 was included with the letter. This information came from our contract with ShareIntel. The participants were delineated, and the "Front Running" that went on around the release of the printed accusations and lies was apparent.

When I received absolutely no response from the Commissioner, I asked our junior senator at the time, David Perdue, to follow-up. Senator Perdue was on the Senate Banking Committee, which has oversight over the SEC. Senator Perdue had previously been the CEO of Dollar General and Reebok which gave him substantial knowledge about these SEC issues. He told me he should be able to get a quick response because these were very straightforward and well-documented questions. Well, the Senator had to admit after a couple of weeks that he had never been treated this way by the SEC staff in that he was getting the "runaround." In spite of his reputation and respected presence, Senator Perdue obtained no response from the Commission.

This is a clear indicator to me that there is a hidden relationship between the regulators and certain short sellers, and they do not want to disrupt what they perceive as a flow of useful information to them. This is occurring, despite the very damaging nature of their partnership with individuals who routinely break federal laws and regulations.

Case 3

Another good example occurred in late 2017 when we were invited to visit with three DOJ investigators at the Southern District of New York to discuss

Cohodes' activities. As previously mentioned, these three investigators began by telling us that they had not been given much credit for the work they had accomplished in discovering Cohodes' previous fraud. It sounded as though they were referring to their superiors or perhaps the DOJ prosecutors. We were told by Kirk Hafer, Criminal Investigator of the Securities and Commodities Fraud Unit, that he wanted us to send him all the pertinent data and information on Cohodes' actions against MiMedx that were possibly unlawful.

As discussed in an earlier chapter, when we extracted that information from our website, we were told shortly thereafter by David Rody, one of the Sidley attorneys, not to send it. Rody claimed that he had a conversation with Assistant U. S. Attorney (AUSA) Brendan Quigley, with whom he had previously worked at the SDNY, about this matter. He claimed that Quigley told him that he did not want the information sent. When I asked for the reason. Rody stated that Quigley was responsible for the investigation, but he admitted within a few minutes that was actually not the case. As my questioning continued, Rody's answers became disjointed and juvenile! I could tell he was not telling the truth, but I did not understand his motive at that time.

If you remember, I later asked my personal attorney to check with AUSA Quigley and Rody to clarify that directive. Quigley's response came back immediately, in writing, basically stating that he never had such a conversation with Rody. It could be that Rody was reacting to an instruction given by King & Spalding to protect Cohodes, or that Quigley actually gave that directive in order to protect Cohodes. Quigley could have been the prosecutor who refused to take action on the DOJ investigators' findings, as described by Kirk Hafer. Regardless of who was directing or lying in this case, this is another indication of federal prosecutors protecting a short seller.

As I have already speculated, what may have happened was that King & Spalding gave our Board of Directors a mandate that would keep accusations of unlawful short selling minimized. I believe Sally Yates was advising Paul Murphy relative to the DOJ's secret policy of protecting short sellers. I do not know how this was discussed at Board meetings as I was not present when the investigation was discussed, but I certainly would not have tolerated any direct discussions or innuendo relative to the government's unspoken policy of protecting short sellers. I would have exposed this corruption.

Case 4

On the advice of the MiMedx attorney in Washington, Marlon Paz, who was a former SEC attorney, our major shareholders filed numerous official complaint forms with the SEC reporting various illegal short selling activities. To my knowledge, I do not think there was a response to any of these complaints. In effect, all communications from these subsequent filings by our large shareholders went unanswered. In addition, I spent some time communicating with FINRA, who regulates all the capital markets as well as NASDAQ who is responsible for FINRA. I never obtained any meaningful communication from either of those parties.

I have come to the rather simple conclusion that, in today's system, the "deck is stacked" against entrepreneurs and public company business executives, primarily because the SEC and DOJ protect short sellers, both legal and illegal, and whistleblowers, both honest and dishonest. They are protected because they bring information that can be used to start an inquiry or investigation, which is relished by the AUSAs and other attorneys for promotion of their future careers. However, this information can be obtained without protecting corrupt people who are conducting illegal actions by paying reasonable fees for their information upon a conviction, but <u>not allowing</u> unlawful short selling to continue to take place or a whistleblower to lie to prosecutors without repercussions.

However, I believe that, when this is called out in the right way by congressional committees, this matter should correct itself because these two federal agencies are doing something they know they should <u>not</u> be doing by allowing blatant illegal short selling to take place in this country. Solving the aligned problem of "Fails to Deliver" for "Naked" short selling is going to be more complex, and that will require competent and zealous leadership.

The key is for the SEC and the DOJ to <u>stop protecting</u> illegal short sellers who create "Naked" short sales and conduct other illegal activities associated with "Short and Distort" campaigns. Also, these agencies need to "clean house" and hold their attorneys accountable for malfeasance with dismissals and even incarcerations. I know the Bureau of Prisons has cells comfortable enough to fit former government attorneys!

King & Spalding Politics

There is an interesting comparison between Paul Murphy completing the MiMedx investigation in May 2019 and moving to a top position at the FBI, and the same thing happening with Christopher Wray, the FBI's current Director who made the same type of career move. I was told that when Wray was an attorney with King & Spalding in Atlanta, he was given the assignment of conducting an investigation into a major Fortune 50 technology company. Wray also brought in KPMG, and they conducted a lengthy and very expensive investigation. I was told recently that when Wray completed that investigation, which was not well received by the Board of Directors, he immediately left King & Spalding to become the Director of the FBI. Murphy did the same when he became the Chief of Staff to Wray at the FBI immediately after completing the MiMedx investigation. It seems there is a pattern at King & Spalding that, when you develop a huge cash "home run" for the law firm, someone in Washington offers you a prestigious position. Of course, they can return to King & Spalding when the timing is right. I do not think these are random events because there have been too many examples! Incidentally, Murphy replaced Zack Harmon, who also returned to King & Spalding.

It would seem appropriate for the head of the most important law enforcement agency in this country, the FBI, to come up through the ranks. Thus, they would have a full grasp of most aspects of the agency, and this person would more than likely be a person of courage and fortitude with the necessary leadership skills. However, we have recently had a series of risk-averse lawyers, who are on a political trip rather than a law enforcement trip, fill top management positions at this agency.

Congress and our Executive Branch need to exert leadership to resolve these matters. If they are not resolved, no company should go public and be subjected to this unfair, unreasonable and disastrous environment.

CHAPTER 16

MIMEDX IS A POSTER CHILD

Unfortunately, MiMedx has become the Poster Child for the numerous abuses and imbalances that now take place in our capital markets. The majority of these problems are the result of illegal short selling, "Naked" short selling with the "Failure to Deliver" shorted shares, abuse of the whistleblower system, the significant changes in public company management and Board responsibilities as a result of the Sally Yates Doctrine and the self-serving behavior of many public prosecutors resulting in the corruption of our justice system. THESE MATTERS HAVE BECOME SO OUT OF CONTROL AND ABUSED THAT MOST ENTREPRENEURS AND THEIR BOARDS WILL DECIDE THAT THEY SHOULD NEVER TAKE THEIR ENTERPRISE TO THE PUBLIC MARKET. That is not an outcome that would be beneficial either to America, in general, or to our capital markets specifically.

There are disclosures in this chapter that will be somewhat repetitive from earlier chapters. However, I felt that is necessary in order for you to have a good comprehension of several significant issues before reading the final chapters of the book.

Over the past 15 years, a substantial amount of time, effort and money have been invested in trying to correct some of these out of balance processes and procedures. Papers have been published, books written, advocacy and congressional hearings held as well as their related meetings with the SEC and DOJ. While there is general acknowledgement of these numerous issues, it will usually take a Poster Child with a story that is absolutely intriguing before focused leadership can make meaningful change.

Most people are aware of what happened to Kate Steinle, the 32-year-old woman who was shot and killed in San Francisco as she walked along the pier with her father. The alleged shooter was an illegal immigrant who had been deported five times and had seven felony convictions. Prior to the murder of Kate, there had been several initiatives attempting to increase the penalties that could be imposed on criminal aliens convicted of illegal re-entry into the country, which would deter and discourage their attempts to return. Not until Kate became the Poster Child for the risk associated with ignoring existing laws and policies did serious movement towards passing a bill through Congress become a possibility. The Poster Child motivation can be the catalyst for meaningful change, particularly when legislation is involved or significant congressional action and review are required.

History

MiMedx Group went from a near-bankrupt biotechnology company in 2009 to the fifth fastest-growing public company in America by 2017, according to *Fortune* magazine. The company grew from approximately 15 employees to a peak of over 1,000 employees. High paying quality jobs for doctors and other clinicians, scientists, information technologists, engineers, sales personnel, production personnel and significantly-sized accounting and legal departments were the result of the growth of this company. This progress took place because a proven entrepreneurial executive stepped into the company in 2009 with capital and specific business experience that would allow this transition to take place.

MiMedx was a unique success story of entrepreneurship and very hard work by about 20 executives who covered all aspects of the company's management needs. However, bad things orchestrated by corrupt outsiders began to happen to the company, and they brought all the successes of MiMedx to a halt. In addition, the related "strike suits," with cooperation from the short seller's legal cabal, attacked the company with numerous shareholder and derivative lawsuits as a result of the stock price declining.

MiMedx suffered almost every negative act a public company could suffer. The remainder of the story will be accurately laid out in subsequent chapters. In the process, we will highlight all the alleged illegal and corrupt activities that took place as well as where our federal regulators, particularly at the SEC and DOJ, "looked the other way" on many issues because some of those alleged illegal activities by short sellers benefited their legal staff.

It is our goal in subsequent chapters to outline "the good, the bad and the ugly" relative to all these issues. I will present information that is truthful and fact-based. In some cases, however, I was not privy to all the specifics. I have only been able to review the results. However, they are very definitive in terms of the causal factors.

As an entrepreneur of almost 50 years, I thought there was not much that I had not seen, experienced or studied in terms of business, and specifically, in the area of healthcare. MiMedx suffered the "perfect storm" in terms of attacks, and I believe the totality of these matters could stimulate some action by our Congress and our Executive Branch to resolve many of these issues. I certainly believe it is in the interest of our capital markets and our country to <u>not</u> subject public companies to these corrupt activities without regulatory oversight and rapid response.

The issues that will again be discussed include illegal short selling, which includes "Naked" short selling and the "Fails to Deliver" (FTDs) with stock lending/borrowing and also the abuses of the whistleblower laws. We have already explained the Sally Yates Doctrine and what that means to executives, investors and Boards. These laws and regulations support unbalanced processes in favor of unscrupulous government employees and self-serving prosecutorial attorneys and law firms.

Today, illegal short selling has grown to embody many sophisticated techniques to include the dissemination of false and misleading information, to the actual manipulation of minute-by-minute trading, and to the lack of proper closure of the short selling activity with FTDs. We have alleged that the broad and sophisticated attack that took place on MiMedx Group embodied about every dishonest practice available.

From a business standpoint, MiMedx had built an excellent asset base, which was producing strong revenue growth, good profits and cash flow. Ordinarily, a company of this nature would not be the subject of a short sale attack. However, after allegations against the company made by sales personnel who were terminated for cause were publicized by their attorney, these former employees began to communicate with the short sellers. They were consummate liars, and the stories they created for the short sellers were often not even plausible. The short sellers began connecting with a few of our other sales employees who had also been terminated for cause, and together they all manufactured a series of false and diabolically negative stories about the company.

This happened about the time the first major short seller of our stock, Deerfield Management, had amassed a loss of probably $50 million by having shorted our stock beginning in 2012. We were told that, in the summer of 2017, Deerfield was looking for other hedge funds and individuals around the country with whom to partner to conduct a concerted short sell attack against MiMedx so that they could recover their losses.

Illegal short selling can develop in a number of ways. One is "Front Running." When this occurs, the illegal short sellers organize and coordinate false and misleading publications and then begin trading on the day of the publication in a coordinated fashion. This is against the law. It is like passing on inside information to someone, which is what happens when the cabal knows there will be a negative publication on a certain date. They preposition their trades, enter the market on that date and use illegal trading techniques to push the stock down. Then, they will tout the accuracy of their false publication by using the declining stock price as proof. The use of the stock price decline to increase their credibility is one of their key coordination activities.

These <u>illegal</u> short selling attacks are quite visible in terms of the daily trading activity and failure to close certain short sales, which turns them into "Naked" short sales. This in itself is <u>illegal</u>. These are called "Fails to Deliver" and are caused by the inadequate stock lending/borrowing rules of the SEC. The SEC seems incapable of correcting this very serious problem. Also, there will be unusual activity in the trading of stock option puts and calls prior to and on the attack day.

This brings me to one key matter that I believe must be corrected. As I have previously stated, I believe I can guarantee that there is an "informal and unspoken policy" at the SEC and the DOJ that they do not "bother" illegal short sellers. I believe this philosophy has come about because these agencies have found that illegal short sellers bring them information that could be actionable. In other words, I believe these short sellers highlight actions from corporate entities that could possibly be investigated. I am certain that is exactly the case. However, many of the short sellers are corrupt, and they will create all types of accusations and innuendo. My experience is that the majority of these allegations will be misinformation and lies.

Now you should question why federal regulators and attorneys would not recognize the fraudulent nature of that type of misinformation and take appropriate action. Well, both the Securities and Exchange Commission and the Department of Justice have young and ambitious attorneys who are working towards furthering their positions within those agencies or having a white-collar crime case that will enhance their resume resulting in their being hired by a large law firm or business. In fact, you can generally trace the departure of these young assistant U.S. attorneys (AUSAs) from the federal agencies after successfully filing, and perhaps, winning such a case.

This simply means that there is strong personal motivation for the investigation and the filing of white-collar crime cases. Of course, that means there are also political and other related motivations by AUSAs to seek and pursue cases with weak or no real evidence of merit.

A rather obvious way to resolve one of the issues of illegal short sellers bringing welcomed information to these agencies is to simply pay them a "whistleblower fee." Whistleblowers are paid up to 30 percent of the amount of the funds the government retrieves from the legal actions that are filed as a result of a their disclosures. There is no reason that illegal short sellers should be paid any more than that; this alone could amount to several million dollars. However, to allow illegal short sellers to continue to conduct unlawful activities to push stock prices down, which will often result in their making hundreds of millions of dollars of profits, as happened with MiMedx, is very unfair and unreasonable. This is particularly the case since those profits come from the losses of the tens of thousands of shareholders of these companies and the related government losses from federal capital gains taxes and state taxes.

The Sally Yates Doctrine has significantly changed the manner in which companies, particularly public companies, have to investigate allegations. Yates was an attorney at King & Spalding in Atlanta, which is one of the largest law firms in the country. She went on to become an AUSA and prosecutor and federal judge. And, in 2014, she went to Washington, D.C. after she was appointed U.S. Deputy Attorney General. During her short tenure in Washington, she developed this Doctrine, which has had a significant effect on corporate investigations. In accordance with the Sally Yates Doctrine, the MiMedx Board would have been advised that it had to retain large law and accounting firms to "target" and investigate executive management regarding false allegations brought by dishonest employees who were terminated for violating their non-compete agreements and by short sellers acting in their self interest.

MiMedx paid King & Spalding, Yates' former and now current law firm, approximately $25 million for a 15-month investigation, supposedly of Cohodes' allegations. However, those issues were not investigated. Instead, the company executives were "targeted" as required by the Yates Doctrine. In addition, MiMedx spent close to $200 million on other law and accounting firms to support this investigation and new audits.

King & Spalding eventually found some emails and a letter that was written in 2015 that they alleged showed executive management knowingly made comments to several distributors that they claimed modified the written contracts; therefore, they caused a revenue recognition issue in these specific quarters. However, the MiMedx distributor contracts had specific language stating that the contracts could not be modified without written agreement by both parties. Our initial General Counsel, Roberta McCaw, drafted these contracts and advised Bill Taylor and me that it would be very difficult to legally modify these contracts with outside verbal and written comments. Roberta McCaw is a CPA and lawyer, and she served our previous companies for about 15 years before retiring while at MiMedx.

When a corporate entity invites experienced prosecutors in to do an investigation, they will get the worst of all worlds. Career prosecutors, as a general rule, have never functioned in the world of business. They have never had business responsibilities. They have neither built nor run businesses. They have never really hired and fired numerous employees. They have never developed business plans and been successful in their implementation. Then, they arrive at the company with an attitude fostered by the Yates Doctrine that, "Executives have done something wrong, and I am here to find it."

The Sally Yates Doctrine requires that an investigation focus from the start on top management. I believe one reason for this is that Yates concluded that larger financial settlements, and particularly legal fees, will occur if top management can be accused of malfeasance. With prosecutors going through company records, what are the chances that nothing will be found that could be twisted into an act that violates company policy, accounting policy or federal regulations or laws? It was really surprising to see the extent to which straightforward emails with distributors on business philosophy were turned into a change in our business procedures that might have modified the written agreements with the distributors. Of course, if those agreements were modified, then one could accuse the company of misstating revenues for that particular distributor over a certain period of time unless the company had booked sufficient "sales returns and allowances" reserves to cover such contingencies. The company did exactly that, but it was ignored.

On February 6th, Ernst & Young's audit partner, Andy Brock, told us that EY would not be able to finish our audit, which was due in two weeks, until the company formally investigated all of Cohodes' current allegations. Of course, the company had already investigated some of these allegations because they were initially made by the employees we terminated for breach of their non-compete contracts with the company. Also, EY accused our Audit Committee of not conducting a thorough investigation of those allegations. I viewed the EY "opinion" as absolutely ridiculous as did some of the other Board members. However, this situation sent a shockwave through the Audit Committee. The Chairman of the Audit Committee, Terry Dewberry, became quite paranoid about his being accused of not conducting an adequate investigation. Thus, Dewberry went into a CYA mode to the detriment of the company, which caused the majority of the subsequent devastation.

I made my recommendations to the Board as to what I thought the company should do to resolve these matters. However, as Chairman of the Audit Committee, Dewberry decided to conduct the investigation, which was driven by his paranoia and CYA motives, and that was the start of all the difficulties the company has endured for the last almost six years. Incidentally, the board should not have allowed Dewberry to manage the investigation because E&Y had accused him of not conducting a proper investigation a year earlier.

A DOJ Inquiry from the D.C. Office

It would be informative to put into perspective the difference in a normal DOJ inquiry into a company's business practices that is triggered by a whistleblower from a qui tam action versus a Sally Yates Doctrine "targeted" investigation driven by numerous other issues, such as politics, vendettas, illegal short selling and corporate opportunists. MiMedx had such a "normal" inquiry in 2016 that resulted from a qui tam action filed by an executive from one of our primary competitors, Organogenesis.

As I recall, in early 2016 we initially received from the Washington, D.C. DOJ office, a notice of the inquiry and a request for documents. I believe we eventually sent over 100,000 documents to the DOJ office. After a few months, our General Counsel, Lexi Haden, and I were asked to come to the D.C. office to answer questions. As the questions unfolded, I could tell that the qui tam action had been filed by one of our competitors. I suspected Organogenesis as they had tried to slow our progress in 2013 by corrupt initiatives, which they orchestrated through the FDA and the VA.

Because of our documentation and straightforward answers, it did not take long for the DOJ D.C. staff to see through the allegations. Therefore, the DOJ refused to join the qui tam lawsuit. When this happens, the whistleblower generally drops the lawsuit, which is what happened in our Organogenesis case. There is generally "due process" of the law in this type of case as the accused gets to answer the accusations. As you will read later, that due process was absent in the King & Spalding investigation and accusations against Bill and me. This is another issue that develops because of the Sally Yates Doctrine.

In the 2013 Organogenesis FDA initiative, their CEO managed to get a meeting with the top four executives who reported to Dr. Margaret Hamburg, the FDA Chief. After the FDA sent us an "untitled letter" saying they believed our micronized product was overly manipulated, I requested and finally received through a Freedom of Information Act (FOIA) request the discussion materials for that meeting. After reading the details of that meeting, I decided to repudiate the FDA's assertion. I knew Organogenesis was on a campaign to damage us because of all our successes so we laid out a strategy to "call out" the issues. The Organogenesis products were clinically inferior to ours and not as cost effective. Our revenues were surpassing theirs, and at that point, we had a 100 percent revenue growth rate.

While Organogenesis was asking the FDA to classify all our products as basically "bandages" with no clinical efficacy, which was ridiculous, the FDA did give in on our micronized product by calling it "over-manipulated" from the crushing process. That was a real stretch relative to the FDA's regulations. While our micronized product was a little more complex regulation-wise than our sheet product, that should not have been an issue.

Once I obtained the FOIA documents, it put the FDA in an awkward position. We began calling the agency's decision unreasonable, and I demanded meetings. Those initial meetings were typical FDA meetings designed to delay and frustrate. After those meetings with us, the FDA called an industry-wide meeting to obtain more support, but that backfired. About that time, the FDA was blessed with a new chief, Dr. Robert Califf, who was a strong leader with common sense. We made contact, and he came to a very logical conclusion with which we did not argue. His solution allowed anyone producing a micronized version of an amniotic membrane to leave their product in the market for three years, but they would be required to complete an FDA clinical trial for "FDA Approval" to be in the market after that date. Well, we were way ahead of all our competitors with our clinical trials at that point. We had about 30 clinical studies ongoing so we just refocused our efforts toward the FDA approvals.

The Investigation

It should be quite enlightening as you continue to read this book, how lies and false accusations caused unnecessary actions by an inexperienced Board who placed their own interests above those of the shareholders. The majority of our Board was intimidated into spending over $200 million on large law and accounting firms, terminating approximately 24 percent of the workforce, or 240 employees, and dismissing 20 of the top 21 managers who built the company into the fifth fastest-growing public company in America. Of course, our shareholders suffered stock losses in 2018 from $18 a share (approximately a $2 billion valuation) to below $1 per share (approximately a $100 million valuation) as a result of the decisions of our first Board of Directors.

As frustrated as I have become with the terrible and destructive decisions that the MiMedx Board of Directors made, I will have to say that, when it comes to governmental interactions, most Boards may succumb to those intimidation factors. The Sally Yates Doctrine has made it very difficult for Boards and their managing executives to work together on solutions that can potentially clear up accusations in an optimal fashion, which would be in the best financial interests of the shareholders <u>and</u> the government. The Board may quickly decide that sacrificing its executive officers, no matter how efficient and productive they may have been, is the easiest way to lift the burdens. Often, it is <u>not</u> <u>the</u> <u>right</u> <u>way</u>, but inexperienced Boards that do not have the courage of their convictions may take the <u>easy</u> <u>way</u>, which will also sacrifice their shareholders, thanks to the Yates Doctrine.

Also, a key point is that regulators have the ability to charge companies in numerous ways. In some cases, that could result in the company losing their ability to develop revenues or other important financial incentives. In healthcare, they could lose reimbursement from CMS for Medicare and Medicaid patients. Changes such as these could force a company into bankruptcy. Therefore, management may be sacrificed rather than have the company come under attack. Often, this easy solution is the most destructive to the shareholders.

The Yates Doctrine essentially requires a company to spend huge sums of money on law and accounting firms to conduct an investigation and then pass that work on to the government and their prosecutors. Hiring an investigative law firm will almost always result in the development of some type of culpability. However, as I previously mentioned, I learned of an investigation of a Fortune 50 public company conducted by King & Spalding in which the company's Board pushed back and took strong issue with validity of the findings from the investigation.

In the 1860s, it took a significant "Poster Child," namely the Erie Railroad, and its trading scandals to motivate Congress into making sweeping changes in the laws associated with the trading of public company stocks. Daniel Drew and his associates had privately printed large numbers of counterfeit shares to sell in order to keep Cornelius Vanderbilt from acquiring the railroad. Vanderbilt figured out what had transpired, and he managed to convince a New York judge to file an injunction stopping the illegal activity. This eventually encouraged major changes by Congress in the regulations and laws associated with publicly trading stock.

At some point, I hope that the MiMedx story will be fully vetted to certain congressional committees in Washington. The company has endured almost every bad process and procedure that is embedded in certain laws and regulations with their misuse by government officials.

It is my hope that the MiMedx Group saga can also have the impact of the Erie Railroad type of change related to illegal short selling, "Naked" short selling, "Failure to Deliver," false whistleblower accusations, overzealous AUSAs filing cases to promote themselves and companies being forced to use the Sally Yates Doctrine to deal with any allegations.

Think of the impact that this book plus all the others I have mentioned might have when "piled" on top of a congressman's desk!

The Story

I wish there were not as many negative aspects to the MiMedx story. However, the advantage is that this story encompasses the vast majority of the corruption that feeds major abuses to our financial markets. While some of these issues are caused by illegal behavior, others are caused by individuals taking advantage of the shortcomings in our systems to perpetuate shameful, self-serving acts. Either way, the current system is going to continue to discourage entrepreneurs and their companies from taking the "Public Company" route for growth.

I implore everyone to understand clearly the issues that I have delineated and are highlighted in these other books and to become an advocate for the necessary changes needed at our regulatory agencies to no longer protect and shelter illegal short selling activities and whistleblowers who lie to federal officials.

After the publication of this book, I will communicate through my website "PetePetit.com," ways that individuals can focus their efforts to see that changes at our federal agencies are being considered and quickly implemented.

CHAPTER 17

OPPORTUNISTS

I define "opportunists" as individuals or businesses that can be a major detriment or positive opportunity for a business. While opportunists can cause harmful issues with mature businesses, the entrepreneurial stage businesses are particularly vulnerable. I will discuss negative opportunists more than the positive ones! Most business executives and entrepreneurs can adequately "size up" opportunists who bring possible positive actions such as financings.

Some of the more famous business opportunists that you have certainly heard of are Carl Icahn and Nelson Peltz. They are sophisticated "corporate raiders" who know what they are doing, and they are very good at it.

Most opportunists are going to be more risk averse than you are as an entrepreneur so they will look for the maturing of your business to the point where they think they can run it better than you! In some cases, prior to their opportunistic motives surfacing, they could be business friends or enemies. The key is for you, as an entrepreneur who is taking all the front-end personal and financial risks required to develop the business, to <u>not</u> be naive about opportunists who are basically <u>predators</u>.

I will discuss some of the opportunists that we encountered during my almost 50 years of entrepreneurship and the lessons we learned. They showed up with various constituents ranging from individuals, to businesses to internal sources.

The Range of Opportunists

The first real opportunist that Healthdyne encountered was an individual by the name of Charles Hurwitz. He was known as the "Redwood Raider" because of a takeover he accomplished with regard to some redwood lumber companies in California. How he developed an interest in Healthdyne he never would explain to me. However, once our stock had a downturn in 1984, I received a phone call from Hurwitz. He was very straightforward. He said he did not know much about our business other than he felt that it was very undervalued. He wanted me to come to Houston and meet with him to discuss what I was going to do to increase shareholder value.

When I met with Hurwitz in Houston, I found him to be very direct and pragmatic. I explained why we had our downturn, what we were doing to correct the issues, and I gave him a timetable for those corrections. Fortunately, we stayed on our timetable and achieved everything I told him we would. From time to time, he would send one of his accountants to visit with us, but the accountant really contributed very little as he was an irritating personality. After about a year and a half, I received a call from Hurwitz saying that he had exited our stock and wanted to thank me very much for giving him a several hundred percent return on his investment. He was very pleased with how things had played out, and he wished us the very best.

My second encounter with an outside opportunist came in 1988. We had heard rumors that Continental Health Affiliates from New Jersey was buying our stock. We did our research and found out that Continental was not a very successful business, and they certainly were stretching matters to try to acquire Healthdyne. Also, there were skeletons in the closet of Continental's CEO and founder, Jack Rosen! But, that did not seem to deter him.

I received a telephone call from Rosen on August 4th, my birthday. He explained that he had an interest in acquiring Healthdyne, and he had the bank financing arranged in order to do it. He explained that I should come to his corporate headquarters and visit with him.

By the time I left for Continental's offices, I had gathered a substantial amount of information about Rosen personally as well as professionally. My visit consisted of spending time with him looking at a letter he had received from Bank Paribas in Paris, France committing to loan Continental the amount of money necessary to acquire Healthdyne at $6 per share. I knew that price would be insufficient, and I told him so. He said, well then, we might have to get into an unfriendly situation. I told him he had to do what he thought he could to be successful, but I explained to him that we were very experienced and would not settle for an inadequate offer. With that, the meeting was over, and I went back to the Newark airport and flew home.

As I recall, Rosen sent us a "Bear Hug Letter," which made his offer public. Our Board met and came to the same conclusion that I had relative to the offer being too low. Of course, we first obtained a "fairness opinion" from our investment bankers. We publicized our decision. Rosen made some other feeble attempts to coerce our Board, all of which were unsuccessful. Finally, he called me on July 3,

1989, to say that he was selling their stock. By that point, Healthdyne was beginning to perform smoothly, and growth was returning again.

Of course, Healthdyne played an opportunist role when we engaged in the unfriendly tender offer for Narco Scientific in 1982. In my opinion, we had the right motives in terms of concerns for their shareholders as well as our own and for the employee groups at their various subsidiary companies. However, I am sure Rudy Garfield, the founder of Narco Scientific, always felt that we were "intruders."

I would like to put into the opportunist category another group of individuals who are called "strike suit" attorneys. Strike suits have become quite a racket in the U.S. capital markets, and they are perpetrated by attorneys and law firms that are the supposed watchdogs over companies whose stock has decreased in value.

A strike suit is a lawsuit brought by a plaintiff who wants to make quick money by filing charges without regard to their truth so that the defendant will simply settle the case to avoid going to trial, even if the claims are baseless. The settlement often costs less than the legal fees for the defendant. I have had a number of experiences with strike suits and have noted the way their tactics have changed over the decades.

We had two strike suits filed against us, one at Healthdyne and the second one at Matria Healthcare. In both cases, we filed for summary judgments with the federal judge, and in both cases, the suits were dismissed. When the same thing happened to MiMedx in 2013, the case should have been dismissed. However, our attorneys told me that the federal judge in the case allowed his legal clerk to answer, and she had no idea what she was doing. She made some comments in her answer that were so far out of the norm that it was ridiculous. Either way, she refused to provide us a summary judgment or dismiss the case. Thus, we had to go through a mediation hearing in New York.

This particular lawsuit came about in early September 2013. As you will recall, the FDA sent us an "untitled letter" stating that they believed our micronized allograft product was over-manipulated; therefore, the product did not meet the criteria to be marketed under Section 361 of the Public Health Act. In addition, they placed that letter on their website within about 24 hours of our receiving the letter. Normally, that would have taken about three to four weeks.

I was suspect of the untitled letter at the start. As I gathered information that day, I became more suspicious. The FDA had given us a planned inspection visit and reviewed all the related information about ten months prior to our receiving the untitled letter. Earlier in the summer of 2013, we had caught Organogenesis, an arch competitor, attempting to manipulate the Veterans Administration into classifying our products as "controlled substances." We called that out immediately and discovered that Organogenesis had an interaction with VA staff on that matter. As a result, we received a letter of apology from the Veterans Administration. So, I suspected that Organogenesis had also attempted to influence the FDA to send us this untitled letter. When we later obtained the Freedom of Information documents from the FDA, we found that there had been significant interaction between FDA executive staff and Organogenesis' CEO and law firm trying to convince them that our product line, in particular the micronized product, was not meeting the proper regulatory standards.

I advised our Washington regulatory counsel that my concern was that this act was improperly motivated, and consequently, the facts had been misrepresented somewhere. Again, that is exactly what occurred.

Either way, because the FDA somehow took a very aggressive posture of posting our letter immediately on their website, I knew they were trying to damage MiMedx. Our stock dropped about 70 percent in one day. But, it essentially recovered within the next couple of months. However, the strike lawsuits were filed stating that management knew this was going to happen and had misrepresented the regulatory status of the product to shareholders. Of course, that was false, as are most strike suit allegations.

As previously mentioned, since we did not get the case dismissed as we had with our previous strike suit cases, we had to go through a mediation hearing in New York. This was quite a revealing day.

Initially, all the lawyers, including the lead strike suit attorney and the attorneys representing our insurance companies, came together in a meeting at which the mediator was going to describe how the day was to proceed. I overheard the strike suit attorney and our insurance attorneys discussing a party in Manhattan at which they had socialized together the previous Saturday night. They were talking about what a nice function it was and how they were involved in all the activities. That told me quite clearly that, with respect to the strike suit racket, our insurance attorneys and the strike suit law firms could be interactive.

As the day went on, our insurance attorneys came back to Lexi Haden, our General Counsel, and me explaining how they had done an unbelievably effective job in getting the strike attorneys' lawsuit demand down to only about $3 million. They said that would be a settlement everyone could embrace, but I commented that we thought we needed to take the case to court. Neither the company nor the executives had done anything improper, and we needed to call out this strike suit nonsense. Our insurance attorneys became very agitated. They claimed that they had done a wonderful job and should be applauded for it. They left the room to counsel among themselves. When they returned, they told us that, if we did not accept this settlement, MiMedx would never again be able to get Directors and Officers (D&O) Insurance, and we would be blackballed by the industry.

Those were very enlightening comments to me. It made me clearly understand that this racket of strike suits had matured to the point that all the attorneys had become comfortable with earning their share from the racketeering.

Of course, I had to relent because I did not want to cause the company future D&O insurance problems. But, this was frankly disgusting.

I wished to discuss this because I want current and future public company executives to understand exactly what a racket these strike suits have become. In these instances, you have to focus your legal activity at federal judges so that cases are dismissed early through summary judgment. Once you get to mediation, the lawyers are all probably cooperating with each other.

Another opportunist story of merit was the Invacare proxy contest against Healthdyne Technologies in 1997. That situation was very clearly described in Chapter 7.

A number of opportunists showed up in the later history of MiMedx. As I have mentioned, some of the outside Board members became opportunists when they found a way to force Bill Taylor, me and other management out of the company. In one case, Charlie Evans found a job as Chairman of the Board. Then, Dewberry realized that he could control matters to cover himself from the EY allegations of his conducting an inadequate investigation. And, in early 2019, as Board members' bad decisions drove the stock price down to around $2 per share, they issued very low priced stock options to themselves.

Relative to MiMedx, the first opportunist who contacted me in late 2018 was a person by the name of Rick Anderson. Rick had been a healthcare executive for many years. He had also been a private equity manager for a wealthy Texas family and then for himself.

Rick came to meet with me in Atlanta. He told me that he had an interest in making a major investment in MiMedx since the stock had dropped from $18 down into the $1 range. He also told me that he had contacted the Board of Directors, and he told them the same thing. He said he would also make a commitment to be the CEO of the company.

As I talked to Rick, I realized that he was a self-made business executive. He had put himself through college on a baseball scholarship at Mississippi State University. After college, he served in the military for five years as an army infantry officer. Then, he started his career in healthcare. He quickly worked his way up into general management roles. By the 2000s, he was on the Board of Directors of ConMed, a company headquartered in London. He had been a general manager at the company for some time and had been elected to the Board of Directors.

I felt comfortable with Rick because he had built organizations, although in a large corporate environment, and he was used to the hard work associated with general management and executive roles. We agreed on numerous issues related to management style, including accepting responsibility. As I got to know him better during the fall of 2018, I communicated with the Board that I felt Rick should be my replacement as the company's CEO. Rick actually began to have conversations with certain Board members on that subject as well.

As Rick's negotiations with the MiMedx Board continued, he would keep me apprised of the general nature of the discussions, which became more and more frustrating for him as they did for me. Rick had experienced a situation somewhat similar to ours at another corporation where certain executives were accused of fraudulent marketing activities. He tried to intervene in that situation so he was very familiar with what transpired there. One of his foremost points was that MiMedx would need some additional capital, in spite of the Board thinking that was not the case. The Board seemed to have no idea or plan for the path they had chosen. No budgets, no schedules, no scope, no control . . . "nuttin!" As it turned out, in the spring of 2019, the Board signed a very onerous loan agreement with a group of investors just prior to the shareholders meeting. Thus, Rick was exactly right.

Rick had proposed to the Board a working capital investment because he was adamant that the Board would potentially need to raise some money, particularly with the huge legal and accounting expenses he knew the Board had committed to fund. The Board kept pushing back on his proposal. I thought his proposal was extremely fair, and I did not think he was being onerous in any way. However, he received some rather immature feedback from this inexperienced group of Board members. Rick told me that he was actually accused by Luis Aguilar as being "just a capitalist!"

Rick finally became tired of trying to negotiate with this self-serving Board and he called to tell me that he was going to have to walk away. I found that very disappointing, and I kept campaigning for him and his proposal. One Board member apologized to me for not taking a stronger leadership role in promoting Rick and his capital infusion. This was at a point when MiMedx stock was trading in the low single digits, and an investment by Rick and one of the large institutional investors that was going to be his partner would have gone a long way towards restoring confidence in the company. Rick was a positive opportunist.

Another MiMedx opportunist would be Ed Borkowski. As I was doing my exploratory work on all of Cohodes' activity, I was introduced to Borkowski through a principal of one of the Canadian companies, Concordia, that had been destroyed by Cohodes. Borkowski had been the CFO of Concordia for several years. Thus, he became familiar with Cohodes' short selling approaches very well. About the time I met him is when EY decided not to complete our audit because of the threatening letter sent to them by Cohodes.

When we met, Borkowski brought up the fact that he knew a number of the EY principals in New York and that he could perhaps be of help. After discussions with a couple of Board members, I thought Borkowski could be helpful in a <u>staff</u> <u>role</u> to me assisting with some of these decisions. So I brought him into the company to assist with accounting and the associated legal matters. After only about 60 days, I realized that Borkowski was a lot of talk, but no successful action. He could not bring to closure any minor projects or assignments that I had given him. I was going to terminate him because he was ineffective. About that time, Dewberry decided he could use Borkowski in his manipulation of the accounting matters. So, he told me not to terminate Borkowski as he was going to use him for support. Later, Borkowski was named temporary CFO by the Board.

That move by Dewberry put Borkowski in an empowering position. He began to campaign for the position of the company's new CEO after my resignation. However, he was <u>absolutely</u> not qualified. He was on a major ego trip and started throwing his weight around within the company. He made numerous blunders. When it became evident that he was not going to be selected as the CEO, he began to work towards holding on to his lucrative temporary CFO position and building up as big a termination package as he could. Unfortunately, the Board succumbed to his "holding them hostage," and they essentially gave him responsibility for all new accounting projects as the company's temporary CFO. This Board allowed Borkowski to work for the company for less than two years and then walk away with over $5 million in cash and stock options. I should not have to say any more other than this opportunist was personally successful, thanks to Terry Dewberry and the other outside Board members.

The next significant opportunist was Eiad Asbahi of Prescience Point Capital Management. Eiad is the manager of a small hedge fund located in Baton Rouge, Louisiana. He had known Marc Cohodes in the past and had seen his attacks on MiMedx Group. He did his own financial analysis and decided Cohodes was actually very wrong on his short position and the bashing of the company. He called me to get my perspective. I suspected that he obtained my phone number from Thomas Pauley, an analyst that had been providing MiMedx coverage for several years.

Eiad initially started the conversation with his interest in buying shares in the company. This was at the point in time when the outside Board's decisions had driven the share price down to around $1. So this was an absolute no brainer in terms of making an investment. Having discussed the investment fundamentals, Eiad began to ask questions about what needed to be done to run the company. I gave him my point of view. He got quite argumentative on points about which I knew he had no experience. I pointed that out to him, but his arrogance then became quite evident. He never realized that he needed more experience to make decisions about the operations of a very complicated biotechnology company.

So Eiad enticed a number of small hedge funds into the MiMedx stock and began to talk to a few of our existing large shareholders. Some of them called me indicating that they did not trust him.

As we entered 2019, Eiad began to realize that there was going to be a proxy contest. He hired a proxy contest law firm, and I knew at that point what his intentions were. Also, as I have previously discussed, I had already made the decision to force a proxy contest for the annual meeting because I and our largest shareholders believed that the Board needed to be changed as quickly as possible.

What Eiad decided to do was go to the company with a slate of three individuals and convince the Board to sponsor his group for their slate, which would mean that they would ask three of the existing Board members to step off the Board in favor of Eiad's slate.

I was told that negotiations went on for a couple of months with a lot of bluster and bravado on both sides. In May, the company finally announced that Eiad's three individuals would be sponsored by the company as their slate, and they would pay $500,000 of Prescience expenses!

Eiad's slate consisted of Kathleen Behrens, a successful portfolio manager or "stock picker" who was Chair of the Board of Sarepta Pharmaceuticals, which had been a success story. Then, there was Rick Barry who was on the Board of Sarepta as well. Barry was a private investor and also a former portfolio manager. Third was Todd Newton, the CEO of a biotechnology company in Austin, Texas. He was a close friend and business associate of Rick Anderson, whom I have previously discussed.

Rick Anderson actually introduced me to Todd in 2018. After several conversations with him, I felt that Todd would make an excellent addition to the MiMedx Board because of his previous experience and his DNA. However, when I brought this up to the Board in late July, I received little response. The only response was that Aguilar felt like they needed a woman on the Board not another male. I reminded them that they needed someone who had the experience that Todd had with a similar investigation like the one they were pursuing.

The Prescience slate came down to these two portfolio managers and an experienced CFO who was now running a small public company and for whom I had some respect. Todd was a CFO for most of his career, but he had some experience with a company that had gone through much of what the MiMedx Board had pushed our company into. So he did have some key experience. Todd Newton was named the acting CEO in September 2022 after the Board finally terminated Tim Wright. This change was welcomed by the large shareholders.

I met with Rick Barry a couple of times as he made the decision to make an investment in the company when the stock was very depressed. I realized he was a very bright individual, but his common sense and business acumen were lacking. That does not mean that he was not successful in picking stocks. He had been a portfolio manager for most of his career. However, he wanted to give me all kinds of advice on running the company, for which he had no experience. And, some of his advice was very immature.

Also, Barry was very devoted to snow skiing. He literally took off two and a half months every winter and was on the slopes every day. So he was certainly not used to the discipline and rigors of managing or even being on the Board of a troubled enterprise.

I do not think Eiad realized, in spite of my comments, what this new Board could or could not get done. As I watched their decisions, these new Board members seemed to be as inept as the other outside Board members. Most notably, they never re-established communications with shareholders, which meant that they were still listening to the bad advice from the Sidley Austin lawyers on that subject. I think they spent most of their time doing exactly what lawyers and accountants told them to do without any focus on running and managing a very dynamic business. When the 2019 and first two quarters of 2020 revenues were finally published, shareholders saw just how much this Board had destroyed the momentum and reputation of MiMedx by its extremely poor decisions. The revenues were down about 50 percent from where 2020 would have been under our leadership.

The Board's actions continued to force the loss of the core group of 21 individuals that ran this company for so many years and made it so successful. You could not lose 20 out of the top 21 people at any major company without causing substantial operating performance difficulties. But, that is exactly what this Board did.

No one was going to ask the obvious question as to why they would do that to this very effective group of operating management. Well, there were other conflicting activities going on as well that the Board or the Board Chair, who was now Kathleen Behrens, never managed. First, Borkowski, during his quest to become the new CEO, wanted anyone who was loyal to either Bill or me out of the company so they could not question his authority and quest for the CEO position. I was told that Mark Landy, who we have previously discussed, was in the same mode of eliminating anybody who would question his decisions, which were often bizarre. Landy was finally terminated, but it was the Board's original decision to place him in a line role for which he was not qualified! Also, they put one of our product managers, who was an extremely bright and qualified individual in terms of biotechnology product management, into the role of Vice President of Investor Relations. Then, the Board apparently decided that some of our female sales employees who were terminated for cause and had begun making accusations, such as the company was "unfair to women," were telling the truth. There could not have been anything further from the truth, but the Board looked for people to terminate who might have fostered that alleged "unfair to women" environment.

So, by the late spring of 2020, the inadequacies and operating inexperience of even the new Board members was beginning to show. Because the March 2020 press release on the 2017 and 2018 financial statements was so confusing and the restatement so ridiculous, the stock price went from about $8 per share down to about $3.50 per share. Of course, Eiad was very upset with that result, but he certainly should have seen it coming with the Board restating revenues to a cash basis. He began having debates with his recommended slate of Board members. I was told that Eiad, and in particular Rick Barry, had clashes because both are very narcissistic, and arguments began developing. Barry told some shareholders that this was too much work for him, and he did not want to put that much time and effort into MiMedx Group in spite of his Board position and investment. Apparently, Eiad forced the Board into taking a vote as to whether or not the company should be sold, or should the Board just continue to flounder at managing it. I was told that there were five members of the Board who realized that this Board was incapable of managing the company, and they voted five to three to sell the company. I do not think there was any follow-through.

Now, it turns out that this third Board finally made the right decision relative to Tim Wright, the CEO at MiMedx since the spring of 2019. On September 15, 2022, they asked him to step down. They replaced him temporarily with Todd Newton as the CEO. That is a move that had been needed for over three years since Wright was never qualified for the CEO role. I was told by numerous employees that Wright was a "nice guy," but he was totally ineffective as a leader and decision maker. Those management issues had showed themselves numerous times over Wright's three years in terms of the company's mistakes and lack of performance. On January 30, 2023, Joe Capper became the company's fourth CEO since the Board asked for my resignation on June 30, 2018. That turnover rate of CEO's does not speak highly about the effectiveness and competence of the various Boards during this transition.

Prosecutors

I have now gained a great deal of experience with attorneys who are or have been prosecutors. My and Bill's defense teams were almost all former government prosecutors. Prosecutors are quite different personalities because of their inherent "skepticism" about almost everything and because narcissism dominates their personalities. I remember thinking at one point how difficult it would be to have a prosecutorial personality and try to build a business! I do not know how you could hire anyone with the degree of skepticism many of them harbor. Then, attempting to manage people as a narcissistic personality and help them grow and flourish would be impossible. Thus, being involved with these types of lawyers has been an interesting and frustrating process. And, they can become opportunists in many ways. Hopefully, your career will not involve prosecutors!

It was also surprising to witness the blatant way the King & Spalding former prosecutor, Paul Murphy, distorted the facts as he built his case. Of course, the investigation taking 15 months and costing $25 million in legal fees plus approximately $15 million in accounting fees was a total surprise as well. And, the accusatory way in which our managers and employees were interviewed by the group from King & Spalding was extremely disappointing and frustrating. Fortunately, I began to read Sidney Powell and Harvey Silverglate's books describing the corruption that can happen as governmental or former prosecutors go about targeting individuals and building their cases.

Your Opportunists

If you are an entrepreneur, I know you have the courage of your convictions. More than likely, because of your courage and self-confidence, you do not harbor a great deal of paranoia about almost anything. However, I want this chapter to instill some degree of skepticism about individuals and their motives. I thought I was generally very perceptive in ferreting out ulterior motives. Please understand that individuals' personalities and motives can change quite dramatically as they age and as their opportunities change. In the process, they can become very destructive.

Now if you have already experienced having private equity partners involved in your business, then you understand how they legally protect themselves and how you will, as a general rule, be the underdog. You may have already gone through a vetting process and the protection of yourself as best you could as you negotiated a private equity investment for your company. However, the private equity partners will always perceive themselves as more experienced and more rational in terms of their abilities than you. Of course, that could be the case. Understand that they may be more astute than you and may be able to bring your business enterprise along at a faster rate or to a better conclusion. That is something that you will have to come to grips with as you arrange your financing.

The bottom line is that you must keep yourself very informed in terms of the individuals that surround you as well as those who could be plotting against you and your enterprise. Remember to devote sufficient time to these Board matters, which is something I did not do effectively at MiMedx because of my time constraints relative to managing our growth opportunities. Superb performance does not preclude issues that can develop from inexperienced Boards with self-serving members.

You should consider having sessions with your Board or other advisors questioning them on what their behavior would be if there were an "allegation" made against the company by a whistleblower as a minimum. That situation deserves some vetting because you want to be in a position to be able to terminate corrupt employees and not have them extort or otherwise damage the corporation. The Sidley Austin attorneys advised the Board to settle rather than fight with any whistleblowers. As usual, the Sidley Austin advice was very destructive because it demonstrated weakness which encouraged further actions by unscrupulous persons.

CHAPTER 18

MIMEDX PROXY CONTEST

Some of the following has been explained earlier, but it bears repeating as I would like to set the stage for why a proxy contest occurred at MiMedx. Shareholders quickly developed a sense of distrust after the executive and management terminations and other Board decisions that drove the stock from $18 down to below $1 per share in the fall of 2018.

As noted in previous chapters, I inherited the MiMedx Board when I stepped into the role as Chairman and CEO in February of 2009. I made some immediate changes, but I never had the time to create a very experienced Board like the ones I had brought together at Matria Healthcare and Healthdyne. We established a staggered Board at MiMedx so that only one third of the Board was elected every year to shield the company from opportunists. The original MiMedx Board was devoid of experienced biomedical technology operating executives and entrepreneurs with public company experience.

In contrast, the Board that I had assembled at Healthdyne and Matria Healthcare over the years included numerous successful entrepreneurial business executives, such as Guy Millner, Jackie Ward, Fred Cooper, Don Weber, Wayne Yetter, Johnny Gresham and former Governor Carl Sanders who built Troutman Sanders, a major law firm. These individuals had the business, and in some cases, legal acumen to manage situations, such as Cohodes' allegations and the EY debacle, quickly and effectively rather than making self-serving decisions that are the wrong decisions for shareholders, employees and customers. Unfortunately, the majority of those excellent Matria Board members were in "retirement" mode by 2009.

By the late fall of 2018, the majority of large shareholders of MiMedx Group were thoroughly disgusted with the decisions that had been made by the remaining members of the original Board of Directors. The Board had basically cut off all meaningful communications with shareholders. They made decisions that took the stock from approximately $18 a share and a $2 billion valuation in February down to below $1 per share at approximately a $100 million valuation by the end of 2018. Shareholders did not have to know many of the details to be very upset with what had transpired, particularly with the lack of communications from the company. As the company's largest individual shareholder, my family and I were also very frustrated.

From the time the resignations of Bill Taylor and me from the company were announced on July 2, 2018, I was in constant contact with the group of the largest shareholders, all of who were responsible for the initial funding of the company. These individuals were generally long-term shareholders as well as sophisticated investors. Many of them knew some of the outside Board members personally, and they would share information with each other when some of the Board members would speak to them.

The shareholders signaled one clear message to me to take to the Board. Recall that I remained on the Board until mid-September when I resigned, primarily because I knew there would be a proxy contest to force an annual shareholder meeting initiated by this group of large shareholders, and I was going to participate with them. Shareholders' primary concerns, which I presented to the Board at the July 26th Board meeting, were the lack of communications with shareholders, thanks to the Sidley Austin attorneys, and the feeling that the management of the company had been turned over to attorneys, accountants and inexperienced executives.

When I presented the consensus from the shareholders, it was received by the outside Board members with neither questions nor discussion; just a "thank you." Over the next many months, I continued to write and communicate with the Board on issues of concern to me as well as to the shareholder group. I do not think any of the issues that I highlighted were ever seriously debated because none of them were implemented. The Board's decisions were so lacking in business acumen that I think they asked the Sidley attorneys for business advice and always took it!

During this stressful period prior to the proxy contest, this group of original shareholders, which became the MiMedx Shareholders Group, was talking to certain Board members as much as possible.

Occasionally, we would get some timely and frustrating information. In one case, one of the oldest tenured Board members told one of our large shareholders something like, "I am furious with Dewberry. He is acting crazy. He has lost it, and he has his own agenda." Apparently, Dewberry, the Audit Committee Chairman, was openly driving the Audit Committee investigation to find fault with prior management to <u>unnecessarily</u> exonerate himself and the Audit Committee from the EY allegations that the 2017 investigation of the whistleblower was not adequate.

It is unfortunate to hear something like that, particularly when the Board would not step up to the Dewberry problem and resolve it. The Board had an excellent reason to remove Dewberry from his role since he had been criticized by EY for not conducting a thorough investigation previously, and he and the Audit Committee potentially had culpability with certain accounting matters. Regrettably, because they were in a "takeover" mode, this Board demonstrated a propensity not to step up to their responsibilities or make logical business decisions to exercise their fiduciary responsibilities to their shareholders. They let the attorneys make many business decisions, and business history is full of those disasters.

The Causes of the Proxy Contest

In pointing out the Board's blunders, let me backtrack to the February 6, 2018 Board call. The first major Board blunder occurred on that date when EY notified the Board that they would not complete the 2017 audit until the Board conducted an additional investigation of all Cohodes' allegations. We should have had a subsequent meeting where the Board asked EY all the detailed questions as to what prompted their catastrophic decision. At that point, the Board should have terminated EY and brought back our previous auditor, Cherry Bekaert, to complete the 2017 audit. Cherry Bekaert had already reviewed the first six months of the year. Therefore, completing this audit would have taken probably 60 days, and that part of the ordeal would have been over. I felt that Cherry Bekaert knew the executives and our accounting practices well enough that they would have told Cohodes "where to go." Subsequently, the Board could have initiated any investigations they so desired. As I mentioned earlier, that was my proposal.

However, I was told that Dewberry hired King & Spalding after a personal phone call on February 8th. He knew that I would not return from vacation until Monday, February 12th. By that time, it was too late to have any meaningful discussion with the Board because Dewberry had locked down the company's decisions on those matters by hiring King & Spalding.

The next serious blunder occurred as a result of the investigation. The Board summarily dismissed the two top financial executives of the company, Mike Senken and John Cranston, on June 7th because the Board had decided, without executive management's participation, that the written distributor agreement with AvKARE had been modified. The allegation/assumption that King & Spalding made was that, because AvKARE often wrote weekly checks for MiMedx invoices that approximated the amount of products that the VA hospitals had supposedly used, the company should only book its AvKARE revenue on a cash collection basis. The idea of changing six years of revenue recognition over a non-accounting and inaccurate document for the FDA that did not change the written agreement with AvKARE was totally ludicrous. However, it matched certain personal CYA initiatives that Dewberry was trying to implement, and it certainly matched the Sally Yates Doctrine, which King & Spalding brought to the company through Paul Murphy, who was a former prosecutor.

The next blunder was bringing in a temporary CEO on July 2nd who had no healthcare experience <u>whatsoever</u> to replace Bill and me. The Board went to Alvarez & Marsal, a business-consulting firm, and brought in David Coles, an experienced "turnaround" manager to become the company's temporary CEO. While Coles had a good track record in the turnaround area, he admitted to me that there was no turnaround required at MiMedx since the company was performing well, growing at 30 percent and rapidly collecting its cash!

I believe the decision to bring in a temporary CEO was probably suggested by King & Spalding in order to get Bill and me out of the way so we could not question or interfere with their corrupt investigation strategy. As things turned out, I learned that this corporate governance investigation process always needs a competent balance to the Yates Doctrine. So exert your leadership and get involved and stay involved until the Board or Audit Committee becomes uncomfortable.

The next issue to develop was that Charlie Evans, who had just been elected to the position of Chairman of the Board, allowed a temporary CFO, Ed Borkowski, to go to NASDAQ in late-September with several lawyers from Sidley Austin to convince NASDAQ that the company could finish its 2017 audit by February of 2019. I was still on the Board at that time, and I asked that the NASDAQ presentation be given to the Board before management was allowed to proceed. Evans overruled the request saying it was a "management prerogative" matter. Of course, Evans had no experience in public company governance. I was concerned that whatever presentation was given could be very flawed. As things turned out, it certainly was!

Within 45 days after the visit, the Board had to admit to NASDAQ that the information that Borkowski and the Sidley lawyers had presented was incorrect, and there would be no audit completed by February of 2019. NASDAQ immediately delisted the company in early November. The stock dropped approximately 30 percent. Also, as I have mentioned previously, there was never a budget, schedule or scope prepared by the Audit Committee and approved by the Board to control the audits or the investigation. Board members told me that Dewberry made <u>all</u> the decisions. I would ask, "Why do you allow that to continue?" I would hear a lot of "excuses," but no valid "reasons!"

The decisions made by David Coles, Ed Borkowski and Mark Landy, with the Board's concurrence, resulted in numerous blunders causing further deterioration in the company's performance and the MiMedx stock price. When Bill and I left on June 30th, the company had strong revenue growth, which was still above 30 percent, and strong cash flow and EBITDA. But, the Board made a decision to terminate 24 percent of the workforce, including the sales organization, on December 5, 2018. This decision to terminate sales employees in particular was devastating to the company. And, the decision to terminate employees on December 5th rather than January 2nd also demonstrated incompetence. That decision sent a shockwave throughout the sales organization so that the December revenues were hurt significantly, which also reduced the 2018 total revenue. And, the stock price dropped approximately another 60 percent when this was announced.

After Bill's and my departure on Saturday, June 30, 2018, we discovered from Coles, the interim CEO, that six weeks prior, the Board had made plans to bring in a professional manager from Alvarez & Marsal on Monday, July 2, 2018, as a temporary CEO. Coles filled that position, but he had <u>no</u> healthcare experience! And, <u>no transition time</u> was allowed for Bill and me to bring him up to speed on the numerous intricate issues that the company's executives dealt with on a weekly basis or the talents and attributes of the staff. Therefore, Coles came in and began to flounder with the complexities of the company.

Coles was allowed to have a short lunch with me. He told me that, when the shareholders saw the new audit and what the revenue changes were, they would be very frustrated with the activity and costs of producing the audit and how the Board was, unnecessarily, just moving revenue around.

The next issue that caused an even larger drop in the company stock was the resignation of Ernst & Young as the company's auditors. This occurred in November just as I had told the Board on February 6th it would. However, there was never any "real reason" given for their resignation. Of course, by this time, EY had probably invoiced the company four to five times the original quote for the audit, but they did not provide one. When I called one of the Board members after EY's resignation, he answered and said, "Do not tell me you told us so!" I simply replied, "Good morning."

When I heard the Board had allowed Coles and the two <u>inexperienced</u> operating executives, Landy and Borkowski, to convince them the company needed to terminate 24 percent of the workforce, including the sales force, I sent the Board a memo asking them to wait until they obtained detailed 2019 budget information at their December 13th Board meeting before making such a decision. As usual, my advice was ignored, and the layoff announcement was made on December 5th.

As I stated, that was a ridiculous date to announce a major layoff for any company. They should have waited until January 2nd or 3rd. That blunder resulted in a disastrous December in terms of revenues because of the morale issues associated with the termination of 24 percent of the sales force. The sales force lost confidence in the company, and they began to leave, even joining competitors! The stock dropped over 60 percent to below $1.00. Because of these continual blunders by the Board with the resulting significant decline in the stock, the long-term shareholders kept asking me what could be done in terms of correcting the Board's incompetency.

After these particular circumstances developed, there was an increasing demand by shareholders to replace the Board of Directors. However, the Board had decided to delay the May 2018 shareholder meeting because of the current circumstances and because they knew one third of them would be replaced. They gave shareholders the excuse that they wanted to wait until they could publish the 2017 audit results, which actually did not occur until March of 2020!

Through the fall of 2018, I worked with the larger shareholders, who represented about 45 percent of the shares, in developing a plan for a proxy contest to call two annual shareholders meetings. The shareholders' goal was to have the 2018 and 2019 meetings held concurrently so that two thirds of the Board could be replaced.

I did not want to call on the company to hold a shareholders meeting too soon because they could have held the 2018 meeting only and delayed the 2019 meeting for another 13 months. However, another shareholder, Hialeah Municipal Fund, filed a petition with the court in Florida to compel the company to hold the 2018 annual meeting in May 2019. When that happened, the other large shareholders and I contacted that group, and we began to work together to hold a proxy contest to force the two annual shareholder meetings. I personally employed law firms in New York and Florida to assist us with our efforts.

Had the individuals on the Board been more experienced and not attempted a "takeover" and had Dewberry not become paranoid and gone into a CYA mode, this situation would have played out in a totally different and much less destructive manner for shareholders. And, it would have concluded very quickly.

Florida Court Action

In spite of the Board's efforts to fight the calling of the 2018 shareholders meeting, the Florida judge, Kevin Carroll, called a hearing in his courtroom on April 3, 2019, to listen to the company's arguments against holding these meetings. The company was represented by Charlie Evans, Chairman of the Board, and two attorneys from the Sidley Austin law firm, Isaac Greaney out of the New York office and Walter Carlson out of their Chicago office.

Carlson was the attorney making the company's arguments to Judge Carroll, and they became quite illogical and nonsensical. He actually told the judge that the company had a staggered Board, like the U.S. Senate, for a reason. He said that the U.S. Senate is constituted so that only one third of the senators are elected each election cycle. And, that is the reason the company wanted to abide by its charter to elect a staggered Board. Carlson's comments made no sense. The judge immediately responded, "Sir, the difference is that the U.S. Senate routinely holds its elections, and this company does not. We are here to see that it does." At that point, Carlson quickly closed his arguments and took his seat, as he needed to do!

Judge Carroll explained that his goal was to see that the company held two shareholder meetings so that the 2019 meeting was held within 30 days of the date it would normally take place. Therefore, he set the date for the 2018 annual shareholders meeting for June 17, 2019. He said he would rule on the date for the 2019 shareholder meeting in the near future. Thus, because of the judge's verdict, the company managed to delay the 2019 meeting at the same time they were required to hold the 2018 meeting. The Board made promises to the court that MiMedx would hold the 2019 shareholders meeting before the end of 2019. That commitment was <u>not</u> met until August 31st of 2020.

We had hoped that Judge Carroll would order the 2018 election to be held in May 2019, which was a year late, but in addition, he would order the holding of the 2019 election. That would have allowed us to elect two thirds of the Board. However, due to delays and manipulations by the Sidley Austin lawyers, what the judge acted on was simply demanding that the 2018 shareholder meeting be held on June 17, 2019. He also called on the company to declare within a few months when they would hold the 2019 shareholder meeting. Thus, the shareholders, including the Hialeah Municipal Fund, had a nice victory in the Florida court over the company's proposal of delay and delay and delay. The battle lines were drawn, and I think most everyone, including the Board, knew that our slate of directors would beat their existing slate of directors.

Since we would only obtain three new seats on the Board at the 2018 election, I decided to select two lawyers, one of which was also an accountant, to run with me. They were both long-term shareholders, and they knew the company well. The first individual was Shawn George, a practicing attorney from Charleston, West Virginia. The second was Dave Furstenberg, a CPA who went on to get his law degree. I felt strongly that we needed two lawyers because we would be having battles with the existing Board and their hired law firms over numerous issues, which would generally be related to legal or accounting matters.

I first met Shawn when I flew to West Virginia in 2010 to raise funds from him and some other angel investors. I left that meeting impressed with his business acumen. While he was a successful practicing attorney, I recognized an individual who had common sense, and consequently, demonstrated business acumen. As I became more involved with Shawn during our proxy contest and in subsequent MiMedx related matters, I became very impressed with his legal acumen as well. In legal discussions, he would point out his lack of experience in certain areas when appropriate, but would listen respectfully to others who may have that specific legal expertise. However, he is not beyond making challenging comments when his business acumen tells him that other legal questions need to be asked. After the frustrations related to my trial, I actually asked Shawn to work with me on numerous business and legal related matters as a "consigliere." He has been so very helpful to me in that role because he knows when to be assertive in discussions where my lack of legal experience might not optimize the outcome of the conversation.

As soon as we could force the company to have the 2019 shareholder meeting, we could elect three more individuals. I knew some individuals who were successful entrepreneurial executives, and I was discussing with them the possibility of their joining the Board at that point in time.

We were well on our way to having a successful proxy contest and three new Board members until a group of opportunists "showed up" late in the process. If the company had not signed up these three new director nominees for the election, MiMedx would have lost the proxy contest to our slate, I certainly believe.

An Opportunist Group

After the Hialeah Fund and MiMedx Shareholder Group convinced the Florida court to take the necessary action to force the company to hold the 2018 shareholder meeting, a group of what I will call "opportunists" appeared. They were led by a small fund manager from Baton Rouge, Louisiana by the name of Eiad Asbahi, who I discussed previously. His company was called Prescience Investment Group, LLC.

As I recall, Eiad was attracted to the company in the fall of 2018 because of all the social media posts by the short seller, Cohodes, and his group of partners and journalistic shills. Eiad contacted me to ascertain some of the real facts about the company. He mentioned that he knew Cohodes well, thought that he had mental issues and, most importantly, thought Cohodes was very wrong about the company.

Eiad also connected with one of our analysts, Thomas Pauley. Thomas was very familiar with MiMedx having covered it as a small fund manager before Cohodes was even involved in his short selling activities. Thomas brought a group of individuals, some of who were already large shareholders, to Atlanta in the fall of 2018 to meet with me to discuss the company.

Let me mention at this point how I view my commitments to corporate entities, their employees, their management, their shareholders and customers. I have always taken my commitments very seriously. I realize that I also have an inordinate sense of responsibility, which goes much further than most. I try to never make commitments to either individuals or organizations that I do not take very seriously. If I were not going to take something very seriously and personally, I would generally not become involved.

So, in the fall of 2018 and into 2019, MiMedx continued to drift along with no communications to the shareholders. This was a demand to the Board from the Sidley Austin attorneys with their inept legal and business advice.

When I received the call from Eiad, he asked for and obtained from me some comments in terms of how the company in late 2018 was doing and how it should be operated. Of course, Eiad had never run an operating company so it was difficult for him to understand the points I was making. However, I tried to help him understand exactly what the company needed to do to quickly turn things around.

Eiad, with the help of Thomas, assembled some investors into a group. I had met with one of his investors, Rick Barry, several times. Barry was a bright person, but he had no experience managing or developing business entities. He was a very successful "stock picker" and portfolio manager. Barry was on a roll because he was on the Board of a company in which he had made an investment by the name of Sarepta Therapeutics, which had been successful.

At that point, the MiMedx Shareholder Group had announced along with Hialeah, the legal action that had been filed in Florida to force the company to hold a 2018 shareholder meeting and elect new Board members for a third of the group. I am certain that caught Eiad's interest, and he told me he was going to talk to Charlie Evans, the Chairman of Board, about changing the Board. I told Earl I had some ideas about those issues, and that we planned to align with Hialeah to support a new slate.

As the proxy contest began to progress, it was evident that I had the support of about 45 percent of the oldest and largest shareholders. These are people who invested in MiMedx Group early in its development stages, and they had seen what we had been able to do in terms of taking the company to be the fifth fastest-growing public company in America. They were incredulous at the accusations being made against me and the other top executives of the company by the Board. They were also very disgusted with the Board's total mismanagement of almost everything. So, these large shareholders were adamantly opposed to allowing the company to delay its 2018 shareholders meeting any longer. They wanted to hold a meeting and change out at least one third of the Board.

MiMedx Shareholder Group

As we began to assemble our list of shareholders and have discussions with them about the proxy contest and the shareholders meeting, it was obvious that we should have no issue at all reaching over 45 percent to 50 percent of the shareholder vote. Since I had participated in proxy contests previously, I had some insight as to how things needed to be orchestrated. Therefore, I took it upon myself to hire New York and Florida law firms and a proxy contest manager. We prepared our announcements as the "MiMedx Shareholder Group." We communicated our intentions through press releases, and we selected two individuals in addition to myself who would be on this slate.

There is another factor that played into this election, which our slate lost. That factor was the huge number of shares that had been sold short against MiMedx at that point. I believe probably 60 percent of the total shares of the company had been sold short, and a huge number of those (40 percent) had been sold short in a naked fashion and had not completed the delivery of the borrowed shares. In other words, there was a very substantial "Fails to Deliver" situation overhanging the company. In a case like that, the brokerage houses are basically in a situation where they can have several owners of a share of stock. Thus, in a proxy contest, many shareholders of the original shares will not receive proper voting documents from the brokerage houses. My shareholder group complained loudly during the last week of the contest that they were not receiving the proxy documents that represented their full holdings. Thus, they were not able to vote their full amount of share ownership.

At the June meeting, three of the original eight outside Board members who asked for the resignations of Bill, Mike, John and me were replaced. Subsequently, another Board member of that group resigned. Thus, there were only four of those original outside Board members left, and at least one was to be replaced, namely Dewberry, at the 2019 meeting, which the company had committed to the court to hold in December 2019. However, as expected, the company reneged on that commitment.

Incidentally, this Board became very 'entrenched' immediately upon the requested resignations of Bill and me. They expected there would be shareholder surprise and rejection of their decisions regarding the termination of executive management. Therefore, they accepted advice from the Sidley Austin law firm, such as not holding shareholder meetings, in order to keep their Board positions intact. Also, that would ensure that the Sidley Austin law firm would continue to be retained, and their legal fees would continue along with their poor advice!

Fails to Deliver

As the MiMedx proxy contest began to build some momentum in the fall of 2018, I was having conversations with over 100 shareholders. They laid out some simple requests of the Board, which I presented. However, the Board had no interest in answering their concerns in any way.

As I previously mentioned, the judge demanded that the company hold the 2018 shareholder meeting on June 17, 2019. The judge was pushing them to also hold the 2019 shareholders meeting. But, the company managed to maneuver its way out of having both meetings at the same time. On August 3rd of 2020, they finally announced their 2019 meeting would be held on August 31, 2020. This was 15 months late.

There are numerous ways to educate yourself on proxy contests. There are some complexities. However, we encountered a new difficulty that I had never before experienced. This occurred because 40 percent of our shares were illegally sold short with a "Failure to Deliver," which means that approximately 45 million shares were owned by more than one individual. As we previously discussed, the "Failure to Deliver" situation is managed by the large brokerage houses on a day-to-day basis, which is corrupt. However, they get by with it until there is a demand for the shares, which happens during a proxy contest. Large numbers of our shareholders had problems getting the proper paperwork from their prime brokers because the brokers were having trouble "locating their shares." So, I believe we had such a large problem that there was no way we would ever have won the proxy contest with the number of our large shareholders having their shares in this position.

Incidentally, unless there are some very extenuating circumstances, many shareholders simply vote with the company because they do not inform themselves of the issues. The odds are with the company winning a proxy contest. I think that, in our case, the extenuating circumstances of having 40 percent of our shares in a "Failed to Deliver" status was certainly the deciding factor because our large shareholders could not obtain all their voting documents.

Other Opportunists

I know the personal involvement and stresses associated with accepting full responsibility for your commitments and that of the organization for which you are accountable. Most opportunists involve themselves in an endeavor with only themselves in mind. Sometimes it is easy to understand their motives, and sometimes it is not. However, if they have never really "walked a mile in your shoes" so they understand the rigors associated with developing an entrepreneurial or even a mature business, they will not really make a full commitment to the endeavor. Most of them will not have put in the 12 and 15-hour days over the years to build a business or put their capital at risk early. In the development of the enterprise, they are <u>superficial</u> in their approach.

Opportunists will often show up as people who have been Board members, management of non-entrepreneurial organizations, portfolio managers or stock pickers, those who have done investment banking deals or whatever. However, you must be suspicious of their motives if they have never expended themselves in an entrepreneurial effort that took major personal commitments and a mature sense of responsibility for all the organization's constituents.

Over the decades, individuals with opportunistic goals have shown up in my life at various times in various organizations. I was generally able to figure out their lack of commitment early on. Often, I would let them do some planning and see how their ideas played out without making personal or corporate commitments to them. As always happens, when the going got tough, these people did not keep going. They were not used to the commitments and responsibilities associated with developing real entrepreneurial endeavors.

As a word to the wise, it is often very easy to poke through the supposed commitments made by these individuals. They may consider the fact that they are investing some of their personal funds as the biggest commitment they should have to make. In many cases, that is the only commitment or responsibility that they want relative to a business endeavor. The really valued opportunists are those who will turn themselves into a committed corporate person who will be ready, willing and able to devote substantial amounts of their personal time, financial resources and relationships to the business in most every way possible. Good luck finding these individuals for your Board or management!

In the spring of 2019, Eiad contacted the Board with the premise that he would propose three new Board members, and he wanted the company's support. Otherwise, he advised them that my slate of directors would win, which is exactly what would have happened. We received word that he and the Board were negotiating, and it was a situation that was on and off, on and off. However, the company finally signed an agreement with Eiad, Prescience and the three individuals who would be the company's slate of new Board member nominees. No one knows exactly the guarantees that were made by Eiad's group or the company in order to bring this unholy alliance together. The company paid approximately $500,000 of the Prescience legal fees. I personally paid the legal and proxy fees for our group, which approached $1.5 million.

The slate that Prescience proposed was two successful portfolio managers, Kathy Behrens and Rick Barry, and one financial executive who was currently the CEO of a small public company, Todd Newton. I had previously tried to get the Board to elect Todd to the Board during the summer of 2018 after I was apprised by Rick Anderson of his background and experience, which was very applicable to the specific complex issues that MiMedx was facing. However, the Board seemed to be very focused on adding a woman to the Board rather than someone who had the specific experience they needed. So, when the Board struck an agreement with Prescience, they elected two portfolio managers and a financial executive. To say that the results of their involvement over the years was a disappointment would be an understatement. Incidentally, the new Board members also decided that they should not communicate with Bill and me in any way at all. This was probably at the advice of the Sidley Austin group with more CYA solutions.

CHAPTER 19

CONTRIBUTING FACTORS TO THE INVESTIGATION

The issues that brought all this disastrous activity to MiMedx were numerous, and generally involved the following:

- the company changing auditors by hiring a Big Four auditing firm, Ernst & Young;
- the unbalanced nature of the whistleblower laws;
- the MiMedx whistleblowers hiring a lawyer who went to the media to see that their false allegations were published;
- the short sellers conducting a "Short and Distort" campaign against the company after seeing the false publications;
- the short sellers collaborating with the whistleblowers;
- certain Board members having their own self-serving agenda and ignoring their fiduciary responsibilites to shareholders;
- the Audit Committee Chairman unnecessarily hiring King & Spalding, to include a former prosecutor, to do a formal investigation of the short sellers' false accusations without Board review;
- the use of the Sally Yates Doctrine, that requires companies who have been accused of something improper to deal with the matter by hiring a law firm to accomplish an investigation that must "target" executive management;
- and the DOJ and SEC attorneys ignoring the alleged unlawful short selling against MiMedx while looking for a white-collar crime case in order to further their careers.

Starting in late 2016, a number of situations developed that were important relative to the downturn in the fortunes of MiMedx, its executives, managers, employees and shareholders. Some of these were beyond the company's control, and others were made worse because of decisions made by the company's

Audit Committee and Board of Directors as well as their outside law firms and auditors.

The first direct event that started the company down this pathway was an email to me from a sales manager who accused MiMedx of "channel stuffing" in late 2016. This was quickly followed by a formal complaint by an attorney that he had retained. This regional sales manager, Jess Kruchoski who lived in Milwaukee, came up with a plan in 2016 that would allow him to sell products from small competitors in addition to the MiMedx product line while still a full-time employee and manager at the company, which was a violation of his employment contract.

Kruchoski had previously worked for a company by the name of Advanced Bio Healing (ABH) as had at least 30 or more of our other salespeople and sales managers. This group had seen the advantages of our product line over what they had been selling, and since they did not have a non-compete agreement with ABH, many of them decided to come to work for us. That gave MiMedx a nice revenue boost early in our building process beginning in 2012.

So, Kruchoski had known these salespeople and managers for a lengthy period of time, and they had some trust in him. When he developed his plan to sell competitive products on the side through his own company, he located a business that represented a number of smaller manufacturers. He worked out a commission plan without that company fully understanding that he was a full-time employee of MiMedx Group. At least, that was what that company told us when we confronted them about his unpermissible activities.

By the time we had proof of Kruchoski's activities in late 2016, he had recruited about 15 out of approximately 350 of our salespeople to work with him. We were told that he convinced them by simply saying that, "Executive management knows what is going on, and they do not see anything wrong with everyone making a little 'extra money'."

What was most disappointing to me was that MiMedx had a very robust and well discussed "compliance system" for employees to report concerns about the company or other employees' behavior. When these individuals were confronted with what they had been doing, many of them stated that they had faith in Kruchoski because they had known him for so many years. Had just <u>one</u> of our salespeople made an inquiry in 2016 about management's view of Kruchoski's plan, the matter would have been quickly resolved. And, I am certain that it would not have developed into the catalyst it did for the short sellers.

Kruchoski certainly had to know he would eventually be caught violating his non-compete contract with the company. I believe it was only in order to protect himself that he attempted to galvanize certain salespeople to join him in accusing the company of doing some type of illegal activity relative to our revenues. He knew the term "channel stuffing" had negative connotations. Channel stuffing, which basically means that a company parks product for long periods of time, is not in itself illegal. It becomes illegal when the company does not disclose to shareholders that some of its revenues will have extended accounts receivable aging because certain product has been sold to distributors that will not be paid for within a normal period of time. This would then be a "consignment" sale and could not become revenues until the cash was received or sale reserves were utilized.

We found out through depositions that Kruchoski was trying to leverage his channel stuffing thesis to intimidate management and break his non-compete agreement. We were told he even had visions of maintaining a distributor relationship with MiMedx after that happened!

Kruchoski made telephone recordings of other sales personnel agreeing with him about supposed channel stuffing at VA hospitals. Most of these individuals viewed Kruchoski as a constant complainer and a manager who was not very proficient. When he would be on the phone with them trying to have them agree with him that the company was conducting channel stuffing, they would reach a point where they just wanted to get off the call. Some told me that they were tired of talking with him. However, if you listen to certain comments in those conversations, you could assume that some of them were agreeing with Kruchoski, which was not actually the case as we later discovered when they were interviewed and gave depositions.

Most importantly, Kruchoski tried the same thing on our President and Chief Operating Officer, Bill Taylor. Bill figured out what was happening, and he called out Kruchoski on his allegations. Kruchoski immediately backed off and said he did not think anything like that was taking place.

Kruchoski Investigation

So, when Kruchoski made his allegations of channel stuffing in an email and his lawyer wrote a formal letter in late 2016, we had to immediately investigate the allegations. In today's regulatory environment, that means the accusations are investigated by an independent committee of the Board, which will normally be the Audit Committee.

I asked our General Counsel to turn over the documents from Kruchoski and his attorney to our Audit Committee, and they conducted, from my view, a very thorough investigation. The Audit Committee asked our existing auditors, Cherry Bekaert, and our outside law firm, Troutman Sanders, to work with them in conducting interviews and reviewing emails and recordings by Kruchoski to determine if the company was engaging in channel stuffing.

The investigation lasted over three months, and it was thorough and specific about the allegations. It was determined very quickly that Kruchoski and his attorney did not know what they were talking about as they really did not know how to define "channel stuffing." They were not familiar with accounting rules and regulations. They were simply making up issues to cover up Kruchoski's unethical activities.

The company filed lawsuits against Kruchoski and others who were the leaders in this corrupt scheme. One of the most important issues was to determine which of these 15 individuals were the followers and which were the leaders. I also needed to determine which ones were remorseful and contrite, and which ones would conduct themselves in some unethical manner again.

I set up an interview process because the information we were getting from many of these individuals was known to be untrue. We conducted interviews by bringing them into our cooperate headquarters. We set up a temporary video recording system in my conference room so that we could ask questions, and we would have a record of their answers since we were getting so many lies and so much misinformation on the matter. We had signs in our building stating "Under Video Surveillance." There was nothing illegal in the state of Georgia about these interviews.

Our General Counsel, Lexi Haden, gave the investigation the name "Snow White" because at the time we thought seven individuals were involved, but that number grew as we broadened our investigation.

The Whistleblower Act

As we previously discussed, the Whistleblower Act and the regulations as they exist today provide corrupt employees with a method of extorting payments from a company in a manner that is quite unbalanced against the company. They can be awarded whistleblower fees, even if they perpetrated the illegal acts themselves!

Generally, the whistleblower will take their allegations to the regional SEC or DOJ office. They do not necessarily have to have any real proof as the agencies will decide whether or not they wish to open an investigation. It is unfortunate that today, if an employee lies to these federal officials, it is "overlooked." Of course, lying to a federal official is illegal, and the whistleblowers that are dishonest should be prosecuted. However, because of the advantages to the federal agencies and their lawyers, whistleblowers are often given special treatment.

Unfortunately, because there is <u>no risk</u> to whistleblowers, many allegations and, thus, actions that should not take place are essentially encouraged. In today's business environment, an employee who is corrupt can cause a company hundreds of millions of dollars in expenses over allegations that are <u>just not true</u>. As I previously stated, there is no balance in today's whistleblower regulatory system.

Coincidentally, in Howard Root's book, *Cardiac Arrest*, he describes a five-year battle with the Department of Justice over this same issue. He had a rogue salesperson that went to work for another company while remaining employed by Vascular Solutions. When Howard found out, the employee was fired. This sales employee struck back by going to the Department of Justice in San Antonio and alleging corporate misconduct relative to their marketing programs. Sound familiar?

Vascular Solutions and Howard Root beat the DOJ after the assistant U.S. attorneys spent five years creating allegations that were ridiculous. However, Root explains that it was all caused by a disgruntled sales employee trying to obtain a whistleblower fee, which he thought would be $5 million in this case. However, the Vascular Solutions Board made the <u>correct decisions</u> relative to their fiduciary responsibilities to the company and shareholders because they supported management.

As I previously mentioned, a whistleblower filed a qui tam case in 2006, which originated at a company we had recently acquired at Matria Healthcare. That company had previously violated some Medicare billing regulations prior to our acquisition. During the negotiations, the federal judge told our General Counsel and me that, "The whistleblower laws are the worst laws that Congress has ever passed. They are so out of balance there is never any fair justice."

The King & Spalding Contract

As we have discussed, the Board call with Andy Brock and other EY managers on February 6, 2018 was the catalyst for the MiMedx "fall from grace." EY staff stated they would <u>not</u> <u>finish</u> our 2017 audit, which was due in two weeks, until the company investigated <u>all</u> the illegal short sellers' allegations. I pointed out that the major allegation, channel stuffing, had been investigated a year earlier by Troutman Sanders and our former auditors, and they found no wrongdoing. MiMedx published a press release on the matter so EY staff should have seen this information during their due diligence in the spring of 2017.

EY then alleged that our Audit Committee, in managing that investigation, had not done a competent job. I asked what was incompetent about it. Brock responded that we did not hire another audit firm to do a forensic audit. I mentioned the allegation of channel stuffing was so easy to disprove that I thought the Audit Committee was prudent to not spend $5 million on a forensic audit. I pointed out that the source of the allegation originally came from a sales manager, who was terminated for enticing about 15 of our salesmen into selling a small competitor's products for his "side" business and that we believed his allegation was simply designed to give him cover. I reminded EY that we had filed lawsuits against Kruchoski and some of the other 15 salesmen who were involved for thier alleged violations.

When EY exited the phone call, I told the Board that EY would never complete our audit because the short sellers would continue to make up allegations, and EY would want them investigated. I recommended that we terminate EY and bring back Cherry Bekaert to complete the audit. Since they had already reviewed the first and second quarter results, I said it should not take more than 60 days, and that would clear the air with shareholders as far as our financial performance was concerned. Then, if there were other matters that needed to be investigated, the Audit Committee could make those decisions. Dewberry, the Audit Committee Chairman, argued that EY <u>certainly</u> would finish the audit and that what I was advocating would "look bad." I responded by saying that what he was recommending would subject the company to a lengthy period of financial uncertainty and confusion, and our fiduciary responsibility to our shareholders called for more certitude about these decisions.

It should be noted that, when EY accused the Audit Committee of not conducting a thorough investigation of the "channel stuffing" allegation, Dewberry went into a very paranoid state of mind. Since he was not a courageous person with much self-confidence, his behavior became very focused on his personal CYA actions. His fiduciary responsibilities to the company were ignored, and he began to let EY dictate all his decisions.

February 6th was a Tuesday, and I was on my normal week's vacation after our late January team meeting (National Sales Meeting). Janet and I were in the Caribbean. I told the Board to consider what had been discussed, and we would have another call the following week to discuss a plan of action. However, on February 8th, Dewberry, probably under advice from EY, had a call with King & Spalding to discuss retaining them to conduct an investigation. Many months later, I was told that Dewberry immediately signed an agreement with King & Spalding. I am not sure if the Board ever reviewed the agreement or understood its implications. I was told much later by a Board member that the agreement essentially turned over control of all investigatory issues to King & Spalding, and the company only had the right to terminate the agreement with no right to dictate what was reviewed!

I had taken Bill and myself out of the investigation discussions because we could have been subjects of the investigation. The Board should have taken Dewberry out <u>also</u> because EY had accused him of not conducting a sufficient investigation a year earlier. Either way, Dewberry had moved quickly while I was on vacation to place himself in control of an expensive and lengthy investigation that would <u>not</u> include himself. I did not fully realize what he had done until sometime later. I did not know the details of the King & Spalding contract until many months later. I kept asking Dewberry and the Board in writing to publish a document outlining the goals, objectives and budget for the investigation. I never received any replies to my numerous requests. As it turned out, those issues were mute because the Board had given total discretion to King and Spalding. That meant King & Spalding could ignore the EY directive to the Board to investigate the unlawful short sellers' allegations and do a "Sally Yates' investigation" instead. That is exactly what happened at a cost of about $25 million in legal fees, about $15 million in accounting fees, and 15 months time! In the meantime, the shareholders were devastated with the stock experiencing a 95 percent decline. Also, EY resigned, as I said they would, without finishing our audit, but they charged the company nearly five times the quoted audit estimate!

I found out later that Marc Cohodes, the primary short seller, had been calling EY exposing his misinformation and had sent a very lengthy and threatening letter through one of his shills to EY executives. However, the SEC and DOJ seem to ignore these notorious short sellers as they can be the source of cases for their prosecutors. Thus, governmental prosecutors benefit, but the American shareholder and the government are fleeced! More on that subject later.

Decline of the Business

Other than the Board of Directors, there are two primary individuals who contributed principally to the decline of MiMedx business after the departure of Bill and myself. These include Mark Landy, who reported directly to me as our Vice President of Strategic Initiatives, and Ed Borkowski, a former CFO who I had recently brought to the company in March of 2018 to report directly to me in a staff role.

Relative to Landy, he was an experienced Wall Street person with a healthcare business background. I had him in a staff role reporting to me because he tended to be arrogant and narcissistic, and he irritated other staff members. Also, I was told that his only previous line responsibility had resulted in a business failure.

However, with some of our Wall Street activities, Landy could be very effective. Since he had no one reporting to him and he had no direct management responsibilities, his narcissism did not frustrate staff. There were not many internal staff at the company that the Board knew very well, but they were exposed to Landy because certain of his Wall Street activities were vetted at the Board level. They very incorrectly assumed that he could also be a line executive rather than a staff executive. Of course, my advice was not sought!

So, someone on the Board must have recommended that Landy take over a number of reporting responsibilities within the company, and he ended up with about 85 of our clinicians and scientists reporting to him. Within weeks, that decision began to be problematic because of the way in which he managed his staff. Again, for a Board to take a staff person with no direct reports and assign him a role managing 85 of the most important individuals in the company was a very serious mistake. I kept pointing out to the Board in writing the problems that Landy's decisions were causing. Finally, after being in that role for almost a year, he was terminated by the Board. However, a lot of damage had already been done.

Some of this information on Ed Borkowski was discussed in the previous chapter on Opportunists, but it is worth expounding on here.

I gave Borkowski several assignments when he first joined the company in the spring of 2018. By that time, the Audit Committee had already hired King & Spalding to do the investigation. Dewberry began to communicate with Borkowski, and it did not take long for Borkowski to realize that he had a real opportunity to advance himself because of where Dewberry was beginning to take things in his CYA scenario. Borkowski found out fairly quickly that the focus of the investigation was on the top executives of the company, and we could very well be replaced. Recall the Sally Yates Doctrine!

Borkowski went to work trying to <u>promote</u> <u>himself</u> to be the new CEO of MiMedx Group. From an experience standpoint, he certainly was not qualified and his business intellect was definitely lacking. That does not mean that he could not be very loud about his opinions, but they were generally bad opinions. So, Borkowski began to work on his own agenda of furthering himself as the new permanent CEO after Coles' temporary CEO role was over.

Borkowski also had a very narcissistic and arrogant personality that was often abrasive. One day he irritated all our top sales managers by walking in on one of their meetings and making some juvenile and absurd comments that were designed to make him look omnipotent. Of course, those comments made him look just the opposite.

Since Dewberry told me not to fire Borkowski, I am certain it was his recommendation to the Board to make Borkowski the temporary CFO. As such, they gave him the power to conduct the audit process. Since the Audit Committee <u>had</u> <u>never</u> <u>done</u> a business plan for the audit with all the proper planning related to scope, budget and schedules, Borkowski was on his own. I thought Borkowski was a terrible planner; he never got anything done to carry out my requests, which were very straightforward. So, the audit process was handed over to a person who demonstrated no abilities at our company to accomplish anything with any degree of complexity. Consequently, the NASDAQ debacle occurred with Borkowski presenting to them along with the Sidley Austin attorneys. They apparently gave NASDAQ misinformation, which had to be corrected within about 45 days, and shortly thereafter, the company was delisted.

Once Borkowski figured out that he was not going to be selected as the new CEO of the company, he continued to work in his own self-interest, but in a different direction. He made statements to the Board that he would not sign off on any financial statements until he had reviewed <u>every</u> <u>invoice</u> the company had issued over a five-year period. That is a ridiculous request by a chief financial officer, or frankly, anyone in an accounting role. Thus, he kept extending the time required to complete the 2017 audits and any adjustments that were going to be made to the earlier audits. Of course, he was very much into attempting to make this process as complicated as possible because it significantly extended his job as temporary CFO. The Board had numerous ways to prevent Borkowski from manipulating the audits and his compensation package, but they took no definitive action.

In one of my conversations with Rick Anderson, he asked me about Borkowski. I inquired as to why he asked. He said, "Because Ed Borkowski used to work at ConMed." I asked, "What happened?" He said "The Board had to fire him." I asked, "For what?" Rick said, "For doing the same thing I know he is doing at MiMedx." My next obvious question was, "And, what do you think that is?" Rick replied, "For making a lot of noise and getting nothing done except something that relates to himself." I replied, "You know him well."

I told Rick that I was about to fire Borkowski because I had really obtained nothing productive from him. He could not seem to manage even the simplest projects. Then, I realized that everything Borkowski did was all about Borkowski.

There are members of our Board who never did take the time to get to know Borkowski or his capabilities. They just turned over large portions of the company and major decisions to him, and the results were catastrophic. He certainly extended the auditing process for a lengthy period of time. It basically took two years to finish the 2017 audit, which was almost complete on February 6th of 2018.

Borkowski and Dewberry managed to turn five or six years of the company's revenues into a <u>controversial matter</u> that required the restatement of <u>all</u> revenues from the normal accrual basis where revenue is booked upon shipment to a cash basis where revenue is only booked when payment is received. Thus, with approximately 3,000 customers that included doctors' offices, wound care centers, hospitals and a few distributors, they turned their self-promoting decision into a very expensive and lengthy accounting project.

For Borkowski, it was another year of a very high salary for his capabilities. Also, it allowed him to leverage our rather naive Board into further compensation and payments. In other words, they allowed him to get to the point where he could "hold them hostage." Remember, he made the comment to the Board that, "If I am going to sign off on these financial statements, then I am going to have to review <u>every invoice</u> that the company has ever issued over the last five years." Of course, that was an utterly ridiculous and self-promoting claim.

With the company's excellent cash collections and low accounts receivable aging, there was no reason to restate <u>any</u> customer accounts to a cash basis. This was done for Dewberry's CYA actions, to extend Borkowski's time in the temporary office of CFO, and to make it look as though the former executives had perpetuated some massive accounting fraud. I was given a document by the company in 2022 that showed the extra direct accounting costs associated with the revenue restatement project alone exceeded $80 million.

Thus, when MiMedx finally released its 2017 audit results on March 10, 2020, they were over two years late. Also, at Dewberry's request, Borkowsk had orchestrated taking over five years of the company's revenues from <u>several thousand</u> <u>customers</u>, and <u>restating</u> them to a cash basis rather than an accrual basis, as previously mentioned. I think this will go down in the history of accounting as a major blunder, not to mention a total waste of $80 million in accounting fees. However, I was told, Borkowski negotiated with the Board an increased severance package so that, not only did he make his $550,000 a year salary plus bonuses, but he also received several million dollars of stock options as he walked away from the company.

The Board of Directors, including its new members, should have clearly recognized what Borkowski was doing, his lack of competence, and his totally self-serving actions. They had plenty of time to deal with the matter and not have the shareholders hijacked by Borkowski and Dewberry!

The Changes In Our Legal System

When key variables become out of balance in any economic system, major disparities, most of them undesired by the majority, will evolve. For instance, there are over 1.3 million lawyers employed in the United States. We graduate about 40,000 new lawyers every year. In Japan, a country with a strong and growing economy that has about 38 percent of our population, there are only about <u>35,000</u> lawyers! So, Japan has approximately 281 lawyers per one million people while the U.S has about 3,769 lawyers per one million.

Now, consider that the majority of our regulations and laws are developed and promoted by state and federal legislators, the majority of whom are lawyers. About 40 percent of our U.S. Congress attended law school. Do you think that could be the reason the U.S. has seen our laws and regulations grow exponentially over the past three decades? Do you think that is the reason the U.S. has 25 percent of all the imprisoned people in the world while we only have 5 percent of the world's population?

And, there are many other examples of the current imbalance in our economy caused by the influence of the overpopulation of attorneys in our country. Even some federal judges are beginning to highlight how out of balance portions of our legal system have become. In fact, our judge, Jed Rakoff, has given the term "the U.S. legal cabal" to describe the current system that we have today. In using this descriptor, Judge Rakoff is highlighting the system that has caused the compensation for lawyers in the U.S. to escalate dramatically over the last 30 years. Thus, federal judges are being paid approximately $250,000 per year while the former government prosecutors, who defend cases in their federal courts, are paid two to six times that amount.

I will now review some other issues that will affect your legal business decisions. Let us begin with a little theme that will permeate many of my comments on these subjects. In years past, I have heard the theme, "Lawyers do not create wealth; they rearrange it."

In further preparation for the details of the MiMedx story, you will need a reasonably broad review of the current U.S. legal system, the Department of Justice and their assistant U.S. attorneys, who are generally their prosecutors, and the defense counsels who are part of the system. My overview will not be very different from what you can read in Conrad Black, Howard Root and Raj Rajaratnam's three books, which I introduced in the Preface. In all four of our situations, even though the circumstances were somewhat different, you can see the same flaws in the justice system as it functions today and the corrupt processes that have developed over the decades. You will be informed about some of the criminal justice problems as they apply to white-collar crime cases and the numerous complexities associated with the relationship between indicted business executives and the lawyers and law firms who represent them.

Hiring Former Prosecutors

It will be informative if we examine the general personality traits of lawyers, specifically prosecutors and their foes, the defense counsels, because there will be considerable discussion on the behavior of these individuals in the following chapters. Also, some of these comments will put in perspective the disclosures that Black, Root, and Rajaratnam made about the various lawyers in their battles with the DOJ. I will make some points for the entrepreneur and business executive relative to retaining outside legal counsel and having them become effective contributors to the legal case and to the business.

Let me start by stating that a very large percentage of lawyers are "risk-averse" personalities. However, that will change slightly as we consider the various legal specialties. The focus and importance for the coming lessons are the prosecutors and the defense counsels who are generally former prosecutors themselves. The "risk-averse" nature of lawyers, as a general rule, precludes them from being business entrepreneurs or executives as they are not comfortable balancing "risk and return" as business executives must do. The few attorneys who have tried entrepreneurship do not have good track records, except Howard Root with Vascular Solutions! Read Howard's book!

Now, I will submit the idea that most lawyers are narcissistic personalities. Simply put, they believe that, "What is in my brain is correct, and what is in your brain is wrong." That belief will develop much discussion when our subject becomes focused on the setting of the "goals and objectives" of a DOJ trial and the "strategy" and "tactics" of achieving those goals. The issue for the business executive becomes one of selecting a defense counsel and support group who can function as a "business team" and not a group of individual narcissists. Black, Root, Rajaratnam and I all had trouble successfully achieving this necessary task. Two of them managed to be able to change lead lawyers and firms several times, which moved them closer to having a "business team." In our case, our trial was expedited so there was no time to change law firms. I was frustrated with my lead lawyers over trying to get a competent planning process in place so that we had a "business plan" for a complex business project - our DOJ trial. However, I finally concluded that getting normal business processes in place with lawyers who are strong narcissists is basically impossible! I warned about the issues of having narcissistic individuals in management roles in earlier chapters of the book.

In Bill's and my trial, we had to have separate law firms. Therefore, we each had at least three lawyers speaking on our behalf during the trial. As I watched, I realized that this was not really viewed by my attorneys as my trial, but rather as a "theatrical performance" in front of this judge and <u>his</u> court. They seemed to forget there was a jury present. Each had their own idea about the "goals and objectives" and "strategies" and "tactics." They were focused on <u>their</u> performances. This was just another Broadway opportunity for them!

Generally, narcissists can fail to be convincing to a jury because they think they are right and should not have to convince someone else of their argument. As such, they spend little time developing "sales skills" and the ability to influence others and change their minds.

In questioning my legal group (I will not call them a team) about their education of the jury prior to the verdict, they all believed that they had done a good job cross-examining the prosecution's witnesses. They gave examples of how they had asked this question or that question. It was as if, simply because they had asked a question, a juror would surely have had their mind changed on the subject. Narcissism? Obviously, there was no significant grasp of "salesmanship" or the real ability to influence a person's mindset. Since there was no "trial plan" highlighting the key points for jury education and mindset change, everyone went their own separate way. I had to remind them that, just because a question was asked or comment made in front of jurors, a "mindset" change does not necessarily occur. Many concepts need repeating and reinforcing with numerous other comments also made by other parties to complete a change of mind. This propensity for a lack of trial planning is very frustrating to business executives because we know the negative issues that can come from shortcomings in the planning and actual influencing processes.

So, if you are ever faced with the task of hiring a law firm, particularly for a complex case, try to obtain a brief from each candidate's firm as a trial plan or business plan. That process might separate the "planners" from the highly "narcissistic" groups, which is certainly a start. You will be fortunate to find a planner! Either way, stress that the first order of business for the project is the creation of a trial plan. See if you can make some progress. When you are told that you do not understand trial dynamics and protocols, remind them that they do understand the process of convincing groups of people, as you have both inside your company as well as outside, to align with your thesis and take positive action on your request. Of course, that is one of the keys to leadership! And, narcissists struggle with effective leadership!

One key business objective should be to influence the jury, not impress the judge!

King & Spalding's Washington Presence

As I previously mentioned, Paul Murphy, former prosecutor and King & Spalding partner, was the individual who managed the investigation at MiMedx. Immediately after his 15-month investigation, he went to the FBI as the Chief of Staff to the Director, Christopher Wray. Wray is also a former King & Spalding partner. He went to his position at the FBI right after he conducted an investigation at a Fortune 50 technology company. It is rather ironic that two King & Spalding partners obtained assignments at the FBI after completing a very expensive investigation of a U.S. public company.

Of course, Sally Yates had just returned to King & Spalding in 2018 after her several years as Deputy Attorney General under President Obama when our investigation began. She was terminated by President Trump for refusing to enforce his border policies. Consider the attitude she must have developed toward Trump, his associates and his 2016 Campaign Finance Chairman for the state of Georgia! Also, think of the bonus payments that King & Spalding partners could have received on this approximate $25 million investigation of MiMedx using the Yates Doctrine!

CHAPTER 20

ACCOUNTING MATTERS

There are numerous accounting issues related to the MiMedx investigation. These matters range from the complexities that public accountants must deal with relative to the Sarbanes Oxley regulations to the existence of the PCAOB as an oversight entity. They also deal with trying to interpret many of the regulations particularly those related to revenue recognition post-Sarbanes Oxley. In addition, there is the natural instinct of accounting firms to force clients into very conservative and costly actions. For instance, the MiMedx Audit Committee decided to restate six years of revenues for every customer as a CYA exercise for themselves, which <u>was</u> <u>very</u> <u>unnecessary</u>. This involved over 3,000 hospitals, wound care centers and doctors' offices, with a few distributors. Why would an accounting firm <u>not</u> go along with a <u>total</u> revenue restatement, particularly when there is <u>no</u> Board leadership, and it will result in over $80 million in extra billings for the firm? Then, almost two years later, the company stated in their March 2020 10-K filing that the "company recovered the majority of its billings made between 2012-2017 with insignificant write-offs recorded."

You should recall that our investigation began when a MiMedx sales manager accused the company primarily of "channel stuffing" in late 2016. Prior to his accusation, he created a scam whereby he enticed about 15 members of the sales force to join him in selling competitive products to our customers <u>on</u> <u>the</u> <u>side</u> while they were still employees of MiMedx. In order to try to develop cover for themselves, he was looking for something that he could use to extort from the company and force the breaking of their non-compete contracts. Once they made the channel stuffing accusation and were told that we had discovered their illicit scam of selling competitive products on the side, their attorney went public with their channel stuffing allegation in the Minneapolis newspapers. That action shut down the final negotiations with the 3M Corporation to acquire MiMedx in early 2017.

However, most importantly, the MiMedx news in Minneapolis caught the eye of certain hedge funds and individuals who were interested in bringing our stock price down. Remember the discussion in Chapter 11 on Deerfield Management. Our sales manager passed on to Cohodes and others the audiotapes that he had made of his discussions with other salespeople. These tapes were discussed in Chapter 19. Cohodes began to disclose the audiotapes through his internet site to further stimulate short selling activities against MiMedx. The MiMedx employees, or "whistleblowers," and their attorney did not even understand the rules and regulations related to public company accounting and what is called channel stuffing. They did not really care about truth; they had their own agenda.

So catalysts were there to start the initial short selling attacks. The principal allegation, that the company was channel stuffing, was explained in Chapter 12. The company <u>did</u> <u>not</u> conduct channel stuffing. These allegations were proven false by the Audit Committee's investigation and report in early 2017 and even by the King & Spalding investigation in 2018.

Cohodes' initial allegations drove the stock price down to approximately $12 a share by the end of 2017. During the month of January 2018, the stock price returned to approximately $18 a share. This occurred primarily because the company began to counter Cohodes' allegations on our website. Answers were given to his major allegations related to the company's violation of regulations and laws, but not to all the superficial nonsense he published about individuals or other activities that were supposedly illegal.

The Cohodes attack had "run its course" by the end of January 2018. He then resorted to sending a lengthy and threatening letter to Ernst & Young (EY), our new auditors in February. In addition, he had previously sent over 200 emails with numerous allegations. Cohodes has also revealed that he had sent notebooks of his allegations to EY and then called them. He is experienced enough to know that there are always issues when a U.S. public company changes auditors. In fact, there is an old adage that public companies in the U.S. should <u>never</u> change auditors. The old and new auditors will begin to argue over their differing "opinions" on accounting matters, and there is no way to mediate those disagreements. The company is stuck in the middle.

I personally made the "bad" decision to change to a Big Four auditor because of the recommendation of some of our largest institutional shareholders with whom I had spoken at the J.P. Morgan Healthcare Conference in early January 2017. These individuals had been investors in my previous companies for many decades, and I respected their input. Therefore, I advised Terry Dewberry, Chairman of our Audit Committee, that I thought we should make that change. Dewberry told me to go into the Atlanta business market, interview the Big Four auditors and bring back a recommendation. I accomplished that task, and I recommended EY.

This was a <u>major mistake</u> on my part in order to satisfy some of our largest and most influential shareholders. However, I thought MiMedx was operating very efficiently, and new auditors would not be a problem. Without the unscrupulous short sellers, a few dishonest salespersons, and lack of governmental regulatory enforcement against illegal short selling, perhaps my decision would not have been a bad one. With the Big Four auditors, particularly under the scrutiny of the new PCAOB and the SEC today, accounting matters are no longer balanced, and a public company will be the victim…cost-wise, time-wise, and otherwise!

EY did their due diligence during the early summer of 2017. They accepted the assignment and stepped in to conduct the third quarter review of our financial statements. They presented a very positive review and outlook to the Board at the October Board meeting. However, Cohodes had just begun making his allegations.

The Cohodes letter sent on *Aurelius* stationary to EY was received in February 2018, and that intimidated EY into demanding that the company conduct an investigation of Cohodes' allegations before they would complete the 2017 audit. EY strongly recommended that the company hire a large and unaffiliated law firm that had the resources and experience to conduct such a broad investigation. They also demanded that a forensic auditor be hired.

In addition, EY faulted our Audit Committee for not conducting an efficient investigation of the whistleblower allegations of channel stuffing in early 2017, primarily because no expensive forensic audit was conducted. That accusation sent our Audit Committee Chairman, Terry Dewberry, into paranoia with a total focus on his own unnecessary CYA actions.

As I have previously discussed, my recommendation was to tell EY that they were terminated, and we should revert to Cherry Bekaert who had already accomplished a review of the first six months of 2017. I clearly told the Board that EY would never complete our audits; however, Dewberry vehemently disagreed. But, that is exactly what happened because EY resigned in late 2018 without completing our audit.

Unfortunately, this Board did not have the experience or courage of their convictions to push back on this very unreasonable request of EY to investigate the allegations from a non-credible source, engaged in questionable short selling. The other allegations made by the sales manager, who was fired for cause, were also from a non-credible source. Remember his dishonest scheme of selling competitive products on the side and his plot to protect himself by trying to extort the company through his allegations. Plus, this was thoroughly investigated by the Troutman Sanders law firm in early 2017. Anyone with a reasonable grasp of accounting could tell from our years of audited financial statements that our DSOs stayed in a reasonable range and did not rapidly increase and remain high. Thus, there was no channel stuffing!

So a fast-growth, very profitable and strong cash flow company was being forced into a process which could not or would not be managed because of its inexperienced and self-serving Board. This would totally derail the revenue growth rate and profitability of the company all because of the actions initiated by a dishonest short seller. Is that the kind of business environment that should exist in the United States of America? The answer is absolutely no. And, this environment would not exist if our SEC and DOJ would do the right thing and not protect illegal short sellers primarily for the benefit of some of their own attorneys who are looking for white-collar crime cases to enhance their careers.

One would think that, after the debacle of the Arthur Andersen investigation, indictments and trial by the Department of Justice, lessons would have been learned by DOJ officials and numerous congressional committees. The verdict in the Anderson case was later overturned by the Supreme Court. But, in the meantime, Arthur Andersen was forced to close their doors with the loss of 85,000 professional jobs. Please remember what prosecutors did to Arthur Anderson!

Cash Collections

All cash collections related to the U.S. healthcare system are more complex because of the involvement of hundreds of health insurance plans. The plans are intermediaries for the patient, and they pay for their obligations. However, the manufacturers of the products must have a contract for reimbursement with the insurance plans also. In the case of MiMedx, insurance plans were making payments to hospitals, wound care centers and doctors' offices for the use of our products. In addition, there are always six to nine subsidiaries from major insurance plans that reimburse and pay for the federal government's obligations to its Medicare recipients. A similar system is used for the reimbursement for the state-run Medicaid programs. Therefore, this means that these third party payers can cause significant issues with healthcare providers being paid in a timely manner, particularly if the health plan does not have a contract with the product manufacturer.

For MiMedx to be paid efficiently for its products by hospitals, wound care clinics and doctors' offices, there had to be contracts for reimbursement with hundreds of health insurance systems across the country. Obtaining product insurance coverage by hundreds of insurers was no easy task. While MiMedx accomplished this in an amazingly short period of time, it was because of the experience that I and some of our top executives had in our previous business relationships. At Matria Healthcare, we had direct contracts with hundreds of insurance carriers for our disease management services. Therefore, I knew many of the medical directors and some of the CEOs of numerous health plans, which was very helpful in gaining their attention to highlight the advantages that the MiMedx product line offered.

In order to obtain insurance coverage for our product lines, we had to provide published clinical studies. This meant we were continually starting company-sponsored clinical research programs or encouraging hospitals or physicians to conduct their own research studies. When the results of those studies were available, we had numerous contacts with medical journals that would review and decide whether to publish the information. Generally speaking, we were consistently successful in having our studies published. More importantly, we were able to expedite the publication of those studies after the completion of the clinical reviews by the journals. So, after about four years of marketing our allograft product lines, almost <u>every</u> major health insurance company in the country was reimbursing for our products, except United Healthcare. Finally, in 2020, after eight years of our products being the leader in the marketplace, United Healthcare agreed to reimburse for the company's well-proven product line. That fact creates the question why did it take United Healthcare so long to begin reimbursement. Unfortunately, it takes just one medical director with some "different ideas" to avoid reimbursement coverage on a product that was as well respected and as broadly utilized as ours.

This discussion should highlight to any healthcare entrepreneur the complexities of getting paid for the sale of your product, even after you have FDA clearances or approvals. I have known many new healthcare entrepreneurs who believed that obtaining FDA approval was the major step that had to be taken in building their company. I would inform them that is often the easiest step and obtaining insurance reimbursement will be much more difficult. In a healthcare related business that will rely on payment to its customer upon use of the product on a patient, health plan reimbursement must be a key focus.

Over the years and decades, I learned many of these lessons the hard way. When the Healthdyne Infant Monitor was introduced in 1973, there was no insurance reimbursement for any product or supporting service of that nature. We had to start with one health plan at a time. Not until the American Academy of Pediatrics published a position paper on the utilization of home physiological monitoring for infants at risk for Sudden Infant Death Syndrome did reimbursement start to build rapidly. There generally has to be some publications of clinical studies showing efficacy or a notable healthcare society publishing similar information in order to obtain reimbursement.

As MiMedx initially began to develop insurance coverage, I set up systems and hired individuals to manage the insurance reimbursement process. We also formed a group that developed and managed our clinical studies. That group of nurses visited our clinical study sites almost every week. Those studies had to necessarily be published before we would obtain any reasonable breadth of insurance coverage. Our accounts receivable group in the accounting department also worked on collecting payment for invoices from our various customers. Of course, if a clinical customer was not being paid by some insurance carrier, they were not very interested in paying us, even though they had used the product. Thus, there was a continuous and complex process for monitoring the status of our accounts receivable.

At MiMedx, I set up a monthly meeting between our top operating and top sales executives, accounting executives and accounts receivable group from the accounting department, and myself. These discussions were necessarily held in front of sales management so that their responsible salespeople could understand the priorities in collecting our cash and the role they must play in that process. We had a very successful accounts receivable collection activity. Occasionally, the cash receivable would get above our 70 day targets, but we would focus additional people on the issues and bring the aging of those accounts receivable down fairly quickly. In fact, our cash flows were very strong. Over a seven-year period, we purchased $132 million of our stock in the open market. In addition, we made significant investments in new production equipment and facilities and all the other asset buildup required to grow the company at the rapid rate we were achieving.

Investigator Corruption

This discussion is important as I will highlight some of the allegations that were "created" by the King & Spalding investigators. You will see the inconsistencies between our business processes and the allegations from the investigators.

One point that needs to be made relates to the difference between revenues being accounted for on accrual basis and revenues being accounted for on a cash basis. GAAP accounting normally requires that revenues be accounted for on an accrual basis. This basically means that revenues are booked when the product is shipped and title changes to the customer. There are some nuances that relate to whether revenues are booked upon shipment from the company's warehouse or whether they are booked upon receipt by the customer. Generally, we wrote our contracts so that our revenue was booked upon shipment to the customer.

Now there are four revenue recognition rules associated with GAAP accounting that have been well known for decades. Simply speaking, they state that there must be a clear indication that a contract exists for the purchase of product, which is generally a purchase order; there is proof that the product was shipped and the title changed; and the obligation for payment was fixed and determinable.

Relative to the actual booking of revenue on an accrual basis or a cash basis, the four basic criteria are where issues normally develop. If a company were to ship to a customer on some basis that did not clearly delineate that the customer owed the money or that title to the product did not change to the customer upon the shipment of the product to them, then questions could arise. For instance, if one were to ship product to a distributor on a "consignment basis," then that revenue should not be booked until the product is paid for. The reason for that is the customer really has no obligation to sell the product because it is in their possession on a consignment basis.

King & Spalding's first allegation was that management had given AvKARE, our distributor for the Veterans Administration hospitals, permission to <u>only pay</u> for our invoices when they had a purchase order from the federal hospital or were actually paid for the product by the VA hospital. This was a trumped up accusation, and I could have disproven that allegation very quickly had I been interviewed. They also alleged that a <u>new</u> GAAP requirement delineated in SAB Topic 13 would require that a distributor have enough salespeople in the VA hospital accounts to do the normal sales functions. AvKARE had contracts with a number of manufacturers for whom they did excellent service because of their very strong <u>internal sales staff</u> and administrative staff. Those individuals served the same purpose as individuals being in the account acting as salespeople because they accomplished the sales function through information gathering and related activities using the hospital staff themselves. Thus, that was another twisted fact from King & Spalding which could have been easily refuted had I been interviewed and given due process of the law.

Because we once allowed AvKARE to return some product a hospital had ruined prior to its application on a patient, we were accused of having a <u>permanent</u> return policy. That was a ridiculous accusation, and that was not the case. We would, from time to time, give a distributor, a hospital, a wound care center or doctor the right to return a product for credit, but that was relatively infrequently. On the other hand, when a customer wanted to "exchange" some product (one set of product sizes for another set of product sizes with the obligation to pay the original invoice), we allowed that because it expedited the use of our product on patients, and we thought it was revenue neutral. However, these decisions were made on an individual basis, and it was not a general policy of all customers having a right for a return or even an exchange.

AvKARE did not have the right to pay MiMedx only when it had a purchase order from one of the hospitals or when it collected the cash from the VA. At times, AvKARE could have been operating like some other distributors may have occasionally done by paying their bills when they collected the related cash. For an auditor to have to determine that a distributor was paying the manufacturer only when they were paid by their customers for that manufacturer's product would be a chaotic situation to manage. Every company pays its bills when it has the cash to do so. In some cases, cash might be running tight so that it has to be collected before payments can be made to other parties. For an auditing firm to decide that, based on very infrequent occasions of these delays beginning to occur, the account needed to be put on a cash basis rather than a normal accrual basis, would be unmanageable! However, that requirement would also involve additional huge accounting fees for auditing firms!

The Investigation is Initiated

After the decision was made by Dewberry as Audit Committee Chairman to conduct an investigation of Cohodes' allegations with an unaffiliated law firm, King & Spalding, and managed by a former prosecutor, Paul Murphy, the die was cast. KPMG was retained as the forensic auditor. Those decisions themselves caused the interest of the SEC and DOJ to escalate dramatically. The company would end up paying approximately $40 million for the investigation and forensic audit, which would be exactly the kind of information that the DOJ prosecutors would relish. Of course, King & Spalding would follow the Sally Yates Doctrine which means that top management would be "targeted" and become the focus of the investigation regardless of the absurd allegations that had been made by the short sellers. And, that is exactly what happened. There was little investigation into the allegations that Cohodes made. They were basically ignored! However, Cohodes had achieved his objective to create more corporate uncertainty to push the stock price down by threatening and intimidating EY to stop our audit.

The first place the investigation went was not Cohodes' allegations, as EY had requested, but a focus on revenue recognition relating to our federal distributor, AvKARE. In 2012, an AvKARE administrator sent a MiMedx administrator an email asking if they could pay MiMedx when they received a notice from the VA that they were being paid for an invoice or an implanted tissue. KPMG decided that AvKARE revenues needed to be recognized on a cash basis because the company was "allowing them to pay only when they were paid." I guess KPMG took that AvKARE email at face value, and pursued building a case by claiming that six years worth of AvKARE revenue needed to be restated based on that one email. Of course, King & Spalding also wanted to claim that Bill and I <u>knew</u> that was the case and that we hid it from our accounting staff, the Audit Committee and the auditors… therefore, we would be guilty of accounting fraud!

Bill and I knew that was <u>not</u> <u>the</u> <u>case</u>. We were working with a distributor, AvKARE, who had a very immature accounting system. In fact, they could not even tell us which invoices they were paying when they sent in their cash payments. AvKARE had directed our internal accountants in writing to credit all of their cash to their <u>oldest</u> <u>invoices</u>. So, the fact that they sometimes wrote weekly checks of approximately the amount that the VA had <u>notified</u> them had been implanted was irrelevant to us. AvKARE could conceal and <u>manipulate</u> the VA implant data to satisfy their cash needs because we had no visibility to that data! We knew <u>no</u> <u>one</u> <u>had</u> <u>given</u> <u>AvKARE</u> <u>permission</u> to <u>only</u> <u>pay</u> <u>us</u> that amount each week. In fact, we rather routinely went back and demanded more payments from them as their accounts receivable would grow above certain limits. But, even more significantly, if AvKARE truly believed that we had given them permission to only pay us when they were paid by the VA, they would have <u>demanded</u> that fact be <u>written</u> into Amendment 4 to their Distributor Agreement. This was <u>not</u> written into their Agreement. Also, there was <u>no</u> email or other communication stating that AvKARE wanted that payment method to be put into the Amendment. Of course, had AvKARE asked for that clause, we would not have agreed to it because of the revenue recognition requirements.

Thus, KPMG and King & Spalding came to the outside Board, probably in late April 2018, with the disclosure that they thought the AvKARE revenue needed to be restated for six years. Their accounting "opinion" was that the revenue needed to be recorded when the cash actually came in. Therefore, there was possibly a timing issue with the revenue that had been accrued for AvKARE.

In addition, to finish out their planned prosecution recommendations, they had to allege that Bill and I had not presented the information that they had just <u>concocted</u> to the auditors, the Audit Committee and our own accountants. Of course, if they had they given us a chance to be interviewed prior to our being terminated, we would have been able to disprove this misinformation. However, I am <u>not</u> <u>sure</u> they wanted us to straighten out the misinformation and <u>ruin</u> their "prosecution story" along with their huge fee opportunity. The accountants at KPMG made and developed an "opinion" on how revenue recognition for AvKARE had no foundational basis because of "the course of dealing." This was terribly unprofessional, and the fact that we were not given a chance to answer the implications of these prosecutorial decisions was very unprofessional, even corrupt, to say the least.

I suspect that, if this forensic audit had not been under the direction of Murphy, the former prosecutor from King & Spalding, there would have been a more objective consideration of the facts. I expect that Sally Yates was reminding Murphy of her DOJ doctrine. However, this particular doctrine "targets" upper management, and it provided Murphy with what he would continue to present to the Audit Committee and outside Board of Directors as executive wrongdoing. Also, the Board must have made up their mind by mid-May to terminate Bill and me because someone from the company approached Alvarez & Marsal, a business-consulting firm, in mid-May about hiring a temporary CEO. They decided to terminate Mike Senken and John Cranston first and Bill and me some weeks later.

In effect, what had been set up was a "takeover" of the company by dismissing the two top executives who were basically the founders. This left the company in the hands of a Board of Directors who had very little experience in managing or running any complex healthcare enterprise or any company for that matter. Their subsequent decisions devastated the company and its shareholders. However, due to the strength of the asset base that previous management had built, the company can regain some of its previous strengths with competent management. Perhaps that will eventually transpire since the Board finally terminated on September 15, 2022, their second CEO, Tim Wright, after three years of significant revenue drops, huge financial losses and failed clinical trials. They hired a fourth CEO, Joseph H. Capper, on January 30, 2023.

Because of the AvKARE accusation flaws, the investigation subsequently focused on four other distributor relationships during a period in mid-2015. KPMG claimed that the purchase orders from these distributors did not meet all the revenue recognition criteria. Therefore, they should not have been recorded as revenue until the cash was received. Actually, with all four of these transactions, the cash was received, but some from a foreign distributor at an extended timing. Much of these 2015 matters related to the launch of a totally new product, OrthoFlo, that had to be marketed through distributors because it had to be stored in freezers.

Again, the prosecutorial plan had to tie Bill and me to these four transactions in a way that made it look like we had kept significant information from our accounting staff, the Audit Committee and the auditors. They claimed that we either verbally or in writing developed "side deals" with these four distributors that made the treatment utilized by our accounting department incorrect. The claim was that our accounting staff was unaware of all of these <u>supposed</u> verbal and written commitments. Without getting into excruciating detail here, that allegation is just <u>not</u> <u>factual</u>. You will read those details in Chapter 21.

However, this is so typical of a prosecutor trying to build a case with false and misleading information. Again, had we been interviewed and allowed to answer questions in front of King & Spalding and the Board before the final decisions were made, all of this would have been debunked. I believe that, even as inexperienced as our Board was, once they heard our explanations and saw our documents, they would have called a "timeout" to this process. By <u>not</u> allowing us to testify and clear up these issues, Murphy got his case to the Board and the DOJ without any "due process." Of course, the Board should be ashamed for allowing an investigation process of this nature to occur with little to no control or overview. Some of them had other goals!

Accounting Reserves

It is very interesting to note that our "sales returns and allowances" reserves and our "bad debt" reserves were given <u>very</u> <u>little</u> <u>discussion</u> and <u>no</u> <u>consideration</u> during the King & Spalding investigation. These two reserve accounts are extremely important particularly when a company is in a fast-growth mode. I always managed my previous organizations by being certain that both of these reserve accounts were very adequately developed. These reserves are to protect for the negative revenue perturbations and profit changes that can occur as a company grows. We had a very disciplined process of developing those reserves on a quarterly basis and always felt that we were more than adequately reserved for any contingencies. For instance, when I resigned on June 30, 2018, the total reserves were approximately $10 million!

Often companies will build up these reserves for what accountants call a "cookie jar." In other words, as they are developing revenues ahead of their forecasts and plans, they will put more reserves in place. If they reach a "dry spell" where revenues are beginning to underperform their expectations, they will reach into those reserves at the end of the quarter, and let some of those flow back into their reported revenue. It should be noted that, at MiMedx, I believe we seldom took any revenues out of our reserves and put them back through the profit and loss statement. Even during the only quarter where we missed our forecast, which was the first quarter of 2016, we <u>never</u> <u>utilized</u> those reserves.

When Bill and I were asked to resign on the AvKARE accusations, we were told that this action was taken because the Board "Wanted to take the company in a different direction." This essentially meant that King & Spalding had not finished developing their "story" on why the executives were guilty of some type of misconduct. Actually, they wanted to prove that we were guilty of accounting fraud, which is a criminal offense. So, this would be a DOJ case, and we could very well be incarcerated if found guilty. Why? I am afraid it was politics from King & Spalding and Dewberry's CYA.

It was not until mid-September of 2018 that King & Spalding told us they had found accounting fraud, and we would be accused of that in the final investigation report. However, we were <u>never</u> officially given <u>any</u> details. In the meantime, Murphy was interacting with both the DOJ and the SEC in terms of passing on his prosecutorial "story" that had been advanced. Remember, his law firm and KPMG were to be paid approximately $40 million for developing this prosecutorial "story."

Sidley Austin Attorneys

As I previously mentioned, we had an incident with two of the Sidley Austin attorneys within a couple of months of them being given assignments by Lexi Haden. When the four of them arrived at the company, they had a very narcissistic attitude. Their attitude was, "Sidley has arrived, and we are taking over." I previously mentioned that their lack of business acumen and common sense caused numerous problems and frustrations even for the Board members.

The major issue was that Greaney and Rody had told me and the Board two blatant lies in order to push their agenda. In both cases, I verified that they had not told the truth, and I called them out to the Board because these were important issues the Board had been discussing. If I had remained at the company, they would no longer have been involved in any of our legal activities. I have never had a lawyer lie to me like these two individuals did. Also, I am certain that, when I exposed their lies to the Board, they developed a hatred for me.

I bring this up because in mid-September 2018, when my remaining on the Board was becoming an issue because I was calling out the numerous poor decisions they were making, I was asked to be on a call with the Sidley Austin attorneys. I knew that I was reaching the point where I needed to resign from the Board because of the upcoming proxy contest, which I expected to become quite antagonistic. The Sidley Austin attorneys advised my attorneys and me that King & Spalding had found out through their investigation that I was a liar and had misrepresented information to the Audit Committee, the auditors and the Board. Of course, I said that was a lie, and the normal due process of the law that I should be given would clarify my understanding of these allegations, and I would be able to respond. They stated that they did not have to provide due process of the law to either Bill or me.

As I thought about that encounter, I believe it goes back to the fact that Greaney and Rody told the Board and me some lies, and I called them out. Thus, they were doing their best to figure out a way "to return the favor." It is a shame that this relationship got off to such a very bad start and was not resolved by the Board by utilizing Simpson Thatcher, the firm I had selected from New York to replace Troutman Sanders. It seems as if there were some people on the Board who were concerned that such a change would have offended Lexi, which should have never been a consideration. Of course, Dewberry was trying to keep Lexi beholden to him particularly in the early phases of the investigation. Remember the 22 percent raise! Lexi later left the company.

Ernst & Young

Recall that, in January of 2017, I recommended to the Audit Committee that we consider retaining a Big Four auditing firm. This was prompted by input from several of our largest shareholders that the only "box" that needed to be checked on our performance was having a Big Four auditor. This suggestion came at the annual January J.P. Morgan Healthcare meeting from large institutional shareholders who had also owned my previous companies.

I explained to these large shareholders that our regional firm, Cherry Bekaert, had done a very satisfactory job and had met all of our requirements. As it turned out, our Cherry Bekaert audit manager had resigned in 2016 to go to a corporate position, and some administrative issues had developed. The Audit Committee became frustrated as well as those of us in executive management. However, as 2016 was completed and 2017 started, those difficulties had begun to dissipate.

I gave this matter a great deal of thought and discussed it with Mike Senken, our CFO, and others. I knew the wise advice that a public company should "never change auditors." However, I thought, as did the others, that the company was doing so well that we should make the move. So I followed Dewberry's request that I interview the Big Four in Atlanta and bring my recommendations to the Audit Committee. I selected EY, and the Audit Committee did their interviews. They decided to retain EY at the beginning of the third quarter. I felt that we should have waited until the start of a new year, but it was the Audit Committee's decision.

EY conducted their due diligence during the spring, and they were very complimentary after their review. They should have reviewed our March 1, 2017 press release on the Audit Committee's investigation of channel stuffing. They subsequently completed the third quarter review and were again very complimentary of our management systems and performance. This was when Cohodes first began his Twitter attacks on the company.

The key unknown with EY was how well their staff would work with our accounting staff and how they would cope with Cohodes' allegations. Relative to Cohodes, I gave Andy Brock, the account partner, a warning in November about Cohodes' bizarre methods of attacking companies and individuals. Actually, with their phone calls and letters to EY, Cohodes and his shills were much worse than I could ever have imagined.

As things turned out, Brock was a very narcissistic personality. He began to assert himself as our 2017 audit was being completed. In particular, he wanted to change the way we booked our revenue from the group purchasing organizations (GPOs). For years, we had booked these revenues as billed to the GPOs as gross revenues, and then booked their small commission of two to three percent separately as an expense. Brock wanted us to book the revenue as net of the commission, and either way, it resulted in the same operating profit for MiMedx as well as the GPOs. Our argument was that our method properly showed the actual revenue and a cost of developing that revenue in which management and many shareholders were interested. Brock's argument was that a high percent of their audit customers did it his way. This brought up the pressure that the PCAOB was putting on the Big Four to attempt to make accounting more scientific rather than just a profession of "opinions." As I have said, that is an attempt to force accounting into a science which will never happen because of the thousands of ways American businesses are managed and their diverse ways of recording data in order to better manage their operations.

Brock's narcissistic behavior quickly surfaced after he informed the Board on the February 6th call that EY would not finish our 2017 audit, which was due in two weeks, until we investigated all of Cohodes' allegations. I have provided the details of that call in Chapter 11. Within a few days, Brock went to see David Ghegan, our outside counsel at Troutman Sanders. He opened the conversation with Ghegan by accusing him of not doing a sufficient review on the whistleblower investigation a year earlier. Ghegan had been involved with all of our companies over the decades because Carl Sanders recognized his promising future and assigned him to the Healthdyne and Matria businesses. Ghegan knew the management team very well. He told me that Brock's comments about his knowledge of the investigation were "way out of line." I believe that Brock reiterated his point that the Audit Committee should have done a forensic audit which would have been very expensive considering the bizarre accusation of channel stuffing that was easily refuted by our years of audited statements and our robust cash flow. The forensic audit was an expensive accounting tool, which would match up with the Sally Yates Doctrine of forcing American companies to hire large law and accounting firms anytime an "accusation" is made!

Within a short time, our Board made the decision <u>without</u> my knowledge, to terminate Troutman Sanders as outside counsel. I expect this was prompted by Brock and encouraged by King & Spalding who Dewberry hired for the investigation.

At this point, MiMedx was going to suffer, just like Vascular Solutions, Hollinger International and Galleon, with unnecessary but huge legal and accounting fees and actions from our corrupt justice system.

To this day, I do not understand how EY could have treated a new client, which was a <u>very</u> <u>successful</u> company, in this manner. I do not know how far up the chain of command this decision to halt the audit went. I do know that Brock pressed people above his direct management on these matters. I do know that the EY demand to have Cohodes' allegations investigated was ignored by Dewberry, the Audit Committee, and Board because King & Spalding implemented a Sally Yates Doctrine investigation, which required all allegations to be focused on top management and not other people.

Regardless of the focus, EY resigned from the audit, as I told the Board they would, about nine months later. By that time, they had billed about four or five times the quote for the audit and had not produced one! To me, this represented a <u>total</u> <u>disregard</u> by EY for a quality client.

Revenue Restatement

It is a shame that the federal officials at the SEC and DOJ look the other way when it comes to illegal short sellers. We have discussed the numerous reasons why this is the case. However, please understand the pressure of being an executive in a fast-growth public company, and in addition, having to cope with the daily harassment from dishonest social media and other publications that are sponsored by short sellers. There is no excuse for regulators to allow this type of <u>illegal</u> action to occur. It is extremely unfair to the millions of devastated shareholders. Also, this type of neglect will result in rapidly reducing the number of companies that are publicly traded on our stock exchanges.

The 2017 financial statements were within two weeks of being finalized when EY called a halt to the audit. Finally, MiMedx published the 2017 and 2018 financial statements in March of 2020 with their 10-K. So it took the company over two years to publish the 2017 financial statements that were almost completed in February of 2018.

The excuse the company will use is that they decided they had to re-audit six years of revenues from 3,000 of our customers to a <u>cash</u> <u>basis</u>. Our customers were hospitals, wound care centers and doctor's offices, plus a few distributors. During those six years, we collected our revenues in a very efficient and effective manner. In fact, if you looked at approximately a billion dollars in revenues during that period of time, you would find that we collected approximately a billion dollars in cash. At the same time, we were so profitable that we managed to repurchase $132 million of our own stock in the market. That clearly demonstrates a very efficient and effective management of our cash flow. Finally, our days sales outstanding (DSOs) in our accounts receivable, when I resigned on June 30th of 2018, were approximately 65 days. That metric is a very strong indicator of our efficient cash collection activities. There should have been little concern about the rate in which we collected our cash from the revenues we published for shareholders. Hence, why all the "noise" about revenue recognition and our cash collections?

Because of the massive additional legal and accounting expenses, there was a great need by the Board as well as the King & Spalding prosecutor to create <u>the</u> <u>myth</u> that there had been this huge mismanagement of the accounting function at the company. Thus, the Board went along with a <u>very</u> <u>expensive</u> <u>restatement</u> of all six years of those revenues from an accrual basis to a cash basis. Apparently, it did not matter whether it was one of the largest hospitals in the country or a doctor's office or a distributor, everyone was assumed to have a problematic or corrupt cash flow issue. All the approximate $1 billion in revenues had to be in doubt. Things could not have been any further from the truth! But, this action supported the CYA approach by Dewberry, the King & Spalding financial goals and the Yates' political agenda.

The most disappointing piece of this revenue restatement was the enormous costs associated with the audit work as well as the legal work. I have mentioned that the investigation cost approximately $40 million, which went predominantly to King & Spalding. The company commented in their March 2020 10-K Report that they expected to spend $125 million on the investigation and final audits. That was later raised to $150 million and then again to over $200 million. I am not certain exactly what the additional restatement process cost, but I was told there was $80 million associated with those costs. All that wasted money, which came out of the pockets of our shareholders, occurred because of the Audit Committee Chairman and his CYA paranoia and the outside Board members not paying attention to their fiduciary responsibility to shareholders. All this has been a pathetic demonstration of a Board's lack of focus on its fiduciary duty to shareholders, but rather a focus on themselves instead.

In questioning accounting experts about the plethora of new rules and regulations, it was revealed that many of them are put in place because some corporate entity found a new creative way to manipulate their accounting. Thus, FASB and their accounting experts decide to add a new rule that all 4,200 public companies in America have to use in order to circumvent one company's creativity, which resulted in producing a new accounting rule!

In many cases, these new regulations can cause immense headaches and problems from industry to industry. It seems as though common sense would prevail such that the PCAOB and Accounting Board (FASB) would simply issue a warning for all auditors to look for these particular types of activities as they go through their audit procedure. That would very efficiently change corporate behavior without forcing 4,200 other public companies to comply with some new rule that probably has nothing to do with the way they account for the same matters in their systems as related to their industry. However, the extra accounting fees to formally investigate a new rule with all clients is certainly a boost to accounting firms' revenue. Those fees fleece American shareholders, but they boost profits for the accounting firms.

Changes in Financial Statements

In March of 2020, MiMedx finally published their Form 10-K annual report for the fiscal year ended December 31, 2018. Since these were the first annual financial statements that the company had published since early 2017, the documents included financial statements for 2016, 2017, and 2018. In addition, some unaudited financials were presented for 2014 and 2015. These adjustments were primarily made because the Board decided that they would restate all revenues from an accrual basis to a cash basis. This document is full of the reasons and/or excuses for determining that those restatements <u>were</u> <u>necessary</u> with the <u>exception</u> of <u>one</u> <u>clarifying</u> <u>sentence</u> on page F-27! I will review that very important statement later.

I have previously discussed the incentives for Dewberry and Borkowski to extend the investigation and the audits for their own personal reasons. In the 10-K document, the Board highlighted their expectation that the auditing and investigation costs were to be approximately $125 million before they were completed. Thus, you can see the motivation for the various accounting firms to agree with the restatements because of the fees that would accrue for their firms. As I just mentioned, I am certain these fees will top $200 million, perhaps even $250 million!

This 10-K document is certainly the longest 10-K that I recall being issued from any of our previous companies. It is approaching 200 pages. There are numerous charts with financial information. There is also an inordinate number of allegations made as to why the Board decided to restate these six years of revenues. The more I read the accusations, the more I want to emphasize that these decisions were <u>supposedly</u> made by former management who <u>knowingly</u> made improper commitments that breached the written contractual agreements with AvKARE and some of our other distributors.

First, all these distributor agreements had clauses that stated they <u>could</u> <u>not</u> be modified without written consent of both parties. Of course, there is a legal concept called "in the course of dealing" which can modify written contracts in certain instances. However, the former prosecutor from King & Spalding and the accountants from KPMG used statements that they found in emails that I would characterize as business philosophy statements as opposed to business process and procedure statements. In other words, they were statements made to new distributors like, "We are the type of business people who would be <u>flexible</u> and understand if you develop cash flow problems. We would certainly take any extenuating circumstances into account and not immediately file lawsuits for collection purposes."

King & Spalding took those types of statements to mean that we had modified the written agreements such that they did not have to pay us for the products we shipped to them for their purchase orders as per their Distributor Agreement. What makes this worse is that the former prosecutor from King & Spalding, Murphy, never interviewed Bill or me to obtain firsthand information on what comments of that nature meant and how we interpreted them for the distributors.

In addition, Murphy's written comments to the Board of Directors stated that Bill and I <u>refused</u> to talk to King & Spalding. That is absolutely <u>not</u> true. An appointment had been set up with us for interviews, and King & Spalding <u>canceled</u> it. This happened two days before we were asked to resign by the Board on June 30th so King & Spalding canceled the appointment knowing that they had already recommended to the Board that we be terminated!

Now several months after Bill and I had been dismissed by the company, King & Spalding submitted another request to meet with us. By that time, we had been told by another MiMedx corporate counsel that King & Spalding had made up their mind about our guilt and had reported that to the Board of Directors so we should not give them an interview at that time.

This is quite unfortunate because no due process was given to us prior to these decisions being made. Due process is one of the basics of obtaining good, clear information and providing a fair and balanced approach to investigations and potential subsequent legal charges.

Recall that the first allegations made by King & Spalding and KPMG were that we needed to restate all of the AvKARE revenues from the inception of the contract because <u>we</u> <u>had</u> <u>allowed</u> them to pay us only when they were being paid by the VA hospitals. That payment history for AvKARE and the related details are absolutely <u>not</u> <u>factual</u>. I previously discussed AvKARE's immature accounting system that could not even tell us which invoices to charge their cash receipts against.

Our collection efforts with AvKARE were basically just as they were with our other distributors and all our accounts. I personally called AvKARE and had them forward to us approximately $2 million on two different occasions. Our staff called and had them forward other payments, which were totally unrelated to any payments they received or expected to receive from the VA. In addition, if it was fact that we were allowing them to pay us only when they were going to be paid by the VA hospitals, they would have <u>absolutely</u> asked us to put that in <u>Amendment</u> <u>4</u> to their contract as we were cleaning things up for the wind-down process. Therefore, the AvKARE situation should <u>never</u> have been allowed to gain any credibility by the Board of Directors. Since we were not given due process, the King & Spalding prosecutor was allowed to build and create this <u>false</u> <u>narrative</u>. As I mentioned, these were the allegations on which the Board asked for Bill's and my resignations. But, <u>most</u> <u>importantly</u>, the DOJ <u>did</u> <u>not</u> even use this particular King & Spalding myth to file charges against Bill and me. I believe they saw the lack of truthful facts and the misinformation. What does that say about the allegation, which was used to request that Bill and I resign? May I use a colloquialism…a trumped up lie!

Now there were some other distributor sales in the middle of 2015, most of which were related to the introduction of our new OrthoFlo liquid product, that were questioned. King & Spalding made accusations about "side deals" which could have modified our contracts with those distributors. Again, due process would have overridden these accusations, but we were not allowed to present the real facts in those cases either. These cases will be discussed thoroughly in subsequent chapters.

Conservatively Reserved

Anytime a public company has to go back and restate any of its previous financial information it always causes concerns. Even if it is related to a relatively minor issue, the speculation from short selling rhetoric will develop rapidly. Therefore, be certain that, as an executive officer of a public company, you do focus on the "sales returns and allowances" reserves and the "bad debt" reserves that are accrued monthly. You should attempt to build those two reserve amounts up as conservatively as possible as we did.

I would like to relate a discussion that I had on this matter with one of our auditors many years ago. When I said something in a meeting where the auditors were present about being "conservatively reserved," I got a lecture from one of them. He reminded me that it was just as bad to be over-reserved as it was to be under-reserved. He stated that we would have to continually verify that the reserves we were carrying on our books were not too conservative because, if they were, some amount would have to be booked back into revenue for that period. I listened to him articulate his position, and then I reminded him that accounting was a "profession of opinions." Also, I stated that he and his staff's opinions on reserves versus our staff's opinions could be different. However, we were the customer, and I expected we knew more about our business activities and the risk profile which we reviewed monthly than they did. Therefore, it would take a lot to change our minds about our reserve positions.

My advice is to be conservatively reserved. If that means overly reserved at times, so be it. You have a strong fiduciary responsibility to your shareholders, and I submit to you that means you should be reasonably conservative with all your accounting activities. In today's accounting environment, there are so many rule changes and philosophy changes that can come back to cause a company problems. Therefore, I believe you need to always have your reserves in a conservative status.

Speaking of reserves, our total reserves in the second quarter of 2015 were about $3.5 million, which was about seven percent of our quarterly revenues. Over the next two years, we built those reserves up to over $10 million, which was over ten percent of our quarterly revenue at that point! We would generally add reserves each quarter depending on the decisions made in a meeting that occurred between our executives, our accountants and sales management. At those meetings, we would discuss our revenues for the quarter and attempt to highlight any potential risks. We would review the accounts receivable from our problematic accounts to see if there could be any possible bankruptcy or other payment delays. Later on, we reached the point where we would generally take a percent of the quarterly revenue and book that into the reserve accounts. Either way, we did our best to stay on top of all those types of issues and to always be conservatively reserved so shareholders were never given inaccurate revenue information.

The Company's Revenue Restatement

Let me attempt to give you some overview of the revenue changes the Audit Committee made when they restated revenues for all 3,000 of our customers from 2012 to 2017. When you do a restatement of this nature, you reduce the revenues in the prior periods and increase them going forward. We were collecting our revenue on an average of 65 days when we were asked to resign. Therefore, I expect they just took every dollar's worth of accrued revenue and delayed it being booked into revenue until it was collected in cash.

The revenues were changed in an unaudited fashion for 2014 and 2015. Revenues for 2014 were reduced from $118,223,000 to $105,257,000. 2015 revenues were reduced from $187,296,000 to $153,131,000. The audited revenues were presented for 2016, 2017 and 2018, which were restated. Revenues for 2016 were restated from $245,015,000 to $221,712,000; 2017 revenues came in at $321,139,000. And, this is interestingly within approximately $2 million of the revenue, which we had booked for 2017 prior to all of this restatement work. The 2018 revenue came in at $359,111,000.

Recall that Bill and I left on June 30th, and the first two quarters of 2018 were still in a robust growth profile of above 30 percent. We had booked revenues of approximately $93 million for the first quarter and approximately $98 million for the second quarter. We had forecast in excess of $400 million for calendar year 2018. Because of the poor decisions and mismanagement by the Board, revenues immediately fell rather significantly in the third and fourth quarters of 2018, and they continued to fall until 2022. However, I am not sure how much of this cash revenue that was taken out of earlier years was put into late 2018 to cover the Board's disastrous management decisions.

The 10-K highlighted that the company expected, when they reported 2019 revenues, they would be approximately 25 percent lower than 2018 revenues. That would mean that 2019 revenues would be significantly less than $300 million. Previously, executive management had given shareholders a five-year outlook on our revenue growth. We expected 2020 to be at $560 million with $1.00 of earnings per share. You can see the major damage that has occurred to the company's revenue growth and profitability, which has been caused by the decisions this Board made. Also, I see that they spent $51.3 million on the investigation and restatement and the related expenses in 2018. Again, they are forecasting to spend a total of $125 million by the time this investigation is over. Recently, they raised that to $150 million, then to $180 million and finally to over $200 million!

This 10-K document is filled with pages of accounting commentary on all the things the Board has done to improve the company from an accounting standpoint. They have long lists of numerous things the new accounting firms decided MiMedx needed to implement. As I read through these suggestions, it is clear that they are taking a company that is now back to less than $250 million a year in revenues and treating it as a multi-billion dollar revenue company. While this is a worthy endeavor, it is a process that needs to be taken a <u>step</u> at <u>a</u> <u>time</u>. Having grown my previous public companies in rapid fashion, I think I have good insight as to when new systems, new procedures and new accounting processes need to be added.

Of course, the new auditors took the "blank check" atmosphere by advising our original inept Board of what else they needed to do to prepare the company to function with perfect accounting and financial controls. I submit to you that this Board was so inexperienced that they may have funded a very expensive accounting system for a company that would not need that degree of sophistication for a decade!

In their 10-K document for 2017 and 2018, the Board has numerous statements claiming that the company's previous revenue recognition policies and actions were inadequate. In the majority of these disclosures, the company has twisted and misrepresented the facts, and in some cases, actually <u>lied</u>. Much of this information could have been easily corrected if they had interviewed us. I will present a few examples; however, this is pretty typical of what we have already discussed related to a prosecutor focusing on an individual they want to charge rather than finding a real crime and then accumulating facts that prove the crime with the proper people involved.

Review of the 10-K

If you plan to review the company's 2018 10-K dated March 2020, please go to page F-27 first and read the top paragraph. The company is saying if you were to review the five years of revenue that were restated from AvKARE and the other 3,000 customers, the effects are not material. That means, they fall within the normal error profile. When you take into account the substantial "reserves" that we developed over the years to cover matters of that nature, those issues should never have been the major consideration for doing any restatements.

For instance, the company commented on established credit limits as having been overridden on occasion by sales personnel and members of management. However, most importantly, their comments were: "DESPITE THESE OVERRIDES, THE COMPANY RECOVERED THE MAJORITY OF ITS BILLINGS MADE BETWEEN 2012 AND 2017 WITH INSIGNIFICANT WRITE OFFS RECORDED; HOWEVER, A SIGNIFICANT AMOUNT OF THESE BILLINGS WERE COLLECTED WELL AFTER PAYMENT WAS DUE UNDER THE CONTRACTUAL TERMS. FURTHERMORE, THE QUANTITATIVE AND QUALITATIVE EVIDENCE GATHERED BY THE COMPANY RAISED CONSIDERABLE DOUBT AS TO THE COLLECTABILITY OF ITS BILLINGS AT THE TIME OF SHIPMENT, BUT THIS EVIDENCE WAS NOT PERSUASIVE ENOUGH FOR THE COMPANY TO REACH A CONCLUSION AS TO WHETHER COLLECTABILITY WAS REASONABLY ASSURED."

Both of these comments clearly indicate that the company's investigation struggled to find instances where its cash flow from its revenue billings was actually impeded by any of these so-called "side deals," credit overrides or inappropriate revenue recognition. The company's collectability statement that, "This evidence was not persuasive enough" in these situations to not book the revenue, shows a lack of business and accounting acumen because they had to admit that the cash was collected. We, as previous management, knew it would be collected, and there was an enviable track record of so doing. These statements are designed as CYA comments for the Audit Committee and the investigators, and they are self-serving and dishonest.

I will remind you again that we built up over the years substantial "sales and allowances" reserves and "bad debt" reserves, which would have certainly covered any minor shortfalls between reported revenue and actual cash received. That is the <u>ultimate determinant</u> in whether a company has reported revenue inappropriately. Also, recall that our days sales outstanding (DSOs) in accounts receivable was at approximately 65 days when we left the company. This is <u>very</u> acceptable, and it is probably below the average of most healthcare companies in our sector of healthcare. Therefore, we were doing a very good job of collecting our accounts receivable. So when they stated that a significant amount of these billings were collected well after payment was due, they are referring to our normal "net 30-day" terms on invoices. In our U.S. healthcare system, <u>very few invoices</u> are collected on those terms by <u>any</u> business entity.

Now, most of the accusations made against former management in this 10-K came from the investigation report prepared by King & Spalding. Reflect back on the comments that have come from Sidney Powell and Harvey Silverglate on how prosecutors focus on individuals, not on whether a crime has been committed when so motivated. Well, I expect the approximate $40 plus million that was billed to MiMedx by King & Spalding and KPMG was motivation enough. King & Spalding made their accusations and never gave management due process to counter their arguments. I can safely say they never presented full information to the Board when they would make their presentations. I have seen numerous "old fashioned lies" given to the Board about former management. This matched well with the directives that were certainly given by Dewberry in terms of his self-interest to not be accused of any mismanagement himself. I will document the King & Spalding misinformation and lies with their actual communications to the Board in Chapter 21.

Unfortunately, in America we are currently going through "The Accusation Era." We have reached the point where, thanks to the national news media, accusations made against an individual are accepted as guilt. We see that happening in so many different facets of American life, and the more accusations that can be made, the guiltier a person must be. You can see this idea pushed by the MiMedx primary short seller, Cohodes. He made 10-plus key accusations in the fall of 2017. Accusations were made that violations occurred relative to numerous healthcare regulations. They range from Medicare fraud to bribing physicians. It is interesting that no mention was made in the investigation report or the March 2020 10-K of how those accusations were false and unsupportable. That gets back to EY asking for Cohodes' accusations to be <u>fully</u> investigated, but the King & Spalding investigation focused on "targeting" the top executives instead, as per the Sally Yates Doctrine. Of course, that matched Dewberry's CYA goals.

When the Board finally had to disclose that there had been <u>no revenue growth</u> after my and Bill's departure, it was another major disappointment to shareholders. The company was maintaining a 30 percent revenue growth when Bill and I resigned on June 30, 2018. I was afraid that the revenues they did not book with the restatements because they went to a cash basis would miraculously show up later when they needed to cover up their lack of management of revenue growth. Those cash receipts which would then be booked as revenue will show up in these later periods when the Board will start being held accountable because they will begin reporting financial statements on a routine basis again. They did not report financial statements for a two-year period.

Where will the $75 million of deferred revenue from 2014, 2015 and 2016 eventually show up? I predicted it would show up in 2020 as the company had to start explaining to the shareholders how badly the original Board's decisions over the last several years have devastated the company, its shareholders and employees. Of course, even after all these years, they will point at the company's significant deteriorating revenue performance as being caused by former management or the COVID crisis!

As I stated much earlier in the book, with the 2017 audit basically complete, Cherry Bekaert could have finished it up rather quickly if the Board had not relied upon the allegations made by an illegal short seller and corrupt employees. This large investigation found that there was not any channel stuffing by the company. However, they decided that there were places in 2015 that the company had not accounted for revenues properly because former management made statements to certain distributors that King & Spalding viewed as violations of the written contracts with those distributors. Although the company had to admit in their 10-K that the <u>revenue</u> <u>was</u> <u>collected</u> <u>in</u> <u>cash</u> with <u>insignificant</u> write-offs from 2012 until 2017. The 2017-2018 10-K document is full of all types of allegations against former management that promotes some type of criminal activity. This is easily understood if you take into account the CYA motivations of the Chairman of the Audit Committee and King & Spalding and KPMG attempting to cover themselves while building very unreasonable fees.

As I have previously stated, this was a diabolical corporate "takeover" by a group of inexperienced, the board, who used the short selling allegations against the company for their own benefit. Our shareholders, employees and even customers were severely damaged by this process that was supported by law firms and accounting firms because of the huge billings they could extract because of the inexperienced and self-dealing Board members.

The Final Revenue Filter

The DOJ's case against Bill and me was based on their claim that in 2015 we allowed the company to recognize revenue from four transactions that were recorded in the wrong quarter. These allegations came from King & Spalding's "supposed" investigation. There was no valid claim that these were not real revenues for real products sold to real customers who paid for the products. There were technical points made about revenue recognition violations, which claimed they should have been booked when the revenue was collected in cash.

King & Spalding and KPMG ignored a key accounting matter, which would have made their allegations <u>baseless</u> which is that very few of the quarterly revenue transactions are seen by shareholders in a company's published financial statements. There is a <u>final</u> <u>step</u> that involves booking the "sales returns and allowances" reserves and the "bad debt" reserves. Generally, this results in a company reducing the final published revenues and profits by certain amounts, depending on that quarter's reserves review by executive management. This key step in recognizing revenue results in only publishing revenue to stockholders that will be collected in cash within a reasonable period of time. At my previous four public companies and at MiMedx, I always tried to be conservatively reserved to be sure that shareholders did not get surprises from hospital or distributor bankruptcies and other revenue and cash collection surprises.

Thus, Bill and I were faulted for revenue recognition issues, which really <u>did not exist</u>. This <u>farce</u> had to be orchestrated by certain Board members for CYA motivations and by King & Spalding to keep the investigation ongoing for 15 months with legal fees of over $25 million. After spending about $80 million on re-audits to cover all of their allegations, the company had to publish a statement with the 2017 and 2018 10-K report that basically exposed all the dishonesty related to their accounting restatements. Also, the company did, for some unknown reason, decide to book the sales commissions paid to GPOs and IDNs not as a sales expense, but as a reduction in gross sales in order to derive net sales. This was not a very logical decision, but it was pushed by Brock and EY.

I will delve into the numerous details of the four supposed incorrect distributor transactions in Chapter 21. I will clearly demonstrate the corrupt manipulations by King & Spalding and the Audit Committee in developing their accusations while <u>ignoring</u> and <u>hiding</u> the reserves and other facts that covered any possible revenue misstatements.

My Thoughts on Revenue Recognition

I would like to give you an "old warhorse" operating executive's overview and definition of "revenue recognition." This subject has been modified and changed over the decades. It used to embody just four main issues. However, as a few companies became creative, a number of other requirements were added. The SAB Topic 13 document came into effect about 10 years ago. I was not even aware of that new publication until our accounting controversy developed.

The public accounting document that contains the revenue recognition requirements is now almost 400 pages in length. It is virtually impossible for an operating executive or even an accountant to have full command of all the specifics. However, with some business experience and common sense, most of these rules, and I will emphasize most, do make some sense. However, many of the new ones beg the question of why does the Accounting Board create rules for all 4,200 public companies when only one or two have devised a new way around a particular issue. Instead of creating a new rule, the Accounting Board should alert the accounting profession what to look out for instead of burdening everyone in trying to figure out if a new rule has any applicability to their business enterprise in their industry. Only my humble opinion!

To me, revenue recognition simply connotes that, when a company discloses it has a certain amount of revenue, everything is in place to be certain that revenue turns into cash in their bank account. Everything is and should be focused on that simple consideration of whether revenue that was booked will, first, turn into cash in their bank or other holding entity, and second, did that transpire in a reasonable period of time.

Over the decades, as I saw the rules changing, I realized this was caused by the increased scrutiny of the various accounting oversight groups. First, I realized that being overly conscious of our revenue reserves would be a practical way to assure compliance. Therefore, decades ago I set up systems in our companies such that there were monthly reviews of our accounts receivable and other revenue and cash flow issues. If we saw any problems that could develop, we would increase our "sales returns and allowances" reserves and our "bad debt" reserves so there was no doubt we were providing shareholders with "reasonably accurate" information on the reported revenues that we expected to turn into cash in that reasonable period of time. Every company will continually make some, hopefully minor, mistakes in these revenue accruals, and they need to be protected by keeping their reserve elements at reasonable levels. Thus, as executives go through their monthly assessments of these particular operating parameters, they should be able to book sufficient reserves in both categories to keep shareholders accurately informed within reason. However, a company's "sales returns and allowances" reserves and "bad debt" reserves are a key element in this effort to keep revenue recognition under control because there are so many new rules being formulated.

By using principles of this nature and remaining very inquisitive on a monthly basis, I was assured that all of our public companies maintained adequate reserves and did not have revenue recognition issues over the decades. To have an individual who is not an experienced public company business executive, such as a lawyer, a prosecutor or accountant begin pouring through revenue recognition criteria in the 400-page document and trying to apply those rules to any complex operating business is a recipe for disaster. It might not be a disaster for their billing fees, but it certainly will be a disaster on decisions they make about these complex business issues, particularly if they are working on their own self-serving agenda.

EY and KPMG Malfeasance

I have been asked several times why I thought accountants would create misinformation and dishonesty like prosecutors. These individuals stated that accountants should not have the same career motivational factors encouraging them to proselyte themselves. My response was, while I never held accountants to the same ethical standards to which I originally held attorneys, the pressure that their firms put on them for more billings is always a threat to ethical conduct.

Also, I have previously discussed the fallout from the creation of the PCAOB by the Sarbanes-Oxley Act. The PCAOB is one of the "watchdog" agencies for our accounting firms. Their particular focus is necessarily on the Big Four auditors because they do the audit work for the majority of the 4,200 public companies in America. Thus, there is a significant amount of pressure on those firms, as I have previously pointed out. This unique focus and undue pressure has caused two of the big four firms, namely EY and KPMG, to recently pay huge fines for violations.

In June 2022, the SEC announced that Ernst & Young will pay a record $100 million penalty after admitting that a significant number of its audit professionals cheated on their certified public accounting exams, and the company withheld key evidence from the regulators. This was the largest fine ever levied against an audit firm.

This SEC investigation determined that EY's audit professionals cheated on the ethics component of their CPA exam as well as other mandatory exams required to maintain their CPA licenses. The SEC found that 49 EY workers sent or received answer keys related to the CPA ethics exam over a four-year period. Also, hundreds of other audit employees cheated on their "continuing professional education" courses. Finally, the SEC said that, "and a significant number of EY professionals who did not cheat themselves, but knew their colleagues were cheating and facilitating cheating, violated the firm's code of conduct by failing to report this misconduct." This is the same breakdown that occurred with MiMedx salespeople not reporting Kruchoski's alleged sales scheme for which MiMedx filed lawsuits.

The SEC pointed out that this EY penalty was twice as large as the $50 million penalty that rival firm KPMG agreed to pay in 2019 in order to settle federal allegations. These allegations included the fact that some of its former employees cheated on their training exams among other purported misdeeds. These charges followed the January 2018 press release from the U.S. Attorney's Office for the Southern District of New York that KPMG executives and recently hired PCAOB employees were involved in a fraudulent scheme to steal valuable and confidential PCAOB information and use that information to fraudulently improve KPMG inspection results by the PCAOB. See Chapter 20 Appendix for these details.

Accounting Summary

The MiMedx investigators or their forensic auditors never considered the company's well-reserved status when they began making accusations about certain 2015 distributor revenues not being properly booked in the right quarter. Remember, these were not imaginary revenues because they were collected in cash. I believe that they were properly reserved at the time they were booked. In fact, in some cases, extra reserves were added during these quarters to cover any possibilities of some of those particular revenues not being collected. Thus, what was orchestrated against MiMedx and its former executives was a diabolical "Witch Hunt" that was out of control from the start because of the terms of the contract that the Audit Committee signed with King & Spalding and the lack of reasonable overview from a competent Board of Directors.

In the 2017 and 2018 10-K that the company published in March of 2020, they clearly stated that between 2012 and 2017 the company collected its booked revenues with insignificant write-offs recorded. Where was the need for this massively expensive restatement of revenues for five years when what was booked was collected in cash in a timely manner because the company's DSOs did not get out of reasonable ranges during that period or <u>any</u> other period? The restatement costs were approximately $80 million on their own! This was a CYA action to attempt to justify the investigation and its huge expenses as well as cover Dewberry's unnecessary paranoia.

As KPMG built their case on our federal distributor, AvKARE, in which they claimed that we needed to restate six years of their revenues, I was surprised and shocked. We were not aware of this situation until there was a large meeting at King & Spalding on May 23, 2018. Three months into the investigation, they had already found and built a case <u>against</u> our booking the AvKARE revenue on an accrual basis rather than a cash basis. I have discussed those issues thoroughly in several chapters of this book. I can simply say that it was quite appalling to see professional auditors manipulate facts so egregiously. I will point out that the DOJ, in filing their indictments against Bill and me, <u>ignored</u> the AvKARE allegations made by KPMG and King & Spalding. I believe they saw through these allegations because there were not any meaningful supporting documents or facts.

I have to say that where there is a corporate investigation with high fees for lawyers and auditors, wrongdoing and fraud can or will be found. I do not think there is any way for an investigation of this nature to take place in which hundreds of thousands of emails from numerous individuals are reviewed that a prosecutor or forensic accountant would not be able to develop some issue that focuses on top management or certainly other executive management. However, when I witnessed the loose nature of the proof of their allegations, <u>it</u> <u>was</u> <u>appalling</u>. In fact, it was so loose and manipulated that I was ashamed in terms of how the practice of American law has deteriorated in certain law firms.

King & Spalding and KPMG apparently saw the weakness in their AvKARE allegations so they continued looking for other possible misconduct. They ended up focusing on some events that happened three years prior in the middle of 2015. That is when we were launching a new product, OrthoFlo, and the launch had to be managed through distributors because it had to be cryogenically frozen. King & Spalding and KPMG developed unsubstantiated proof of their allegations that certain distributor transactions during the second and third quarters of 2015 did not meet GAAP revenue recognition criteria. They alleged that Bill and I had made verbal and written statements to these dealers that changed their written agreements and did not disclose that action to our accountants and auditors. Those allegations are <u>not</u> true, and they will be detailed and refuted later.

Also, what happened to a review and public rebuttal of all the Cohodes' allegations that EY requested? Apparently, that was not done in order to protect the short seller and implement the Sally Yates Doctrine at MiMedx! Hence, the "targeting" of the top executives.

The lessons to be learned here by entrepreneurs, executive management, Boards and shareholders are simply just how destructive this type of expensive investigatory process can become, particularly when it is not managed by the Board. While the Sally Yates Doctrine is dictating that this is "standard operating practice," I think that, with the MiMedx case as a Poster Child, an astute Board needs to push back on such a process. You need to engage a law firm that has the experience and courage to go head-to-head with the regulators, and then decide if a Yates investigation is required. A Board has a business to oversee and where appropriate, manage. Also, they have fiduciary responsibilities to shareholders, and those responsibilities are not met by turning the enterprise over to lawyers or accountants! A Board should remain aligned with management as much as possible and as long as possible. Boards should provide the <u>benefit of the doubt</u> to their management and give them due process of the law.

I have mentioned several times the significant overreach of the Audit Committee's decision to restate the company's revenues for a six-year period because of the AvKARE distributorship. I have called out how out-of-line and ridiculous that decision turned out to be. I have discussed several reasons why I have drawn that conclusion. First was the fact that there was no mention of an alteration in required payment terms for AvKARE in Addendum 4, which was the last change to the AvKARE contract. There had been a change in the payment requirements for invoices in Addendum 2 in which the payment terms were extended to 75 days from 45 days. However, this major change that the Audit Committee and King & Spalding alleged was not factual because there was no mention of those changes in Addendum 4 nor were there any emails or other communications asking for those changes to be made and put in Addendum 4. In addition, the company clearly stated in their March 2020 10-K filing with the SEC that, "the company collected all of its revenues in 2012 to 2017 with inconsequential write-offs." Finally, the Department of Justice did <u>not</u> file any allegations of fraud against Petit and Taylor for the AvKARE case. I have also said that this would go down in accounting history as one of the most ridiculous decisions made by an Audit Committee. That is certainly reinforced by the following comments that come from "Audit Analytics."

A recent Wall Street Journal article citing Audit Analytics data noted that the period of time affected by the MiMedx restatement is four times longer than the average, indicating a substantial longstanding problem. In 2017, on average, companies necessitating restated financial statements had to go back about 500 days, while a period of non-reliance from MiMedx spans nearly five years. Where was Dewberry and our Audit Committee?

Remember, Bill and I were indicted for a "scheme" to report revenues to shareholders in the wrong quarters of 2015. These "misreported" revenues were basically collected in cash, and they amounted to approximately $9 million out of approximately $187 million in revenues for 2015. Even if you <u>assume</u> this $9 million was <u>purposely</u> reported incorrectly, the company spent $80 million on accountants to do the unnecessary restatements. Does that make sense? Also, I estimate there has been another $140 million spent on all other aspects of the investigation, primarily with law firms! This will prove to be one of the most out of control, absurd and corrupt corporate governance actions in recent history. Remember, they <u>ignored</u> our <u>revenue reserves</u>.

As I previously stated, if I knew that I or any other executive had purposely created accounting or any type of fraud, why would I have recommended to the audit committee to change auditors? That recommendation would have been absolutely idiotic!!

In ensuing chapters, you will see more details on how travesties of this nature can develop, why they develop and what you can potentially do to be certain it does not happen in your organization.

Chapter 20 Appendix

Ernst & Young to Pay $100 Million Penalty for Employees Cheating on CPA Ethics Exams and Misleading Investigation.

5 Former KPMG Executives and PCAOB Employees Charged in Manhattan Federal Court for Fraudulent Scheme to Steal Valuable and Confidential PCAOB Information and Use That Information to Fraudulently Improve KPMG Inspection Results

KPMG and Atlanta Auditor Pay $6 Million-Plus to Settle SEC Charges.

CHAPTER 21

MIMEDX'S ALLEGATIONS AGAINST EXECUTIVES

There were many causal factors related to the MiMedx investigation, the re-audits and related matters. They evolved from an unethical whistleblower to a deceitful short seller to a self-serving Big Four auditor to a paranoid Audit Committee Chairman in a CYA mode to an inexperienced and somewhat uninvolved Board to large self-serving law and accounting firms conducting the investigation and finally to the government's attorneys trying to further their careers. All of this resulted in essentially a "corporate takeover." Over 15,000 shareholders were fleeced, and 24 percent of the 1,000 person workforce was dismissed. The following chapters will be full of many lessons for business executives, their boards and their shareholders, which should be extremely informative.

One self-inflicted factor that certainly drove a number of the decisions was the Audit Committee's Chairman, Terry Dewberry, going into a state of destructive paranoia over being accused by Ernst & Young of "not conducting a sufficient investigation" of the allegations made by our unscrupulous sales manager and whistleblower who was terminated for cause. This is demonstrated by Dewberry making the same comment at two Board meetings, which was, "I'm not going to let the SEC put me in jail." Dewberry was chastised by legal counsel and me when these comments were made. Incidentally, the Securities and Exchange Commission (SEC) files civil cases against individuals. However, in spite of Dewberry's many years of being on audit committees, I believe he was so fixated on his <u>nonexistent</u> problem and his <u>CYA agenda</u> that either he was not thinking clearly, perhaps due to aging, or he was being malicious. That type of behavior exhibited itself over the course of this "corporate takeover" and investigation, and his behavior unnecessarily caused a number of the company's major problems, huge expenses and shareholder devastation.

In reading through the Brady and Jencks information, which was given to us before our trial, and by talking to Board members, it is very clear that Dewberry over-controlled the investigation from the start. He had a phone call with Paul Murphy, a former prosecutor and attorney at King & Spalding who would conduct this investigation, within two days of EY telling us that they would not finish the 2017 audit until <u>all</u> of Cohodes allegations were thoroughly investigated. I was told that the call with King & Spalding occurred on February 8, 2018. On that call, I was told that Dewberry committed to contract with King & Spalding for the investigation. The Board was not involved, and I was still on vacation that week.

In addition, Dewberry never established an investigation scope, goals and objectives, budget or schedule to be presented to the Board of Directors. He went off on his own, and that was probably motivated by his paranoia to be certain that he was not faulted in any way. I was told over a year later that the King & Spalding contract was so broad and complex that the Board had no input relative to the investigation! Can you imagine?

I suspect Murphy or his staff advised Dewberry very quickly of the Sally Yates Doctrine. Her doctrine required an investigation of this nature to "target" top management regardless of the allegations or credibility of the accuser. In fact, as the investigation proceeded, I was told that there was very little to no focus on Cohodes' allegations, as had been specifically requested by EY.

I believe Dewberry realized that, if the executives were not accused of accounting fraud, then he and the Audit Committee might be accused of accounting mistakes. Therefore, a "theme" developed that, even though Bill and I were not accountants, we must have conspired to withhold important accounting information from our accountants, the Audit Committee and our auditors. Not only was it a myth that management had agreed to allow AvKARE to pay their accounts payable to MiMedx only when they were paid by the VA, but the myth went back to the start of the contract in 2012. Remember, that myth began as the result of an email from one of the AvKARE administrators basically saying that is what AvKARE would like to do. There was never any confirmation from anyone at MiMedx that we accepted such a process, and we did not.

In fact, you could probably accuse most American businesses of only paying their bills when they have sufficient cash. Does that mean that the PCAOB and the SEC are going to dictate to public accounting firms that accounting for corporate revenues on a cash basis becomes required, particularly with revenues from distributors?

Some of the numerous new additions to the revenue recognition requirements put forth in SAB Topic 13 do not align with how American business routinely works. One of the new criteria is that a middleman, namely a dealer or distributor, cannot pay the manufacturer only when they are paid for that product by the final customers. Frankly, it is practically impossible to be assured that every distributor or middleman is not waiting until they get paid for a product before they pay a specific invoice. If that were the case, SAB Topic 13 would require revenues to that distributor to be on a "cash basis" and to be booked only when the cash is received!

In effect, that is what some of these new revenue recognition rules require. Of course, it would be possible for an auditing firm to spend an enormous amount of time and money to determine if a distributor is actually conducting business in that manner. What would probably be determined is that sometimes they are and sometimes they are not. I think that the problem with some of these new revenue recognition requirements is that they do not have a "common sense" business basis, but they do develop many new fee opportunities for audit firms!

Please understand that this latest change in revenue recognition rules and other accounting matters is headed towards the accounting profession attempting to become an "exact science" versus a profession of "opinions." Since the accounting profession will always be a profession of "opinions," the accounting professions' oversight agencies, the SEC and the PCAOB, which was created by Sarbanes-Oxley, will always be in debates, particularly with the Big Four, over accounting matters of this nature. So the Big Four firms are attempting to get their accounting criteria into an "exact science mode" in order to reduce their conflicts with the PCAOB and SEC. I could see that from the discussions we had with EY. Some of that is understandable since they are literally being graded and harassed by the PCAOB and SEC over their auditing practices and "opinions."

As I have previously mentioned, I participated along with our other top executives basically every month in a review of our accounts receivable with our CFO and his accounting staff. Of course, we reviewed in particular the accounts that seemed to be giving us collection problems. By 2018, we had approximately 3,000 customers, which included doctors' offices, wound care centers and hospitals in addition to a few distributors. We also were in the process of eliminating most of our distributors and replacing them with direct salespeople by 2016.

At these monthly meetings, we would get into the details of the reasons certain accounts were not paying in a timely fashion and the promises that had been made to our staff in terms of payment being made. Occasionally, Bill or I would interact with a customer if we knew the situation sufficiently. In particular, I knew the AvKARE business operations fairly well, and I could call the principal owner, Steve Shirley, and ask him to pay down his accounts receivable balance with us. Also, other accounting staff members would call their staff and insist on payments. Therefore, in my opinion and overview, we were managing the AvKARE account just as we did all the other distributors. We monitored their days sales outstanding (DSOs) and accounts receivable, and when they exceeded a range we had agreed upon as their payment terms, we would call and ask for additional payments to be forwarded immediately. In fact, that is the way the American business system really works!

As a side note, I was involved in a discussion at one point with one of the EY partners from New York on our accounts receivable and its aging. I pointed out that our 65 days of DSOs was better than the healthcare industry average. We had kept our accounts receivable in a very manageable range over the years so we should be judged as very competent in managing that part of our business and in the collecting of our cash. In addition, I told the EY partner that we were well reserved in terms of "sales returns and allowances" reserves and "bad debt" reserves. We increased those every quarter in order to take care of the perturbations and uncertainties in certain revenue groups. That is the way I had managed my accounting responsibilities with public companies for almost 37 years.

The New York EY partner said that, if we had set specific DSO aging metrics for a customer and they exceeded that number, then that placed their accounts receivable at risk and <u>might</u> require us putting that customer on a <u>cash</u> <u>only</u> revenue accrual basis. I told him I thought that was absurd in light of our company's reserves. If we took that approach, we would be flipping back and forth between a normal accrual and a cash accrual every quarter for any customer that pays over 90 days from time to time. Frankly, most of our customers, or almost any business in this country, will occasionally behave in that fashion. Everyone has variations in their cash flow and ability to pay bills in a specific period of time. Thus, you can begin to see how frustrating today's interpretations are of some of these revenue recognition matters, particularly when a company has set aside sufficient reserves for sales returns and bad debts already. It goes even deeper than that, but there is no point in taking up any more time on this somewhat out of control subject, thanks to the PCAOB and SEC.

The Investigation Process

It took awhile for me to realize that this investigation was not being conducted to determine the facts relative to the Marc Cohodes allegations, but rather it was focused on Bill as the COO, Mike Senken as the CFO and me as the CEO in particular. I had not yet read the Sally Yates Doctrine, and I did not understand the implications of investigations of this nature being focused on the top executives for reasons that were supposedly beneficial to the U.S. Government. Again, no focus on finding truth and justice, just on the targeted individuals and the large legal fees that will accrue. No focus on the thousands of shareholders who will be significantly hurt by this unbalanced and corrupt process.

As the King & Spalding investigation unfolded, a number of our managers came to me and expressed concerns related to the fact that the lawyers who were interviewing them had no comprehension of business practices or other normal processes and procedures within a business. I initially took this as lawyers merely trying to understand our business operations, which was going to be difficult for them to do because they had no experience in this area. Also, MiMedx was a very complex business. While they might have been able to comprehend many business activities, they certainly did not have the experience to understand how to manage them.

As an example, Jim Dozier, the head of all our information technology operations, came to me rather frustrated after his first interview with King & Spalding. He told me that the lawyer who interviewed him would "roll her eyes" at him on most of his responses to her questions. Jim told me that he finally asked her to stop as her behavior was unprofessional, and if she did not stop, he would not continue the interview.

Well, Dozier was given one more interview, and then he was summarily dismissed from the company. This occurred after I had left the company and resigned from the Board of Directors. To have an individual as experienced and talented as Jim Dozier be summarily dismissed was frustrating. Dozier was an eleven-year veteran of our companies. This gave me another hint as to what the investigation was really about.

We had a "Witch Hunt" going on, not a well-managed investigation. A "Witch Hunt" to benefit Dewberry, law firms, auditors, short sellers and certian federal prosecutors.

As things continued to unfold, it was obvious that anyone who did not become aligned with the King & Spalding themes would be potentially terminated. In actuality, the Board terminated or ran off 20 of the top 21 managers who were responsible for making MiMedx the fifth fastest-growing public company in America. The company's operating performance has <u>never recovered</u> from that mistake five years later!

For any company to lose their top 20 managers is tremendously destructive. For a very successful medium-sized company with a fast-growth rate, it is even more destructive. The fact that the company today is still in business and producing $250 million in revenues is a credit to the strength of the product line and the supporting systems that were developed by management as the company was built. However, the current revenues are about 50 percent of what they would have been! For 2020, they were at the company's 2016 revenue level. The majority of the top salespeople have left, and many went to work for competitors. The company ignored their non-compete contracts until 2021, which was too late. I expect the Sidley Austin attorneys advised the Board that these contracts were hard to enforce so do not bother. Former management had success with every action we brought! Again, bad business decisions caused by bad legal advice.

When we finally obtained written portions of the King & Spalding investigation as a result of our DOJ trial, it was appalling to see their commentary. Their accusations clearly demonstrated little in the way of actual truth, business experience or business acumen and common sense. Their allegations were easily refutable had we been given "due process" of the law and had a chance to respond.

I was also given some printed information, which highlighted that the Board had requested King & Spalding give us time to respond to the allegations. However, that never happened prior to our terminations. This corrupt prosecutorial pattern became very apparent, and it is quite clearly explained and documented in Sidney Powell and Harvey Silverglate's books.

Therefore, executive management was never told of the accusations, other than AvKARE, which were going to be made by the King & Spalding investigation. Thus, no "due process" of the law occurred whereby the executives were allowed to understand the accusations that would be made against them and be given time to explain their counterarguments to the Board and the investigators. All the shortcomings of this out of control process were clearly delineated in a press release made by the executives' law firm, Quinn Emanuel. This press release is referenced in Appendix 21 under the title *MiMedx Audit Committee Tries to Avoid Criticism by Making Special Findings of Misconduct by Former Management, According to Attorney William Weinreb*.

Mistake on Accounting for Exchanges

Please recall that I previously explained MiMedx had made a minor mistake in accounting for "exchanges" from distributors since this revenue first began in 2011. This was a mistake that was not highlighted until early 2017 when we were interacting with Scott Taub, a nationally recognized revenue recognition expert.

However, the Audit Committee, the Board and the outside auditors were all aware of the fact that the company was not increasing "sales returns and allowances" reserves that were specifically related to each exchange taken from a distributor. Those reserves were increased each quarter in a significant manner, but that was not specifically related to the quarterly exchanges that took place with distributors. In all of the King & Spalding investigational materials, I never saw a mention of this mistake which was made by our accountants, our Audit Committee and our auditors...certainly not by executive management because we were following the direction given to us by accounting.

Taub clearly stated that it was <u>not</u> very logical to require "sales returns and allowances" reserves to be increased on an exchange that is made from a distributor versus an end customer. While it did not make much sense, he said that is the way this particular SAB Topic 13 rule was written. Thus, the company had continued to make this "mistake" from 2011 to early 2017. However, by our continually adding additional "returns and allowances" reserves and "bad debt" reserves each quarter, the company covered itself from these minor revenue perturbations caused by the new SAB Topic 13 rules.

AvKARE Allegations

At the beginning of the investigation, I felt somewhat positive about the investigators taking each of Cohodes' allegations, which we had highlighted on our website, investigating them and publishing the findings in a press release. If our shareholders could have seen press releases every several weeks essentially refuting accusation after accusation that was made by Cohodes, that would have been a practical and reasonable way to approach matters. However, Isaac Greaney of the Sidley Austin law firm convinced the majority of the Board to shut down <u>all</u> communications with shareholders, which basically lasted over two years. The Board did not initially deal with the massive void in corporate information flow and did not realize how damaging that was. Of course, they did not want to expose how destructive their decisions were on revenue growth. I know what the Matria Healthcare Board would have done with the legal recommendation of <u>no</u> communication! That would be the last recommendation that attorney would have made!

As I have reviewed some of the written accusations and backup materials presented by King & Spalding to the Board, I find them very inaccurate and biased towards a finding of corporate wrongdoing and executive wrongdoing. The lack of business experience and acumen of King & Spalding is quite apparent, and numerous mistakes in their assertions occurred because of those issues as well as their focus on accusing the top executives of accounting fraud while ignoring the accounting mistake made by the company. Remember, making an accounting mistake is not fraud, and thus, not a criminal act. There must be scienter for a criminal act to have occurred.

The investigation initially began to focus on the ways that Bill and I somehow breached the contractual language that we had with all our distributors. They also focused on a <u>few</u> situations where a salesperson had apparently told a healthcare practice that they would not have to pay us until they were paid. Those types of communications through 435 salespeople were certainly not visible to us, or probably even to sales management. There would be a comment in a few of our collection files of customers trying to use that as an excuse. However, in healthcare that is an "old excuse" often used by slow paying customers, particularly doctors' offices because frequently they know their salesperson.

Apparently, the King & Spalding investigation first concentrated on the manner in which Bill and I had "conspired" to violate the contractual terms of our federal hospital distributor, AvKARE, who was our largest distributor. This meant that we <u>might</u> <u>have</u> allowed shipment and the booking of revenues when all of the revenue recognition criteria had not been met and that we <u>hid</u> these changes or "side deals" from our accountants, the Audit Committee and auditors. This would mean that we were guilty of accounting fraud, which would allow the SEC to charge us civilly and the DOJ to charge us criminally if there was scienter. I was told that the King & Spalding attorneys began to have conversations with the Southern District of New York DOJ by late summer of 2018.

Please recall that I had managed public companies for 34 years prior to this MiMedx situation developing in 2015. The SEC published their new revenue recognition document, SAB Topic 13, in 2009. When significant changes such as this are made, are the top executives of public companies supposed to obtain the information by osmosis? In other words, while the accounting profession will get notifications, there were no registered letters sent to the 4,200 public company executives. I was totally unaware of the new changes, which are extremely complicated. It would make sense if federal agencies, when making complex changes of this nature, would simply forward a registered letter to all the public company officers who are the ones that are <u>finally</u> <u>held accountable</u>. That matches with the common sense solution I presented to Commissioner Mary Jo White after the SEC spent four and a half years harassing me over the supposed passage of inside information. I highlighted this matter in Chapter 8.

Now, to <u>totally</u> <u>refute</u> that early AvKARE allegation, one fact is paramount and very straightforward: <u>no</u> <u>change</u> was made in the contract amendments to AvKARE payment obligations. We had several amendments to the AvKARE contract, which AvKARE wanted, and in most cases, we did as well. When we told AvKARE that we were going to terminate our relationship with them because we had obtained our own federal supply schedule (FSS) contract, they were very upset. To some extent, that is understandable. However, having business frustrations is different than having business vengeance, which was not called for in this case.

The last two amendments made to the AvKARE Distributor Agreement took place in 2014 and early 2016. The 2016 amendment clauses were numerous, and we were focused on improving the "wind-down" aspects of the contract since MiMedx had acquired its own FSS contract. There were a number of issues clarified and modified in order for there to be a smooth transition. The AvKARE contract was finally concluded on June 30, 2017.

The key fact related to the AvKARE agreement supposedly being <u>verbally</u> modified to allow them to pay MiMedx only when they received notice that an allograft had been implanted at a VA hospital or that they had been subsequently paid is that AvKARE would have <u>absolutely</u> asked for that supposed verbal agreement (the "side agreement") to be placed into <u>one</u> <u>of</u> <u>the</u> <u>written</u> <u>amendments</u> to their contract. AvKARE was so focused on their cash flow that they would <u>not</u> have allowed MiMedx to come back later and claim that they must pay based on the date of our invoice to them <u>if</u> <u>that</u> <u>was</u> <u>not</u> <u>the</u> <u>truth</u>. Thus, that one point should totally refute the accusation that we had given AvKARE verbal permission to only pay MiMedx for our invoices after they were paid by the Veterans Administration. There was no mention of those supposedly new payment terms in email communications or in the last two amendments to the contract! Therefore, we did not disclose this change in payment methodology for AvKARE because <u>it</u> <u>did</u> <u>not</u> <u>exist</u>!

The accounting expenses over the next two years were exorbitant. EY resigned in November of 2018 after billing the company over four times what their original quote was for the 2017 audit fee, and their audit was <u>never</u> <u>provided</u>. I was told the re-audit of all the revenues cost approximately $80 million!

It is also <u>very</u> <u>pertinent</u> that the DOJ ignored King & Spalding's AvKARE allegations. I am sure they recognized all the weaknesses. However, the AvKARE issue is what the Board used to ask for Bill's and my resignations and those of Mike Senken and John Cranston. Fair? Reasonable?

My Recommendation to Change Auditors

I will reiterate again a strong underlying fact that we were <u>not guilty</u> of <u>knowingly</u> violating revenue recognition rules as published in SAB Topic 13 and concealing those from the accountants, thus being guilty of scienter. There are numerous other facts that the King & Spalding investigation refused to utilize, and the DOJ must have understood that issue. But, there is one other key point that should make it clear that I did not knowingly violate these rules and regulations.

That point is this. Remember that I recommended to Terry Dewberry in early 2017 that we move to a Big Four auditing firm. I had just returned from the J.P. Morgan Healthcare Conference in San Francisco in mid-January, and a couple of our large institutional shareholders, who had been investors in my former companies over the decades, told me that MiMedx was very professionally checking every possible box in terms of investment criteria, except that we did not have a Big Four auditor. They felt strongly that it was time for the company to move to a Big Four auditing firm.

I thought about that recommendation a great deal. I knew the <u>very wise</u> philosophy that a public company should "Never Change Auditors." I had seen the headaches associated with that at Guy Millner's company, Norrell, which I have previously discussed. However, in my opinion, MiMedx was "humming." I felt that we really had our processes and procedures working very well, particularly relative to accounting.

The simple point that I have made is: IF I KNEW THAT WE WERE CREATING FRAUDULENT ACCOUNTING TRANSACTIONS, WHY WOULD I HAVE RECOMMENDED TO TERRY DEWBERRY THAT THE COMPANY HIRE A BIG FOUR ACCOUNTING FIRM? Any <u>idiot</u> would have known that all of the "supposed" fraudulent transactions would have been discovered.

Therefore, I did not believe then nor do I believe now that the company was guilty of infractions, particularly those that required a <u>total restatement</u> of six years of its revenues to a cash only basis for 3,000 customers! That will go down in accounting history as a process that was <u>way</u> out of control because there was no focused management by the Chairman of the Audit Committee, Terry Dewberry, on the investigation or the ensuing audits. Neither was there sufficient Board oversight or interaction. So another hard lesson learned about personality types, CYA syndrome and the results of lack of competent leadership! All this related to me not making a priority of attempting to more aggressively change Board members because of my time constraints and how well the company was performing.

Of course, since Bill and I were <u>never</u> interviewed by King & Spalding for the investigation, none of these issues were disclosed. King & Spalding was free to review and process the information they found to support their involvement for a <u>lengthy</u> <u>period</u> <u>of</u> <u>time</u> and bill the company substantial amounts of money while satisfying Dewberry's wants and desires. Again, no "due process" of the law occurred.

I <u>do</u> <u>not</u> believe that even our 2018 Board members, who I have admitted were not experienced enough to manage very complex situations of this nature, were informed early enough about Dewberry's intentions or by King & Spalding as to where they wanted to take this investigation. Had the Board been able to sit in on an interview conducted by King & Spalding with Bill and me, this situation would not have become <u>out</u> <u>of</u> <u>control</u>. So I have to point my finger at Dewberry's lack of management and transparency as to what he was doing and where he was trying to take the investigation. As I have stated, I believe he was primarily in a paranoid CYA mode with a "takeover" of the company as a goal!

Also, I think that I have determined Dewberry was the only Board member who really reviewed the King & Spalding contract. The other Audit Committee members were possibly not fully informed, and the rest of the Board was not initially informed at all. I do not think that was proper corporate governance, and I would never have allowed a situation like that to develop without being sure the full Board was totally informed. As I have mentioned, I could <u>not</u> be involved in the investigation details so the Board was easily manipulated and swayed.

Over a year later, I was told by one of the Board members that the King & Spalding agreement that Dewberry signed was extremely one-sided for King & Spalding. Apparently, it was not really negotiated, and it gave full control of the investigation to King & Spalding.

The King & Spalding "Witch Hunt" Documents

A few weeks prior to the start of the trial, our attorneys received numerous documents from the prosecutors. These documents were classified as information that should be given to the defendants because of the Brady and Jencks rules.

In those documents, I noticed one entitled *Investigation Update* that was written by King & Spalding and had been given to Dewberry and Joe Bleser, a member of the Audit Committee. It was also given to the temporary CEO, David Coles, and Borkowski, the temporary CFO. There were no other Board members mentioned in terms of the attendees of the meeting at which this document was disseminated. However, King & Spalding should have forwarded it to all Board members, and they were probably all involved in a conference call. This document was dated September 26, 2018. There should have been a later document that King & Spalding prepared and distributed to the Board as well discussing the 2015 distributor supposed "side deals."

A Board member told me that a 12-hour conference call was held with King & Spalding promoting their investigation findings to the Board.

Another Board member told me that the investigation was over (probably after the AvKARE accusations), but it was re-opened by Dewberry. This could have happened when the DOJ did not think the AvKARE information was worthy of an indictment. Thus, the 2015 allegations developed!

This investigation document clearly shows the way the allegations were developed and what they were. If this document is carefully reviewed, it becomes very evident that there was a "Witch Hunt" going on without real substantive facts that had been given "due process" of the law. That would have required Bill and me to answer and give further input to these twisted allegations.

In this section, I will present numerous comments from this investigation document followed by truthful explanations to clarify matters. There are numerous places where King & Spalding makes statements as though they are facts, which in most cases they are not. This is similar to the way a prosecutor twists facts and testimony in trials to match their own agenda.

One of the most revealing comments relates to King & Spalding absolutely verifying that they are using the Sally Yates Doctrine for this investigation. They stated that they were not focusing on a definition of "channel stuffing" due to the lack of a "true definition" and were instead focused on the conduct of former management. As you will recall, EY was very specific when they advised the Board that they would not finish the 2017 audit until all the Cohodes allegations were investigated. That is what King & Spalding should have been retained to accomplish. Channel stuffing was Cohodes' first and primary allegation.

Our shareholders were very aware of the Cohodes situation and deserved to have his numerous accusations discredited. I believe most of the Board truly understood how Cohodes' shorting campaign had developed, but as soon as King & Spalding was retained by the Audit Committee, the Board seemed to become disinterested and allowed whatever was going to take place to happen. There was no questioning of the process. In fact, as I mentioned, there was never a business plan, which would have required a budget, a scope and schedule developed by Dewberry and the Audit Committee. Thus, the company was in effect turned over to the whims of a couple of law and accounting firms. In so doing, MiMedx spent well over $200 million to investigate about $9 million of <u>actual</u> revenue that was <u>alleged</u> to have been booked in the wrong quarters of 2015!

What follows should be a clear indication of the intent of the activities that took place relative to this "investigation." With all the investigators being lawyers and certain ones being former prosecutors, the twisting and ignoring of facts in order for King & Spalding to achieve their goal to document dishonesty of certain company officers while developing huge legal fees was going to happen.

I believe, after reading this section, it will be quite evident how King & Spalding was successful in making accusations by misinterpreting and misrepresenting the facts, which were never questioned sufficiently by the Board of Directors. I have never seen or heard of any issues where our Board pushed back on the accusations and asked for more information, including testimony from the two individuals who would be later charged by the DOJ and SEC based on the King & Spalding allegations ... Taylor and Petit.

Note: All the following investigation statements are the <u>exact</u> <u>wording</u> and <u>punctuation</u> of the King & Spalding documents:

Investigation Statement: "Quinn Emanuel letter makes the argument that AvKARE was not really paying only when it got paid." King & Spalding concluded that this argument ignores that MiMedx regularly accepted credits for tissues that had been paid for even when the VA had not received a purchase order. Additionally, even when AvKARE had been paid for tissue there was a right of return for product if an issue arose."

> First, MiMedx allowed customers to <u>ask</u> to return a product for credit or <u>ask</u> for an exchange. In each case, we took the entire situation into account before making a decision. That did not mean that we had a blanket policy of allowing credit for <u>all</u> returns, which could cause a "course of dealing" issue. We were prudent business people who took into account the fact that our customers would occasionally have extenuating circumstances where we needed to provide some type of full credit or at least an exchange where they still had an obligation to pay us.

The remainder of the comment is totally <u>incorrect</u> because the VA did not receive purchase orders; they issued them! The last sentence is factually incorrect because any right of return or right for an exchange was only granted on a situational basis. You can tell how inexperienced the King & Spalding staff were relative to understanding business processes and procedures from these two comments that make no sense…first, the VA receiving purchase orders, and second, if AvKARE had been paid for an allograft, that meant it had been implanted so how could it be sent back for credit! You can see the lack of knowledge of MiMedx standard business and clinical practices by King & Spalding staff <u>and</u> apparently our Board!

Investigation Statement: "King & Spalding obtained evidence to support former management's knowledge of the AvKARE course of dealings and the GAAP implications: Taylor email to Bobby Lindsay at AvKARE on March 8, 2013 Regarding payment, we have established a history over the past six months, and we're satisfied with the arrangement. Although it is slightly different from the way the contract is written, we see no need to change what has become our standard practice."

This comment refers to MiMedx giving AvKARE 75 days for payment rather than 45 days, which was in the original contract. Most importantly, this change in payment terms was included in a subsequent amendment to the AvKARE Distributor Agreement. This demonstrates that we were diligent about process and procedure changes being put in amendments to the Distributor Agreement. Again, King & Spalding misinterpreting words to suggest a possible crime!

Investigation Statement: "King & Spalding stated that the Taylor email resulted in a discussion between Shirley and Petit leading to MiMedx offering to extend AvKARE payment terms to 75 days."

As discussed above, we extended AvKARE's terms to 75 days as a result of this discussion. That change appeared in either Amendment Number 2 or 3. We were dealing with the practicality of the slowness of the Veterans Administration in paying their accounts payable to AvKARE. Most importantly, <u>we documented</u> those changes in an amendment to their Distributor Agreement. This certainly highlights our discipline in placing changes in payment terms in a contract amendment.

Investigation Statement: "On August 29, 2016, Petit's email to Cranston: I do not think this is what was promised. He told me he would forward us half of what was sold each week since he would eventually collect that."

My comments relate to a promise that I had received from Steve Shirley that they would start bringing their DSOs down since they had become too high. He was saying that he would forward "more cash" each week to bring the accounts receivable aging down. I asked him to quantify what "more cash" meant. He said about half of what they sold that week. This is merely a discussion from my calling him, which I did from time to time, asking him to bring his DSO levels down because they were out of an acceptable range. I did this on a number of occasions, and in two incidents, Shirley sent checks of approximately $2 million. This is the point where I had begun to mistrust AvKARE and their activities. They were upset with us because we had obtained our own FSS contract, and we were now selling with our own sales force in all these accounts. We were in the process of winding down the AvKARE relationship so they were holding as much of our cash as they could without us calling them out.

As far as the allegation that AvKARE only paid us when they were paid or received a purchase order that would indicate they would be paid is a false narrative. We had no insight into the communications between AvKARE inside sales personnel and the VA facilities. We had no idea what their revenues and collections were from their VA accounts other than what they told us. What they told us and what was actually the case were two different things. AvKARE managed their cash flow by simply putting in this weekly report, which was developed for the Food and Drug Administration, information about the tissue that was supposedly implanted. However, those reports were inaccurate as we proved during our detailed investigation of many of these particular sets of numbers.

I do not know what King & Spalding was trying to insinuate with this former statement of mine. They were just twisting the meaning of normal business comments.

Investigation Statement: "A letter from Petit & Taylor's attorneys, Quinn Emanuel, said on June 29, 2018, downplayed what they understood and what their role was in the AvKARE process through the following statements: No information was presented to Mr. Petit and Mr. Taylor that AvKARE paid MiMedx for particular tissues only when those tissues are sold to the VA." "Petit and Taylor do not recall when they first heard about this practice and still do not know the full extent of it. Neither one of them were involved in collection at that level."

> The reason that MiMedx never granted, formally or informally, AvKARE the right to only pay us for invoices that had been paid to them by the VA is that it would have violated GAAP revenue requirements. We held AvKARE as well as all our other customers to a set of payment terms that involved their DSOs. If AvKARE was holding our money for too long, we demanded payment. That is when I would get involved in the process and call Steve Shirley and others. Things went relatively smoothly for the first couple years until we told AvKARE we had obtained our own FSS contract and would be winding down our involvement with them. Then, they started holding back our funds. We had no way of determining what was owed to AvKARE by VA hospitals. Their accounting system was very immature to the point that they could only tell us to credit any cash payments that we received to their oldest invoices. Thus, we were holding them accountable for their DSOs. How much they were paid each week by the Veterans Administration was irrelevant. This was a very efficient credit policy, and we never had any significant credit or DSO issues with the vast majority of our accounts.
>
> Again, just insinuations from King & Spalding without proper vetting – and proof.

Investigation Statement: "December 11, 2015, Lou Roselli emailed to Petit, Taylor and others: Credits for tissue implant or lost. Each quarter we credit AvKARE a significant amount of revenue." Petit's response December 11, 2015, "These problems are caused by one thing ..... lack of management. Again, routinely focusing on these issues and holding your subordinates accountable. We are monitoring these metrics and so should you. The metrics will move in the right direction quickly if they are managed."

> I made a sales management recommendation. Most importantly, you see no reference by King & Spalding to the substantial "sales returns and allowances" reserves that the company booked each quarter to cover issues of this nature. Roselli would not focus on this because he was in sales management. To my knowledge, there was never an instance where we felt we were significantly under reserved, and therefore, shareholders were being given misinformation on collectible revenue and its trends. I imagine the Board members, when hearing

comments such as these, were totally oblivious to what was being discussed, but certainly picked up on the allegation of management misconduct. Incorrect accusations were always driving the King & Spalding investigation.

Investigation Statement: "Investigational evidence showed three things: AvKARE paid MiMedx after receiving payment from the VA; MiMedx retained significant responsibility of the product after the sale to AvKARE; AvKARE had a right of return throughout the relationship with MiMedx even in situations in which tissue got lost, or implanted. (Note: products could have a right to return following being implanted in instances where there was not a PO)."

Like any distributor, AvKARE could have paid MiMedx on occasion only after receiving a payment from their customer, which was over 160 different VA hospitals. Many distributors would make payments after they received payments. That is a common U.S. business practice if working capital is tight. However, there was absolutely no written or verbal policy from any authorized officer at MiMedx allowing any customer to only pay the company after they had received payment from their customers.

If auditors of all U.S. public companies had to verify that there had been no payments made to the company by intermediaries, such as distributors or dealers, after they were paid by their customers, we would have billions and billions of dollars of extra accounting fees every year. That assumption, and it was absolutely an assumption, cost MiMedx probably in excess of $80 million because it gave the Audit Committee the ability to restate six years' of AvKARE revenues from an accrual basis to a cash basis. Again, the Audit Committee Chairman, Dewberry, was still in a destructive CYA mode at this point, and these allegations matched his plan to be sure he was not called out in any way.

Can you imagine the chaos that would accrue to U.S. publicly traded companies if they had to verify annually that all their distributors or middlemen were paying them upon the terms of their invoices or contractual agreements versus holding payment back until they received payment from one of their customers? This would be total chaos. That is what was forced upon MiMedx by taking six years of revenue and restating it to a cash basis. This was a huge windfall in fees for King & Spalding, KPMG and other accountants and law firms. Again, the Board should have managed this process and held Dewberry accountable for demanding a restatement process that resulted in over $80 million of unnecessary accounting costs.

Also, according to some of the new revenue recognition rules, if a company sells product to a distributor and retains significant responsibilities to see the product is sold after shipment, then that will require that particular sale to be booked on a cash basis rather than an accrual basis. King & Spalding alleged, because AvKARE did not have a significant field sales organization whereas we had a portion of our sales force (probably 50 out of 450) specifically selling to the VA hospitals, that created a second reason that MiMedx would have to book our AvKARE revenues on a cash basis.

It is factual that MiMedx had salespeople in most of the 160 VA accounts on a routine basis. We were continually training doctors and nurses on the clinical aspects of our products. No distributor will ever know the product line as well as the manufacturer so there are numerous situations in American business where representatives from the manufacturer are present in the final user accounts primarily for training purposes. This is particularly true in healthcare because of the complexities of the pharmaceutical products as well as medical devices.

Just because our salespeople were playing those types of roles does not mean that we had to only bill this customer, AvKARE, on a cash basis after they had actually sold our products. I believe the purpose of this accounting rule is more than satisfied by the fact that AvKARE had a substantial size inside sales and administrative group, and they were very familiar with their counterparts at all the VA hospitals. These individuals conducted a considerable portion of all sales and administrative activities related to our product line as well as the product lines of other companies they were representing.

In addition, after 2015, we had our own federal supply schedule authorizations, and we were selling our product line into the VA hospitals along with AvKARE salespeople in those hospitals. Our sales force tended to concentrate on the new departments in the hospital where we wanted to introduce and sell our products, such as the surgery and dermatology departments. Because both companies were selling product into the same VA hospitals, we added some Addendums, Numbers 3 and 4, to the AvKARE contract to help sort through what we called the "wind-down" process as we took over all the AvKARE business. Both companies thought through the issues very carefully and placed issues that needed to be resolved in those two amendments. There was <u>never</u> any discussion or wording put into those amendments that AvKARE was allowed to only pay MiMedx when they were paid by a VA hospital for a product.

King & Spalding made the allegation that our AvKARE revenue needed to be on a cash basis from the start of the contract in 2012, which was ridiculous. I believe this accusation by King & Spalding is what convinced the Board of Directors to terminate me, the CEO, Bill Taylor, our Chief Operating Officer, Mike Senken, our Chief Financial Officer and John Cranston, our corporate Controller.

I believe that the DOJ, when preparing their indictments against Bill and me, reviewed the AvKARE revenue restatement issue and the evidence associated with it, and they decided to <u>ignore</u> that charge because of the lack of <u>any</u> credible evidence. That should speak very loudly to the lack of professionalism, legal acumen, business acumen and honesty of King & Spalding in making those and other allegations against the executives. All four executives were terminated over these false AvKARE accusations.

Neither AvKARE nor any of our other customers had a "right of return." That does not mean that on occasion the company would not grant a right of exchange (which is different from a return) or even a return for full credit. However, that grant was not a "guarantee" of any kind, and it depended on a determination by MiMedx executives of whether there were extenuating circumstances that meant we should grant a return or an exchange or neither.

We developed a very robust sales channel because we were viewed as fair business people who would work with our customers to be certain that they were able to market or use our products properly. If any issues arose, we would certainly consider the circumstances before denying the ability to exchange or return a product. This flexibility certainly did not warrant the company going on a cash basis for the disclosure of its revenues. There was no policy in place that guaranteed the company would <u>ever</u> make those types of commitments, particularly on a routine basis.

The King & Spalding comment about products having a right of return after being implanted is laughable. Why would MiMedx or any other manufacturer give credit for a product that has been properly used by the final customer? Other comments made by King & Spalding about this happening in instances where there was not a purchase order is also incorrect. First, MiMedx never shipped any products to anyone without a purchase order, and in some instances, a Distribution Agreement. However, MiMedx had no insight into when a VA hospital issued a purchase order to AvKARE. We were never privy to that type of information unless some type of conflict arose where we would try to help resolve the matter. I doubt if King & Spalding staff could explain either of these two issues with any degree of comprehension.

Again, King & Spalding was presenting incorrect facts or just had no concept of MiMedx or American business processes. Either one is very unprofessional!

Investigation Statement: "King & Spalding do not believe that 'channel stuffing' is the right terminology to describe the allegations and instead believe that 'earnings management' is a more accurate phrase."

So a second opinion that there was no channel stuffing!

Now business executives are compensated to manage the earnings or profits of any business! They are also compensated to manage revenue growth for the corporation. King & Spalding must be alluding to executives falsifying revenues or earnings/profits. That is something that executive management at MiMedx did not purposely do. As a start, you can see that the allegations relative to AvKARE revenues being falsified, meaning were booked ahead of the cash being collected which is not the normal accounting practice, was a farce. I think that, in this section and in previous and future chapters of the book, you will clearly see that the accusations of incorrect revenue recognition for AvKARE, which resulted in the termination of four of the top corporate executives and $80 million for a six-year revenue restatement, were false allegations. Evidently, the DOJ also thought this was the case because the AvKARE matter was not used in their indictments!

Investigation Statement: "Former management engaged in overseeing the company's revenues resulting in inconsistencies with GAAP."

Of course, executive management of public companies is responsible for managing and overseeing the company's revenues, profits, investments and other processes, and those are demanding and complex responsibilities that lawyers would generally not understand. King & Spalding's allegations about inconsistencies with GAAP are overreaching and not factual. Just this one example relating to AvKARE makes it very clear how they misinterpreted or even twisted facts which led to inaccurate allegations. And, many of their comments make very clear their lack of business acumen and experience.

Investigation Statement: "King & Spalding believe that the misstatements and omissions (from executive management) occurred as a result of: issuing quarterly revenue guidance; a top-down attitude; the belief that the value of MiMedx hinged on its growth rate; and misstatements and omissions, which drove revenue growth, such as recording revenue upon shipment."

Having been the CEO of several public companies, I always did my utmost to provide shareholders with guidance on quarterly revenue and other pertinent information, whether it was good, bad or ugly! Many CEOs choose not to make those disclosures or take any forecasting risk, and I believe their companies would suffer lower valuations because of that approach. Shareholders like to see management that is open and clear about company activities, able to make forecasts and then execute. MiMedx had an impeccable track record of making quarterly revenue forecasts and meeting them. There was only one quarter that MiMedx missed its revenue forecast by a few percent over this almost eight-year period.

A "top down attitude" is a ridiculous accusation made by attorneys who have never built or managed any business enterprise. They have no idea what they are saying about the way in which MiMedx was managed or any company for that matter. It is evident they never read my management booklet entitled *Management-MiMedx Style*. In that booklet, we discussed our management philosophies and the way the company was to be operated. It was an extremely detailed book that very few public companies could have published. We had a policy of "participatory management" that involved all employees in the decisions of their various departments. I believe that many of our successes were due to this philosophy where employees felt respected and their opinions on company business listened to and considered.

I have said numerous times to shareholders, the Board and employees that the value of a company like MiMedx, which had new technology and was in a growth mode, was based on their revenue growth rate. That is business common sense and a well-known Wall Street valuation technique. The higher the growth rate, the more valuable the company will be in the future assuming other valuation variables remain constant.

The vast majority of all American public companies book revenue upon shipment of their product or the completed execution of their services. It takes some really odd scenario to force a company to book revenues only upon the receipt of the payment for the invoices. I do not know what normal GAAP procedures have to do with King & Spalding's claim that we made misstatements and omissions. They had no real facts to back up that statement.

This is the point where a competent and properly motivated Board should have called out the prosecutorial bias within in the investigation. This King & Spalding statement is one of its most bizarre and dishonest!

Investigation Statement: "King & Spalding have interviewed both Senken and Cranston. Taylor and Petit have refused to speak to King & Spalding; however, their lawyers Quinn Emanuel have sent a letter to King & Spalding."

This is an <u>absolutely false</u> and very misleading statement. Bill and I had a two-day session scheduled for our meeting with King & Spalding on June 27th and 28th of 2018. The day before those meetings were to begin, King & Spalding canceled them without any explanation. On the 29th of June, I was advised by Charlie Evans that the Board intended to ask us to resign at the Board meeting on Saturday, June 30th. That was the first indication I had that King & Spalding had advised the Board to terminate us. Therefore, we did not refuse to talk to King & Spalding until a request came some months later. At that point, we were advised by a member of one of MiMedx's other outside counsels that we should not meet with King & Spalding as they had already made up their minds about our guilt. Remember, King & Spalding had told the Board that we should be terminated because of the accusations they had already <u>created</u> about AvKARE in May 2018. Also remember, the DOJ did not use those allegations!

Investigation Statement: "Previous statements by former management have referred back to the contract (AvKARE) to justify actions which are consistent with the contractual terms but do not reflect the course of dealings. King & Spalding stated management understood the course of dealings but rarely distinguished between the two."

First, our distributor contracts required signatures from both parties in order to change any of the terms of the agreements. That is why we utilized amendments to contracts to make necessary changes. Our first General Counsel, Roberta McCaw, had advised me that it would take an actual written amendment signed by both parties to change the course of dealings. However, there is corporate law that clearly dictates that, if there is a guaranteed, routine and continuous course of operating, then that action can modify the contractual terms of written agreements.

It is my view that these <u>alleged</u> changes to distributor contracts from these <u>alleged</u> "side deals" were <u>not</u> sufficient to modify the contract by a course of dealings, even if the allegations were true! In every case where there was some change or adjustment, management considered each situation <u>individually</u>. Therefore, there was not a contractual or <u>guaranteed</u> <u>arrangement</u> with AvKARE relative to exchanges or returns, relative to their requirement to not pay as per invoice and contract terms and relative to the risk of loss remaining with AvKARE unless we reviewed each individual situation. Also, we had no obligations for resale of the products, even though our salespeople were in the accounts training doctors and nurses.

King & Spalding did not interview either of us so I believe the quote "'previous statements made by former management" does not refer to us and I do nor know to whom it could refer.

Investigation Statement: "February 10, 2017 videotaped meeting between Dean, Petit, Taylor and Cashman: The four individuals discussed crediting AvKARE for lost inventory and the group decided to credit 2013 to 2014 and look for purchase orders for products shipped in 2015 and 2016. The risk of loss did not transfer to AvKARE for the tissues."

First, please recall that this video system was installed to assist with interviews of the salespeople who were involved in the scam to sell competitive products on the side, and the switch was not turned off after the last interview. Thus, the motion detector turned the system on any time there was conversation in the room. So numerous conversations were recorded without my knowledge for many months.

I do not remember the meeting, but I am certain these lawyers did not interpret the conversations properly as usual. I do not know why in 2017 we would be discussing 2013 and 2014 shipments. The same thing goes for 2015 and 2016. Either way, the allegation that the risk of loss did not transfer to AvKARE for these tissues because of these discussions is certainly a gross misrepresentation. If AvKARE had this right given to them, why would we not have credited this revenue in 2013, 2014 and 2015? Why is this discussion going on several years later? There were no <u>routine</u> returns granted to AvKARE or anyone else without discussions with executives going through the extenuating circumstances at the time. Therefore, all requests of that nature were <u>not</u> granted, and reviews were on a case-by-case basis.

Investigation Statement: "King & Spalding state that this recording highlights the importance of what was being played out by the account executives at the VA's."

King & Spalding had listened to conversations between the four top operating executives at MiMedx. They obviously did not understand numerous aspects of the conversation. They misinterpreted terms and the situation in general. I have explained that our account executives were much more present in these accounts than were any AvKARE people. However, AvKARE had a very proficient and effective <u>inside sales force</u> and administrative staff that worked with VA managers and personnel. Until we obtained our own federal supply service number, we did not have that type of contact with the VA purchasing staff or their administrative staff. Therefore, AvKARE was doing more than its share by being certain that the products went through the pipeline smoothly and were finally implanted in patients.

Our sales force was in those operations for our selling activities, and that primarily included the training function. Of course, that meant they could occasionally track down some issue that no one at AvKARE had been able to resolve. However, that did not mean that we were <u>relieving</u> AvKARE of any of their sales or administrative function related to our products going through the utilization pipeline smoothly and efficiently.

Investigation Statement: "May 8, 2015 email about Osiris revenue recognition issued from Senken to Taylor: "At a certain point this should become a revenue recognition issue"... Taylor to Petit on May 8, 2015: "quote from their CFO 'Our DSOs' are about 150 days, because we give generous payment terms."

> This was a discussion that came up when Osiris finally had to disclose they had been guilty of channel stuffing. The clear determinant of that was their days sales outstanding moved from about 80 days to 150 days in a matter of a few months. That is always a clear indicator of channel stuffing and customers not paying in a timely fashion for the products they have recently received. Testimony was presented in our trial that, in this particular instance, Stability Biologics was the culprit. They were accepting products from Osiris <u>without</u> purchase orders or any documented proof for shipments that met revenue recognition standards, and Osiris booked revenues for these shipments. Recall that our DSOs never got over 90 days, probably averaged 75 days, and were down at 65 days when Bill and I departed MiMedx.

Investigation Statement: "King & Spalding's interview with Cranston led to his parse around the language of side agreements needing affirmative assent from both sides and that he was never aware of MiMedx affirmatively agreeing with the side agreements."

> Cranston's statement was absolutely the truth. There was never any written or verbal commentary stating that we had agreed to any "side deals" with any distributor, much less AvKARE. However, King & Spalding wanted to ignore Cranston's comments in order to continue to pursue their allegations on revenue recognition. I think the DOJ believed Cranston! King & Spalding did not want to believe him for obvious reasons.

Investigation Statement: "King & Spalding identified instances in which Petit would claim that providing information of the AvKARE sales would be too difficult a procedure despite being relatively easy to perform. (That is certainly a lawyer's view.) Examples included December 26, 2016 response to Dewberry's request for AvKARE sales data: "If you could describe a process that you're trying to assess, that might be helpful...""

> Dewberry made a confusing request that was going to be difficult to complete, particularly the last week of December, which is one of the most hectic times of the year for our accounting staff. I was trying to get more clarity from Dewberry so that our accounting staff would

not be put through a rigorous exercise that would prove to be of little value at a time where their time was very constrained.

Also, note the misrepresentation of the plural "instances" when this was <u>one</u> <u>instance</u> representing my memo to Dewberry.

Investigation Statement: "Once Troutman Sanders' investigation began, Petit pushed back on information the Audit Committee was requesting. August 29th, 2018 Petit emailed the board: "In the 37 years that I functioned as a public company Chairman of the Board, I never recall telling any board member that I would not provide to them information they requested. On many occasions I thought the information was inconsequential and of no value but I would provide it if it was requested."

King & Spalding has developed another set of <u>inaccuracies and lies</u>. The Troutman Sanders investigation WAS OVER IN EARLY 2017! During that investigation, I never withheld any information whatsoever, and there is no evidence that I did so. My email of August 29, 2018 was sent to the Board in order to try to expedite some information from management that would have been very beneficial, particularly related to the presentation that Borkowski and the Sidley Austin attorneys were going to make to NASDAQ.

I explained to the Board that this was a very serious issue that needed to be vetted in front of the Board before management presented it to NASDAQ because it could result in the company being delisted. I was told by Charlie Evans, the new Chairman of the Board, that management was <u>not</u> going to supply the Board with that information. So this communication was my caution and chastisement to the Board that this information was extremely important, and it should be distributed to the Board. It was <u>never</u> fully disseminated.

What transpired is exactly what I was concerned about. Borkowski and the Sidley Austin lawyers misrepresented information to the NASDAQ staff in mid-September, and within a few weeks, they had to go back and tell them that the information was faulty. NASDAQ immediately delisted the company on November 5, 2018.

There is no reason whatsoever, other than an attempt to misrepresent the facts, for King & Spalding to take my August 29, 2018 memo and use it to state that I was pushing back on information the Audit Committee was requesting from me in early 2017 during the Troutman

Sanders investigation. I had been asked to resign on June 30, 2018 so I was merely a Board member on August 29, 2018.

The confusion of these dates is another indication of King & Spalding's misrepresenting facts or incompetent investigatory work!

Investigation Statement: "During his interview Senken acknowledged that Petit was distorting his picture to the board and is an occasion where Petit made omissions to the board about what AvKARE was saying."

This is another case of twisted facts and information. First, the Board of Directors had their own documents that were provided by AvKARE's attorney in answering these questions. So there was not any distortion by Petit in any way. I suspect that Senken's statements are twisted and distorted by the King & Spalding legal staff. This type of behavior is so disappointing, but it matches with many other published cases of prosecutorial misconduct in the many books that I have recommended.

Investigation Statement: "January 27th, February 8th, April 18th, 2018 letters to the SEC did not disclose the AvKARE's right to return."

The reason those disclosures were not made is because that statement is not factual. AvKARE did not have the right to return product. If AvKARE made those requests, they would each be evaluated for some extenuating circumstances. Occasionally, they were allowed a right of exchange, not necessarily a right of return, which are very different. However, there was no guaranteed right to return. That was not in their Distributor Agreement or its amendments.

Investigation Statement: "In October 31st, 2017 Petit, Taylor and Senken signed a rep letter stating that there were no side agreements and other arrangements (relative to AvKARE)."

That rep letter was signed because there were no "side agreements" with AvKARE. If "side agreements" were in effect, they would have been negotiated and placed into Amendment Number 3 or 4 to the AvKARE contract. King & Spalding never found any email or testimony relative to those requests being made or those types of requests being placed in the amendments. Remember, the DOJ ignored the AvKARE allegations. I hope you can see why!

Investigation Statement: "Information provided to Scott Taub by former management did not reflect the normal course of dealing. Taub relied upon this information to come to his conclusions on the accounting for AvKARE beyond 2016".

> King & Spalding continued to misrepresent the "course of dealings" with AvKARE. I do not believe that any reasonable legal argument could be made that, when occasional situations are reviewed by management as individual actions would require, that those particular courses of dealings would have modified our written contract. Again, the DOJ certainly saw weaknesses in these allegations relative to the course of dealings so they did not bother to bring any legal action relative to AvKARE. I believe that fact certainly eliminates any credibility to the allegation of "side deals" with AvKARE and "side deals" being caused by the "course of dealings." You can clearly see the corrupt bias with this King & Spalding investigation.

Investigation Statement: "Email on November 2nd, 2016 Kruchoski email to senior management: Also based on these conversations, as well as past conversation with upper management regarding the company's revenue reporting as it relates to third-party distribution companies, specifically but not limited to AvKARE Inc., we believe the company's practices are violations of Sarbanes-Oxley Act."

> This is the email in which Kruchoski was alleging channel stuffing. Within a few days, we obtained a similar, but much more lengthy and detailed letter from his attorney. I do not think Kruchoski even knew what the Sarbanes- Oxley Act required. These are words probably given to him by Clayton Halunen, his attorney. Halunen requested $14 million be paid to Kruchoski and Tornquist for them to basically "go away." However, he also wanted them to be released from their obligations under their non-compete contract.

> These allegations and the Audit Committee's prior investigation conducted by Troutman Sanders are thoroughly discussed earlier. They found no evidence of incorrect or fraudulent accounting. King & Spalding's allegations of violations of the Sarbanes-Oxley Act obviously intimidated an inexperienced Board! This was so <u>unprofessional</u>! King & Spalding later agreed in writing to the board that channel stuffing <u>did not</u> take place! However, the CEO, COO, CFO and Controller were asked to <u>resign</u> over their AvKARE <u>allegations</u>.

Investigation Statement: "Sole focus of this effort, referred to as 'Project Snow White' was to find the individuals who are selling on the side as well as additional evidence to support a lawsuit. It is not clear to King & Spalding what prompted this email review process."

The investigation of the whistleblower's allegations was the responsibility of the Audit Committee. They would check the allegations to determine if there was any validity to corporate or executive malfeasance. That was completed in early 2017, and there were no findings of malfeasance. A press release was made.

It was the responsibility of executive management to determine the guilt and culpability of the individuals that were found to be participating in selling competitive products on the side and breaking their non-compete agreements. It was important for executive management to understand who the leaders were behind this dishonest scheme and then who were the individuals who were "carried along by the crowd."

It was felt that there would be differences of culpability, and consequently, differences in the way the company disciplined and managed certain individuals. These differences would range from terminations and lawsuits to fines and reprimands. These were management judgments based on the fault that each individual had in this scheme and just how contrite they were about the situation. This had nothing to do with GAAP or other accounting matters. It was an executive management process, and it was the reason I set up an interview video camera in my conference room so that, during these interviews, we could go back and refer to what was being said. This would allow us to thoroughly vet the range of guilt for these various individuals, and hopefully, make the right decisions relative to the disciplinary processes. The video camera being used in the interview was known by our General Counsel, Lexi Haden, as well as outside counsel.

The last King & Spalding sentence makes no sense because review of emails and text messages allowed this type of evidence to be gathered! I believe that this demonstrates a lack of business acumen and common sense from the King & Spalding staff.

Investigation Statement: "Other MiMedx employees and are found to be selling on the side that did not receive the same sorts of discipline as Kruchoski and Tornquist."

That is certainly the case. The leaders of this scheme were disciplined more harshly than the followers, particularly because the followers were contrite and settled with the company.

Through our interview processes and video reviews, we were able to sort out the levels of guilt in this situation. It is hard to perceive why a lawyer or a former prosecutor would not understand the difference between the leadership and the participants in a business scheme of this nature. King & Spalding had no grasp of business management or normal business practice! Also, I know that prosecutors are accustomed to indicting as many people as possible with their "conspiracy tools" as they build their conviction record and resumes. We were only interested in determining their level of guilt and propensity for recidivism.

Investigation Statement: "Lexi Haden and Wargo French were in Minneapolis to mediate with Kruchoski and Tornquist attorneys. Haden and Wargo French were informed later that a settlement was possible with the employees. Petit was informed of the possibility of settlement and he proceeded to file lawsuits against the employees."

The majority of this statement is absolutely <u>false</u>. Lexi and Joe Wargo were in Minneapolis to mediate with Halunen for Kruchoski and Tornquist. The mediator told Lexi and Joe that she had conducted several mediations with Halunen in the past, and she spent the majority of her day trying to convince him that he had no case. She said she expected our mediation to go the same way.

Halunen wanted $14 million for what I called "hush money" but our attorneys called that a settlement proposal! I told Lexi and Joe that the company was not going to pay any settlement to these individuals, and they absolutely agreed. They continued negotiating during the day and kept me informed on what was transpiring. Halunen dropped his demand from $14 million down to $8 million at the end of the day. The <u>consensus</u> of Lexi, Joe and me <u>before</u> they went up to mediate was that we would do our best to explain to Halunen that they had <u>no</u> <u>countersuit</u> here, but at the end of the day if the matters were not settled to our satisfaction, MiMedx would file lawsuits the next day against Kruchoski and Tornquist for violations of their non-compete contracts with the company. And, that is exactly what transpired.

When Halunen was advised that we would be filing lawsuits based on his clients' behavior in allegedly violating their non-compete contracts and leading others to do the same, he flew into a rage. He said that he was going to expose MiMedx in the Minneapolis press the next day with all his clients' allegations. Halunen did exactly that.

As I have previously mentioned, MiMedx Group was in the final negotiations of being acquired by the 3M Corporation. Since 3M is headquartered in Minneapolis, their executives saw the article with all the false allegations in the newspaper, and they put the acquisition on hold.

Investigation Statement: "Directionally Kruchoski and Tornquist allegations were in the right ballpark but some of the specifics were inaccurate."

Well, basically <u>all</u> the specifics were false, regardless of a King & Spalding "ballpark" comment. Their major allegation was that the company had a channel stuffing scheme related to Veterans Administration hospitals. They claimed that we were shipping product to these hospitals without purchase orders and were overstocking them. Then, we were somehow booking these revenues.

That was absolutely <u>not</u> <u>factual</u>. Neither of these individuals nor their attorney understood the revenue recognition accounting practices that were utilized to properly book AvKARE and VA revenues at MiMedx. The Troutman Sanders investigation in 2017 clearly delineated that there were no channel stuffing activities at the company. Also, our accounts receivable stayed in a reasonable range over the years. King & Spalding basiclly admitted in the next document that channel stuffing was not occurring!

At the VA, our sales management was pushing the sales group to train staff in the surgical suites as well as the dermatology department. Kruchoski did not want to follow that instruction because he was selling competitive products in the podiatry department where he had over a decade of experience. So he was pushing back on our sales management's ability to know where the products he was responsible for were being utilized and why they were not being exposed to the surgical and dermatology departments in these hospitals. Kruchoski had been called out for this violation of management's directives.

Incidentally, this King & Spalding comment certainly should have concerned Dewberry because it insinuated that the Audit Committee investigation's findings were incorrect! This probably caused him more paranoia!

Investigation Statement: "King & Spalding have not been focused on the definition of channel stuffing due to the lack of true definition and have instead been focused on the conduct of the former management individuals."

King & Spalding has clearly stated my contention that they never really focused on fulfilling EY's request to investigate all the Cohodes' allegations (primarily channel stuffing). They used the Sally Yates Doctrine to come into the company and do exactly what the Doctrine requires. Which is to "target" top management and develop accusations around their activities. I believe they did so with a biased prosecutorial and polictical approach. This approach would result in a more significant engagement for King & Spalding with massive fees for numerous other law and accounting firms.

King & Spalding did not focus on "channel stuffing" because they found no proof!

Very few boards will have the experience to adequately deal with this investigatory and governmental overreach.

Investigation Statement: "King & Spalding concluded that former management played an active role in managing earnings and used the following in order to reach their conclusion."

This statement clearly demonstrates the lack of business experience and naivete that was brought to this investigation by King & Spalding. With all of their investigators being lawyers and one being a former prosecutor, this is the level of naivety they showed on their knowledge of how well-run businesses actually function.

Executive management is compensated to develop optimal revenues with achievable growth rates and the resulting profits or earnings per share. The management of revenue and earnings growth is a very key part of business management. If those two parameters are not managed well, executive management will be replaced by any normal Board. There were a number of occasions where King & Spalding tried to take issue with good business practices because they did not know what they were! Their investigation seldom used normal business practices as guidelines because they were on a "Witch Hunt" and busy twisting facts.

The King & Spalding innuendo was that, if revenues and earnings were "managed," there was wrongdoing! So naïve…or diabolical!

Investigation Statement: "King & Spalding stated that the bottom-up forecasting in 2015 was not very mature. The revenue numbers published to the street were based on what Petit thought they should be as opposed to bottom-up from the sales teams. The forecasting later improved."

King & Spalding <u>never</u> found any written documents or valid commentary about my forcing the company to meet revenue goals because of what I thought they should be. <u>This was basically a lie</u>.

Very early, I initiated the company's development of a sales management system that would mature into a very effective means of forecasting revenue from the territory, to the region, to the area and up to the sales executives. This "bottom up" system matured each year because our very talented information technology group, under the leadership of Jim Dozier, continued to add new applications to enhance the effectiveness and breadth of sales forecasting. If we had not developed such a system, then there would have been numerous flaws in the estimates that we gave to our shareholders. As I have mentioned, we only missed a sales forecast that we gave the shareholders one quarter out of 30. This was a <u>very</u> <u>exceptional</u> record.

We were later told, as we were investigating the practices of Kruchoski and others, that this group decided to "hold back" orders in the first quarter of 2016 in order to "teach management a lesson." The lesson they wanted taught was that they did not want any management oversight into their activities as the new and improving sales management system was allowing us to do. This is the same type of bottom up sales management process I had used with my previous companies, but we were more effective at MiMedx because of the information technology that had been brought to bear on managing all of the sales variables.

Investigation Statement: "Petit, Taylor, Cashman watched the revenue numbers closely and assured that the company hit the revenue number."

That statement is called "sales management," and yes, we conducted that function very successfully! MiMedx became the fifth fastest-growing public company in America by 2017…a truly laudable result.

Also, the "revenue number" was the primary responsibility of the sales organization, not Petit and Taylor. We did review the sales forecasting process every Monday morning because it was a very important business variable that had to be managed in a timely fashion.

Such a naïve King & Spalding statement! I hope some Board member called them out on this obvious "naivete!"

Investigation Statement: "In 2014, it was no later than three days before the end of each quarter (that guidance was met). In 2014, there were very few sales at quarter end with 5% of revenue coming in the last seven days. In 2015, the company hit the revenue target on the last day of each quarter. The last seven days 16% of quarterly sales, with the top five customers comprising 20% of quarterly revenue in the last seven days. Had the company not made any sales on the last day of each quarter in 2015, the company would have missed the low end targets."

These statements clearly delineate the lack of reasonable business experience and acumen of the King & Spalding legal staff. The major differences between the 2014 and 2015 sales activity related to two product issues. One, we lost our extra reimbursement as a new Medicare product for Epifix from 2014 into 2015. So the revenue per unit for that product was reduced. Also, we introduced a brand new product, OrthoFlo, in 2015, which changed the sales parameters somewhat. The fact that the company's five largest customers strongly participated in sales during the last seven days of the 2015 quarter should be an <u>attribute</u>! Again, King & Spalding lawyers have <u>no</u> experience in developing sales for medical products or anything else so they have no perspective on business issues of this nature.

Another very idiotic statment is that if the company had made no sales on the last day of each quarter in 2015, it would have missed the low end of the revenue guidance range! That is why we reviewed the revenue forecast every Monday morning. Also, because management was so efficient at planning production of our over 30 SKUs and matching those with our sales forecasts, we only missed our forecast in one quarter when some sales employees held back their orders at the end of the first quarter of 2016. We discussed that previously. Many of these comments would be humorous were it not for the terrible destruction this King & Spalding "Witch-Hunt" unnecessarily brought to the company. What a bargain…only about $25 million in investigation fees for King & Spalding and $15 million for KPMG.

Investigation Statement: "No email searches were performed to investigate channel stuffing or revenue recognition (by management). Email searches were performed on Jess Kruchoski, Luke Tornquist and other employees to investigate: selling on the side, violating their non-compete agreements and disclosing confidential information."

This is a typical King & Spalding comment that has, once again, twisted the facts. An extensive email and text message search was done in order to review the information from numerous documents for the Audit Committee investigation in early 2017 and again for the investigation by management of the non-compete violations.

Any issues that would indicate corruption by these or other individuals or the company would have certainly been highlighted by the Troutman Sanders and Audit Committee investigation in 2017. However, as we thought, that investigation found significant documentation on the sales employees' behavior, but nothing discussing any significant issues that would delineate channel stuffing or revenue recognition issues. That certainly is logical because these sales employees had no idea about the revenue recognition criteria or company processes and procedures that would cause revenue recognition or channel stuffing issues. After having known a number of these sales employees for years and understanding their personality traits, it was fairly easy to determine what had happened relative to employee dishonesty and who the leaders were. I know King & Spalding staff knew the difference, but these misrepresentations matched their "Witch Hunt" goals.

It was the Audit Committee's responsibility to investigate the "allegations" of accounting fraud caused by management while it was executive management's responsibility to investigate employee culpability for breaking their non-compete contracts.

Investigation Statement: "The investigation into the substance of allegations performed by management was limited to Haden having an interview with Kruchoski's lawyer."

This statement is factually <u>incorrect</u>. Actually, another lie!

It is the Audit Committee's responsibility to investigate allegations made against management or the corporation. This was done over a three-month period in late 2016 and early 2017 with the assistance of Troutman Sanders and Cherry Bekaert.

I could have quickly corrected this twisted comment had I been interviewed. All emails and text messages from employees who were suspect were reviewed. Anything that seemed to be a corrupt action or abnormality was brought to management's attention. The innuendo that management did not want to make this corporate investigation is absolutely false because this investigation <u>was not our responsibility</u>. It was the Audit Committee's responsibility! More King & Spalding misrepresentations and lies!

Investigation Statement: "February 3, 2017 AvKARE response to Troutman questions: The only written agreement between the parties is a main contract as amended. ... The companies have a course of dealing pursuant to which AvKARE <u>generally</u> does not make payment to MiMedx until after the VA issues a purchase order. MiMedx also credits AvKARE for all product returned by the VA and for all lost inventory."

AvKARE had recently hired a new and much more experienced attorney in Nashville when these questions came up in early 2017. This lawyer was merely looking after his new client and repeating what he had been told. He knew nothing about the "course of dealing" because he had represented the company for only a few months. As I have stated many times, if these terms of the selling process were truthful and so critical to AvKARE, they would have insisted that they be put in Amendment Number 4 to their Distributor Agreement. There are no emails, suggestions or conversations related to these terms being changed in Amendment Number 4. So the statements from the AvKARE attorney should be discredited as the new representative of an irritated distributor merely trying to gain leverage with MiMedx.

It is interesting to note that King & Spalding took the word of a Nashville attorney who had only recently begun to represent this client over the top three officers at MiMedx and the outside counsel at Troutman

Sanders. It is also interesting that, when Troutman Sanders queried AvKARE's new lawyer, they saw through his comments and motivations. King & Spalding did not want to see through those allegations because they were trying to build their case against the top officers at MiMedx Group. Even an inexperienced Board should have seen through this charade and accepted their responsibility to call out the flaws in this investigation process just as the Board of the Fortune 50 technology company did to a King & Spalding investigation a couple of years earlier.

We did not credit AvKARE for all product returns or lost inventory. There were no guarantees for any customers as that could have caused a revenue recognition issue. We reviewed each situation on its merits.

Investigation Statement: "Petit stated ... there were many instances in which AvKARE had paid prior to receiving a payment from the VA."

King & Spalding also stated that this turned out to be a misunderstanding on Petit's part as instances where AvKARE had an accelerated payment when MiMedx offered special financing terms. The special financing terms were merely a discount for early payment. This is done frequently by American business, and it is not a violation of GAAP. As we have previously mentioned, if AvKARE really believed that these terms were in place as a result of the course of dealing, they would have asked for them to be documented in Amendment Number 4 to their distributor contract. There was no written or verbal discussion about that issue whatsoever. I believe this was just the AvKARE attorney trying to impress a new client by repeating what he could have been told. Also, it should be evident that King & Spalding was more than happy to take statements from a non-credible source as it matched their Sally Yates doctrine theme of "targeting" the top executives.

The King & Spalding motives are so evident!

Investigation Statement: "MiMedx investigation focused on revenue recognition with the audit committee concluding that the company needed to refile financials for 2012-Q3 through 2017 due to: MiMedx business practices with AvKARE varying significantly from the contract and extended payment term for First Medical."

The decision was made by the Audit Committee that the company needed to refile its financial statements for 2012 to 2017 primarily because they decided that AvKARE had been paying MiMedx based on what they were paid weekly by the VA hospitals. Because AvKARE presented to MiMedx a weekly report, which went to our compliance department and consisted of a list of the implanted tissue serial numbers for the previous week (or months), the Audit Committee decided that meant AvKARE was given permission by the executives to pay MiMedx when they were paid by the Veterans Administration hospitals. That allegation was absolutely <u>false</u>, but the King & Spalding investigators ignored all information pointing clearly to that not being factual.

As I previously mentioned, the weekly FDA report that came in from AvKARE was something that MiMedx had no way to verify. We never received the communications that were sent to AvKARE from VA hospitals with this information. We were told that it sometimes took three months for VA hospitals to send in this data, which was required for the FDA, and AvKARE had the ability to not disclose that information to us. AvKARE's accounting system was so immature that it could not even tell MiMedx which invoices were to be credited when a check was sent. They just told us to credit every dollar to the <u>oldest</u> invoice that existed. Therefore, this FDA report was a very inaccurate document that had very little pertinent information related to accounting.

Also, as I have said, if AvKARE had been given permission to pay MiMedx only after they had been paid by the Veterans Administration hospitals, they would have <u>demanded</u> that those procedures be put in Amendment Number 4 to the AvKARE contract, which included all the issues required to wind-down our relationship.

There was so much misinformation coming from King & Spalding to the Audit Committee and Board stating that they believed our course of dealing with AvKARE overruled our distributor contract, even though our contracts stated very clearly that it took an amendment signed by both parties to make any changes to the contract. As a final "nail in the coffin" to this allegation, the DOJ <u>did</u> <u>not</u> <u>file</u> <u>any</u> <u>indictments</u> against officers of the company related to AvKARE. I believe they looked at the information that King & Spalding had developed, and they also saw the flaws in the allegation.

However, it was the AvKARE allegation that encouraged the Board of Directors to terminate four of the top officers of the company. I believe that Dewberry pushed this accusatory theme because he felt that it would eliminate any question of the Audit Committee possibly not performing some of their duties correctly as was alleged by EY with regard to the whistleblower investigation in early 2017.

Relative to First Medical, Bill had some significant negotiations with them at the end of 2015. They wanted us to ship a large order to them in Saudi Arabia, but at that point they had not received an anticipated tender from the Saudi government. They thought they would get the tender in March, which they did. However, we pre-filled the order they wanted and made the shipment in December. Bill made some commitments to them that, if the government did not order in March, we would reconsider their billing terms. The order was received in March as expected. However, MiMedx was not paid in a timely manner by First Medical as had occurred with their previous orders because the Saudi government had stopped paying all their suppliers and vendors because of the oil crisis and their war with Yemen. This was a very unusual situation with numerous extenuating circumstances.

We eventually collected the First Medical invoices. However, this situation certainly did not warrant a restatement of our financials from an accrual basis to a cash basis. Recall our large revenue reserves which, if we had determined there was a question of revenue recognition, they would have covered the First Medical December 2015 invoice in its entirety.

The total revenue restatement will go down as the most ridiculous and bizarre decision that could have been made by this Audit Committee and Board in the process of taking control of the company and terminating management on June 30, 2018.

Investigation Statement: "Various statements by former management have referred back to the contract to justify actions, which are consistent with the contractual terms, but do not reflect a course of dealings. King & Spalding stated that management understood the course of dealings but rarely distinguished between the two."

The management at MiMedx had dealt with distributor relationships for decades and had a track record of selling to distributors and booking revenue on an accrual basis (upon shipment) with no issues developing. King & Spalding was the first to raise questions about the "course of dealings" with distributors when they found a few instances where certain rights had been given to a distributor to exchange one product size for another product size or where there were actual returns for credit. However, neither AvKARE nor any of our distributors had any written or verbal agreements with the company or management guaranteeing that they had a right to make these returns or exchanges. In every situation that came up, management was involved in the decision-making to determine if the circumstances were such that we would make the change, even though our contract did not require us to do so. Thus, our "course of dealing" was on a case-by-case basis and not routine! From the legal advice we were given, this random course of dealing was not sufficient to modify our written contracts. Also, our sales "reserves" covered any potential reported revenue inaccuracies

In most of these cases, we would always tell our distributors that we wanted to be with them as a partner, and we would do what was reasonable on occasion to help them through situations that may have extenuating circumstances. This was just good business practice, and it was one of the reasons we had so many sales successes over the eight-year period as we grew to be the fifth fastest-growing public company in America.

Investigation Statement: "King & Spalding concluded that by at least 2016, former management understood and were aware that the GAAP rules were applicable to both MiMedx and AvKARE and that similar revenue recognition issues occurred at Osiris."

The first part of that statement is extremely disingenuous. I had been the Chairman and/or CEO of public companies for 35 years, and I understood the GAAP rules that I had been exposed to over those decades. However, there were some new rules added in SAB Topic 13 with which I was not familiar.

The similar revenue recognition issues they refer to for which the SEC found Osiris liable, did not occur at MiMedx, and King & Spalding later verified that in writing. Osiris was accused of "channel stuffing," which means shipping product to distributors without purchase orders or other agreements, and booking the revenue. That violates some of the four primary revenue recognition requirements. When something like this occurs, the accounts receivable for the manufacturer move up very rapidly as had happened at Osiris. Their days sales outstanding went from about 80 days to approximately 150 days. At MiMedx, we never had any issue like that with our accounts receivable. When we left the company, the DSOs were at approximately 65 days.

King & Spalding finally admitted that channel stuffing did not occur at MiMedx in their written statements to the Board.

Investigation Statement: "Petit claims that he was unaware of the loan. However, there's email traffic of him receiving a loan agreement, accidentally being copied in by the family's lawyer, to which Petit requested his assistant to print the attachments."

I <u>never</u> stated that I was unaware of the loan. I stated that I was unaware of the <u>terms</u> of the loan or other financing arrangements. I maintained an arm's length between myself and my family members who were negotiating the loan to SLR. My service to SLR was to merely make an introduction to my son-in-law, Todd Campbell, and to a former Matria Healthcare executive, both of who were doing business with small companies and might be interested in making a working capital loan.

King & Spalding stated here that I was accidentally copied, which was the truth for a change. They often parsed words and left out facts to press their agenda.

Investigation Statement: "Disagreement was not tolerated or encouraged at MiMedx."

Nothing could be further from the truth. If the lawyers had taken the time to read and could understand the "participatory management" principles that we articulated in our management booklet, they could not make this statement. Again, this is just a case of King & Spalding attorneys not understanding how normal American business is managed and functions or not wanting to understand. More misrepresentations! And, frankly more lies!

Investigation Statement: "King & Spalding learned that Legal and Finance were excluded from weekly Monday morning staff meetings, something that is inconsistent with a company with healthy tone at the top."

I sincerely suggest that having King & Spalding attorneys opining to proper and balanced business management is <u>absurd</u> due to their total <u>lack of experience</u>. Our Monday morning staff meetings were primarily related to review of the weekly sales activities, the weekly activities related to our production of product, our clinical studies and other critical issues that had significant <u>timing</u> implications. I had conducted these meetings for decades at my other companies, and I found them to be very effective in making certain that none of our managers in these various areas were talking past each other and were very focused on managing the proper variables while not missing any deadlines.

Our legal organization, who would have been represented by our General Counsel, and our financial organization, who would have been represented by our Chief Financial Officer, were never "excluded" from weekly Monday morning staff meetings. However, that does not mean that they were invited to the majority of these meetings. At MiMedx, we were all working very hard and for our General Counsel and CFO to sit for three hours listening to people discuss issues for which they really had no background would have been very wasteful in terms of their time management. If there were specific issues that needed accounting or legal expertise, I would involve those executives, or we held separate meetings. These King & Spalding lawyers <u>did</u> <u>not</u> <u>know</u> <u>how</u> to properly assess the management skills required to become the fifth fastest-growing company in America in just eight years!

I have seen enough to state that the King & Spalding attorneys should <u>never</u> discuss or opine to "Tone at the Top" for a business entity since they have <u>never</u> functioned in that environment! In other words, they have no real background or experience on which to base such opinions or make such statements and allegations.

If we had been given these investigation documents and allowed to respond, it probably would have created, even with our inexperienced Board, a very strong negative response to the management of the investigation. This is what occurred with the Fortune 50 technology company that I previously mentioned that had undergone a similar King & Spalding investigation about six years ago. I was told that their Board trashed the investigation's findings.

When you read through these twisted allegations with the real facts presented and explained, it demonstrates the extent to which a law firm with former federal prosecutors can distort facts and information. Again, having now read numerous books on this subject, I am very, very disappointed in what I have seen in terms of the results of the Sally Yates Doctrine and the behavior of our investigatory law firm and the DOJ assistant U.S. attorneys assigned to the case. As has always been said, a federal prosecutor can "indict a ham sandwich!"

However, in most cases, an experienced Board will punch through any misinterpreted facts or misconstrued sentences. This would be particularly true if accused management were given a chance to respond to the accusations. Thus, the Board and management should <u>work together</u> to ensure that both their fiduciary responsibilities to their shareholders are met.

I think these investigation statements and my comments should be sufficient for clarity on how our "Witch Hunt" was conducted. You can see how not being given a chance to respond was detrimental. I hope these disclosures put in stark perspective the half-truths and manipulation of facts and lies that can come from lawyers who are prosecutors or former prosecutors. As I have said, "This is not America." But it <u>is</u> today.

New Financial Statements

When the company finally published the 2017 and 2018 financial statements in their 10-K dated March 10, 2020, it was unbelievably complex. For the motivation of Borkowski, the temporary CFO, to continue to remain employed, he and Dewberry must have agreed to resolve revenue recognition questions by placing <u>all</u> revenues for <u>3,000 different customers</u> on a <u>cash</u> basis rather than a normal accrual basis when the shipment took place. Borkowski's motivations were always directed at himself, but I cannot understand, other than his paranoia, why Dewberry and also the Board allowed such a wasteful and ridiculous accounting process.

When Bill and I left the company on June 30, 2018, the revenues were annualized at approximately $400 million. MiMedx's actual revenues were below $250 million for 2020. We had given shareholders a forecast of $560 million for 2020! These accounting and investigation matters became <u>totally</u> out of control. Inept Board decisions caused the revenue to stop the 30 percent growth rate and to significantly decline by almost 40 percent from the first two quarters of 2018. There has been little annual growth since.

MiMedx had a very acceptable cash collection process over the years. If the auditors had done an analysis of the approximately $1 billion dollars of revenues and the approximately $1 billion of cash collected in this period, they would <u>not</u> have developed the opinion to place all of those revenues on a cash basis. However, it was <u>not</u> in their <u>self-interest</u> to do such an analysis because not doing so allowed them to do a very complicated re-audit that cost $80 million. Of course, had Dewberry and Borkowski been properly motivated, they would have gone down a very different path. And, had the Board been experienced, attentive and fully involved, this travesty of investigations, re-audits and expenses would <u>not</u> have taken place.

As previously mentioned, another major argument against this expensive accounting foray was the fact that the company was generally very <u>well</u> <u>reserved</u> with our "returns and allowances" reserves and "bad debt" reserves. Neither the Board nor King & Spalding <u>ever</u> mentioned these very <u>extenuating</u> <u>circumstances</u> in the findings of the investigation. We routinely added to those reserves every quarter, and if we perceived a potential weakness in our revenue or accounts receivable for that quarter, we would add additional amounts to the reserves. THUS, ANY PERTURBATIONS IN REVENUE RECOGNITION, CASH COLLECTIONS AND BAD DEBTS SHOULD HAVE BEEN MORE THAN ADEQUATELY COVERED BY THE COMPANY'S BUILDUP OF BOTH TYPES OF RESERVES. When we left the company, these reserves were at about $10 million!

Again, it was <u>not</u> in the financial interest of EY, KPMG or the other accounting firms to take that approach. Huge accounting expenditures occurred over matters that should <u>not</u> have been worthy of a re-audit! Also, most importantly, MiMedx was "taken over" by an inexperienced Board manipulated by Dewberry. Even after the election of three new Board members, nothing much changed since they continued to take the "easy way" rather than the "right way" when making decisions, and I think they relied on "business advice" from Isaac Greaney and the Sidley Austin law firm. This was a serious mistake!

Now the King & Spalding investigation turned up the fact that neither Bill nor I <u>knew</u> <u>about</u> <u>the</u> <u>changes</u> <u>in</u> <u>revenue</u> <u>recognition</u> brought about by SAB Topic 13 until early 2016 when Mark Anderson, our new Controller, brought it up to Mike and the Audit Committee. Dewberry conducted an Audit Committee investigation on the matter, as he should have. There were complicated revenue recognition and accounting procedures that we did not understand because we were not familiar with SAB Topic 13. However, the Audit Committee and Dewberry decided that Anderson's issues were "merely a conflict between members of the accounting department." The report also stated there was nothing the company needed to do to resolve the matter. Dewberry did state that he wished to talk to executive management about the matter, but he never scheduled such a meeting!

In early 2017, some revenue recognition issues were brought up by Cherry Bekaert, which <u>should</u> <u>have</u> <u>been</u> <u>questioned</u> because of the changes we made in the AvKARE contract by Amendment 4. The company retained a very experienced revenue recognition expert, Scott Taub, to assist with the education process and resolution of all the questions. Taub's counsel was superb. We reviewed on a number of occasions all the issues that Cherry Bekaert was concerned about relative to what revenue recognition for AvKARE needed to be because of the changes to their contract from Amendment 4. Taub came to the same conclusions that management had reached, and there were no changes made going forward in the "Rev Rec" criteria for AvKARE through the end of the contract.

During these lengthy discussions with Taub, neither Dewberry nor the Audit Committee <u>ever</u> <u>participated</u>. That was in spite of my encouraging Dewberry to talk to Taub. He said he did not think the Audit Committee needed to be involved. So we were left with the opinion that we had no concerns on this matter with AvKARE. But, with that conclusion, King & Spalding would have had <u>little to</u> <u>investigate</u>.

As Sidney Powell often points out in her books, misdirected prosecutors do not focus on whether a crime has been committed, but on persons they want "to get." Paul Murphy, the investigation manager and former prosecutor, decided that Bill and I <u>withheld</u> information from the accounting department, the Audit Committee and the auditors. We supposedly did not reveal the <u>concocted</u> King & Spalding "imaginary side deal" with AvKARE to let them pay us only when they were paid! Thus, we were guilty of accounting fraud, which is a criminal offense. In order to keep the investigation going, we became potential criminals! King & Spalding and KPMG had financial motivations to create allegations plus there were the possible political motivations against me.

Recall that Cohodes and one of our former sales managers who violated our policies alleged the company was doing channel stuffing. We discussed that matter in Chapters 12 and 13. The first Audit Committee investigation did not find that the company had conducted any channel stuffing, and eventually King & Spalding had to admit the same. However, King & Spalding also made allegations about "side deals" in the second and third quarters of 2015 where management had reassured some distributors that our "business philosophy" was that we would work with them on any problems, including cash flow, which might develop. In other words, we were not a litigious organization that would file lawsuits without first trying to work through their business or cash flow problems. Also, we were introducing a new product line in the third quarter of 2015, which required frozen storage so we had to market through distributors. To us, this business philosophy was basically good business practice!

In the next chapter, we will get into the details of those other four allegations, which were actually turned into charges in our indictments. While the DOJ did some of their own investigative work, they predominantly utilized the majority of the work that King & Spalding had prepared, with the exception of AvKARE. Thus, King & Spalding was paid an exorbitant amount of money to do the work that would normally be accomplished by the DOJ attorneys…more of the Sally Yate's Doctrine and much more money for King & Spalding and the associated law firms, which we will discuss later…well over $100 million!

Guilt by Accusation

In Alan Dershowitz's book entitled *Guilt by Accusation,* his very last paragraph says it all. "This is everyone's battle, not just mine. It is a battle for justice for all. It is a struggle against those who bear false witness. The Bible commands, 'Justice, justice you shall pursue.' The word justice is repeated, because there must be justice for both the victim of false accusations and for those who falsely accuse. Dershowitz commented that he will not rest until 'justice' comes to me as well as to those who have born false witness against me.

In Dershowitz's case, he is seeking justice through the court system where he is able to file defamation claims against a number of individuals. However, if he gets the wrong makeup of jurors, he could very well not achieve justice, even in a fair court system. Decisions made by many jurorss today may be either very politically motivated or driven by disclosures from the media, which can be very deceiving and even untruthful. Also, what has happened to our right to have a jury of our peers?

Key Goal

One key goal for writing this book is to educate as many individuals as possible as to how the U.S. judicial system has changed. Even as a very experienced business executive, I continue to get surprises and disappointments about how our system of justice has deteriorated. The same realization happened to Conrad Black, Howard Root and Raj Rajaratnam when they went through their trials.

As Americans, I think we need to clearly understand that, in the last couple of decades, there have been numerous changes in key governmental agencies, in our justice system and our access to sources of information, principally the main stream media and social media, which have dramatically affected many of our mores and traditions. In general, the changes in our justice system have had many negative consequences.

There are a number of books available to inform you of these various changes. Please avail yourself of all these materials and attempt to balance your information gathering. Then, start talking to family, friends and politicians about the need to bring back the lost balance to our American values and our way of life caused by "our" lawyers.

Chapter 21 Appendix

MiMedx Audit Committee Tries to Avoid Criticism by Making Specious Findings of Misconduct by Former Management, According to Attorney William Weinreb.

Former Chairman and CEO "Pete" Petit Highlights Flaws in Revenue Recognition Allegations.

Parker H. "Pete" Petit Responds to Charges by the DOJ/SEC.

CHAPTER 22

GOVERNMENT CHARGES AGAINST EXECUTIVES

As a public company officer, entrepreneur or not, you need to understand the world of a federal prosecutor in today's business and regulatory environment. Over the 37 years that I presided over my entrepreneurial public companies, I have seen the regulatory environment and enforcement processes change dramatically in America.

On April 1, 1940, Attorney General Robert H. Jackson made comments to his Department of Justice federal prosecutors that have stood the test of time. Attorney General Jackson commented, "If the prosecutor is obligated to choose his cases, it follows that he can choose his defendants." In other words, "the most dangerous power of the prosecutor: that he will pick people that he thinks he should get, rather than pick cases that need to be prosecuted." This can take place by prosecutors "picking the man and then searching the law books, or putting investigators to work, to pin some offense on him." I am afraid that, over the decades, more and more of our federal prosecutors are behaving in just the way Attorney General Jackson warned.

Attorney General Jackson became a Supreme Court Justice and also served after World War II as the Chief United States Prosecutor of the International Military Tribunal for the Nuremberg trials. Obviously, he was a man of legal wisdom and integrity.

This is a very simple issue: FEDERAL ATTORNEYS CAN BECOME VERY FOCUSED ON TRYING TO OPTIMIZE THEIR CAREERS VERSUS BEING FOCUSED ON ADMINISTERING JUSTICE. In other words, it is very obvious that the federal attorneys who are fortunate enough to involve themselves in a significant white-collar crime case will be of increased interest to one of the large law firms. Thus, if they can find a way to manipulate themselves into a notable white-collar criminal investigation and trial, that almost guarantees a job offer from one of these larger law firms. This means they can become a partner and potentially make millions of dollars more than their annual federal salaries. I believe there are not many young government lawyers who do not succumb to that desire.

What I have described is a very simple concept. There is little accountability in most federal agencies so that, if a case is brought that is an injustice, the young attorneys will not be faulted or terminated. So, in many cases, these attorneys will take the risk of filing cases for their own benefit that should not be brought.

As I have now had my experiences with two regulatory agencies, the SEC and DOJ, I have gained quite an education. Frankly, even after 37 years of public company stewardship, I have been quite shocked at some of the actions of the lawyers and federal prosecutors at these two agencies. Also, remember that there are former federal prosecutors working at numerous law firms across the country who represent defendants in federal cases. Does that "rehabilitate" the prosecutor?

Investigatory Techniques

As I have been able to go through the investigation material that King & Spalding developed, it is evident that they were quite thorough in that they viewed approximately a million emails and text messages from over 50 employees for about a six-year period. However, as most prosecutors do, they went into this case with a preset notion of where they wanted to be in terms of their optimal outcomes. As we have previously mentioned, Dewberry, became quite paranoid about being "sent to jail." He had the initial interaction with Murphy from King & Spalding without all the members of the Audit Committee or Board being very involved. I believe he was advised about the Sally Yates Doctrine of pursuing top management with any set of allegations. And, I believe that suited Dewberry's CYA paranoia very well. So nothing was vetted with the Board members in terms of the scope of the investigation.

Actually, I saw in writing where the Board was concerned that Bill and I be given "due process" so we could educate and correct the numerous misconceptions that Murphy and his team of lawyers developed about our business processes which they had <u>never</u> before experienced themselves. However, that <u>did</u> <u>not</u> <u>take</u> <u>place</u>, and consequently, the concerns that Attorney General Jackson expressed many decades ago actually took place. From the situations I have reviewed, I believe that Dewberry was the cause of the mismanagement of the investigation primarily because of his initatives for his own CYA agenda.

What will generally transpire during an investigation is that there will be a very expensive review of all pertinent written documents and other materials, which is certainly in the prosecutors' interest. In the case of MiMedx, there were numerous and very complex business processes, particularly with one distributor,

AvKARE, who had the contract with the VA hospitals. The manner in which I have seen the King & Spalding as well as DOJ and SEC lawyers build their cases is that, while they may turn up all the key facts, they very selectively emphasize and manipulate particular ones that build their case. There may be compelling facts that shut down an allegation the lawyers want to advance, but that information is de-emphasized as the investigation proceeds, and they drop discussions of it.

That is exactly what happened in our case since Bill and I were not allowed to counter the AvKARE case they initially developed. For instance, King & Spalding never had anything in writing stating that we were allowing our federal distributor, AvKARE, to only pay us when their products were implanted and sold at the VA hospitals. They had one email from an AvKARE administrator in 2012 merely stating that they would like to pay us when they obtained the weekly reports from the VA that a specific product had been implanted. There was not a reply to this message from any members of the MiMedx staff agreeing to that request. In fact, we had numerous examples where we managed the AvKARE accounts receivable as we did with all our other distributors and customers. That is, we monitored how many days sales outstanding they had in their payables to us (our receivables), and we held them to keeping those within an acceptable range.

On two occasions, I personally called and demanded that AvKARE send us approximately $2 million, and they complied with my request. That certainly demonstrates that they were not paying us only when they were paid. However, when King & Spalding made their first presentation to our Board on AvKARE, the cash collections information was never really discussed, or the fact that MiMedx accounting staff had done the same thing as I had done in terms of asking AvKARE to reduce their receivables by sending payments. We did not give AvKARE permission to wait on the VA to implant our allografts or pay for them in order to pay us.

So the technique that is used by prosecutors is to determine the facts, all of which they would like to have made available to them, and then decide which facts match their prosecutorial goals. In the case of a corporate investigation, this generally means they will make a recommendation that an executive has violated some rules, regulations or laws, as the Sally Yates Doctrine requires.

Going forward, the prosecutors will selectively discard the facts that do not fit their narrative. Of course, relative to federal prosecutors, I believe those who supervise them generally do not carefully review the cases they want to file and do not prevent them from going ahead with potential cases, which "keeps the peace" because it works towards building the prosecutors' resumes.

Of course, in today's environment, Sarbanes-Oxley gives Audit Committees substantial new duties and responsibilities. Therefore, when any allegations are made against a company, the top executives must turn them over to the Audit Committee for their review and deliberations. Also, as a general rule, that means the executives are pushed aside, and the investigation can go forward without the top executives having any knowledge of the scope, goals and objectives. Also, no "due process" of the law has to be given under the Yates Doctrine.

If an executive tries to question matters or become involved, that is seen as an immediately suspicious act. Therefore, I never did that, and consequently, we had an Audit Committee Chairman and other individuals acting in their own self-interest. I did not pick up on this behavior until the AvKARE investigation was essentially complete. So, with the Sarbanes-Oxley requirements and the tendency of prosecutors to manipulate the facts to meet their desires, that leaves public company executives in an extremely weak and debilitating position. Of course, the Sally Yates Doctrine is the "coup de grace."

After having experienced this investigation, I think I can generally say that, if a Board hires a law firm particularly with a former prosecutor to manage an investigation, there will not be many public companies in America where a case could not be developed against executive management. Particularly when you pay $40 million and allow 15 months to investigate. In reading Harvey Silverglate's and Sydney Powell's books, you could summarize by saying, "Corrupt prosecutors don't look for justice; they focus on one official and begin to build a case, using only their facts."

Would most astute and experienced entrepreneurs and business executives want to accept the responsibilities of being a public company executive in this current unbalanced regulatory and business environment? I would not think so! However, much more to expose!

Our AUSAs

The Assistant U.S. Attorneys (AUSAs) that tried our case were Edward Imperatore, Scott Hartman and Daniel Tracer. Imperatore left the DOJ rather quickly for a large law firm after our sentencing. Hartman received a promotion to Chief, Securities and Commodities Fraud Task Force in June 2022. Tracer went to work for Neuberger Berman, an investment managment firm in New York.

The DOJ Prosecutor's Allegations

First, after all the work that KPMG and King & Spalding put into the AvKARE allegations, I believe the DOJ attorneys saw through the fallacy of that accusation just as we have outlined. The DOJ did not include any AvKARE allegations in their indictments against Bill and me.

Murphy put in a lot of time and effort to develop the AvKARE story and allegations for the Audit Committee investigation. As we have discussed in numerous parts of the book, all of that was an absolute concoction of misinformation. However, the MiMedx Board, unfortunately, bought the story and terminated Bill Taylor, Mike Senken, John Cranston and me based on those inaccurate and untrue AvKARE allegations.

Remember, the one very obvious fact that destroyed the King & Spalding allegation that we gave a "side deal" to AvKARE so that "they did not have to pay us until they were paid by the VA" was that there were no communications that mentioned placing those business terms into Amendment Number 4 of the AvKARE Agreement. Thus, that first alleged "side deal" was totally fabricated and false. Incidentally, you are going to hear the term "side deal" numerous times as we discuss the other allegations because that is one of the prosecutor's favorite ways of trying to cast aspersions and allege fraud.

Now the company's investigation through King & Spalding continued past the AvKARE allegation. The investigation continued on for another 12 months. During that period of time, I was told by a Board member that they thought the investigation was complete, but that Dewberry opened it up again, probably when the DOJ informed him and King & Spalding that they would not use the AvKARE allegations to file indictments.

In the last round of investigations, King & Spalding made accusations about transactions in 2015 with several distributors. We were never told about these issues until the company used some of the allegations in a press release during the proxy contest in May 2019. The comments were very derogatory towards me, and they were just not true.

King & Spalding subsequently picked the second, third and fourth quarters of 2015 as a place to focus their attention, which resulted in our indictments by the DOJ. During these quarters, we were having negotiations and modifying and creating Distributor Agreements with four different distributors. These four distributors were CPM Medical from Dallas, Texas, SLR Medical from

Dallas, Texas, Stability Biologics from Nashville, Tennessee and First Medical from Saudi Arabia.

At that point, we were still adding some distributors to our national presence. However, from that point forward, we began to add our own sales force in areas where we might have previously considered distributors.

These distributors will be discussed in detail to make it clear that we were conducting what we considered to be normal business activities, and we had no intention of modifying any distributors' contracts or changing any of the accounting processes that had been in place for several years.

This very detailed information is what should have totally stopped our investigation had Bill and I been given "due process" of the law. However, the individuals controlling those decisions were not interested in determining the truth. They were interested in seeing their "targets" being indicted, tried and convicted.

CPM Medical

CPM was MiMedx's second largest distributor, and they had an exclusive territory for the state of Texas. MiMedx's management required CPM to purchase certain amounts of product each quarter in order to meet the requirements of their distributor contract and to continually grow the company's presence in the Texas market. Generally speaking, by 2015 their quarterly purchases were in the $2 million range. If this distributor made a $2 million purchase, they were given an additional five percent discount, which is something that their principal, Mark Brooks, was adamant about receiving.

Brooks' relationship with the company had soured over the years because of the violation of several of the key requirements in the CPM Distributor Agreement which included not selling MiMedx products outside the state of Texas and not selling competitor's products in the state of Texas. Also, most importantly, some of CPM's doctor customers were gouging health plans with prices that were two to four times our suggested retail price. I had received calls from the Chief Medical Officer at Blue Cross Blue Shield of Texas with whom I had a previous relationship at Matria Healthcare. He told me that they were receiving bills from doctors that were marked up substantially over the MiMedx suggested retail prices.

I understood the seriousness of such an issue, and I made a commitment that I would be certain this distributor did not allow the alleged price gouging to continue. However, it did. I received another phone call from the Medical Director's subordinate explaining that other violations had occurred. I knew that MiMedx could not only lose its relationship with Blue Cross Blue Shield of Texas, but also these violations could result in losing contracts with all of the 48 Blue Cross Blue Shield organizations in the U.S.

I had warned CPM's principle, Marc Brooks, on several other occasions about the situation. His solution was simply to deny that he knew anything about the specfics of these problems. I had previously met some of the doctors that were customers of CPM, and I could tell from their conversations that they would follow whatever CPM suggested.

When I received the third phone call from Blue Cross Blue Shield about price gouging in mid-2015, I made the decision that the company could no longer take the risk of being involved with CPM. I started moving towards cancelling the contracts. First, I sent Brooks a letter dated June 25th terminating his consulting contract. I immediately began to work on canceling the CPM distributor contract by June 30th.

About the same time, Bill and his sales management staff were working on trying to fulfill the CPM second quarter order. As usual, Brooks had waited until very late in the quarter to place an order, hoping he could avoid some contractual obligations. This time, Brooks waited so late that some of the product sizes that he wanted were no longer in inventory. These unavailable sizes amounted to $1.2 million. Thus, the sales staff began to work on a solution to be able to ship CPM their $2 million order requirement, which would give them the additional five percent discount that Brooks desired. They made a very logical decision to talk to Brooks about buying some product sizes that CPM had routinely sold in the past to substitute for some of the <u>new</u> sizes that he <u>thought</u> he wanted with this second quarter order. That certainly made business sense.

Sales management expected that CPM would be able to readily sell the alternative products that it had previously purchased. To mitigate any concerns, sales management reminded Brooks that he could exchange some of the products, if necessary, as MiMedx had allowed some customers to do over the years. Recall that Brooks was adamant about his five percent discount, which required a $2 million purchase.

An "exchange" is simply the return of product and the immediate shipment of replacement product, generally in different sizes. Since 2011, MiMedx had been allowing hospitals, wound care centers, doctor's offices and distributors to "exchange" products because they were merely replacing one product size for another that doctors had decided they preferred to use. No change in the financial obligation took place.

Bill and I had been working with information given to us by our Chief Financial Officer, Mike Senken, several years earlier that "exchanges" of this type were "revenue neutral," meaning that the product merely came in and a similar dollar amount of different product was shipped out to the customer. The payable to MiMedx did not change. However, even though this process was clearly known to the company's accounting staff, the Audit Committee and the company's outside auditors, it turned out there was one flaw.

As we previously mentioned, in February 2017 MiMedx contracted with one of the foremost revenue recognition experts in America, Scott Taub, to discuss an issue that our auditing firm, Cherry Bekaert, had some concerns about relative to the wind-down of the AvKARE contract. After several discussions with Taub, he told management that we were correct in the way that we thought the AvKARE revenues going forward should be booked until the contract ended. However, in the process of those conversations, Taub brought up another issue that he said had given some of his other clients a surprise relative to "exchanges." He told Bill, Mike and me that an exchange was revenue neutral only with the final customer which, in the case of MiMedx, would be a hospital, wound care center or doctor's office. He said an exchange with a middleman or distributor was not revenue neutral. Taub said this rule does not make business sense, but that is the way it is written in SAB 13. Thus, with a distributor, the product must be taken in as a "return," meaning the items are placed back into inventory. Then, the company ships other products out on, essentially, a new order. Because there is a return, the company has to issue a credit and to slightly increase its reserve for "sales returns and allowances." While this would be a very minor matter in the company's financial statements, it was a change in the way exchanges with distributors had to be booked in the MiMedx accounting system. This mistake was caused by Dewberry, as Audit Committee Chairman, not being inquisitive about MiMedx's treatment of exchanges and returns, and not desiring to talk to Taub.

Fortunately, as I had always done over the decades, the company had been taking a certain amount of revenue each quarter and placing it into our "reserve" account. Thus, basically every quarter the accounting department increased our "sales returns and allowances" and "bad debt" reserves significantly. So shareholders were being protected from revenue surprises that could take place, such as these exchanges with distributors or a possible hospital bankruptcy. According to the auditors, there was no significant impact on the company's past financial statements on this distributor exchange issue when we changed our approach because of the information we had learned from Taub.

However, once the formal investigation was started by King & Spalding in February 2018 at the direction of the Audit Committee Chairman, management was accused of doing <u>undisclosed</u> exchanges in 2015 with distributors when the company and auditors thought this process was revenue neutral and adding additional "returns and allowances" reserves was not required. Thus, Bill and I were accused of manipulating accounting rules and the company's accountants, Audit Committee and auditors when we made business decisions related to exchanges, and these decisions were not formally disclosed. These were not formally disclosed because we operated in 2015 with the previous direction given in 2011 that these types of transactions were revenue neutral. So that fact eliminated the requirement that exchanges be disclosed because we all thought there was no revenue or other accounting impact.

With this particular CPM order at the end of the second quarter of 2015, the DOJ claimed that the part of the order where exchange discussions had occurred, which related to product CPM had previously purchased, was a "side deal" that created fraud relative to the company's quarterly revenue disclosure. However, they did not take into account or ignored the fact that the company, in almost every quarter, had increased its reserves by <u>reducing</u> revenue in general. So, in the second quarter of 2015, the company increased its reserves by $580,000 over the first quarter. These quarterly reserve increases were always developed through discussions between me and our other executives toward the end of every quarter.

As it turns out, CPM was terminated for the final time at the start of the fourth quarter of 2015. They sent back all product that had not been purchased by their customers. That returned amount was $392,000 of which about $323,000 was from the <u>alternative</u> <u>second</u> <u>quarter</u> purchase. Therefore, of the $1.2 million of alternative product that CPM ordered in the second quarter that they <u>supposedly</u> did not want, they had already sold about 70 percent of that product. With that return of only $392,000 of product, it was certainly covered by the increase of $580,000 of new reserves that were added in the second quarter. Thus, the company was <u>not</u> misrepresenting its revenues from CPM in the second quarter of 2015 to its shareholders.

The other issue with CPM related to the fact that the government accused me of "bribing" Brooks in order to obtain their second quarter order. First, CPM was required by its Distributor Agreement and management to place quarterly orders in a certain range in order to grow MiMedx's presence in the Texas market. If they did not, they ran the risk of having their Distributor Agreement canceled.

Second, as has already been discussed, I was in the process of canceling their contract at the end of June 2015 because of their not controlling their customer's price gouging of the MiMedx products to health plans. However, one of our sales managers, Mike Carlton, came to me on the 26th of June to explain a critical issue where CPM had a business complaint against MiMedx.

That complaint related to the fact that MiMedx had begun to sign contracts with group purchasing organizations (GPOs) and independent delivery networks (IDNs) across the United States. These were organizations that purchased manufacturers' products at minor discounts and resold them to hospitals where they had contracts. Some of those GPO/IDN contractors had sold product to Texas hospitals; therefore, MiMedx had violated the exclusivity clause in the CPM Distributor Agreement. MiMedx owed CPM restitution for those previous sales, and we also needed to set up a process whereby the company kept up with those GPO and IDN sales and reimbursed CPM on a monthly or quarterly basis.

I obtained from our sales administrative department the dollar amount of product that had been sold into Texas by the GPOs and IDNs. I was given a figure of approximately $317,000. On a phone call with Brooks, I took that figure down to $200,000 because CPM had not actually had to buy the products from MiMedx or sell them so that would have been costs they would not have incurred. Subsequently, I informed our General Counsel, Lexi Haden, about the resolution of this business issue and asked her to bring the matter to closure.

However, Lexi did not develop a separate "Settlement Agreement" for the GPO and IDN incursions. She simply instructed accounting to send the $200,000 as a part of Brooks' existing consulting contract. Lexi later admitted to the DOJ (I read her proffer) that she had made this mistake, and she should have written a separate "Settlement Agreement." Therefore, there was <u>no</u> <u>violation</u> of any type relative to accounting or otherwise in the way that the company handled this payment. It was certainly <u>not</u> <u>a</u> <u>bribe</u>. But, the government <u>continued</u> to use that term in court in front of the jury in spite of the fact that the AUSAs knew, because of their conversations with our General Counsel, that this was a legitimate settlement for a business matter. It was most disappointing to see federal prosecutors continue to <u>lie</u> about this matter throughout the trial. They used the "bribe" word throughout the trial because of the negative implications it gave to the jury.

Actually, the bribe term was not applicable to distributor negotiations anyway because it was perfectly legal to give them discounts. The real issue would have been that MiMedx would have had to reduce their revenue for the quarter by that $200,000 figure. However, this had nothing to do with my bribing a distributor. In fact, we had approximately $3.5 million in revenue reserves at that point. So the bribe story was all a prosecutors' lie!

Thus, there should be no accounting or securities fraud allegations related to the sales to CPM in the second quarter of 2015. Witnessing the self-serving actions of the King & Spalding lawyers and the AUSAs at the SDNY on these matters was very disappointing and disgusting. Remember my continuing thought, "This is not America."

SLR Medical

Jerry Morrison was one of MiMedx's most effective and astute sales managers. He joined MiMedx in 2013, and since he lived in the Dallas area, he was given management responsibilities over CPM, the company's second largest distributor that was owned by Mark Brooks. Jerry managed the CPM distributor relationship as well as could be expected under the circumstances. Brooks was an extremely difficult personality to get along with, much less manage.

Before Jerry joined MiMedx, he had set up a medical products distributorship with his fiancée (now wife). They built that operation into approximately a $1 million a year business. When Jerry joined MiMedx full-time, Joyce continued to build and manage the business on her own.

In August 2015, Jerry came to Atlanta to discuss with management that he was tired of the battles he had to fight with Brooks, and he was seriously considering resigning from MiMedx and joining Joyce in their business, which was called SLR. At that point, I knew the relationship with CPM was going to be short-lived. I was certain that CPM's doctors would continue the gouging of the health plans, and that would result in severe repercussions for the company. I also knew that MiMedx was launching a brand new product for which we had great expectations. The product was called OrthoFlo, and it was an injectable product for osteoarthritis. However, it had special logistical issues because it had to be kept frozen until it was ready for injection. This meant that the product would be managed predominantly by the company's distributors who had the capacity in local cities to keep the products frozen. Thus, I proposed to Jerry that he consider carrying the OrthoFlo product line in Texas on an exclusive basis. I told him that I also expected I would ask SLR to step into the CPM distributor role shortly as I expected they would be terminated. Thus, I presented Jerry with a nice business opportunity. I asked him to put together a business plan and come back and present it to Bill and me.

Bill and I seriously reviewed the SLR business plan, and we were quite impressed with the possibilities. We knew Jerry well in terms of his management skills and ability to run this type of business. We came to an agreement to initially give him the exclusive rights to the OrthoFlo product line in the Texas area and provide a 50 percent discount for a substantial purchase of the OrthoFlo product as an initial stocking order.

In order to extend a $4.5 million credit to a relatively new distributor, I knew I would have to make the credit decision myself. I explained that to Mike, our CFO. General agreement was reached that Jerry could accept such an order and would rapidly build the sales of the OrthoFlo product in Texas with high profit margins for SLR because of the discount rate. I had no real concern that Jerry would not be successful and pay off his initial stocking order in a relatively efficient manner.

So, in the third quarter of 2015, MiMedx shipped a substantial order of the OrthoFlo product line to SLR. There were some logistical issues in terms of being certain that SLR had sufficient freezer space to store the product. MiMedx loaning Jerry one freezer to supplement what SLR already had was certainly not anything out of the ordinary.

After a couple of months, Jerry called me for some financial advice. He said that his banker was not going to be as flexible with him as he had previously told me. But, he was going to contract with a factoring company to pay down his accounts receivable and free up his working capital. I advised him not to use a factoring company based on my prior experience. I suggested that he find some individuals who would loan him some additional working capital or a few angel investors to provide SLR with some equity investments. But, Jerry stated that he and Joyce did not want to have shareholders because they thought the business was going to grow and rapidly increase in value.

Then, Jerry asked me if I knew anyone who would consider loaning SLR some working capital. After some brief thought, I told him that I knew two people in Atlanta, but did not know anyone in Dallas. I told him I would give my two contacts his phone number and a recommendation. Other than that, I said that I could not be involved because this needed to be an "arm's length transaction." I gave my son-in-law, who had been a very successful investor in small companies, and my former Executive Vice President of Sales at Matria Healthcare, who also had made some successful investments in small companies, Jerry's contact information. Todd Campbell, my son-in-law, made immediate contact with him and started discussions relative to a working capital loan, although Todd also was apparently interested in some equity in the company, which made business sense.

Unbeknownst to me at the time, Todd ultimately set up a new partnership with his wife (my oldest daughter) and her siblings (my son and youngest daughter). Each of the partners then took a loan against a trust fund I had set up many years earlier for their benefit. Importantly, once these trust funds were set up, I had no further access to or control over the corpus of the trusts. Each of the partners funded this new partnership so that it could make the loan to SLR.

I did not give much thought as to whether I needed to disclose my limited knowledge of the transaction to anyone at MiMedx. I did not in any way benefit from the loan, and in my mind, it did not matter whether Jerry received financing from my son-in-law, a factoring company or anyone else. I had never been told that I was obliged to disclose any knowledge I might possess about a distributor's working capital financing. As far as I was concerned, any information that the company needed to know regarding SLR's financing could be obtained in the ordinary course, through D&B and the kinds of research and due diligence that I believed was routinely undertaken by MiMedx's management and our accounting department.

I remained at <u>arm's length</u> as the parties negotiated. While I was mistakenly copied on a few emails, I took no action whatsoever, and most importantly, I never read any documents or gave any significant advice.

I maintained what I believed to be a satisfactory arm's length from this transaction. I also knew that MiMedx <u>never</u> asked for working capital financing information or proof of financing with any of its other 15 distributors. If we had, we would have probably been told, "It is none of your business." Market intelligence was obtained on distributor sales activities and from D&B information, and our <u>credit decisions</u> were made. I certainly made the credit decision on SLR, which I had the authority to do. However, it certainly would have been prudent for me to disclose my recommendations of these two angel investors to our auditors.

The key point about SLR is that it became an <u>extremely</u> efficient and effective distributor for MiMedx. Within two years, SLR developed over $15 million in revenues for MiMedx and had replaced the CPM distributorship very effectively. I certainly do not believe that I or anyone else ever misled the investing public regarding MiMedx sales to SLR in the fall of 2015.

At the trial, the DOJ devoted considerable time and focus on the loan from my family members to SLR. Without calling a single witness to testify about the loan and without any evidence that there was anything illegal about the partnership, the way it was funded or the loan itself, the prosecutors used loaded words like "sham," "shell company" and "cover up" to describe the arrangement.

I believe the AUSAs knew there was no fraud so they had to rely on a conviction by "name calling."

The one issue that eventually required a return of some product from SLR to MiMedx related to the large-size OrthoFlo product. MiMedx offered the product in one milliliter, two milliliter and four milliliter sizes. The four milliliter size was relatively expensive compared to the other two, and it never sold well. Jerry asked to return those products after about a year of trying to be successful with the sale of that large- size. He sent back for credit approximately $1 million of the large-size OrthoFlo product.

As it turns out, MiMedx increased its "sales returns and allowances" and "bad debt" reserves in the third quarter of 2015 by $1.127 million. Thus, the return from SLR of about $1 million of product was covered by that increase in the reserves in the third quarter when the SLR order was shipped and the revenue booked.

The MiMedx shareholders were not given revenue information that was improperly inflated or incorrectly reserved in the third quarter of 2015 because of the SLR order. A very simple situation when the true facts are used!

Stability Biologics

Stability Biologics was a distributor of medical products primarily for spinal procedures. They had been discussing with the company becoming a distributor for the MiMedx product line for about six months when the final negotiations began in September 2015. Their sales executive had been negotiating with MiMedx sales executives, and Stability Biologics developed a specific interest in the new OrthoFlo product line, which was just being offered in the third quarter of 2015. As mentioned, this product required some extra logistical support because it had to be frozen until delivered to the customer. Therefore, MiMedx was going to use distributors predominately for the distribution of this product.

As usual, when a distributor signed the MiMedx contract, they would schedule a meeting at our headquarters to meet with corporate executives. That meeting took place in mid-September with Brian Martin, Stability Biologics' CEO, and Tom Johnston, their President who managed sales for the company. Martin and Johnston explained that they expected to do $27 million in revenue in 2016, up from around $20 million in 2015. Therefore, they were a substantial-size medical distributor who should have had strong profits and cash, which they alluded to having.

At that meeting, some discussions took place about a new product that they were just beginning to manufacture. They had developed a bone growth product called "Physio," which struck my interest. I asked them to come back and do a presentation to MiMedx doctors and scientists on that product because we might have an interest in distributing Physio. I also thought that MiMedx might have an interest in buying the product line from Stability Biologics, but I did not mention that interest. At that point, I certainly had no interest in buying the company because they had just become a tissue bank processing operation, which was generally a low profit operation and full of logistical headaches.

The Stability Biologics executives came back in October for some serious discussions on their Physio product line. At that meeting, MiMedx scientists and doctors also developed an interest in the product so they began to examine all Stability Biologics' clinical and scientific studies. As it turned out, Stability Biologics was giving MiMedx personnel fraudulent information on Physio.

We visited their tissue processing operation in San Antonio to understand the production techniques for the Physio product. We also reviewed the rather limited product line Stability Biologics was offering from human tissue and cadavers. That product line being so limited gave me some additional comfort in their not being a broad processor of human cadavers.

As the fall played out, MiMedx executives did make the decision to acquire Stability Biologics. During December, we negotiated the terms for a staged buyout or "earn out" of Stability Biologics.

During the fourth quarter, I could not understand why Martin had not signed the Distributor Agreement, which should have been signed in late September. I queried the legal department on the matter and was told that Martin was continuing to negotiate rather ridiculous points. The standard MiMedx Distributor Agreement had never really caused any problems because it was well balanced for both parties. But, Martin seemed to have a particular fetish for these negotiations. As it turns out, Martin apparently had a scheme in mind, which he had perpetrated with a previous Stability Biologics supplier, Osiris Therapeutics. Some years earlier, Martin apparently conspired with the Osiris officers to commit accounting fraud. The Osiris officers were indicted.

While MiMedx's sales to Stability Biologics were very straightforward, Martin had an understanding with Osiris Therapeutics that he could accept their product without any terms and conditions. Thus, Martin had total flexibility to pay Osiris when he so desired. However, the MiMedx invoices that were sent to Stability Biologics after fulfilling their purchase orders had sufficient terms and conditions stated on them. Of course, the distribution agreement had additional terms and conditions, but they were not required to perfect what would be necessary for normal recognition of the revenues when MiMedx products were shipped because of their purchase orders and our invoices.

Because a Distributor Agreement had not been signed at the time of the third quarter 2015 shipments, the DOJ accused me of allowing the company to book this straightforward transaction as revenue in the third quarter when it should not have been. Another case of twisted facts developed by King & Spalding and given to the prosecutors at the DOJ.

Most importantly, the DOJ later called Martin out as being a participant in some accounting fraud they had found at Osiris Therapeutics <u>after</u> we had acquired Stability Biologics. The AUSAs told Martin that he was going to be indicted for being a <u>participant</u> with Osiris in allowing them to ship product to Stability Biologics with no commitments for payment and no supporting paperwork. They told Martin that Osiris was booking revenue fraudulently because they did not require the normal paperwork for their transactions with Stability Biologics, which violated the revenue recognition rules.

Therefore, the DOJ turned Martin into a very manipulated witness in the MiMedx case. As such, Martin made numerous statements at the trial as a prosecution witness that were not factual; <u>they were lies</u>. For instance, he said that, at his second meeting at MiMedx, I told him that MiMedx would be interested in acquiring his company, and he needed to be a "good partner." When asked what that meant to him, he said he thought I was telling him to give MiMedx a big order in their initial stocking situation. He also insinuated that I told him that Stability Biologics did not have to pay for the product until they sold it. All those comments were <u>absolute</u> <u>lies</u>. That was only the second time I had met Martin, and common sense would dictate that I was astute enough not to be making comments of that nature to basically a stranger. At that point, we certainly had not decided that MiMedx should acquire Stability Biologics or Physio as we had not conducted <u>any</u> due diligence!

On cross-examination, Martin had to admit that I called him before the end of the fourth quarter asking him for a million dollar payment on his account. When asked why he thought I would do that if I had given him permission at the beginning of the relationship to not pay, he said he did not know! Also, under cross-examination, Martin had to admit that he was a consummate <u>liar</u> and <u>fraudster</u>. Thus, I think the jury gave little credibility to his testimony. If they really understood the indictment, they would have probably ignored the Stability Biologics situation totally. However, it was pointed out that MiMedx did acquire Stability Biologics in January, which meant the balance sheets were merged and the remaining payable from Stability Biologics to MiMedx was absorbed. There is nothing illegal or immoral about a company acquiring one of its distributors. Unfortunately, Martin was a shrewd and corrupt individual who lied frequently and temporarily convinced me and a number of our staff of his misrepresentations.

Because of the scam the Stability Biologics principals perpetrated against MiMedx by providing fraudulent data and information on their Physio product line, I recommended that MiMedx force them to repurchase their company in 2017. By that time, we had obtained enough clinical information on our own to realize that we were initially given fraudulent data on Physio.

Martin's manipulations caused another question to develop. The legal department had the responsibility to finish negotiations with Martin and get the Distributor Agreement signed, and as I checked with the legal staff, I was told that Martin was being very unreasonable on the terms of the Agreement. As it turned out, Martin was trying not to sign the MiMedx Distributor Agreement so that, if MiMedx did not acquire Stability Biologics, he could <u>claim</u> that they had the right to not pay for the products until they sold them, as he did with Osiris.

At the very end of December, MiMedx had made substantial progress in negotiating the terms for the acquisition of Stability Biologics. The final terms had been agreed to, and the documents were being prepared. Martin called and asked me to give him a letter stating that, if the acquisition did not close, Stability Biologics could return <u>some</u> of the product they purchased because they <u>might</u> want to develop their own amniotic membrane product and compete with MiMedx. This was a very frustrating and out of the ordinary request this late in the process.

However, I did dictate a letter that had "if" clauses…<u>IF</u> the acquisition did not take place, and <u>IF</u> Stability Biologics could produce a competitive product to EpiFix and AmnioFix, I would allow them to return their equivalent inventory on those particular products. I knew that Stability Biologics could not produce competitive products because of MiMedx's patents and Stability Biologics' lack of development staff and manufacturing expertise. Thus, I believed that <u>no meaningful</u> commitments were made, and we had substantial "sales returns and allowances" reserves to cover their purchases. Regardless, the acquisition was closed on January 13, 2016.

Thus, MiMedx should have had <u>no issues</u> booking the Stability Biologics distributor purchase in the third quarter of 2015 as valid revenue.

First Medical

I was not involved in the negotiations with First Medical at all. In fact, I did not know about some of the discussions and outcomes until the allegations by the DOJ were made.

First Medical had been a distributor for MiMedx for a number of years. They were located in Saudi Arabia. MiMedx had spent a lot of time and money sending doctors and sales educators to the country in order to create demand for our product line. The Saudis particularly had major problems with diabetes and the resulting diabetic foot ulcers and venous leg ulcers.

First Medical managed to have the Saudi government purchase the MiMedx product line. They gave MiMedx their first order of a couple of million dollars in early 2015. They were asked to provide a letter of credit from a bank so that MiMedx was assured of payment. That went very smoothly. On their second order, MiMedx provided an open credit line.

The third order that was questioned by the DOJ arrived in December of 2015. It was for about $2.2 million. The Saudi government was getting ready to issue a new tender for this amount of product. First Medical wanted MiMedx to begin manufacturing the product so it would be available by March. As it turned out, MiMedx had almost sufficient product in December to ship the sizes that they needed for the tender. Therefore, the sales staff began to negotiate to obtain the purchase order for a December shipment. I was totally uninvolved since I seldom participated in the routine negotiations of sales orders.

The MiMedx sales organization reported to Bill, and he became involved with them as they desired to ship the First Medical order in December. Bill had to get involved in the process because communicating with First Medical and their personnel was often confusing and difficult. Often the Saudis did not understand what MiMedx was requesting them to do.

Finally, Bill worked out an agreement whereby First Medical would pay for this shipment within four months after the tender offer issued, which was expected by March 1st. As it turned out, the tender did issue on March 1st. In the process, Bill had to give First Medical specific payment terms in order to meet GAAP revenue recognition criteria. However, Bill also reminded them of the MiMedx "Business Philosophy" which was simply that the company would not routinely sue their distributors or other customers until the company had given them all the flexibility that was possible. MiMedx called that our "Business Philosophy."

Bill sent two emails. One was confirming the payment terms that MiMedx would accept on their purchase order. The second email was a discussion of the MiMedx business philosophy to explain to them that, if they wanted a shipment in December, the company would consider flexibility if for some reason the tender offer did not issue. While that was taking some degree of risk, Bill's assessment of the situation was that there was <u>very</u> <u>little</u> <u>risk</u>. He turned out to <u>be</u> <u>correct</u>. However, the prosecutors took his second email as a "side deal" which meant that First Medical did not have to pay for the product and could return it all. As I later read the document, I agreed that the second email was a corporate philosophy statement and not a corporate process and procedure statement. However, that did not keep the prosecutors from alleging that MiMedx shipped $2.2 million of product to a distributor and booked the revenue that did not meet revenue recognition rules. As it turned out, MiMedx collected every dollar of the billing except for a small discount. However, it did come in late because the Saudi government began paying First Medical and <u>all</u> of its contractors late due to their war with Yemen and the major drop in oil prices.

Again, I believe that the prosecutors were overreaching in their allegation that the First Medical sale should not have been booked in the fourth quarter of 2015 due to Bill's second email describing MiMedx's business philosophy. Most importantly, I believe MiMedx met <u>all</u> the revenue recognition requirements for this shipment because of our "sales returns and allowances" reserves which were totally ignored by King & Spalding and the DOJ prosecutors!

We missed our first quarter of 2016 revenue forecast by a few percent. I was later told that certain sales people (guess who) were frustrated by management's focus on having them give attention to all the medical departments at the VA hospitals so they held back on their late quarter orders to "teach management a lesson." That caused our stock price to decline about seven percent for a couple of weeks, and then it retraced itself. Over the next 20 months, the stock climbed to over $18 per share as the company continued its 30-plus percent revenue growth.

Final Point

At this point, you have absorbed a tremendous amount of information on what transpired at MiMedx Group that resulted in termination of at least 20 top executives and managers and caused the five-year decline of the company. You have heard me use the word "Witch Hunt" and other descriptors to describe how this takeover by an unqualified Board was orchestrated. You have seen me describe the motivating factors for several different individuals, including short sellers, former employees, an Audit Committee Chairman in a paranoid state of mind, a politically motivated law firm and corrupt prosecutors.

I realize that this has been a tremendous amount of information to absorb and assimilate. I also realize that it does not seem like something that would take place in the America that most of us grew up in. But, it is all factual, and in the current environment, you see displays of this occurring in all aspects of our politics, business and personal lives.

I want to give you one comment from a very knowledgeable individual that should summarize all of these bizarre and corrupt actions. I think this comment will solidify the way I have characterized what played out as a "Witch Hunt".

I want to introduce a gentleman by the name of John Staton. John was a Georgia Tech graduate who went on to obtain his law degree at Emory University Law School in Atlanta. Upon graduation, he became employed with the King & Spalding law firm in Atlanta and retired as a partner.

I met John when I joined the Georgia Tech Foundation Board. John remained on that Board for decades, and at one point, he was Chairman of that Board. He and I became friends. I visited his home in Aspen, Colorado when a small group of Georgia Tech Foundation members had a long ski weekend together.

John and I had used the same doctor in Atlanta for decades. This doctor, Dr. William Whaley, is an internist, oncologist and hematologist. Bill Whaley is one of Atlanta's most respected physicians. His credentials are wide and broad. Thus, John and I both enjoyed Bill as our physician and friend.

John passed away on June 26, 2022. This was a surprise to all of us. When I next visited with Bill Whaley, I mentioned John's death. He began to talk about John. In the process, he told me John had said to him, as related to my MiMedx situation, that I was treated very unfairly in the legal process. Acually John used the "F" word.

Since John knew his former law firm well and their politics and business practices, I believe his comment was quite clear on what had transpired. Also, this probably ties into what another very respected attorney from that firm said to me many decades before. That was when Rusty French, a Healthdyne Board member, thanked me for giving him the ability to earn sufficient capital to resign from King & Spalding.

CHAPTER 23

PRE-TRIAL ACTIVITIES

During the late summer of 2019, Bill Taylor and I received communications from our attorneys that they had been contacted by the Southern District of New York (SDNY) prosecutors stating they intended to file criminal indictments against the two of us. At that point, our attorneys, Bill Weinreb, Bill Burck and Mike Packard with the Quinn Emanuel law firm had been representing us since the initiation of the King & Spalding investigation at MiMedx. They were deeply into the details of the situation, and they were rather incredulous that the Department of Justice (DOJ) thought scienter, or intent, could be proven relative to the numerous allegations that King & Spalding had made about accounting issues on certain distributor contracts from 2015. They did not feel that there was any evidence indicating that Bill and I purposely developed schemes to create false revenue in the MiMedx accounting system and not properly inform our accountants, our Audit Committee and auditors.

Bill and I would be required to have separate attorneys, even though we would be tried together as one case. So I sought out additional attorneys to represent me, and I let Bill retain the representation of the Quinn Emanuel group. My new attorneys were Eric Bruce and Jennier Loeb of the Freshfields law firm and later Matthew Menchel of Kobre & Kim who was recommended by Eric Bruce.

The consensus of the Quinn Emanuel group was that the DOJ was way out of bounds in terms of indicting us because of the requirement for them to prove scienter, or intent, in order to have a criminal act.

Of course, the first recommendation from our lawyers was that we seek relief by seeking appeals to the U.S. attorney at the SDNY offices. If we were not successful, we would go straight to the Department of Justice in Washington, D.C. So, in the fall of 2019, our law firm, Quinn Emanuel, visited with the U.S. attorney and his staff at SDNY. Our appeal was rejected, very much to the surprise of our legal team. Consequently, they made an appeal to Deputy Attorney General Jeffrey Rosen and his staff at DOJ in Washington, D.C. Unfortunately, we received the same rejection from Rosen.

I told my attorneys that I felt the influence of King & Spalding would be wide and deep with political undertones at these agencies. I believe it is safe to say that was the case. There have been more recent changes as King & Spalding attorneys have become a larger part of the Washington D.C. infrastructure and vice versa, which we discussed previously about Wray and Murphy going to the FBI. Also, I think the fact that King & Spalding had supposedly accomplished a very lengthy and expensive investigation to prepare these allegations gave DOJ officials a great deal of confidence in what they would pursue. Remember, the cost of the investigation alone was approximately $40 million!

The indictments were issued in late November. As I read the charges, I certainly became very frustrated. I had begun to realize just how corrupt the judicial process could be. I was quite surprised at how the lawyers at King & Spalding and SDNY and the forensic accountants at KPMG had framed the indictment. I know that their being rather uninformed and never involved in a business enterprise can result in some confusing allegations, but some of the things that were twisted into lies were very obvious. To me, there was a serious integrity problem here.

In reading Sydney Powell's and Harvey Silverglate's books, I began to put in perspective what could take place in situations like this. Of the 4,200 publicly traded companies in the U.S., there are probably not many, even those in the Fortune 100, that have Boards that could stand up to a Sally Yates Doctrine investigation. Our federal government should clearly understand that what they have allowed to develop is a very unbalanced system, which is going to continue to discourage companies from going public. At one time, there were approximately 12,000 public companies in America! Now there are only about 4,200. These are some of the reasons why!

Of course, in the MiMedx case, we had some particularly inexperienced and paranoid individuals on the Board initially and then some additional inexperienced individuals joined the Board. That made matters worse, particularly when they were being manipulated by the Chairman of the Audit Committee and the temporary CFO, Borkowski.

So, after the rejection of our appeal by the DOJ office in Washington, D.C., the realities began to settle in. We rolled up our sleeves and set to work. I observed the management process of this complex case as it began to unfold. As I patiently watched, which is unlike me, I developed some frustrations over what I would call inept business/legal process management. Eventually, the legal team took some of my suggestions and modified the administrative approach in order to establish weekly meetings and reviews, enhance communications between all parties and set goals and objectives related to timing.

Early in this process, our case was assigned to Judge Jed Rakoff at the Southern District of New York. I immediately went onto the internet to see what I could find out about this judge. Our lawyers were advising us that he was tough on lawyers. Rakoff put up with no legal shenanigans in his courtroom. They also said he was reasonable in terms of sentencing. However, we were to find out that he was <u>very</u> biased for the prosecution, or the "hometown boys."

I found a video of Judge Rakoff participating in a panel discussion. He used the words something like the U.S. "legal cabal." As I listened further, he was bringing up some of the issues that I had heard about 12 years ago from a federal judge in Roanoke, Virginia when Matria was working on settling a case. I mentioned that situation in Chapter 14. Rakoff's issues were simply that the U.S. legal system has reached the point where law firms are so entrenched and the laws so dramatically modified that many of the legal decisions simply relate to compensation for the law firms and their lawyers. As the judge in Roanoke mentioned, he was being paid about $225,000 a year, but the lawyer representing our former employee, who herself had actually caused the crime, was probably making four times that annually. So you can see the frustration that federal judges have with legal fees that are generally paid by individuals and businesses and how it is way out of balance with what they are paid as senior federal legal officials.

My first reaction when I saw the video was that I believed Judge Rakoff on this subject and that I would certainly think similarly on many issues. I witnessed him telling our lawyers in our first pre-trial meeting that he would listen to their motions, objections, etc., but he would not have a lot of patience with them because of the U.S. "legal cabal." He pointed out that we would be in his courtroom, and it would be his wants, desires and rules that would prevail. Narcissism? Just wait!

The judge set our first trial date for July 7th. Unfortunately, supposedly due to the coronavirus and the associated chaos in New York City, the trial was moved to October 5th. It was subsequently moved to November 9th and finally to October 26th. I will discuss the probable cause of these numerous date changes as related to trial manipulations later.

By this time, I had begun to put a number of things into perspective. I reviewed the March 2020 10-K that the company had published when they finally issued the 2017 and 2018 financial statements. I decided that their latest auditor, BDO, had gone through many headaches attempting to get the new audits completed. While they were asked to restate six years of revenues for approximately 3,000 customers to a cash basis, I believe they probably had things to say to Borkowski, Dewberry and the Board like "We see no accounting need to do this restatement." As I previously mentioned, there was a statement made by the company in their 10-K document that put everything into <u>stark</u> <u>perspective</u>. Their quote was, "DESPITE THESE (CREDIT LIMIT) OVERRIDES, THE COMPANY

RECOVERED THE MAJORITY OF ITS BILLINGS MADE BETWEEN 2012 AND 2017 WITH INSIGNIFICANT WRITE-OFFS RECORDED." They went on to state that the company (Dewberry, the Board and Borkowski) had developed some doubt as to the collectability of those billings at the time of shipment, but there was not enough <u>persuasive</u> <u>evidence</u> to reach such a conclusion. They had <u>no</u> <u>involvement</u> in those decisions! The final conclusion was that the cash resulting from the 2012 to 2017 revenues was basically collected with non-material differences. This confirms that the King & Spalding former prosecutor, Paul Murphy, had constructed a <u>false</u> <u>narrative</u> over the 15-month investigation that cost the company $80 million in accounting fees and over $100 million in legal fees. Many of these fees were a result of covering up the many false accusations made by Murphy through King & Spalding.

This is a clear indication that what took place at MiMedx as a result of the pressures from the illegal short sellers ended up being a "Witch Hunt" and a corporate "takeover" by a self-serving Audit Committee Chairman, certain Board members and a new executive, namely the temporary CFO. This group had to find some type of evidence that would substantiate their illicit and selfish actions. Of course, the King & Spalding team was very capable of reading enough emails and creating enough imaginary scenarios to convince the Board as well as the DOJ that these criminal indictments should be filed.

In other chapters of the book, we have had several discussions about the motivations of government lawyers and why they would lose their integrity over prosecuting white-collar crime cases. The DOJ assistant U.S. attorneys (AUSAs) at the SDNY were more than happy to take all the King & Spalding information and turn it into indictments. And, that is exactly what happened except for the AvKARE accusations, which were ignored. Thus, there was little effort required on the DOJ side, except for their witness preparation, or tampering! More later!

Jury Consulting

After a great deal of review, we selected DOAR to be our jury consulting firm. During the late summer and early fall, we planned three mock jury trials. The first "trial" was simply having DOAR personnel explain to the "jurors" the prosecution and defense themes as we knew them at that point. From those discussions, we solicited input from the various "jurors" in terms of the effectiveness of our arguments and what information was confusing to them and what was enlightening.

We had planned two other sessions to present videos of Bill and myself being questioned and cross-examined. However, the judge moved our court date, which was then November 9th, back to October 26th. That pushed us to expedite the process. Therefore, we combined the last two sessions into one three-day session, and things worked out fairly well.

We selected Ankura to be our accounting consulting firm. The government decided <u>not to bring</u> in an accounting consultant as a witness because there would have been a debate between the accounting "experts." That is because the prosecutors built their case not on facts, but on "ugly words," such as greedy, bribers, liars, etc.

Our legal teams became very excited when they received the Brady and Jencks information from the DOJ. These are documents that are required to be given to the defendants, which delineate witness proffers (discussions) the DOJ has gathered in their process of developing the indictments and interviewing potential witnesses.

I had encouraged our legal teams to read Howard Root's book, *Cardiac Arrest*, in which Howard explains how the Department of Justice AUSAs had intimidated and actually threatened employees of his company, Vascular Solutions. That happened to numerous employees in Howard's case. I told our lawyers I would bet that this was happening in our case too. However, I was told that until the Brady and Jencks information was received our attorneys would be "skeptical," as usual. Once the legal group reviewed the interviews of some of our distributors and employees, they realized that there was a great deal of corruption in our case by these AUSAs. It was blatant and in print.

In one case, the DOJ had the principal from CPM, one of our distributors whom we had to terminate for cause, come in and testify to them. In the first lengthy session, Mark Brooks' answers to their questions were exactly what we would have said, and they were truthful. He had four more lengthy sessions with them for a total of 23 hours of interrogation. In the end, they gave Brooks a non-prosecution agreement, but his testimony had totally changed to the story that the AUSAs had wanted to portray relative to my supposedly "bribing" him to get his required second quarter order in 2015. There were several more of those similar situations with other people.

This type of behavior is extremely disappointing. You do not want to believe that employees of our DOJ who are paid by taxpayers' money, would act in this fashion. However, there are too many personal motivations, and there are numerous AUSAs that have ethics issues. Thus, there needs to be some type of

DOJ oversight and review that would quickly make examples of this misbehavior and bring this AUSA misconduct to a halt. Most judges just ignore this corrupt behavior as a benefit for the home team! Also, our government seldom holds its employees accountable.

New York Rules

As trial preparations began at a feverish pitch in early October, we found out that the New York federal court had ruled that anyone coming to New York from any of the 35 states who were considered high COVID-19 risks must be quarantined for two weeks in New York before they would be allowed into the courthouse. Well, this required our attorneys as well as Bill and myself to do exactly that. We all arrived prior to October 11th and began our two-week quarantine. Of course, we were rapidly working on trial preparation throughout that two-week period.

Fortunately, my wife, Janet, and I managed to obtain a small one-bedroom efficiency apartment about two blocks from the courthouse. We set up housekeeping like a young couple! Most of the restaurants nearby were closed because of COVID so Janet became very proficient again at light cooking, or we would often order food for delivery. Also, they would not allow us to use the apartment gym until we had been in New York for two weeks. Thus, we got very little exercise, and that was one of the most frustrating parts of this stay.

Developing Our Trial Strategy

When King & Spalding began their investigation in February 2018, they utilized the Sally Yates Doctrine as their mode of investigation. Yates had just returned to King & Spalding after being terminated by President Trump for disregarding his instructions relative to border security. Thus, there would have been some additional motivation at the firm to use her Doctrine with this investigation opportunity. As has been discussed in a number of the books that I have recommended, an investigation that is improperly conducted will not necessarily focus on determining justice, but according to the Sally Yates Doctrine, will "target" the top executives since that is supposedly where the largest payoffs for the government will result. However, as we explained in Chapter 14, with a Yates investigation, the government can lose hundreds of millions of dollars in tax revenue while the law firms make hundreds of millions in legal fees.

That is what occurred in our case. The twisting of the facts was started as the investigators built their case. One of the key issues in our case, where it was finally alleged that we made "side deals" with four distributors that modified the quarters in which their revenue should have been booked, was the fact that the company's "accounting reserves" were totally ignored. In all the information we obtained from the company relative to the investigation and DOJ indictments, there was never any discussion about the company's accounting reserves. Their basic allegation was that we allowed the company to book approximately $9 million of real revenue from four distributors in the latter part of 2015 in the wrong quarter.

The company's SEC 10-K filings in 2020 stated this revenue was real and it was basically collected in cash. Also, as King & Spalding got into the specifics of why they thought this revenue was booked improperly, they never took into account the "reserves" that the company added each quarter and added when these supposed fraudulent transactions took place. The facts are, in two of these instances, we took extra reserves in the quarter to offset any risk associated with these distributor purchase orders not fully meeting revenue recognition standards. However, I will always deny there was any fraudulent revenue published in those three quarters of 2015 or for any quarter in which I was the CEO if for no other reason than the "sales returns and allowances" reserves properly covered any mistakes.

Of the strategic issues for our trial defense, I think that scienter, or intent, was most important. In order for a transaction to be fraudulent and fall into the criminal category, there must be intent. If there is not, then the action could potentially be a civil violation, but it does not fall into the category of a criminal violation, which is the responsibility of the DOJ. Civil violations are overseen by the SEC. In those situations, there will be fines and other restrictions on the defendant, but generally no jail term.

Thus, scienter should have continually been raised in the trial and explained to the jury at every possible opportunity. I do not believe our lawyers achieved that goal. I believe most of the jurors probably finished the trial not even understanding the word "scienter." They all should have understood that there might have been some minor mistakes made in the accounting of some of the transactions, but it was because of the manner in which the company had been booking its distributor exchanges for years. Recall that Scott Taub pointed that out to all of us in early 2017. Also, the auditors, accountants and Audit Committee were all knowledgeable of that fact so how could there have been any intent on Bill's and my part. That "no scienter" fact could very well have won the trial for us and a not guilty verdict.

The second most important issue was convincing the jurors that the three AUSAs had a different agenda other than that of serving justice. While there are numerous reasons that AUSAs push outside their integrity limits in settlement discussions and trials, I believe the number one reason relates to their future careers. One of the older AUSAs at SDNY, who was in charge of the Osiris Therapeutics trial, immediately left SDNY after he had success with that case. His resume now had a white-collar crime case that was successfully won, and he was hired by one of the large New York law firms. At that point, his salary probably tripled, and he would be in line for the benefits of a large law firm partnership in the future. Also, almost immediately after our trial, one of the AUSAs left the DOJ for a large law firm. So why would not a young AUSA push the trial rules and their integrity in order to change their employment for the benefits of a large law firm career. Unfortunately, the motivations are there. And, as I have said, with most federal agencies, there is little accountability.

We were ready to show that the transactions were not fraudulent and that they resulted in no real shifting of revenue during this period of time. We were also ready to discuss who was hurt, really hurt in all these supposed fraudulent transactions.

Finally, we were going to discuss and educate the jury on both "returns and allowances" reserves and "bad debt" reserves. That would have helped jurors put in perspective that the fraudulent transactions that the government was alleging were not actually fraudulent. We would have shown how these possible mistakes were actually offset by the actions taken by the executives and the accounting department by routinely increasing the revenue reserves on our quarterly financial statements. However, we never had the opportunity to present any information of that nature. Why? I will fully explain shortly!

Actual Trial Preparations

As we began to coordinate and have discussions between my and Bill's law firms, I was beginning to have concerns about the administrative process I was seeing. There was a great deal of focus on obtaining large amounts of documents and getting them organized and categorized. However, the disciplines that I had always used in managing complex business processes and programs were absent. Setting strategic and tactical goals and objectives for the trial and then developing responsibilities and schedules were not being utilized. My greatest concern was setting the strategic goals and objectives because the majority of the focus seemed to be on the tactical minutia.

Now I know using the word "minutia" is not complimentary, but it goes along with lawyers' basic personality trait of being very risk averse. Thus, they focus on the exquisite detail of each document, but they often miss the big picture embedded in the strategic objectives.

I finally determined that this focus was supposedly because they never wanted the prosecutors to call Bill or me a liar upon cross-examination. Well, the prosecutors called us liars from the moment AUSA Tracer began speaking in his opening remarks. Not any evidence or confirmation was needed. Liars was part of their mantra, which included using numerous suggestive words and phrases, such as being liars, greedy, bribers, cheaters, using shell corporations, creating sham transactions, lining our pockets and a few other choice names. Those words were used routinely because they would have a strong influence on the jury.

Throughout the trial, I attempted to focus our two groups of attorneys on our strategic goals, which included establishing that there was no scienter in any of our activities with the four distributors. And, there was a strategic need to call out the three AUSAs in this trial as being not only corrupt, but also naive with regard to never having had any business experience. We needed to stress that the $9 million dollars of alleged fraudulent revenue from the four distributors was not fraud. We also needed to introduce to the jury the concept of "revenue reserves" that came under the accounting heading of "sales returns and allowances" reserves. The company was conservatively reserved in this area so it could take a reasonable loss of revenue in a quarter before there was any overstatement in the revenues that were reported to shareholders.

The Dewberry Debacle

In earlier chapters I have mentioned a few of the issues that came about because of Terry Dewberry's paranoia and his intense focus on his CYA actions. I also mentioned the fact that in February 2017, Mike Senken, our CFO, Bill and I had a conversation with a nationally recognized consultant on revenue recognition by the name of Scott Taub. We were calling Taub to obtain advice on the approach that the company was taking relative to the wind-down of the AvKARE contract. Our Cherry Bekaert auditors had some concerns that we might need to defer any AvKARE revenue that took place in 2017 because we had clauses in Amendment Number 4 to their contract which determined how MiMedx would pay them for any remaining inventory after the contract expired in mid-2017. Cherry Bekaert thought that might require us to put all the revenue from the signing of that amendment on a cash basis rather than an accrual basis. Management felt differently so we agreed to obtain an opinion from Taub.

After we gave the information to Taub, he agreed with management's assessment of the situation. However, in some general conversation, he brought up an issue that had caused some problems for one of his other clients. As I mentioned in Chapter 21, this related to how "exchanges" were booked for a distributor, who would be a middleman. Exchanges were revenue neutral for final customers, but Taub explained that for a distributor, the exchange needed to be booked as a "return." This meant that the "sales returns and allowances" reserves would have to be increased for that exchange from a distributor. This is a mistake that the company had made since 2011 when Mike Senken told management and the Audit Committee that, in his opinion, exchanges were treated the same for a final customer as well as a middleman or distributors. Our auditors, our Audit Committee and our accounting staff all agreed. Dewberry should have done additional research!

This is another example where I think Dewberry, as the Chairman of the Audit Committee, felt a great deal of paranoia. This GAAP treatment of distributor exchanges was not very logical, thus our accountants, audit committee and auditors made a mistake in 2011. However, my decisions covered our reported revenues for issues of this nature by our building up "sales returns and allowances" reserves so no restatement of revenue was required. However, in his paranoid frame of mind, Dewberry saw a situation for which he thought he might be held accountable. So he added this to his list of transgressions for which he must accuse management so that he and his Audit Committee would not be questioned. Also, he probably carried some guilt because I tried to encourage him and the Audit Committee to get on the phone with Taub when we were having our discussions in the early part of 2017. Dewberry commented to me that he did not think that was necessary! Taub was an extremely astute financial and accounting executive, and he could have helped our Audit Committee with numerous things, but Dewberry did not think that was necessary.

In the early stages of the investigation, Dewberry supported the King & Spalding conclusion that Bill, Mike, John and me did not report the AvKARE revenues properly. King & Spalding alleged that we gave AvKARE permission to pay us only when they were paid. That was absolutely not factual. We managed AvKARE as we did all our other accounts receivable by keeping their days sales outstanding (DSOs) in a certain range that was acceptable to us. On several occasions I called and had AvKARE send in substantial amounts of money because they had let their DSOs get too high. Our accounting staff did this also. Most importantly, there was no written or verbal confirmation anywhere that we would allow them to pay only when they were paid. However, Dewberry used that allegation to have the Board terminate all four of us, and he also went to the ridiculous extreme of having the company restate six years worth of revenues because of that allegation. That was another costly mistake designed to point fingers at management. So Dewberry wasted $80 million on an unnecessary financial restatement to give him unnecessary CYA protection!

As I read the company's public information that they filed with the SEC and their press releases, it is quite evident now that Dewberry was so paranoid and trying so frantically to protect himself that he pushed the Board into doing things that were totally out of line with reality and their fiduciary responsibility to the shareholders. In effect, this investigation allowed Dewberry to control the Board and company and force decisions that any experienced Board would not have made. However, he was here in Atlanta and those Board members who were not in Atlanta seemed to defer to him. I heard numerous criticisms from those Board members about Dewberry's behavior, but when I would challenge them to do something about it as a Board, they just made excuses! No courage of their convictions!

Prosecutors and the New Justice System

I discussed in Chapter 21 my experiences with prosecutors who are focused on business/corporate governance, accounting and other related white-collar crime cases. I have mentioned eight books that discuss the unscrupulous means through which some prosecutors build their cases and careers. Yes, careers that depend on their efficiencies in winning cases and developing incarceration years for the convicted. For federal prosecutors, this generally means obtaining the career changing offer from a large law firm and having their annual compensation quickly double, triple and quadruple as they become a law firm partner. Unfortunately, their integrity may become compromised or lost on building their resume. As they transition from a public prosecutor to a defense counsel at a firm, those traits may become muted, but still exist due to their narcissistic personalities.

I believe the corruption that has developed in this particular part of our justice system is driven by two major factors: first, the public focus and concern on the growth in crime rates with the resulting "tough on crime" political actions, and second, the very rapid growth in law school graduates over the last several decades.

Today the population of the U.S. is five percent of the world's population, but we have 25 percent of the incarcerated prisoners in the world. Obviously, we have the highest incarceration rate, which is two to four times the rate of the liberal democracies in Europe. In 1970, our incarceration rate was only 20 percent of what it is now.

In this same period, the rate of law school graduates has escalated very rapidly. In 1970, there were 325,000 practicing attorneys in our country. In 2020, there were 1.35 million practicing attorneys in the U.S. We have been graduating approximately 40,000 attorneys per year for the last couple of decades. As a comparison, Japan has 35,000 practicing attorneys, and its population is about one third of ours. Quite a difference!

My business experience and common sense (whatever is left at age 84) indicate to me that any program, business or government, that grows as fast as our incarceration rates and law school graduations will get "out of control" because of the many aspects that can be improperly influenced or manipulated. In this growth scenario, there are many oversight elements lacking, and over time, the development of such abhorrent processes are difficult to correct. Also, they are easily manipulated by those in control, in this case, the prosecutors. As all these factors began to develop, the prosecutors clearly saw how to grow this system for their own benefit.

Prior to my personal experiences and reading books on prosecutorial misconduct, I would have argued that lawyers employed by the government should have no reason to have their integrity questioned. I have to admit now how naive I was on that subject and how our justice system has changed while I was very busy as an entrepreneur.

My experiences with the justice system will be described in some detail in the following chapters. However, I believe it would be informative to give you some thoughts from several of the authors of the books I mentioned in the Preface. While their experiences with the U.S. judicial system vary somewhat, they have all reached the same conclusions about the corruption in the prosecutorial processes in America with regard to business and individuals.

In his book, *A Matter Of Principle*, Lord Conrad Black highlights how his prosecution in federal court was caused by some large individual shareholders of Hollinger International pressing he and the Board to sell off certain company assets. Although Black had controlling interest in the company, he was still taken to task because he set up a "special committee" to examine the allegations of these shareholders, and the special committee soon hired a large law firm to do an investigation. The rest is history. I believe his major mistake was taking his company, Hollinger International, public in America! His description of his long onerous process clearly highlights again the corrupt nature of the U.S. prosecutorial system and how it particularly treats entrepreneurial executives. Eventually, this long and corrupt process bankrupted his company, Hollinger International. The primary prosecutors all went on to positions with large law firms.

In Howard Root's book, *Cardiac Arrest*, he describes the particularly egregious prosecutorial behavior of threatening his company's employees. Fortunately, Howard and his company beat the DOJ in their trial in San Antonio, Texas! I believe that was primarily because their attorneys attacked and called out the corrupt actions of the prosecutors in a manner that was clearly understood by the jurors and not fought or manipulated by the judge.

In his book, *Uneven Justice*, Raj Rajaratnam delineated his lengthy battle with the DOJ over their accusations that at his very successful hedge fund, Galleon Group, he engaged in insider trading. Raj was one of the most successful hedge fund managers on Wall Street, and he had an impeccable reputation of honesty, integrity and philanthropy. Frankly, that is what made him the target of the DOJ because those qualities had resulted in him becoming a billionaire only about eight years after the formation of his very successful hedge fund.

In Raj's case, the lead U.S. attorney for the SDNY used his trial to make a name for himself in numerous ways. The DOJ was looking for ways to place blame for the 2008 financial downturn, and they just happened to pick Raj. After Raj's conviction, the prosecutors all went on to much higher paid positions, as is typical.

Witness Tampering

A brief discussion on this subject is in order because it clearly demonstrates another way in which our American judicial system has become more corrupt. Many of the laws related to this subject came about because of the way the Mafia threatened and manipulated witnesses and juries in the 1930s. There were certainly many instances where government prosecutors lost good cases because of this type of behavior. In some cases, witnesses just lied or disappeared, and some who did not cooperate with the Mafia were murdered.

Once I realized that the King & Spalding investigation, which the Audit Committee authorized, was not going to investigate the allegations made by the illegal short sellers as requested by Ernst & Young, I became very frustrated. I realized they were on their own "Witch Hunt" following the Sally Yates Doctrine. I began to read all I could find on similar cases. I read all the books that I mentioned in the Preface.

Initially, Howard Root's book, *Cardiac Arrest*, provided an excellent overview of how DOJ prosecutors utilize actual "witness tampering" to an extreme to build their cases. Conrad Black's book, *A Matter of Principle*, added numerous examples of different types of tampering, and Sidney Powell's books clearly demonstrate the corrupt nature of how today's DOJ prosecutors behave with respect to threatening and manipulating witnesses.

In our trial, the prosecutors accused me of witness tampering with Mike Carlton. They wisely did not charge me with such an offense, but brought it up to the jury to add to their long list of my supposed faults, such as being "greedy" and a "briber." Of course, they had to carry out a personality assassination because the blue-collar jury would not understand the supposed accounting fraud that was charged. Therefore, Bill and I were accused of anything that could make us look like greedy, selfish, self-serving men who would do anything for money.

Why was I accused of witness tampering with Carlton? It started with Carlton calling me to fret and seek advice about the small amount of his termination package. As I recall, he called me at least twice about that matter. My advice was to write a letter to Charlie Evans, copy the Board, and make your points. He seemed to want me to write the letter, which was not appropriate for his one case. As the purge of management continued to be pressed by the Board's new management for their self-serving desires, I did communicate with the Board because it was so evident what was occurring and how destructive it would be. I was ignored, and finally 20 of the top 21 managers and executives were dismissed or left the company. These were all very experienced and successful managers. But, they were viewed by the potential future CEO as "Pete and Bill's people" so they must be terminated. The company has never recovered from the loss of these personnel who built the company into its industry leading position. The Board should have known better, but they were still acting in their own self-interest and were still taking business advice from all their legal firms!

Either way, I had read Howard Root's book during the time that Carlton continued to ask for assistance. I felt that he needed to read Howard's book to understand what MiMedx would potentially be put through. So I told him to meet me at our joint property fence so I could give him the book and answer any more questions. This meeting lasted about five minutes.

Under Carlton's cross-examination at the trial, he admitted that I did not ask him to do anything inappropriate or illegal during our phone calls or fence meeting. He said that I did not ask him to lie. He did say that he did not read Howard Root's book. He claimed he threw it away! Where was the truth? Well, this comment could have been well rehearsed!

Now let me compare my supposed witness tampering with what the federal prosecutors did with Carlton. The prosecutors recognized that Carlton was a person with little courage and no business acumen other than in sales. So he was the ideal candidate to be manipulated into a government witness. Carlton's two bosses between himself and Bill were not going to allow themselves to be manipulated by the DOJ as were other sales persons. That only left Carlton and his subordinate and friend, Jeff Schultz, as possible government witnesses.

We had access to the prosecutor's written notes as they interviewed Carlton. He was initially told he could be indicted for conspiracy related to accounting fraud because he had interactions in one or more distributor transactions in 2015. That was about all it took when Carlton was offered immunity to "tell the truth," which means the "truth" as defined by the prosecutors! Now, it took a few meetings with the prosecutors to accomplish "witness tampering" government-style with Carlton. Carlton had to finally admit at the trial that he had 18 meetings in person and on conference calls with the prosecutors. At a minimum, that probably represents 60 hours of time for the manipulations that took his testimony to a rehearsed and memorized presentation! So let us compare my supposed witness tampering that took five <u>minutes</u> and the government's witness tampering that took certainly over 60-plus <u>hours</u>. This is certainly a joke, but it is not funny!

Please reflect on how corrupt this government witness manipulation process has become since the 1930s! This is a key reason that 95 percent of the government's cases in most districts are won. In the Southern District of New York, the percentage is even higher than that! That huge percent of successes is equivalent to the legal system in Russia and China.

The only way to counter this travesty is to have defense counsel call out what has happened with each witness in a way the jury will understand and repudiate. However, the judge may take up for the system. Our judge instructed the jury that a witness meeting with the prosecutors 18 times is normal. Our defense counsel should have continued to bring out the fact that the government gave immunity to a witness testifying to the government's definition of "The Truth." Most jurors would be very skeptical of a government witness' testimony if they understood the process. However, most defense counsels are former prosecutors, and they do not want to bash their former life or the federal legal system. Howard Root's attorneys did attack the prosecutors, and they won.

Our attorneys seemed to think that their cross-examinations of the government's witnesses had been very much to our benefit, and they thought that would carry the day in terms of the knowledge that had been absorbed by the jury. I certainly argued the opposite case. I did not think the jurors had anywhere near sufficient background information on what had transpired to be able to put our facts in perspective, beginning with the scienter, or intent, issue.

When the judge told us that he wanted the trial over by the Thanksgiving break, that left us with only a week to put on our case whereas the prosecutors had four weeks. Our attorneys advised us that Bill and I would not have time to testify; therefore, we should refuse to testify. That was the "coup de grace" for us! More details in the next chapter!

In addition, our attorneys should have raised the issue of our loss of defense time. That would have allowed us to use that manipulation in our appeal. By the time I started asking questions regarding the appeal, I was told that we lost the opportunity to use that issue because our trial attorneys did not raise the issue when it occured. This was most frustrating!

CHAPTER 24

THE TRIAL

As I gave some thought to how this chapter on the trial should be developed, I kept reminding myself that the primary focus of this book is for entrepreneurs, business executives and their investors. They are and should be the major beneficiaries of the potential successes and failures that have been described. There are some crucial issues to be absorbed from the MiMedx debacle and focusing on lengthy trial testimony would be unproductive. In fact, I would think it would be very boring and frustrating to most business people. It certainly was to me!

The key issues of this chapter are the manipulations by the judge and prosecutors that took place. Of course, the key is how those manipulations interfered with the administration of truthful disclosure and fair justice. The other issue is how shrewd the Southern District of New York (SDNY) is throughout the entire process in terms of achieving their desired outcomes. While our trial demonstrated numerous ways the legal process can be manipulated against the defendants, I am certain that there are many other subtle, but shrewd techniques that we did not witness in our trial. The major lesson is that any defendant going into a SDNY courtroom is significantly disadvantaged by the processes that have been developed over the decades to benefit their prosecutors and the SDNY track record.

I will highlight some of the testimony specifically and then try to explain my conclusions. These conclusions will sometimes be relevant to the specifics of our particular trial, and at other times, they will be more general in nature. Either way, you will be astounded by some of the things you will read that emanated from federal prosecutors and this court through Judge Rakoff. Relative to the issues being discussed, I will try not to over-analyze, but rather I will point out the flaws of this "justice" process as I saw them.

Prior to the trial discussions, I want to convey some broader issues pertaining to the U.S. legal system and its constituents.

Our Legal System as Related to Business

For the entrepreneur or business executive, the rapid growth in U.S. regulations and laws presents a major challenge. Over the last 30 years, the regulation and laws governing business conduct have soared. At this point, there are approximately 4,500 that significantly affect the way business must be conducted in this country. In the healthcare sector, the regulations have grown even faster. Managing your business in this increasingly complex regulatory environment will continue to be demanding. I will provide some commentary relative to my experiences in this area and what business executives can possibly do to protect themselves from this increasingly hostile regulatory environment.

Obviously, business executives turn to knowledgeable experts when they are confronting management issues on regulations and laws. Thus, the legal profession becomes much more embedded in today's business activities. With that being said, this opens up the additional challenges of the business executive making normal business decisions, which involve managing "risk and return" with legal matters. Often, when legal advice is sought, the business executive is given the pragmatic "don't, don't, and by the way don't." The general risk averse nature of the legal profession always presents a challenge to balancing "risk and return" which is the responsibility of the business executive. Thus, lawyers will play a key role in some of your business decisions, but you must figure ways to accept reasonable business risks and sometimes even bold ones without violating regulations and laws in order to produce the returns that your shareholders expect.

With business activities today being so challenged by increased government rules and regulations, your selection of legal staff or outside law firms is a critical decision. Therefore, it would be helpful to have experience in doing so. I am now going to give you some thoughts that I have developed over the decades pertaining to legal staff and the personalities of the various disciplines in the legal profession.

First, you must understand that a person becomes a lawyer for several reasons, but one is that they are generally risk averse personalities. You will not find very many courageous and bold personalities in the legal profession. However, some of the most successful trial attorneys are people who are bold, but they also possess sales abilities. Most lawyers do not have those qualities, and after law school, any tendencies in that direction have probably been discouraged.

Thus, most business executives will likely develop certain degrees of frustration with their legal staff and outside legal expertise. I will reveal some of my experiences with the legal profession, which might be helpful as you encounter similar situations. There have been several books written, some of them by lawyers, involving attorneys who were very clearly problematic personalities, particularly in the area of the prosecution of federal justice. My recommended books are a good start.

My experience with the legal profession began in 1970 as I set up my first corporation and began my entrepreneurial activities. The first lawyer that I ever hired was the friend of a very good friend of mine who had gone into the construction business and was beginning to have his initial successes. And, he recommended the lawyer that had set up his business for him. I used this individual, but I had no way to really determine whether he had "dotted all the Is and crossed all the Ts." It was not until several years later I discovered that when he searched the name of our corporate entity which was to be Life Systems, he did not search trademarks. He only checked corporate names.

We were about to launch our first product when I noticed, while testing some of our products in the neonatal intensive care unit of Northside Hospital, a competitive product that had the name "Life Systems" on the front panel. While that was not the name of the corporation that produced the product, they had trademarked the name "Life Systems" to cover one of their product lines. Thus, we had to do a substantial amount of rework to not only change our corporate name to Healthdyne, but to also change our new product training and marketing materials. I highlight this example because it taught me my first lesson, which was that I needed to know enough about the laws and regulations so that I could ask sufficient questions to be certain that most of our legal advice was reasonably correct.

The second significant situation occurred when our first attempt to take the company public in 1973 was stopped by the Atlanta Regional SEC Office. They had received a letter from an individual who had been solicited by a brokerage house and had placed an order for our stock. In his letter, he stated that he did not place an order to purchase the stock. He later admitted that he did place the order so there was no issue. However, the SEC opened an investigation right at the point that our offering was subscribed and funds were ready to be distributed. At this point, we were represented by one of the largest law firms in Atlanta. I became quite frustrated with the fact that nine months of work was going to go to waste because of one individual initially not telling the truth to the SEC. The SEC quickly made the correct determination relative to the witness, but the incident gave them the ability to open an investigation, which they seemed to relish.

I asked our Atlanta law firm to be more aggressive in their questioning of why this federal agency would open a full investigation over something so trivial as this, particularly when the individual admitted to the agency that he did not mean to cause any trouble; he just did not want to buy the stock. He should have merely called the brokerage house from which he ordered the stock and canceled his order.

However, in the process, I was told by the partner at our law firm that they would not ask the SEC to terminate this investigation because it could endanger their relationship with the Atlanta SEC office, and they had other clients for whom they had to interface with this agency. So what I heard was, "Healthdyne, you are too small a client and too unimportant to us." I decided that I would have to fire my first law firm over this matter. And, that is exactly what I did! To me, this example represents the lack of risk taking capacity that most lawyers demonstrate. I think there were numerous ways the law firm could have dealt with this at the Atlanta Regional SEC Office. However, they were too risk averse to do so, and they were fired by a small company who went on to become a major business success.

I turned our legal activities over to a Healthdyne shareholder, Richard (Dick) Thomason. I was introduced to Dick by a friend. He quickly made a major investment in Healthdyne and became a member of our Board of Directors. Dick was a courageous personality, and he would think things through using his legal background, but also with a degree of business acumen. He continued to interact with the SEC, and within a couple of months, they advised us that they were dropping the investigation. However, by that time we had refunded everyone's money who had invested in the offering and taken another pathway for fundraising. Investors in that offering would have seen their stock appreciate in value by 500 times over the next ten year period!

There are very few lawyers who have been very successful business managers. The basic risk averse personality precludes their taking the necessary business risks to increase returns significantly. Therefore, history shows lawyers' attempts at becoming business executives have not been rewarded by significant successes. So be careful of allowing lawyers to make or overly influence your business decisions.

Prosecutor's Personalties

I would like to discuss in more detail one other legal personality that I now know very well. That is the prosecutor. Most defense attorneys start out as federal or state prosecutors. This gives them a chance to understand the system and the type of individuals they will be defending after they leave their position as a government prosecutor.

My experience with the DOJ Assistant U.S. Attorneys (AUSAs) and the former prosecutors who represented Bill and me in this DOJ case has given me a great deal of insight into their personalities. In addition to having the normal risk averse characteristics, they are, what I began to call during the trial, "super skeptics." Some of that skepticism is certainly warranted when working with "criminals." With the focus on criminal acts, such as murder, drug dealings and related matters, you can understand why skepticism is important. Generally, those laws are very straightforward and the criminal actions clear. However, in many white-collar crime cases, the actual case facts can be confusing due to the massive number of regulations and laws. For instance, when a lawyer is trying to understand the business decisions made by an executive that supposedly violated a regulation, it can be difficult. It can be difficult because the lawyer has never been involved in business transactions or decisions. So the lawyer who is trying to make an assessment as to whether or not their client is being honest and has integrity or whether they are attempting to change the facts, which would cause additional criminal actions, they will use their normal skepticism.

With no business experience, it is generally very difficult for an attorney to grasp what their client was thinking at the moment of any business act much less an illegal act. That is very important in determining if scienter was present.

My experience was that our group of attorneys did not fully understand Bill's and my description of what transpired relative to the accusations that were made against us. Fortunately, Bill and I are men of integrity, and the stories and facts that we presented at the very beginning of the investigation were basically the same as the ones we gave throughout the three-year period.

However, the skeptical nature of the attorneys and their risk averse personalities led to their attempting to find "business experts" to validate what Bill and I were saying about the facts in the case. These outside consultants attempted to give the legal team some degree of comfort that their clients would not give them bad surprises during the trial because of a change in their testimonies.

As an example of this, I will mention the accounting consulting firm that was retained by my lawyers. Without discussing the accounting matters with me, an individual who has gone through annual accounting audits and quarterly reviews over the decades that numbered into the hundreds, they selected what I call an "academic accounting professor" to give them advice. This particular individual had never been involved in public company audits. Thus, the attorneys received a very precise interpretation of the accounting regulations rather than what happens in reality in the tens of thousands of quarterly reviews and annual audits that are accomplished in this country. Once my lawyers heard the academic approach, they were rather confused about the practicalities of how audits really worked, and how the regulations were generally interpreted. I finally stopped trying to "educate" and decided that when I testified at my trial I would clear up those matters.

As I began to realize the magnitude of the "super skepticism" of my legal team, I became quite frustrated with the process. However, as you will find out as you read further in the book, no one on the defense side ever testified during the trial due to the schedule being changed because of manipulations by the court.

In talking to Howard Root about these types of issues, he stated that he had time, in terms of developing his case, to terminate one law firm and have the other resign before he settled on the third one to try his case. Bill and I did not have that flexibility so we were basically stuck with the teams we had originally selected.

Legal Counsel Narcissism

I discussed earlier in the book the issues associated with narcissism. Narcissism can be destructive no matter who exhibits that type of behavior. However, when it exists in a corporate lawyer or outside legal counsel, it can be particularly destructive. As I previously characterized it, narcissism basically shows up as an individual who has a "know it all" attitude with the thought that, "What is in my brain is right, and what is in your bran is wrong." And, they generally have little compassion for others.

My trial lawyers demonstrated this characteristic at times. When appropriate, I would remind them that I happened to be the client whose life was going to be dramatically affected by the outcome of the trial. As such, I expected them to listen to me and respond to my concerns in a professional manner. However, I cannot state that I was very effective with my arguments. In talking to other executives who have been in a similar situation, they state that they have encountered the same results. When you combine the skeptical outlook with narcissism, you get a pretty intractable personality.

Now the lesson to be learned is to try to keep yourself in a position of being able to change outside legal counsel as rapidly as necessary. When you think you are "stuck," you will be in a very awkward situation. Unfortunately, you will not really know the personalities until you become involved with them and go through some debates and battles.

In preparing for the trial, I tried to focus our legal team on using proven business practices that are used for project management. I asked them to set the strategic goals and objectives and then the tactical plans associated with attaining those goals. They never really focused on the strategic issues, in spite of me trying to bring them back to the ones that I certainly emphasized. They were very focused on all the technical nuances and having stacks and stacks of books of emails, letters and case law documents. They were tacticians and not strategists, which caused some of the issues and problems we had in our trial.

Due Process Violation

The fact that Bill and I were given no "due process" of the law in any activities related to this investigation or DOJ trial is one of the pivotal issues in our case. As we have previously stated, King & Spalding never interviewed or confronted us with all of the allegations that they eventually took to the Department of Justice at the SDNY. In fact, as I mentioned, we never knew the accusation details other than the ones pertaining to AvKARE until the indictments were published. As previously mentioned, the AvKARE accusations were the ones over which the Board asked Bill Taylor, Mike Senken, John Cranston and me to resign, but the DOJ did not think they were worthy of an indictment.

We were in the fourth week of the trial when the judge announced that, due to COVID, the court would be closed after Thanksgiving, and we needed to finish our case before then. We were totally shocked and surprised. Judge Rakoff first asked the prosecutors, who were still presenting their case, how much longer they would need. The prosecutors said they would need another week. The judge countered with, "I will only give you three more days." Then, he asked our attorneys about how long they would need to put on our defense. They were basically silent. They mentioned having a meeting that night to discuss the matter. There should have been, in my humble opinion, objections from our attorneys the moment that change in timing was given to us. The prosecutors in essence had four weeks to present their case in an efficient manner. We would only have about a week to present ours, which was blatantly unfair and violated the "due process" requirements of the judicial system.

This disclosure by Judge Rakoff was the first item on the court's agenda that morning of November 12th. The discussion lasted about five minutes. However, in the official transcript of the trial, this particular conversation is omitted. That was the first time I witnessed the judge make comments from the bench that did not appear in the official transcript. Why would that have occurred? Maybe a CYA action! Either way, this is the beginning of another violation of due process of the law.

The Poster Child and the AUSAs

You have seen me call MiMedx a Poster Child because of all the unethical problems that can evolve around a publicly traded company today. What transpired at MiMedx is a sad and tragic story involving almost every negative issue that can arise as a result of the shortcomings of our whistleblower laws, the failure of certain federal agencies to enforce their well-documented laws and regulations particularly against illegal short sellers, the Department of Justice allowing their prosecutors to take advantage of individuals or corporations in order to further their careers, the flaws in a judicial process that allow prosecutors to manipulate cases, the manipulations that can actually take place during a trial and in the courtroom, particularly in districts like the Southern District of New York, and finally, the politics that have infected our judicial system and encouraged our "accusation" culture.

Let me start by explaining what I mean by certain federal agencies not maintaining reasonable discipline and not holding individuals accountable for their actions. It is well known that there are certain types of governmental prosecution cases that, when conducted by the AUSAs, will result in the AUSA being acknowledged by a large law firm with an offer of future employment which generally results in them becoming a law partner.

Thus, most of these young AUSAs are motivated by anything or anyone that brings them a potential white-collar crime case. Those cases may come to them by their own initiatives or by reading or hearing of situations in which they believe federal laws were broken and should be investigated with possibly charges filed. Or more often, information is brought by individuals who also have a vested interest in seeing that the AUSAs will investigate, file subpoenas and later indictments against individuals who they have determined would be to their benefit. Also, often these investigations are started because a short seller brings their accusations to the Department of Justice for them to investigate. Overzealous AUSAs never seem to be held accountable by their supervisors for aberrant legal behavior patterns, except in rare cases.

In addition, the new Sally Yates Doctrine requires companies who have accusations made against them to hire a law firm to do an investigation that "targets" top management and for the company and that law firm to bring all the information to the Department of Justice. In the Sally Yates Doctrine, it clearly states that this is the way the government wants these cases investigated, even though it is the DOJ's responsibility to do their own investigations.

The Sally Yates Doctrine states that companies will be given certain legal flexibility from the DOJ if they react in this manner. The Doctrine is not clear what happens if the company simply says they have done their own investigation and see no issues in terms of federal laws being violated. Of course, there are some strong personal relationships between prosecutors, lawyers in private practice who used to be prosecutors, large law firms and the Department of Justice.

Frankly, without this ability to expedite their legal career by working at the DOJ or SEC, these AUSAs might never consider going to work for the government. Thus, the system has this strong built-in bias that is detrimental to American citizens and corporate entities, and it undermines real justice.

One great example of the problems associated with unsupervised and unfettered AUSA investigations came as a result of the indictments brought against the late Senator Ted Stevens of Alaska. This story has been well-documented by Sidney Powell in her book entitled "Licensed to Lie." The legal actions against this senator were brought because of political reasons. He was facing re-election, and DOJ officials were possibly members of the other political party.

DOJ attorneys were guilty themselves of numerous violations of federal regulations in the way in which they hid exculpatory information and created false information against the senator. They were guilty of lying and were <u>called out</u> by his attorneys and finally <u>the court</u>. This book is well worth reading to help put in perspective how the lack of oversight and management help create corruption from the AUSAs who work at the Department of Justice.

An example of the judicial system being controlled by accusations is outlined in Professor Dershowitz's book called *Guilt by Accusation*. His book clearly highlights that accusations, which are picked up and encouraged by the news media for their own political and financial benefit, cause immense distortions in our judicial system today. In our case, alleged illegal short sellers were the primary source of the accusations, which was then reinforced by their media pawns.

Pre-trial Activities

Before the trial began, the prosecutors and our defense lawyers had sessions on pre-trial motions where each side presented to the judge certain issues that they wanted put into evidence or kept from being put into evidence. Our lawyers lost almost every one of our important motions in this process. It was quite evident that the judge was very favorable to the prosecution. The AUSAs obtained about 80 percent of their pre-trial motion requests while we only received about 20 percent of ours. SDNY judicial fairness again!

One significant point that the prosecutors did not want mentioned at the trial was that I had a very strong track record of philanthropy. The judge granted the prosecutors' request without much discussion. So the part of my personality related to generosity and lack of greed was not to be discussed by my lawers, but the prosecutors were allowed to say, and did say, dozens of times that my supposed "illegal" actions were all motivated by my alleged "greed." My attorneys could not respond with the truth in any way! Typical court manipulations!

Another key loss was when the judge ruled that the MiMedx financials could not be discussed after 2015 year end! The continuing superb performance could have been very revealing to the jury, particularly the disclosure of *Fortune* magazine's ranking of MiMedx as the fifth fastest-growing public company in America in 2017.

There were also situations during the trial where the judge assisted the prosecutors with their witnesses. For instance, Mike Carlton, one of our former sales managers who was testifying for the government, was asked by our attorney on his cross-examination about how many times he had met with the AUSAs either by telephone or in New York. We knew that it had been at least 18 times because of the Brady and Jencks information that was given to us by the prosecution. We also had some handwritten transcripts of Carlton's conversations with the AUSAs. Either way, Carlton was initially trying to be evasive, but when my attorney finally dragged out of him that he had been up to New York or on conference calls with the AUSAs at least 18 times, the judge immediately stepped in to tell the jury that there was nothing wrong with Carlton visiting with these government attorneys 18 times. However, for a witness who had been threatened with conspiracy indictments, who had obviously been very intimidated by the AUSAs and who had been given immunity if he would align with the government's story, it was quite revealing to listen to the judge support this obvious misuse of judicial power.

The Jury Selection Process

As we were preparing for the trial, we conducted several mock trials with actual jurors from the New York City area. These "trials" were very informative in terms of verifying what I would call common sense outcomes, depending on our particular presentations.

In each of these mock juries, we always had about 30 percent who were Wall Street business and salespeople, then we had another 30 percent who were classical blue-collar workers and finally about 40 percent who were currently unemployed or had been underemployed during most of their careers. However, having 30 percent of the individuals who had some Wall Street experience was very beneficial as we learned when we listened to how the jurors deliberated on specific issues. There were some reasonably complex accounting issues that were being alleged against us, and it took people with some business experience to put those things in perspective for the others who did not.

My only previous experience in a federal court was in the late 1970s in Atlanta. I remember the jury selection process well because it took about two days. My company, Healthdyne, was the plaintiff so our attorneys had first choice. But, the two groups of attorneys went back and forth eliminating the jurors that they felt were not going to be supportive of their case. As I recall, we had a fair balance of jury candidates both blue-collar as well as white-collar individuals. It took two days to select a jury, which was done by the two groups of legal counsels. However, Judge Rakoff stated that he would select the jury down to a certain point within an hour, and then the two legal groups could fine tune matters.

After being quarantined in New York for two weeks, our trial started on Monday, October 26th. Judge Jed Rakoff entered his courtroom promptly at 9:30am and began to immediately explain the processes and procedures of his court. He made it clear that this was *his* court, and there were certain ways that he demanded his court would function during a trial. After about a half an hour of learning our rules, he explained the jury selection process in which he would select the jury.

So we all went over to a very large room where there must have been over 200 people seated. Judge Rakoff went to a microphone and began to call people up to the jurors' microphone from a list. As he interviewed each of approximately 50 potential jurors, he would question them about their situations in life and their work experience. And, he would thank them for making themselves available to sit on his jury.

Judge Rakoff pared the group of jurors down to 16. There would be 12 jurors with four alternate jurors who would fill in if we lost anyone during the course of the trial. As it turned out, we lost four jurors, and we had to use all the alternates.

Relative to Judge Rakoff's jury, it seemed to me that every one of his 50 initial interviewees were blue-collar people. There were no Wall Street managers, analysts or accountants brought to the microphone for the initial interview. While the room was filled with a couple of hundred people, no white-collar people were called to the microphone. Thus, we ended up with a jury of blue-collar people and no one with any relevant business or accounting experience.

When I asked my attorneys about the judge selecting the jury, they told me that, in the Southern District of New York, the judges have the right to do so. I said that seemed to be different from the previous experience I had in a federal court trial, and it could be very influential in the outcome of the trial. My attorneys reassured me that the judge had the right to select the jury in the SDNY. I pointed out that we essentially had an all blue-collar jury. I asked how that could happen with a couple of hundred people in the room. Obviously, no one was called to the microphone that had business experience. One of my attorneys stated that the judge does not actually pick the jurors to be interviewed; the clerk of the court is responsible for that activity.

Well, my next thought was how "naïve" that statement was. If an inexperienced law clerk has the ability to pick the group that the judge will screen, then the judge simply needs to say to his clerk, "I want blue today." I believe that is what happened in our case. Needless to say, the trial did not begin with my feeling very comfortable about the balanced process of justice that we were supposed to receive in a federal trial in America.

The jury selection process was over by approximately noon. So, as Judge Rakoff promised, he had a very quick and efficient process. However, I realized I was not going to be involved with a jury of my peers in the weeks ahead! More significant manipulations by the court!

Back in the courtroom, we went right into the opening statements. Of course, the prosecution went first. I do not know what I was really expecting to hear, but as I sat listening to AUSA Tracer's lengthy analysis of their twisted facts and lies, I was continually saying to myself, "This is not America."

I was really surprised by the name-calling by AUSA Tracer as he presented the government's case. While there were not many facts pertaining to the allegations, there was a tremendous amount of name-calling relative to Bill and me. Tracer was using words, such as liars, cheaters, greedy, lining their pockets, bribery, sham and secret transactions. The AUSAs had put into perspective the fact that the court had selected a blue-collar jury who was not going to understand very well any of the allegations, but would understand those words. They stressed that we were guilty of fraud because we had planned all the "schemes" that they had twisted into violations of accounting rules. Of course, that was not factual. And, most importantly, did any of these acts involve scienter, which meant they were planned acts that created fraud and criminal acts?

My and Bill's attorneys took a more genteel and educational approach to their opening remarks. My attorney suggested that the prosecutors were asking the jury to look at this case through "dirty windows" so that everything looked dirty! After the opening statements were closed, I was left with the feeling that we were being painted as wealthy criminals who were selfish, self-centered, dishonest and greedy. I made a mental note of how much work our attorneys had to do to get across the fact that we were honest and hardworking individuals with integrity who had built very efficient companies in the past that employed thousands of individuals, and the same had occurred at MiMedx.

Personalities Who Testified and Did Not

It is certainly very important for entrepreneurs and business executives to understand their personnel relatively well, but it is very difficult to obtain real facts and details on someone's prior employment in today's environment. Most companies are fearful of being sued if they pass on to a potential future employer any information pertaining to negative job performance of a former employee. My HR executives told me that it is becoming more and more difficult to extract any type of information. Thus, the legal profession is making it more difficult for a company to hire people who do not have personality disorders or corrupt tendencies.

Thus, when we hired over 450 sales employees from 2011 to mid 2018, we were bound to make a few mistakes in the process. Of course, we had a very efficient program of monitoring the performance of salespeople. It was a two-step process with reviews by sales management and human resources. Also, we had an efficient compliance system, which allowed concerns to be brought to me personally and privately or to the Board of Directors independent of management. However, I have found that many people were concerned about using such a system because they were fearful of the possible repercussions, even though they did not have to disclose their names. While there was never an instance of that occurring in any of our companies, it is human nature to have a fear of the unknown.

It is wise to continue to emphasize to all employees the need for reporting instances or situations that are uncomfortable or possibly illegal that may be transpiring within the corporate entity. However, that is not a perfect solution so you have to be keenly aware of the personal traits of your employees as they cause problems.

A matter that was extremely important in the indictments and trial was the people the AUSAs decided they would use as witnesses. As you know by now, the major allegations were all related to misstatements of revenue in several quarters of 2015. Basically, they alleged that Bill and I had specific and improper negotiations with distributors in terms of their quarterly orders and some that related to the introduction of our new product line.

The sales chain of command at MiMedx went from me to Bill to Chris Cashman to Kevin Lilly to Carlton and then to Schultz. No testimony was given from Chris Cashman or Kevin Lilly during the trial. Everything came from Carlton and Schultz, who were at the bottom of the sales management chain. They became government witnesses and did testify at the trial. Why did we not hear anything from Chris, Kevin and other sales and marketing managers.

The reason is that when Chris, Kevin and several other managers were interrogated by King & Spalding investigators and the AUSAs at SDNY, they were not intimidated by the threats of being involved in fraudulent activities. They knew the facts and stuck to the truth. These individuals had intregrity and were courageous in nature. Chris Cashman is a former Naval Officer who served on a submarine. Kevin Lilly's father was a very experienced Air Force officer and pilot. Kevin certainly inherited the courageous nature of his father. Thus, these individuals told the investigators or the AUSAs "where to go." However, the AUSAs realized that Carlton would be easily manipulated and would respond to threats. They realized that Schultz would follow Carlton's lead because of their long-term relationship. The fabricated stories that were told by Carlton and Schultz could have been easily refuted if Chris or Kevin had testified at our trial. They would have told a very different story because of their integrity and common sense. I certainly would have done the same had I been able to testify.

Unfortunately, in a trial of this nature involving complicated business and accounting principles and with a jury who had little to no business experience or background, the jurors could be easily influenced as they had no idea how to separate fact from fiction. AUSA Tracer told the jurors numerous times to just use their "common sense." Well, when an AUSA is able to twist facts and is relying on a blue-collar jury's lack of business experience and potential negative attitude towards entrepreneurs and business executives that may be all they need to do.

I bring this up to simply point out that there were several other very important individuals in the sales chain of command that I am sure would have given much different testimony than Carlton and Schultz. The absence of Chris, Kevin and others from the prosecutors' possible witness list is a very telling clue about honest justice in the SDNY.

I have made the point that Schultz has followed Carlton in his sales career. Both these individuals were terminated by MiMedx in late 2018 by the original Board. Carlton immediately called me with his typical "the sky is falling" description of the situation. I gave him some suggestions on what to do in terms of going back to officials at the company to demand a termination package. He was afraid they were not going to give him anything, and they would cut off his medical benefits. I could tell he was in his normal panic mode and not thinking very clearly at all.

I subsequently received other phone calls from Carlton, and at some point, suggested that he meet me at the fence that adjoined our two properties. I had been told that the company was advising terminated employees not to talk to Bill or me. However, at that time, that was really very biased advice, and it was designed to protect the Audit Committee during this CYA process. There was no critical involvement to my knowledge of the DOJ or the SEC with any of the company's activities at that time so I should not have been accused of trying to influence a witness. In Carlton's case, I was trying to help him get through his "panic period" and receive his termination pay.

I can certainly use Carlton, our first sales manager, as an example of someone with personality weaknesses and the propensity for dishonesty, particularly when under the pressure of being jailed by federal prosecutors.

Carlton was an effective person in terms of developing relationships. He was one of the best "relationship builders" that I recall in any of our previous sales organizations. He developed trust rather quickly with his subordinates, and he could maintain that trust. However, he was a weak manager because his propensity for building relationships required him never to hold people accountable or be critical of their performance. At least that was his thought process. This behavior caused problems for us as we grew our sales organization. Thus, Carlton was moved from total responsibility for all our sales activities to a position of being responsible only for our foreign sales activities to a position of being responsible only for our European sales activities. Carlton went through those transitions seemingly without much of an observable problem. However, I am certain it bothered his ego. We never changed his compensation plan or made it appear that he had been "demoted." The company's growth took care of situations like this, and everyone realized that changing responsibilities was taking place throughout the corporation rather routinely.

One of Carlton's real management issues was that anything that disturbed his "peace" was attributed to "the sky is falling." Bill and I were subjected on a number of occasions to meetings with him where he described his "the sky is falling" scenario. We would suggest rather simple management solutions to resolve the problems. Generally, he would follow those, and his issues would be settled. Carlton really did not have the "courage of his convictions" in most situations, and he would put himself into a "panic" mindset. Frankly, his behavior was much like Terry Dewberry's, our Audit Committee Chairman!

I believe the prosecutors at the SDNY recognized Carlton's personality very quickly. They interviewed a number of our sales and marketing executives from Chris Cashman, who was Executive Vice President of Sales and Marketing, on down to Jeff Schultz, who was four levels below Chris. Schultz and Carlton had been friends for decades. Schultz was a different personality than Carlton with a little more courage, but less common sense. He looked upon Carlton as a "big brother."

In the case of Carlton or any person who has little courage, the threats prosecutors can hurl at them can become overwhelming. They will be told, as happened in our case, that they can be indicted because they were in a chain of command that <u>supposedly</u> committed accounting errors with revenue recognition issues that involved scienter, or purposeful fraud. They will not understand the reality of the situation or their actual legal risks, and they will become concerned only for themselves. I can see how Carlton and Schultz were very easily manipulated by the AUSAs, even though they were represented by counsel.

Testimonies

Relative to lying, the prosecutors always tried to get their witnesses to claim that Bill or I lied to them. In some cases, they did not obtain that testimony, even from their coached witnesses. As a matter of fact, at one point, Carlton was being cross-examined by Matt Menchel and within an hour or so he perjured himself in a rather bizarre fashion.

Right before lunch on October 27th, Menchel questioned Carlton:

MENCHEL: "And your testimony on direct examination was that your understanding was that he (Petit) was professing these things to you because he wanted you to say the same thing as well; is that right?

CARLTON: The impression I had was he wanted to make sure that, you know, that was the story on CPM.

MENCHEL: But he never asked you to lie, correct.

CARLTON: He did not.

MENCHEL: He never asked you to shade the information that you were going to share with the government, right?

CARLTON: He did not say that, no.

MENCHEL: Or minimize?

CARLTON: He didn't say that either, no.

Menchel continued to question Carlton on a telephone conversation we had. Menchel basically asked the same questions about those conversations, and Carlton responded the same way.

After lunch, AUSA Imperator started his final examination of Carlton. His first question to Carlton related to the immunity that he had been given by the prosecutors for his testimony. Recall that the immunity could be cancelled if Carlton lied under oath, but the definition of a lie was determined by the prosecutors! Imperator started by making this inquiry:

IMPERATOR: This is labeled an immunity and compulsion order for your testimony. Is that correct, Mr. Carlton?

CARLTON: That is correct.

IMPERATOR: If we can flip to the second page. It says here: "It is further ordered that pursuant to Title 18, United States Code, Section 6002 and 6003, no testimony or other information compelled under this order or any information directly or indirectly derived from such testimony or other information may be used against

Carlton in any criminal case, except a prosecution for perjury, giving a false statement, or otherwise failing to comply with this order."

Mr. Carlton, what is your obligation onto this immunity order? What is your job on the witness stand?

CARLTON: Tell the truth.

IMPERATOR: Does your immunity order give you any protection if you don't tell the truth on the stand?

CARLTON: No.

IMPERATOR: By the way, is there someone in this courtroom who has pressured you not to tell the truth to the government?

CARLTON: Yes.

IMPERATOR: Who is that?

CARLTON: Pete.

IMPERATOR: Is that Mr. Petit?

CARLTON: Yes.

So, within about two hours, Carlton changed his testimony about my interactions with him. I asked my attorneys about this amazing change that took place after our lunch break. I suggested that during lunch with the prosecutors, Carlton was reminded that his answers were not what they had coached or wanted him to say. When I asked, my attorneys immediately said that the prosecutors and Carlton were not permitted to have lunch together during his testimony or have discussions about it. My reply was simply, "Does that mean this conversation did not take place? Why did the prosecutors even bring the subject back up at this point? If they did not have that conversation, why did Carlton change his mind and perjure himself?" There was no response from my attorneys, and they <u>did not</u> formally call out this perjury to the judge.

In fact, it was disclosed to us from the government's Brady and Jencks information that Carlton had met with or had conference calls with these AUSAs 18 times. That shows the extent to which they had opportunities to mold his testimony. Also, as he was being questioned by the prosecutors in court, it was evident that his desired testimony was essentially memorized.

Relative to Jeff Schulz, we had a little different set of testimony issues. Schulz was much more of a "BS artist" than Carlton. He was often too creative with his sales pitches and had to be reminded to stay within bounds. On the stand, you could tell he had his answers well memorized, but he would often begin to embellish, and that is where you could see the "BS artist" come out.

One issue that was particularly irritating was when Schulz was asked if he thought that some of our conversations with Mark Brooks of CPM was out of balance and possibly illegal, why did he not use the two compliance system communication links to get that information to the Board of Directors or to Pete Petit. MiMedx actually had two systems. One went directly to the Board, and one went directly to me. Thus, an employee could select to whom they wanted to expose their concerns. Schultz stated that he was concerned about retribution and being fired, but he <u>did</u> <u>not</u> have to put his name on these documents. Also, he knew that had never happened to anyone using this system. There was <u>never</u> any type of retribution at MiMedx based on an employee using our compliance system. Of course, employees had been terminated for violations of company policy or federal regulations.

Another interesting part of Schulz's testimony came on November 12th. He was on a roll answering Hartman's questions very quickly and rapidly because they were basically memorized. Apparently, Harman changed the wording in one of the questions, and Schulz gave a quick affirmative answer. As soon as he did that, Hartman realized that Schultz did not recognize the word that he had used. This was rather embarrassing as they both tried to clean up the obvious memorization faux pas.

The conversation went like this:

QUESTION: And was making records like this a regular practice, contracts like this?

ANSWER: No.

QUESTION: Was this something that was generated through a quasi-automated process or was this something that was done in a bespoke way.

Answer: It was done in a spoke way.

Question: Well, I mean, you understand what I mean by that?

Answer: No. Please rephrase this.

Question: Was this through an automated process or did somebody put this together specifically to send to Mr. Brooks on this occasion:

Answer: Somebody put this together to send to Mr. Brooks.

Schultz made numerous misstatements, misrepresentations and lies during his testimony. The prosecutors had worked diligently with him, particularly on trying to prove the "bribe" aspects of the $200,000 payment to CPM in the second quarter of 2015. Of all the prosecutors' claims, this is the most ridiculous, especially because the prosecutors took a proffer from Lexi Haden, our General Counsel, about her making a mistake of not papering that transaction as a "Settlement Agreement." So the prosecutors <u>knew</u> what the $200,000 payment was. They knew that MiMedx had made an honest legal mistake, and this payment was compensating CPM for the GPO sales into Texas, which was required because they had an exclusive contract in Texas. Now for Schultz to testify that he knew nothing about the GPO issue is just <u>blatantly</u> dishonest. In fact, Schultz and Carlton brought the issue to me on or about June 26, 2015. They were both aware of the problem because it was their responsibility to know about these matters, and they disclosed the issue to me.

I immediately expressed my concern to Carlton and Schultz that it was an obligation that we needed to correct. I asked Mark Diaz, our sales administration vice president, to provide to me the revenue that the GPOs and IDNs had made in Texas because we needed to compensate CPM for those lost revenues. As I recall, the total was about $317,000. After I took out the costs that CPM did not have to pay for the product, the number was approximately $200,000 of damages. That is where the $200,000 number came from, and it had nothing to do with some of the gibberish that Schultz was making up about a bribe. That was all constructed around the prosecution's desire to claim that I had bribed a distributor. In fact, the bribe term was not even applicable to distributor negotiations because it was perfectly legal to give discounts to distributors when appropriate. The accounting issue was that we would have had to reduce our revenue for the quarter by that $200,000 figure. This had nothing to do with me bribing anyone. The bribe idea was concocted in order to use a derogatory word to describe me to the jury.

During his testimony, there was a lot of complaining from Schulz about how Bill and I set the revenue goals for each quarter so high that it was tough on everyone in sales. Nothing could be further from the truth. The revenue numbers that we forecast from MiMedx were developed from the bottom up. We had a very sophisticated system that took every territory, every region, every area and allowed salespeople and sales management to forecast at the beginning of the quarter from the bottom up. Sales management was given about ten days to analyze their numbers and correct any overages or underages that they saw. I never heard any complaining because these were sales management's own numbers. They were not Pete's or Bill's numbers. In fact, we would take their quarterly revenue forecast before we gave it to our shareholders and cut it back several percent, depending on the situation as we saw it.

The prosecution's third most "interesting" witness was Brian Martin. Martin was Chairman, CEO and one of the founders of Stability Biologics. We discussed the history of our acquisition of Stability Biologics in earlier chapters. We also discussed the fraudulent clinical data and information they presented to us to entice us to acquire this company. We realized after the acquisition, unfortunately, that the majority of that clinical data and information that we had been given on their Physio bone growth stimulator product was fraudulent. Thus, we forced them to repurchase their company from us.

During that time, I realized that Martin was neither an honest person nor a person with integrity. Even his third largest shareholder saw the issues as we began to uncover the fraud. That shareholder, Marty Hall, was just as disgusted as we were about Martin's propensity for lying and fraud.

Why the prosecutors decided to bring a self-proclaimed fraudster to testify in our trial was a mystery. However, they gave him a non-prosecution agreement, which basically said that he would not be prosecuted if he testified to their story about Petit and Taylor. Under cross-examination, Martin admitted that he had perpetuated fraud against Osiris Therapeutics some years before meeting us. Then, he claimed that he committed fraud with MiMedx and tried to implicate me in the process. However, there was one key question that was asked that essentially took away all of his credibility.

In effect, Martin had stated that when Stability Biologics became a distributor for MiMedx in the third quarter of 2015, I supposedly told him that they would not have to pay for the products they purchased until they were sold. That was a bold-faced lie. In fact, at that point, I had only met Martin twice, and I did not know him well at all. I would not have made a comment or offer like that to anyone because I knew the revenue recognition implications. So I called him in mid-December after our monthly accounts payable meeting as their accounts payable were aged out to about 75 days. I asked him to send us at least a $1 million payment. When my attorney asked him under cross-examination why I would call and ask him for a payment if I had given him extended payment terms, Martin replied, "I do not know."

In addition, our attorneys were notified a few months after the trial by the AUSAs that Martin's mistress had reported to them that he admitted to her that he had lied while giving testimony. Thus, he disclosed to her that, for whatever reason, he was presenting information that was not truthful in his testimony. I suspect some of this was a result of his being instructed by the prosecutors as to what they viewed the "truth" to be. Therefore, in order to maintain his immunity agreement, he would have to stick to their "truth," which were actually lies!

During the testimony of Matt Urbizo, the Cherry Bekaert auditing manager, he was asked if I should have disclosed to him the fact that there had been a working capital loan made to SLR through a partnership set up by my children. Matt's response was that I should have notified the auditors of that fact. Upon cross-examination, my attorneys did not ask Urbizo a very key question. He should have been asked whether or not any of our other 15 distributors had been requested to give information on how they obtained their working capital. The answer to that would have been "never." If they had, I expect the majority of our distributors would have told us that was "none of your business," and that there was plenty of information available to ascertain whether or not they could cover the anticipated accounts receivable from our business transactions. So, from a disclosure standpoint, there was no precedent to highlight the SLR working capital loan. I was helping a person, Jerry Morrison, with whom I had developed a great respect and who I knew would be successful. I took some calculated risk, and MiMedx achieved a significant return!

I was very conscious of maintaining an "arm's length" from this loan. I had no personal financial benefit from it being made by this partnership, which was controlled by my three children. And, I was not knowledgeable of the terms and conditions of the contract. If this loan had not been negotiated, Jerry Morrison would have had to sign an agreement with a factoring company so he would have had approximately the same amount of cash available, but it would have been much more costly to SLR. Thus, my offering the names of two individuals who might be interested in making a loan of this nature to Jerry was very beneficial to SLR, and it was not illegal. However, at the time, I did not think I was required to make a disclosure to our auditors. Of course, that would have been the "safe" thing to do, even if there was no legal issue. However, I did not give this matter much thought because of the very hectic time of the year involving our National Sales Meeting.

It has been disclosed that this loan functioned very efficiently. It was paid off according to the terms of the loan agreement in a timely fashion. Most importantly, it gave SLR sufficient working capital to make the necessary commitments to market the MiMedx product line broadly in their territory. They certainly did so. Within the first two years, SLR developed over $15 million in revenues and certainly proved to be an excellent replacement for the CPM business in Texas. This business success was never discussed by the prosecutors. In fact, the judge had decreed that there would be no discussion of MiMedx's business successes or activities after the late 2015 period. Does that make sense when trying to properly assess the reasons we made our decisions, which were in question? Absolutely not. More SDNY manipulation of fair and reasonable justice.

Curtailing Available Court Time

When Judge Rakoff brought up the change in court schedule on the morning of November 12th, he did not allow time for the parties to leave the courtroom and have discussions. I still do not know why our attorneys did not at least voice serious objections at the time. They were certainly warranted. However, I guess they wanted to conference together and make a joint decision. That occurred that evening.

When we convened in a conference room after the court session that day, our attorneys had already discussed the situation and made their decision. They told Bill and me that they believed we needed to tell the judge that we would not testify. And, they would tell the judge that no witnesses would be called to testify either. They stated that they believed they had done an excellent job of cross-examining the government's witnesses, and they would have a superb closing statement so our testimony was not needed. I vehemently disagreed with their conclusions. I told them that I did not believe this jury was well enough informed on the key issues and that they had heard nothing but twisted facts and lies. I said that I did not think there was any way to fully correct that misinformation except with Bill's and my testimonies. I remember saying that I did not believe this jury even understood what the word "scienter" meant or its implications. One of my counsel members spoke up and said that they had mentioned it several times. I replied that just mentioning something does not bring finality to the learning process.

Our attorneys' arguments that we not testify were related to the amount of time remaining to finish the trial. About eight days would be left in the trial after the prosecutors finished. Then, there would be two days allocated to the AUSA's closing statements. Our attorneys felt that five days would need to be allocated to my testimony, four days allocated to Bill's, two days for our closing, and we would still not have time to bring up any witnesses. Therefore, my attorneys' conclusion was that we should simply tell the judge that we were not going to offer any testimony at all.

Our attorneys certainly understood that I wanted to testify. However I reluctantly changed my mind, particularly in light of our legal team being so adamant that Bill and I did not need to testify because of their supposedly good cross-examination results. I felt that this obvious manipulation by the court would serve us well with our appeal. As it turned out, it did not because our attorneys did not appropriately document this incident during the trial!

I felt that this timing change had been contrived by the court. I remember the trial date being moved around four different times in the last couple of months before trial. I could not figure out why the SDNY could not set a trial date and maintain it. It may have been that they realized they were going to shut down the court after Thanksgiving, and thus, were trying to set a start date that would be detrimental to us when that stop date was finally disclosed during the trial. In fact, this court's manipulation of the trial schedule put us in the position of not being able to offer any counter testimony, which was the coup de grace for our case.

Closing Statements

Relative to the closing statements, AUSA Imperator made the government's argument. It was even more frustrating than their opening remarks. Bill and I were characterized as consummate liars. Imperatore even insinuated that our attorneys were dishonest as well because they had called out the prosecutors and their programmed witnesses for not telling the truth. Our attorneys did not call out the corrupt behavior of the prosecutors as effectively as did Howard Root's. Remember, they won the Vascular Solutions case in San Antonio.

At that point, I felt strongly that the prosecutors would win the final argument as neither Bill nor I nor any of our witnesses had been able to testify because of Judge Rakoff's surprise that the trial would be cut short and ended by Thanksgiving. I had received a real education reinforcing things that I had read and been told about the legal process at the SDNY and the court and prosecutors' behavior.

The prosecutors were still throwing out the accusation that I had bribed the CPR principal, Brooks, into making his required quarterly order in the second quarter of 2015 because we had sent him a check for $200,000. The prosecutors knew that this check was for MiMedx violating Brook's distributor contract for exclusivity in the state of Texas. Our GPOs had sold into numerous hospitals in Texas, and until the end of June of 2015, no one had brought that transgression to my attention. I knew it was irrefutable and must be resolved, or Brooks would sue us. The relationship was bad enough without leaving a major issue of this nature overhanging the financial activities.

Prosecutors knew this fact because our General Counsel, Lexi Haden, had given them a proffer to that effect. When they gave us the Brady materials, it included Lexi's testimony, or proffer, to the prosecutors. Lexi stated that I told her what had happened with my negotiations with Brooks. I had written him a letter of apology and began to discuss and negotiate a settlement, which turned out to be the $200,000 for lost CPM business as a result of our national GPO contract. Lexi made it very clear that I had explained the matter to her and how I had resolved it. She said she made a mistake in not papering the transaction as a "Settlement Agreement." She just told the accounting department to send the $200,000 check.

Now for these government attorneys to have continued to call that $200,000 a bribe on my part to obtain the CPM quarterly order, when I had already essentially written CPM off because I was terminating our relationship, is an absolute blight on the integrity of those prosecutors. There were many other issues that they brought up, and all of them had the same dishonesty associated with them in terms of the way they twisted the facts. This particular issue was especially onerous to me because they took testimony from another attorney. While they had no respect for business executives, they certainly should have for our General Counsel, particularly when compared to the lies and confusing statements we heard from two former salespeople who became manipulated government witnesses.

The prosecutors also spent time in the closing remarks attempting to make the jury believe that I was some type of business criminal because I had told employees as well as shareholders that the revenue growth in MiMedx was very important relative to the evaluation of our stock. The faster a business entity is growing, the bigger the multiple that shareholders should place on their revenue and earnings because in a future period of time, the company will be larger and more valuable. It is a very simple business concept, and it is a well-known basic valuation technique used by investors. To these prosecutors, this was valuable to help twist facts…nothing more!

It was disgusting that these attorneys sought a way to make it look as though I was so obsessed with this growth metric that I would commit crimes to falsely inflate it. I had served for 37 years as a public company officer, and MiMedx had been one of the absolute stars. You do not manage the fifth fastest-growing public company in America according to *Fortune* magazine by not having a great deal of business experience and knowing how to apply that experience. I was paid to manage the company to produce revenue and earnings growth and increase the company's value! And, our team and I did so with honesty, integrity and very hard work.

The Verdicts

Late on the morning of November 17th, the jury notified the judge that they had reached a verdict. They were called back to the courtroom along with all of us.

Judge Rakoff's meaningful comments began with, "I will open the verdict envelope. It appears to be in proper form. I will give it to the foreperson. Mr. Foreperson, please rise."

"On count one, the charge of conspiracy to commit securities fraud, making false filings with the Securities and Exchange Commission, and/or mislead MiMedx's auditors, do you, the jury, find Mr. Petit guilty or not guilty?"

FOREPERSON: Not guilty.

THE COURT: On count two, the charge of securities fraud, do you, the jury, find Mr. Petit guilty or not guilty?

FOREPERSON: Guilty.

THE COURT: On count one, the charge of conspiracy to commit securities fraud, make false filings with the Securities Exchange Commission, and/or mislead MiMedx's auditors, do you, the jury, find William Taylor guilty or not guilty?

FOREPERSON: Guilty.

THE COURT: On count two, the charge of securities fraud, do you, the jury, find William Taylor guilty or not guilty?

FOREPERSON: Not guilty.

The judge went on to tell the jury that they did not have to talk to anyone, including lawyers, about what transpired during their deliberations. Judge Rakoff stated that it was his personal recommendation that if they (our attorneys) wanted to talk to them, they should say no, and they will, of course, not pursue it further. But it was their decision to make.

More lack of transparency in the SDNY justice system!

After our verdicts were delivered, the judge began to detail some of the administrative issues that needed to be addressed. Most importantly to me was when the sentencing would take place. I was told that it generally took 90 days for that process to play out.

In the courtroom that day, the judge gave us the dates that he would announce our sentences. I was told that my sentence would be given on February 23rd, and Bill's would be announced the next day. Therefore, we did have approximately 90 days for the court to receive additional documents and for the judge to administer his sentences.

Company Request

After the trial was over, MiMedx's lawyers came forward with a request that Judge Rakoff grant the company restitution for the legal fees they had paid for Bill Taylor's and my defense. The judge asked a few questions, and then he quickly made up his mind. He basically said that the company had no right to request legal fees as restitution because we were both acting as agents of the company. Of course, that is not what the company wanted to hear. I do not know if Judge Rakoff even realized that the company had already taken all of our stock options and stock grants, and they had not provided severance to us.

The company decided to file a lawsuit against us to retrieve those legal fees. This case was filed in Florida, which is where the company was founded. Subsequently, I decided to file a lawsuit against the company to re-institute some of the stock options that the Board took from me about 75 days after I agreed to resign. Many of those options were initally granted on the basis that I worked for several years at about half the salary I had at my last company, Matria Healthcare.

The company recently attempted to have my lawsuit dismissed, and the judge ruled that was not in order. Thus, these suits are still in effect as I complete the book.

Sentencing

In the ensuing weeks and months, we were instructed by our attorneys as to the documents that we needed to prepare prior to the sentencing. Most importantly, we were told to obtain letters of recommendation from approximately 20 people, including family members, which were to be sent directly to the judge. We were told that we would have a great deal of interaction with a parole officer in New York City. In that process, our detailed financial statements would need to be prepared and provided. Also, they would take testimony as to our childhood and upbringing, our lifestyle and our current personal situation. In other words, a thorough personal and financial analysis would be prepared by the parole officer in New York City. Subsequently, the parole officer would make a recommendation to the judge as to the sentence he felt the judge should impose.

In addition, my lawyers explained that my philanthropy should give the judge reason to consider my being given home confinement, particularly if I could provide consulting benefit to the numerous charities that I was supporting financially. At that point, there were three charities with which I interfaced routinely that were in their growth phases where perhaps my management expertise could provide important advice. Therefore, I connected with the founders of these charities, and all three executives said they would welcome my involvement in any way the court would allow. Of course, there would be no compensation to me for contributing time to these charitable enterprises.

This certainly appealed to me because <u>my</u> <u>major</u> <u>concern</u> about being incarcerated was that I would be "wasting time." At this point in the book, you probably understand that I am not an individual who "twiddles my thumbs," but I am generally involved in some type of business or philanthropic deliberations on a day-to-day basis. The founders and Board members of these three charitable organizations wrote very strong letters of recommendation asking that I be allowed to have home incarceration so I could routinely consult with their organizations.

Thus, we went into the day of the sentencing with some positive thoughts about my being able to provide free consulting services to three very worthy charities at a point in their growth where my experience would have been valuable. However, I would be under "house arrest" during that period of time, and I would have to work out, with a parole officer, the times I would be allowed to visit with management at the facilities of these organizations.

Bill and I were given the choice to return to New York, be quarantined again and appear in person in Judge Rakoff's court for our sentencing or appear by video-conference. We were told by our legal counsel that the judge would probably be more favorably impressed if we were to appear before him face-to-face. Bill decided to return to New York and be in Judge Rakoff's courtroom for his sentencing. I decided that I did not want to go back to New York because of their quarantine requirements and other odd COVID 19 processes. I decided that I would appear on video in front of the judge. I felt the judge would be able to look me very carefully in the face as my video appeared on his screen. Therefore, I did this by video-conference sitting in my dining room at my home.

One very important part of providing the judge information prior to the sentencing was the personal letter that Bill and I were allowed to send him. I received a good deal of advice from my lawyers in terms of what the letter should and should not say. As I would have expected, they were very wary of me speaking my heart in a sincere manner to Judge Rakoff. They reminded me of his personal characteristics, and how I would probably do myself serious damage if I spoke to him honestly in the way that I wanted to do. I had presented to my lawyers a draft of what I was going to say to the judge very early in this process. I could tell that none of them had anything positive to say about my comments. By this point in time, I fully realized that my legal team was not very astute in the matter of influencing people!

In my letter, I spoke my mind very honestly and frankly with my normal degree of courtesy, which was certainly warranted in this situation. While my legal group made numerous cautionary comments, a few of which I accepted, the letter that I presented was very frank and straightforward. After the judge finished giving me my sentence, he actually added a complimentary statement. Judge Rakoff said, "With respect to specific deterrence, this is an unusual case because Mr. Petit still denies his guilt. In some ways, I admire that because in so many cases I face the crocodile tears of people who are saying, 'Oh, I'm so sorry, your honor,' and all like that when what they really mean is 'I'm so sorry I got caught.'" I believe that says it all as to how my letter affected Judge Rakoff's sentencing in my case.

Relative to the sentencing, I was given one year of incarceration in a federal prison camp and a $1,000,000 fine. The prison camp is the lowest level of correctional imprisonment. Also, due to my bladder cancer, the judge was going to recommend that I be sent to the federal facility in Lexington, Kentucky, which had a federal medical center (FMC) supported by the University of Kentucky College of Medicine, or as a backup, their facility in Butner, NC, which had a relationship with the Duke University School of Medicine. Later, the decision was made to send me to the Butner facility in the Durham area.

As I have previously stated in this book, you know that I have strong feelings and frustrations over the fact that this trial in the Southern District of New York was so unbalanced in favor of the prosecution. You also know that neither Bill nor I nor any of our witnesses ever testified during the trial. This was primarily because the judge waited until the prosecution had used up over three quarters of the time that, unbeknownst to us, was going to be allocated. Then Judge Rakoff announced that his court would be shut down by Thanksgiving due to Covid. He asked the prosecutors how much longer they needed, and they said another week. He told them they could not have another week, but he would give them three more days. Well, the prosecutors had opened the trial, and this was the fourth week of the trial. Therefore, they were going to get four weeks, and we would get what was left prior to Thanksgiving. It really came down to our getting less than seven days. This shows you the very unbalanced nature of the way a trial can take place when a federal court has a propensity to manipulate.

So, considering what we had been through and the total lack of "due process" from the King & Spalding report and the justice system, I considered the sentence the judge administered to me as fair. Since our jury heard nothing from Bill or me or our witnesses, but only from the prosecution and their witnesses, I am surprised we did as well as we did with half of the indictment charges against Bill and me being eliminated. I firmly believe that, had we been allowed to testify and clear up the confusion that the prosecution created, we would have been exonerated. However, as I just stated, my feeling was that we received a fair sentence considering the information a jury of blue-collar individuals managed to assimilate and make a judgment on without any testimony from the defendants.

Vengeance

I have been reasonably at peace with what has transpired in our trial, our sentencing and incarceration. While there are a number of individuals whom I consider to be dishonest, corrupt, without integrity, involved with self-dealing, and in some cases incompetent, I realize that what has happened to Bill and me can unfortunately happen to any public company executive in this country. While there were circumstances that could have played out somewhat differently, once issues come together with the same abhorrent motivations of a number of individuals, there will be some, "Bad things that happen to good people."

I have been asked numerous times as to what I would like to see happen to the individuals that caused the trials and tribulations for the company, the management and employees as well as the 15,000 MiMedx shareholders. During my adult life,

I have always managed to tell myself that, "Vengeance is the Lord's." Thus, when I find myself getting upset with the behavior of one of the several individuals that caused this corporate tragedy, I simply go back and repeat that any retribution or vengeance associated with MiMedx becoming this Poster Child is none of my business. I am to do what I can to learn from the experience, explain clearly to as many people as possible exactly what transpired, and, hopefully, help others never suffer the same tragic circumstances. Also, as often happens with a Poster Child, larger groups of people with influence will become involved and begin to clarify and change the numerous problems that cause these types of personal and corporate tragedies.

Closure

Generally, every new business start-up encounters enough challenges in becoming a growing and profitable business without the added burden of excessive legal and regulatory issues. Today, there are many examples of new federal regulations and laws that severely curtail new business development and hinder existing businesses effectively operating in certain environments. Healthcare is particularly susceptible to these various new mandates.

When business executives begin to seek advice on these regulations and laws, they necessarily turn to lawyers and law firms. The real challenge is that most lawyers are going to say, "Don't, don't, and by the way, don't." The executive who is compensated to manage "risk and return" must balance the "no" environment created by lawyers and the "go" environment requested by shareholders.

I have stated many times that Bill Taylor and I were never given due process of the law during the King & Spalding investigation or in our trial. These were obvious corrupt manipulations by the court prosecutors and former prosecutors. This is something you will probably encounter. You must be proactive if you find yourself confronting such an experience.

I have discussed some of the frustrations in our trial with my attempts to have our lawyers conduct their activities in a way that somewhat paralleled business processes. However, I found out, as did Conrad Black, Howard Root and Raj Rajaratnam, that it is a very difficult thing to accomplish. Lawyers have their way of preparing for trials and their "theatrical performances," and that will not align with the ways that business executives bring success to their numerous projects.

Relative to actual testimony in the trial, I gave some examples of how our two former salesmen, who had been manipulated into testifying against Bill and me, gave their testimonies. The extent to which prosecutors can intimidate and threaten witnesses into testifying to "their truth" is really beyond imagination. We have many examples in our case, unfortunately. So did Conrad Black, Howard Root and Raj Rajaratnam.

In their closing remarks, our prosecutor continued with their "name-calling." Since the jury never heard or received testimony from Bill and me, they had no idea of the type of people we were or how corrupt the trial has been. Had we been allowed to testify, I believe our honesty and integrity would have been evident. However, we had been called all kind of names during the trial, and I am sure there is often a resentment of anyone who has accumulated some wealth during their career. Thus, we had that built-in bias.

Our Trial Appeal

We did appeal the results of our trial.

My insights are that most initial appeals are a waste of time because they generally go back to a panel of three judges who are part of that trial district of the Department of Justice. Therefore, the judges are all part of the "fraternity." I thought we would have an excellent appeal opportunity because of the way in which we were manipulated into not being able to give any defense testimony and the perjury from at least two DOJ witnesses. However, because of legal technicalities, those issues could not be brought up in our appeal. My appeal attorney developed some highly sophisticated legal nuances, and the panel of judges created some very confusing counter-arguments. Therefore, our very expensive legal appeal really went nowhere.

Just be careful if you get to the point of deciding whether or not to appeal your court decision. I believe that positive outcomes are very rare in most DOJ districts.

CHAPTER 25

INCARCERATION

As I began to prepare for my incarceration on September 21, 2021, a number of issues began to surface that reflect back on the justice system. I was given the names of two institutions, one of which would be where I would serve my time. Both had a federal medical center (FMC) on the premises. Because of my bladder cancer, which had been described to Judge Rakoff with some degree of detail, he rightly decided to place me in one of these FMC facilities. One was in Lexington, Kentucky, where most of the non-staff medical professionals were affiliated with the University of Kentucky College of Medicine. The second one was located in Butner, North Carolina where the medical professionals came from the Duke University School of Medicine. I was initially told I would be going to the Lexington facility.

As I recall, it was in July when I received another communication from the Bureau of Prisons (BOP) stating that I would now be going to Butner FMC in North Carolina, which was about 20 miles north of Durham. When I looked up the facility and began to gather information, I noted there was a lawsuit against the institution filed by 20 inmates because a COVID epidemic had been allowed to develop in the prison. Because of my weakened immune system due to my cancer, I was very concerned that going to a facility, which had an epidemic that possibly would take some time to control, would not be a wise thing to do. Therefore, we asked Judge Rakoff to delay my reporting for a month or two. He granted a one-month delay until October 21st.

Then, we found out through our BOP consultants, all of who were generally former BOP managers or wardens, that I would not be allowed to take the adjuvant drug for my bladder cancer that had been so successful in keeping it in remission. We were in contact with a retired manager who had been responsible for all the medical activities at BOP facilities across the United States. He told us there were specific medical product protocols that the BOP would never violate. One of these protocols was that any product used in a federal prison would have to be "FDA Approved" or "FDA Cleared." The drug I was taking was being used "off label." I will not go into all the details associated with that descriptor, but it did not meet BOP standards and criteria, which is understandable.

After a year and a half of the standard treatment for bladder cancer failing to put my cancer in remission, I began taking Fenbendazole, which is a drug that is used in veterinary medicine in the U.S. Once I started taking Fenbendazole, my cancer went into remission. A derivative from this family of drugs, Mebendazole, has been approved for human use in some European countries for removing parasites from the intestinal tract just as it is used with animals. If I could not take the Fenbendazole in prison, we were hoping the BOP would allow me to take Mebendazole.

As expected, the BOP responded with numerous excuses as to why they would not allow me to take either form of the drug while in their institution. They claimed that, if my cancer returned while I was incarcerated, they would administer the approved treatment for bladder cancer, and their care was going to be excellent. That is what I was told when I started the normal protocol for bladder cancer in June of 2018, but my cancer returned and was removed every 90 days.

So, we contacted the judge explaining to him that I, like 30 percent of the other individuals who had my type of bladder cancer, had been unable to stop the return of the cancer using conventional protocols and treatments. The cancer continued to recur, even after having been surgically removed from the bladder. Subsequently, the cancer can become embedded in the wall of the bladder, which requires removal of the bladder. After that, this cancer generally escapes into the rest of the body, and one's life expectancy is modified considerably. Regardless, I was denied this adjuvant drug during my incarceration.

Now, let me explain a concern that I had at this point. Because the facility to which I was to report had been moved from the Lexington, Kentucky FMC, where the female warden had been liberal in giving CARES Act releases, to the Butner federal facility, where the warden had given very few, I began to get suspicious, particularly since that venue change came right before I was to report. It seemed as though I was being set up to be unable to obtain a CARES Act release because of the change of venue to Butner and the attitude of the warden there. I had been told by numerous knowledgeable former BOP managers that I was the epitome of a candidate who would be eligible for a compassionate release under the First Step Act or CARES Act. However, the warden at Butner was not granting many of those releases so it would not matter that my situation matched perfectly with the criteria for those releases. Therefore, I would remain incarcerated for the full year. I though that one year without Fenbendazole or a similar off-label drug could have been my death sentence.

As it turned out, I was released under the CARES Act to home confinement after six months. I had an appointment with my urologist in Atlanta two days after I came home. He checked me and found my cancer was still in remission, but it unfortunately returned some months later.

Prison Camps

As you may recall, Bill and I were both given a one-year sentence to be served in a federal prison camp. A prison camp is the lowest level of security. Bill was sent to a camp on Maxwell Air Force Base in Montgomery, Alabama. I also would have gone there had I not had bladder cancer. I was sent to a medical care unit on the Butner Federal Correctional Complex in North Carolina. We had very different experiences in a number of ways!

Bill's confinement was largely with white-collar criminal inmates. Since I was in a facility that cared for critically ill patients, I was with inmates that had sentences all the way up to life imprisonment. I began acquiring a real education on how our justice system has changed for individuals since 1994 when the "Crack Law" was passed. This law has become another financial windfall for state and federal attorneys and the legal support structures for those accused of a crime as well as those who are already incarcerated. The Supreme Court has ruled that incarceration for individuals processed under the 1994 Crack Law has resulted in violations of the U.S. Constitution. More thoughts on these issues later.

Facilities

My experience at Butner left me with the feeling that the hospital facilities were reasonably adequate. I was on a floor with about 150 other cancer patients. There were two patients to a room.

I felt that management of the staff and their communication systems were inadequate. Primary communication with staff, other than medical staff, was through a form called a "cop-out." The problem with this process was that the form was a single piece of paper. It was filled out specifying a problem or a request, and then it was dropped in a box. There was no way to determine if it had been received or if any action could be expected. Now, where there was some accountability was the facility email system. I had much more staff response because there was a record in the email system that could be called out. The problem with the email system was the difficulty in getting to a computer to send the communication because you could not leave your room when you or the unit was in "lockdown," which was quite often.

I was in lockdown for over 30 percent of my time at Butner. It started with my first 17 days of incarceration for COVID quarantine, then another 11 days when I contracted COVID. Another 16 days was due to overall COVID lockdowns and about seven days for a national prison lockdown because of a murder in a Texas prison. There were numerous other lockdowns as well because of staff absences and other administrative issues.

COVID Issues

Because of the COVID epidemic, most prisons were having numerous problems providing their previously available services, which is certainly understandable. Lunchrooms, gyms, visitation, and all education programs had been shut down at Butner. My biggest frustration was the lack of communication during lockdown. I was unable talk to my wife for about 20 days at one point.

Were it not for the COVID epidemic, the prison programs were broad and more than sufficient to fill most prisoner needs. There were religious, educational, psychological, exercise, healthcare, occupational and entertainment programs. However, during my "internment" most of these programs except healthcare were canceled. Some were beginning to be reopened when the Omicron variant hit, and the shutdowns started again.

I was one of the first inmates to be tested for COVID after the Omicron variant developed. I tested positive. Of course, my cellmate did also. In fact, he brought the virus to our cell probably from the staff of an outside medical care vendor that he had spent some time with a few days prior. He developed a cough, but he thought it was caused by the chemotherapy treatments he had been given for his lung cancer. I quickly developed the worst sore throat I have ever had which triggered my visit to the medical staff on a sick call.

Incidentally, the Butner medical staff was highly trained members of the U.S. Public Health Service. My interactions with those staff members were always very professional. Their involvement, interactions and activities with inmates were managed by Butner staff, which is where issues would develop.

Incarceration Friend

I would like to briefly mention an individual who became my best friend during my six months of incarceration, and who I expect to remain a best friend for the remainder of my life. I will call him "Nat." "Nat" has been incarcerated for 28 years. He is serving a sentence of 32 years. I have listened to his explanation of his incarcerations. I have heard him tell of the various manipulations by prosecutors, public defense attorneys and the system in general. He should never have gone to jail particularly for half his life.

I found "Nat" to be a caring and compassionate individual. In fact, the Butner warden called him the "mayor of the fourth floor," which was the cancer unit, because of the way that he continually demonstrated compassion and assisted all inmates. He was our leader, and he went out of his way every day to help his fellow inmates with their personal problems as well as legal matters.

I spent a lot of time during my six months of incarceration trying to understand clearly what was right and what was wrong with the prison system as it exists today. I heard many discussions about how unfairly prosecutors had treated these individuals, all who were trying to use public defenders in their cases. Basically, the public defenders are dependent on the prosecutors for their cases. Therefore, what happens to the accused? Well, I have been told that the public defenders are "forced" to advise their client what the prosecutor wants them to do so they can <u>win</u> their case with extended prision sentences. It is all about the prosecutors!

I spent some time with "Nat" teaching him basic accounting principles. He is very set on starting a small trucking company when he finishes his incarceration. I also gave him some insight on how to write a business plan. He and I discussed some of his business thoughts, which proved to be very good, frankly. He has a lot of common sense and no PTSD even after 28 years of incarceration. "Nat" is a "blessed" human being!

Halfway Houses

As I have previously mentioned, the United States has 25 percent of the world's incarcerated prisoners while being only 5 percent of the world's population. Our incarceration rates are many times those of the major European countries on a per capita basis. We have 14.40 times the number of practicing attorneys as Japan,

2.10 times as many as Germany, 3.94 times as many as France and 1.85 times as many as England.

Our overpopulation of lawyers has resulted in extreme dislocations in numerous places within our economy. This particularly affects our overly litigious nature and, more importantly, our federal justice system. Finally, over-incarcerations bears heavily on certain segments of our populations where distortions in their family life have left them more susceptible to crime and even more liable to receive unbalanced incarceration. While we MUST be tough on crime, leaving sentencing basically up to prosecutors has left the US with <u>unreasonably lengthy</u> prison sentences.

Under the halfway house program, there are many benefits. If you have the right credentials and no behavior issues, you can find a job and become fully employed. However, you will still have your ankle monitor, and you will still have to report in as you move around the city with your job. They do not provide opportunities for what I would call recreational meetings. However, if you hold a job, you are generally given substantial leeway to conduct your business activities. I certainly applaud the halfway house program. It should be used <u>much more broadly</u>.

The First Step Act and The CARES Act

We should all be thankful to President Trump for taking the initial steps in focusing on some of these factors that have distorted our life and economy so dramatically. President Trump's first initiative was called the First Step Act. This act is formally known as the Formerly Incarcerated Reenter Society Transformed Safely Transitioning Every Person Act. The passage of this act resulted in several changes in U.S. federal criminal law aimed at reforming federal sentencing laws in order to reduce recidivism, decrease the federal inmate population and maintain public safety. This act was passed in December of 2018.

As a means of further providing opportunities for early release of prisoners to home confinement because of the COVID pandemic, the CARES Act was passed with the specific eligibility requirements set forth in memoranda from Attorney General Barr on March 26th and April 3rd of 2020. Attorney General Barr's providing specifics related to this program made it very effective.

Once I was incarcerated at Butner, I began to finish my research, and I had numerous questions answered on these two laws. What I determined was that, at Butner, the definition for eligibility for transfer to a home environment was relatively strict. The way it was defined at Butner was that a prisoner needed to be terminally ill and expected to pass away within the next 18 months before they were eligible for release to home confinement under the First Step Act. I was told that numerous other prisons had much less stringent requirements for early release to home confinement.

I found out that the CARES Act, as defined through Attorney General Barr's memoranda, contained more specific rules. For instance, his memoranda stated that a prisoner was eligible for transfer to home confinement after they had served at least 25 percent of their sentence and had less than 18 months left to serve. That aligned with Bill and me only having a one-year sentence. Thus, after being imprisoned for 90 days, we were theoretically eligible for home confinement. However, there was certain paperwork that had to be filled out and approved in order to start the process. Generally, the prison was required to notify the inmate of their eligibility and give them the paperwork to complete. At Bill's institution, the federal prison camp at Maxwell Air Force Base, Alabama, one case manager was very focused on matters of this nature. Bill was given his paperwork within two days of his eligibility date. At my institution, the administrative processes were either not well managed or were manipulated. I did not obtain my application until several weeks after my eligibility date, and it only arrived after my attorney wrote a letter to the warden. I subsequently experienced several other unreasonable delays. Consequently, I was not released to home confinement until I had served approximately six months of my sentence. Bill was released to home confinement after he had served about four and a half months.

I think the CARES Act is a real opportunity for wardens to considerably reduce the overpopulation of our prisons. However, there will be different philosophical attitudes about early release depending on the warden's experience and even their DNA. Please recall that the United States has 25 percent of the world's incarcerated prisoners, but has only five percent of the world's population. That says it all!

After having met and becoming friends with a number of my fellow inmates, I believe that many of them should already be eligible for home confinement under the CARES Act and this process should be expedited due to over incarceration. As far as release under the First Step Act, if a prison requires that the criteria for early release be a terminal illness with an expected death within 18 months, I believe that criteria should be much less restrictive.

I believe that our prison system is ridiculously <u>over</u> populated because of <u>over</u> sentencing which primarily stems from the use of the 1994 Crack Laws that allow a current sentencing to be significantly increased if prior convictions exist. Many prosecutors use this law to over incarcerate for their own benefit.

Released

I was released from Butner Federal Medical Center to home confinement on April 20th of 2022. I was incarcerated on October 21st, 2021. Therefore, I served basically six months of my one-year sentence in a prison hospital. I flew back to Atlanta from the Raleigh Durham airport by myself. My wife picked me up at the airport, and we drove over to the Atlanta halfway house. This halfway house is one of about 40 houses run under the Dismas Charities organization.

I was told that I would have to be there for several hours while I filled out paperwork and sat through some education programs. However, after being there for many hours, I was told that I was going to have to remain there for several days because they did not have any ankle monitors. I asked some of the normal questions because I could not quite understand why an operation with so many halfway houses across the country could not manage their inventory sufficiently well to keep ankle monitors available. It took six days before I was fitted with the ankle monitor so Janet could pick me up and take me home!

It was wonderful being home with my wife. On the next Saturday, visitation by my children and grandchildren began. And, very soon thereafter, we had a dinner party for a number of our former managers at MiMedx, Matria Healthcare and Healthdyne.

For me, being able to have a cell phone and iPad was the restart of my life! I realize that sounds a little narrow, but I love to interact with people, and I love to have something productive to do on a daily basis. This book has certainly provided that opportunity... as you can tell!

CHAPTER 26

THE SUMMARY

I have looked forward to writing this chapter for a long time. By now, I am sure many of you have been looking more and more forward to reaching this portion of the book! I know there were a lot of facts in the book. That was because numerous issues created this story. Each needed to be told, and there were a number of details within each issue. Much information to be assimilated and many lessons to be taught! Also, I apolgize for the repetition, but hopefully, it has improved your retention!

I primarily wrote this book for entrepreneurs, future entrepreneurs, business executives, particularly those involved with publicly traded companies, and their shareholders. I was the Chairman and/or CEO of public companies that I basically founded for over 37 years. Thus, I have had a chance to see the U.S. stock markets change in many ways. A few of these changes benefited American investors, but most only benefited Wall Street firms, government prosecutors and other opportunists.

I briefly reviewed the results of the passage of the Sarbanes-Oxley legislation that was designed to prevent financial misinformation being disseminated by publicly traded companies, such as happened at Enron. The Enron situation resulted in the demise of the Arthur Andersen accounting firm and the loss of 85,000 jobs. However, the Supreme Court ultimately overturned the DOJ's case against Arthur Anderson! You should now understand the self-serving reasons DOJ prosecutors caused that legal debacle and the resulting business loss of all those professional jobs.

Over the last 40 years, I have watched as Wall Street changed their trading systems, processes and procedures and some of their "schemes." I have witnessed the development of our "new" justice system. There are a number of these changes that make being an officer of a public company much more difficult and very risky. I believe that MiMedx has been a poster child for the majority of the negative issues that have developed and matured in the current stock market and justice system we have today.

These numerous legal and regulatory issues are easily discovered by following the money trail to the organizations or individuals. They occur in the heart and soul of individuals, the personalities of corporate entities and in federal governmental agencies who have little accountability. With such a diverse set of causes and effects, correcting the trends will not be easy.

I believe that resolving the significant loss of honesty and intergrity in our justice system will require a change of political leadership. Also, the chronic misrepresentations by our mainstream media can only be corrected by a well managed boycott of their advertisers. Therefore, it would be beneficial if I briefly review some of the key issues that bear so directly on these matters.

Whistleblower Laws

The Whistleblower Protection Act was modified by President Obama in 2012 to give whistleblowers more protection! A federal judge told me in 2006 that he thought the whistleblower laws were "some of the worst laws that Congress had ever passed." He felt they are unfair and unreasonable and do not provide a balanced environment for corporate entities. He said too much power has been given to people who could also be corrupt themselves…employees, other individuals, other opportunists plus their attorneys.

I believe we gave several examples of the power that whistleblowers have today, particularly if given questionable advice from their legal counsel. Unfortunately, since whistleblowers themselves are not held accountable for violating specific federal laws or regulations, such as lying to federal officials, the situation is bordering on being out of control. Any corporate employee who is dishonest enough can create a situation in which the company may be given advice by certain law firms to just pay a settlement and move on. That is what I call, "Doing the easy thing, not the right thing."

I think I made it clear that it is very difficult for a corporate entity and its executives to protect themselves from this type of behavior. While the regulations and laws are fairly straightforward, a corporate entity has no advantages in a situation of this nature. Frankly, I do not know how you can effectively prepare yourself for whistleblowers. I do not believe that business executives will ever have sufficient screening ability to determine if a potential hire will behave in a corrupt manner or be dishonest at some point in their career. For top-level management and even Board members, please consider using an industrial psychologist to do a thorough personality analysis.

It is my belief that the only way the Whistleblower Act will be fully fair to all parties is for our laws to be equally enforced. In other words, when a whistleblower brings false information or lies to a federal agency, they should be held accountable. This means that they understand clearly the penalties for misrepresenting facts to the government.

Now, I certainly realize that there are corporate entities in America that may need and deserve to have whistleblower actions filed against them. However, I believe whistleblower cases have grown immensely over the last 10 years because of employees who are dishonest and the lawyers who have little scruples representing them. Another look at the whistleblower regulations is necessary to ensure that they become balanced in a way that assures all allegations given to the government are true and honest. In order to make it clear that corrupt whistleblowers <u>will</u> <u>be</u> prosecuted, many legal cases of misinformation being given to prosecutors would have to be brought. Otherwise, whistleblowing will become another destructive "racket" that primarily benefits certain lawers and their dishonest clients.

Illegal Short Selling

The problems associated with short selling and illegal short selling are well known in <u>all</u> <u>the</u> <u>right</u> <u>places</u>! Congress and federal regulators have supposedly attempted to make changes to correct the unwanted issues associated with illegal short selling. However, nothing effective has transpired, and those previous efforts have been a waste of time. There has been no real attempt to prosecute the corrupt individuals who are attracted to this process. The Securities and Exchange Commission has overall responsibility, but they have demonstrated no real interest in bringing significant cases that would help resolve this travesty. There are other semi-governmental entities that have also abandoned their responsibility related to illegal short selling.

The SEC and DOJ are well aware of the problems that illegal short selling causes and the huge profits made by certain individuals, hedge funds and other entities. These matters have been called to their attention by Congressional committees and numerous individuals over the years. I sincerely believe the primary reason that this agency does not want to stop short selling is because <u>alleged</u> white-collar crime allegations, which are routinely brought by illegal short sellers, are cherished by the government staff attorneys. I believe there are numerous lawyers at these agencies who are willing to listen to the lies and innuendo of short sellers just to be able to file a case against an individual or corporate entity. In my research, I was <u>unable</u> to find a <u>major</u> illegal short selling case brought to trial by the SEC or DOJ. I have presented several instances that occurred in the MiMedx situation where it was quite evident that the SEC did not want to pursue our short sellers and neither did DOJ prosecutors at the SDNY, in spite of their own investigators feeling different.

Regulator Transgressions

First and foremost, I have commented a great deal about the problem of federal prosecutors misusing their positions and their power. A prosecutor represents the key position in our justice system. As federal prosecutors, these attorneys have extremely broad discretion and little effective supervision or accountability. They are immune from lawsuits, even when they orchestrate deliberate wrongdoings. Prosecutors have unlimited discretion when it comes to obtaining and executing search warrants and the resulting arrest. When they do <u>their job</u> of "witness tampering," they develop cooperation agreements that produce less than accurate testimony. These acts would amount to extortion if they were not made by a prosecutor. I gave you an example of my five-minute meeting with Mike Carlton and the prosecutors meeting with him for probably 60 hours. Yet, it was insinuated that I did the witness tampering!

With the publication of the Sally Yates Doctrine, America now has a new issue relative to prosecutorial abuse, and that is called "targeting" which requires prosecutors to focus on the top executives of companies that are the subject of allegations. Targeting is one of the <u>corrupt issues</u> that Attorney General Robert Jackson so eloquently highlighted to his prosecutors. I do not believe that Sally Yates ever read any of his very wise documents and comments on this subject.

Again, relying on the wisdom of Attorney General Jackson, he commented on the ability of a prosecutor to find a violation of some act on the part of almost anyone. He stated, "Prosecutors can easily succumb to the temptation of first picking the man and then searching the law books or putting investigators to work to pin some offense on him." Attorney General Jackson strongly condemned this unscrupulous behavior back in 1940. However, these "targeting" actions are now <u>encouraged</u> by the Sally Yates Doctrine.

I also highlighted the rapid rate at which new regulations and laws have been passed by Congress over the recent decades. Prosecutors have become very creative at turning minor or no violations of federal regulations into crimes. That occurs when they allege a "conspiracy violation" or invoke the "aiding and abetting statute." I noted where our judge, Jed Rakoff, had commented in an article in the New York Review of Books "It is the prosecutor, not the judge, who effectively exercises the sentencing power, albeit cloaked as a charging decision." The federal sentencing guidelines are the basis for this abuse by federal prosecutors.

The Arthur Andersen case turned out to be one of the most far-reaching in terms of the prosecutors' new view of the law in recent years. In its decision, the Supreme Court noted that the Department of Justice as well as Congress shared the blame for the demise of a presumably innocent firm, Arthur Anderson. Justice Anthony Kennedy commented that the "DOJ's definition of a crime in this case amounted to a sweeping position that will cause problems for every corporation or small business in this country." Those condemnations from the Supreme Court should make it very clear how much damage narcissistic prosecutors have done and will continue to do to the U.S. judicial system as well as this country's business and economic environment without some Congressional action.

One could argue that prosecutors with the strongest narcissistic personalities could be those individuals who decide they would like to be a federal judge. Either way, the arrogance present in these personalities certainly carries its way into judgeships. While there may be a little more accountability as a federal judge, there are still numerous ways for their narcissistic tendencies to prevail and cause substantial injury to citizens who are on trial. Remember, narcissists have little compassion. This should not be a personality trait of a judge who ideally should balance their decisions involving the fate of our citizens. Also, a judge should stay out of politics, in spite of their narcissism!

It is certainly incumbent upon those of us who understand the issues and have common sense solutions to play active roles in resolving these matters. You will now have numerous books and a poster child to use with your senators and representatives to assist in making clear and common sense arguments about the overwhelming negative trend of prosecutorial over control of our judicial system and our business enterprises.

Of course, there is also the undue control of individual rights by overzealous and narcissistic prosecutors. That is another subject in which I have developed some interest through interaction with my fellow inmates at the Butner Federal Medical Center. I will work toward attempting to influence some changes in individual judicial rights in the years ahead.

There is a significant problem when one group of federal regulators, such as the investigators that called us to their DOJ office in the Southern District of New York to exchange information on Marc Cohodes, does not effectively communicate with the prosecutors in their agency, or more than likely, they are ignored. At that visit, they clearly told us that they knew there were legal issues with Cohodes, and they were in contact with European and Canadian officials. They also said money laundering was taking place as well as securities fraud. Even Senator David Perdue, who was a very respected member of the Senate Banking Committee, could not get the SEC to properly respond to his inquiries regarding our letters and documents about Cohodes. This issue is probably not the investigators fault. I believe the SEC and DOJ prosecutors ignore their own federal investigators as they do everyone else. We should now know they are generally seeking cases to build their resumes. Where is management oversite?

I have made some comments that I believe the MiMedx investigation was primarily orchestrated with some political motivations by individuals, law firms and DOJ prosecutors. I mentioned that former Deputy Attorney General Sally Yates had returned to King & Spalding about the time our investigation was started. It was general knowledge in Atlanta that I was President Trump's 2016 Campaign Finance Chairman for the state. Thus, I have always felt strongly, with what ensued and with the related publicity, that I had become another prosecutorial target simply because of my association with the President. This was brought to clarity when our prosecutors attempted to have Bill Taylor turn against me and endorse "their truth." Of course, Bill gave them the same message that the vast majority of our other managers gave to the DOJ's prosecutors. From what I have been told, these individuals clearly explained where these prosecutors, King & Spalding and several others "could go." I think it is easy to realize the frustration that I have felt by witnessing this wonderful organization and its personnel and shareholders badly damaged by political motivations directed at harming me and possibly President Trump.

Accusations

The accusation culture that America has allowed to develop is another important matter about which you should have serious concerns. Professor Alan Dershowitz discusses this very thoroughly in his book, *Guilt By Accusation*. If that type of dishonesty begins to develop around your company or in your life, you must take it very seriously. It will be a time in your life where you should not trust even some of your closest friends if they can somehow be dragged into the process. Very few people have the courage and strength of character to cope with these type of situations, and they will take the "easy way out." So go after these false allegations aggressively and professionally so that they do not build up momentum that will overwhelm you and your organization.

The Healthdyne Era

In the early part of the book, I went through the success stories of Healthdyne, Healthdyne Technologies, Healthdyne Information Enterprises, Home Nutritional Services, Narco Scientific and Matria Healthcare.

Those early years of founding and building Healthdyne, a medical technology company that later matured by adding healthcare services and healthcare informatics companies, was rather smooth. We also managed to continue to achieve higher than normal revenue growth rates and profitability. This was a result of my maniacal focus on sales territory management with supporting data. We focused on hiring talented people who demonstrated common sense. We also tried to keep narcissistic personalities out of the company. Our participatory management philosophy helped to build a talented and loyal employee and management base around our companies. Our successes came rather easily because at that time the Wall Street and regulatory environments were not out of control.

Healthdyne did have a couple years of poor performance when Congress enacted the Diagnosis Related Group (DRG) legislation. That totally changed the way Medicare was reimbursing hospitals and doctors for their services. It focused on paying only certain amounts for certain procedures and not paying whatever were the institution's or doctor's invoice amounts. While that made a tremendous amount of common sense, it took several years for those changes to work their way through the system so that this legislation no longer affected suppliers of medical devices, services and pharmaceuticals.

During this problematic period for medical device manufacturers, we divested some of our acquisitions. We sold all of the Narco Scientific subsidiaries. I especially hated to divest the Air Shields subsidiary, but we received a good offer. All of the Narco subsidiaries were sold at nice profits, as were all of our subsidiaries at later points in time.

The Matria Healthcare Era

Matria Healthcare's growth relative to its disease management and health enhancement programs came rather quickly because of the results of our previous experiences in medical product manufacturing and healthcare information technology development.

Matria's disease management programs involved connecting individuals with a nurse telephonically who acted as a healthcare coach, mentor and coordinator with their physician. Sophisticated care plans were developed and goals set, and those were routinely monitored. These programs developed into what Matria eventually termed "health enhancement" programs, which included all processes that improved the health and status of a patient. These processes ranged from specific clinical services, such as disease management, case management and utilization management to services that improved wellness, lifestyle and productivity.

As usual, Matria Healthcare grew rapidly. By 2007, Matria had nearly 370 wellness and disease management business clients who were members of the Fortune 500. Their clients were serviced out of 12 care center locations across the country. Matria was serving more than 1 million participants under our disease management programs, more than 4 million participants in our 24/7 nurse triage program and more than 250,000 online participants that had completed our healthy living programs. Matria was aquired in May of 2008 by Iverness Medical for $1.2 billion, and they later sold it to United Healthcare.

The MiMedx Group Era

By the time I began to manage MiMedx Group in 2009, there were major changes in the justice system and many more new regulatory issues related to healthcare. The Sarbanes-Oxley Act, which was prompted by the Enron and Arthur Andersen debacle, changed corporate governance dramatically. As to be expected when emotionalism drives decisions, that Act exceeded what would have been prudent and balanced regulation in a number of areas. Those excesses were a license for prosecutors to ramp up their abhorrent behaviors. Then, the Sally Yates Doctrine was signed in 2015, and prosecutors began to work off of those directives to "target" all their allegations towards top management of corporate entities. Many of the new prosecutorial techniques of <u>threatening</u> and manipulating witnesses now parallels some of the jury malfeasance of the Mafia in the 1920s and 1930s. It is really disgusting relative to how far our judicial system has become unbalanced and deteriorated.

I have called MiMedx a "poster child" because of the takeover of a quality company as a result of numerous factors, most of which were unscrupulous. These factors possibly included illegal short selling, employees making up false whistleblower allegations to cover their own misdeeds, an Audit Committee Chairman working in his own unnecessary CYA self-interest, the majority of the Board members ignoring their fiduciary responsibilities to shareholders, an outside law firm following the Sally Yates Doctrine to "target" top executives with false and politically motivated allegations that will become a financial windfall for their firm as well as many other law and accounting firms and finally several DOJ prosecutors acting in their own self-interest to try a notable white-collar crime case so they will secure job offers from large law firms or businesses. As you have seen, all these issues were prevalent in this unnecessary debacle. That is why the MiMedx story has exposed so many issues that need to be addressed primarily by congress taking prudent action to assist our regulatory agencies and by the justice department in cleaning up their dishonesty.

Coping

I have been asked numerous times about how I managed to cope with all the various matters associated with MiMedx becoming this Poster Child. Well, as a start, I reflected often on Mother Teresa, Teddy Roosevelt, and Rudyard Kipling's words of wisdom. Remember, "Do It Anyway."

First, as a very experienced individual relative to managing public companies, I never thought that MiMedx or our management had any issues that would rise to being fraudulent accounting matters. Thus, the investigation was over three months old when I first realized that Dewberry and King & Spalding had orchestrated a "Witch Hunt." That occurred on June 7th when the Board announced they were going to terminate Mike Senken and John Cranston for issues related to the supposed AvKARE payment modification. To finalize my concerns, Bill Taylor and I were asked to resign three weeks later on June 30th. This is when I had a reasonably full perspective on what was being orchestrated. I realized that the investigation was being orchestrated to satisfy Dewberry's unnecessary CYA paranoia, and this would involve a takeover of the company by an inexperienced Board and their unqualified executive management appointees.

While I developed some significant frustrations, I merely went about my business of finding ways to protect our shareholders from what I knew would become an absolute debacle. That is now probably an understatement. Therefore, I focused my attention on the proxy contest to initially replace as many of the Board members as possible and satisfy our large shareholders.

While it was a disappointment that our slate did not win the proxy contest, there were three new board members elected to replace some of the initial board members who had made these aberrant decisions.

During the development of the proxy contest, it was evident that the goal of King & Spalding was to serve the Department of Justice and the SEC with enough information so that they would file indictments against me and Bill Taylor, and the SEC would charge Mike Senken.

From that point forward, I was concentrating on understanding the dynamics of a federal trial in the Southern District of New York. I read numerous books, which clearly documented the legal shenanigans and misconduct that would take place in a SDNY trial.

The trial was extremely frustrating because of the issues I raised in Chapter 24. However, I was quite calm during this process because I realized this same type of manipulation of our legal system had taken place at the trials of numerous other people.

When Judge Rakoff delivered our sentences in mid-February of 2020, I was still very comfortable. While I did not like the idea of being away from my wife and family for a year, I knew that I would use that time relatively efficiently in continuing to write this book. Thus, my real concern was wasting a year, but I thought I could make efficient use of my time, which I did.

I looked upon my incarceration time as an opportunity to meet and understand some individuals that I had not been associated with during my life. I was very curious as to how their incarcerations came about, and if there was as much legal manipulation relative to them as individuals as there was relative to corporate entities.

I became relatively well educated on the issues my fellow inmates had to deal with which were very similar to ours in terms of the legal manipulations and malfeasance. Thus, I had an opportunity to understand clearly some additional issues relative to our judicial system. I made some plans relative to bringing those matters to light in the years I have left.

In summary, I think that I absorbed these frustrating matters relatively efficiently by focusing on what I could do to learn from them, help resolve them, and keep others from suffering similar fates. I had served my country in the military so I was used to being away from family and sometimes living in rather spartan conditions. So I did not let the incarceration time concern me. As an optimistic personality, I always focused on what I could do for the benefit of others during those particular periods. I used these five years as a learning experience where I could expose to fellow members of the business community and other Americans the issues that have developed that make managing American public companies extremely different and difficult today. I think I have accomplished that goal as I have completed this book. I would simply ask you, as a reader, to recommend the book to any and all business people whom you know and educate your senators and congressmen on the issues.

Resolution of Lawsuits

Just prior to publication of the book, I made an offer to the company that they accepted in terms of settling both my lawsuit against them and their lawsuit in Florida against me. Other than one other lawsuit against the company and Bill and me, my issues with the company are settled, I believe!

Problems and Solutions

As I composed sections of the book, I tried to emphasize specific problems and specific solutions. I hope that, in all cases, the problems and solutions were clear in my book as well as the other books I recommended.

I hope that this book, along with a focus on the other three books that relate to the corporate trials, will be utilized by hundreds of individuals to encourage their senators and representatives to review the key issues that are now out of control. While I am not qualified to speak necessarily about all the solutions, I can tell you that the individuals who have written the other books certainly are. When you read the books written by Harvey Silverglate, Sidney Powell, Wayne Jett, Suzanne Trimbath and Professor Alan Dershowitz, you will be extremely informed on the details of these issues and how they have grown to become a crucial matter for all Americans relative to the deterioration and politicalization of our judicial system. In fact, imagine how productive it would be to have hundreds of business executives, and perhaps even a few lawyers, begin to approach senators and representatives with these books. As discussions develop, the books could be placed on the congressman's desk, one at a time! That would certainly be a clear sign that these are valid issues that should be addressed, and these books have exposed the majority of the problems as well as <u>THE SOLUTIONS</u>.

The Entrepreneur's Dilemma

I am certain you have already come to some conclusions as to "The Entrepreneur's Dilemma." I have discussed dozens and dozens of key decisions that you will have to make as your entrepreneurial organization matures. Many of those decisions will cause a dilemma. However, I hope you have realized that "THE" dilemma is whether to take your company public. My recommendation is that generally no small or even medium-sized company should be publicly traded in America until there is a major change in certain policies at the SEC and the DOJ. Unfortunately, the prosecutors and other attorneys in those agencies view public companies as a "place to be plundered." A prosecutor working in their own self-interest will always find some issue to twist into fraudulent activity. So it is my recommendation to finance your growth through angel investors, venture capital and private equity sources. Then, shop your company to the most logical acquirers and give your shareholders their payoff through an acquisition. Your life and your entrepreneurial endeavors will be more richly and peacefully rewarded.

I am truly sorry to make this recommendation. However, to have such an experienced and successful management team with such exceptional corporate performance as MiMedx and to be rewarded by what you have read about says it all. Today, no business executive can fight an effective battle against our corrupt justice system unless they have an exceptional board of directors who will unselfishly fight the battles with their fiduciary responsibilities to the company as their primary goal. As you now know, MiMedx did not have a sufficiently experienced and properly motivated Board, and that is absolutely required to do battle with all the enemies that public companies face today – particularly the Sally Yates Doctrine and our "new" justice system.

The last five plus years have been frustrating at times, but also very much a blessing. I primarily focused on this book and the enlightenment and blessings it could bring to many entrepreneurs, business executives and shareholders of American businesses. Thus, I have prayed that my book could serve many individuals in their quest to accomplish or support successful entrepreneurship that will continue to improve and bless our country and all our citizens.

What has happened to America through the politicization and weaponization of our Department of Justice and other Departments is truly beyond belief and is a tragedy. However, this has occured, and it will eventually affect all of us very adversely regardless of our political affiliations. As I have said many times:

"THIS IS NOT AMERICA."

ACKNOWLEDGEMENTS

First, I want to thank all the employees, supervisors, managers and executives who worked so very hard to make our "Entrepreneurial Adventures" the successes that they were over the decades. You should all be very proud of our achievements, and I thank you very, very much.

My next tribute is to my wife, Janet, who has intimately lived through more of my "entrepreneurial adventures" than any other person. Now, she has coped, not only with my being incarcerated for six months, but also with almost six years of my fighting accusations and legal battles.

Janet is a devoted Christian with a very kind spirit. We met at her Baptist church. She still claims that I, being a Presbyterian, was attending her church's singles meeting for the wrong reason because of what I confessed when I noticed her. I exclaimed to a friend who was with me that we were in a "target rich environment!" Remember the movie "Top Gun?" Well, it took awhile, but I finally convinced her to go out to lunch and eventually to marry me when she became an instant grandmother to our first grandchild. Now, all seven grandchildren adore her and call her "Janny."

Relative to this book, Janet transcribed about half of it from my dictation. At that point, she wisely found an internet transcription service to complete our work.

So, to my wife, I thank you with all my heart for being my soul mate <u>and</u> my transcriptionist: I love you dearly.

Relative to my last company, I wish to give a special thanks to the MiMedx staff for what you accomplished by becoming the fifth fastest-growing public company in America in 2017 according to Fortune magazine. Unfortunately, that astounding success was brought to a halt by a few self-serving, unprincipled individuals both inside and outside the company. The last part of the book will put in stark perspective the travesty of the MiMedx saga – a debacle that included the termination or resignation of the top 20 out of 21 managers and executives who were the heroes that made our extraordinary achievements possible. All the MiMedx staff should be very proud of your successes and commitment to the very effective MiMedx product line for wound healing that improved and even saved lives.

I owe a very special thanks to Bill George, a former Georgia Tech classmate and the former Medtronic Chairman and CEO. I asked Bill, who is the author of several management books, to look over my very early draft. He encouraged me to include more details on the Healthdyne successes in addition to the MiMedx challenges. He said something like, "I do not know anyone who has been so 'foolish' as to be an entrepreneur for 48 years so the whole story should be told." Then, he properly criticized the book's first title as it was negative in nature. He suggested the current name because it leaves questions to be answered. I thank you, Bill.

Now, to the proofreaders… First, Nikki Istwan, one of our talented medical writers who was generally involved with our dozens of published clinical papers for MiMedx and Matria Healthcare. You were a blessing, and you deserve a special thanks.

Next is Margaret Martin, the longest employed person at all my companies. She started as an executive assistant at Healthdyne in 1982 and eventually began managing our sales and clinical meetings and travel functions. She was a manager at MiMedx until June of 2022 when she finally retired. A very special thanks to a special lady!

Then, James and Laura Trivette, both former managers at Matria Healthcare, and to Laura, who was also at MiMedx. Thanks so very much.

Next, Meredith Martin, my youngest daughter, who has always been into "the details" of all her activities. A loving thank you.

Then, Chuck Torres, a long-time friend and owner of a sales and marketing organization. Chuck, thanks for your talent and oversight!

Finally, Shawn George, a large MiMedx shareholder and attorney with business acumen and common sense…a rare combination! Thank you.

All these talented people brought their own special perspective to the book, and all were effective contributors. I thank you all.